"Joshua Moritz's excellent and user-friendly *Science and Religion* accomplishes two interrelated tasks. First, it dispels the myth of the conflict between religion and science by showing that no science can be done without some important presuppositions and that any good theology incorporates critically and sympathetically the best results of scientific investigation. Second, it covers in a most up-to-date manner all key topics in science-religion conversation from the 'beginning' to the 'end.' Footnotes and a glossary further strengthen this book's value for classroom and self-study."

—Veli-Matti Kärkkäinen
Professor of systematic theology, Fuller Theological Seminary,
and docent of ecumenics, University of Helsinki, Finland

"Joshua Moritz's *Science and Religion* is a stunning contribution to the dialogue between the scientific and religious communities, laced with enormous scholarship and marvelous humor and driven by a passion to put aside the reported conflict and contribute to creative interaction. Moritz first argues that the purported warfare between science and religion is actually a myth propounded by a collection of outspoken, antireligious scientists. He then provides a detailed and promising assessment of several key areas, including Big Bang cosmology, evolutionary biology, and creation theology; the human person and the image of God; science and miracles; God's relation to suffering in nature; and the far future of the cosmos and Christian hope. I strongly recommend *Science and Religion* to both the general reader and the scholarly community. It is a must-read for scientists, religious scholars, high school teachers, clergy, and the general public interested in the possibility of a creative interaction between science and religion."

—Robert John Russell
Center for Theology and the Natural Sciences
Graduate Theological Union

"One of the many virtues of Joshua Moritz's well-structured and wide-ranging introduction to the relationship between science and religion is its resourceful use of historical scholarship to illuminate the origins and demonstrate the limitations of an all-pervasive conflict model. Ambitious and controversial in its bid to replace conflict with peace at every opportunity, *Science and Religion* will be accessible and stimulating for a general audience and will prove to be a successful student text."

—John Hedley Brooke
Andreas Idreos Professor of Science and Religion
University of Oxford

Author Acknowledgments

This volume would not have been possible without the invaluable participation, specific expertise, critical feedback, and support of my family, friends, students, colleagues, and editors.

I would first like to express my sincere gratitude to the editors at Anselm Academic—Bradley Harmon, Maura Hagarty, Jerry Ruff, Beth Erickson, and Paul Peterson—for enthusiastically supporting this project and for diligently working with me to see it to fruition. I thank the various anonymous peer reviewers for their critical acumen on numerous aspects of my discussion and for pointing out weaknesses in an earlier draft of this text—thereby giving me the opportunity to make this a better book.

I owe a considerable intellectual debt to a number of individuals who over the years have been particularly influential in helping to form my way of thinking about the interrelationship between philosophy, religion, and the natural sciences. I particularly thank Ted Peters, Bob Russell, Marty Hewlett, and Ralph Stearley for their conversations on these topics and for their expert feedback on various chapters of the manuscript.

I am exceedingly grateful to my students at the University of San Francisco for being my continuing dialogue partners in the search for truth, for raising important philosophical, theological, and scientific questions that I would have never thought of on my own, and for offering valuable insights from the wealth of their learning and the diversity of their personal experience.

I am especially thankful to my lovely wife and best friend, Melissa. In addition to enthusiastically encouraging me throughout the research and writing of this volume, Melissa has—through reading numerous versions of the manuscript, asking key questions, offering prudent editorial suggestions, and critically engaging my work—significantly helped to shape and clarify the overall discussion. I also thank my little son, Xavier, for inspiring and encouraging me in countless ways. It is my sincere hope that the impact of this research will help to bring a brighter day to his future horizon.

Publisher Acknowledgments

Thank you to the following individuals who reviewed this work in progress:

Joseph A. Bracken, *Xavier University, Cincinnati, Ohio*

Celia Deane-Drummond, *University of Notre Dame, South Bend, Indiana*

Andrew Lustig, *Davidson College, Davidson, North Carolina*

Science and Religion

Beyond Warfare and Toward Understanding

JOSHUA M. MORITZ

ANSELM
ACADEMIC

Dedication

To Mom, Dad, Mel, and Xave

Created by the publishing team of Anselm Academic.

Cover images: © shaunl / *istock.com*; © Markus Schieder / *istock.com*

Printed in the United States of America

7071

ISBN 978-1-59982-715-5

Contents

Introduction

Some people, in order to discover God, read books. But there is a great book: the very appearance of created things. Look above you! Look below you! Note it; read it. God, whom you want to discover, never wrote that book with ink; instead He set before your eyes the things that He had made. Can you ask for a louder voice than that?

—*Augustine of Hippo*[1]

Both religion and science require a belief in God. For believers, God is in the beginning, and for physicists He is at the end of all considerations. . . . To the former He is the foundation, to the latter, the crown of the edifice of every generalized world view.

—*Max Planck, Nobel laureate in physics*[2]

Within the global culture of the twenty-first century, two of the greatest forces for change and sources of inspiration—whether for good or for ill—are science and religion. The relationship between science and religion is complex.[3] Today, many think there is potential for only conflict when faith meets fact. Others, however, including more than half of practicing scientists, have discovered a way to build a working relationship between the two.[4] Bringing science and religion into conversation, whether in one's personal life or in the academy, requires a vision that can see beyond many popular misunderstandings. Whenever the topic of science and religion is broached, many myths abound. References to the Catholic Church's excommunication and torture of Galileo are typical, as are allusions to Christianity's perennial rejection of Darwinian evolution. Even publicly funded endeavors for scientific education seem to have storylines peppered with the meme that science and religion are at war.[5] For

1. Augustine, quoted in Clarence Glacken, *Traces on the Rhodian Shore: Nature and Culture in Western Thought from Ancient Times to the End of the Eighteenth Century* (Berkeley: University of California Press, 1967), 203–4. Original source uncited.

2. Max Plank, "Religion and Natural Science," in *Scientific Autobiography and Other Papers*, trans. F. Gaynor (New York: Philosophical Library, 1949), 184.

3. Historian of science John Hedley Brooke notes, "Serious scholarship in the history of science has revealed so extraordinarily rich and complex a relationship between science and religion in the past that general theses are difficult to sustain. The real lesson turns out to be the complexity." John Hedley Brooke, *Science and Religion: Some Historical Perspectives* (Cambridge: Cambridge University Press, 1991), 5.

4. Edward J. Larson and Larry Witham, "Scientists Are Still Keeping the Faith," *Nature* 386 (1997): 435–36. See also David Masci, "Scientists and Belief," Pew Research Center (website), November 5, 2009, accessible at *http://www.pewforum.org/2009/11/05/scientists-and-belief/*.

5. For example, Carl Sagan, Ann Druyan, and Steven Soter, "Standing Up in the Milky Way," *Cosmos: A Spacetime Odyssey*, season 1, episode 1, directed by Brannon Braga, Ann Druyan, Bill Pope, aired March 9, 2014 (Los Angeles: 20th Century Fox, 2014), DVD.

instance, the television show *Cosmos*, which has been broadcast to a viewing audience of over a hundred million,[6] weaves timeless tales of scientists being burned at the stake for defending their scientific beliefs. It might come as a surprise to the general viewer when historians of science point out that "no scientist, to our knowledge, ever lost his life because of his scientific views,"[7] that the church has been generally supportive of the natural sciences through-out the ages,[8] and that evolution has been embraced by many key Christian thinkers and numerous church denominations since even before the days of Darwin.[9] Yet, a good story dies hard, and the story that science and religion have been perpetually at war is one of the most enticing. This book illustrates how the narrative that science and religion are at war is a *myth* in two key senses of the word: it is *foundational* to a certain anti-religious worldview, and it is historically *false*. Introducing the topic of science and religion by examining how the warfare myth arose, *Science and Religion: Beyond Warfare and Toward Understanding* also examines why the myth persists, and why the myth is mis-taken. Moving beyond the warfare myth, this text explores numerous dimen-sions of the complex and creative mutual interaction of science and religion in an endeavor to achieve a better understanding of their relationship.[10]

---

6. The viewing audience of *Cosmos* was 135 million. See Rick Kissell, "'Cosmos' Draws Biggest Global Audience Ever for National Geographic Channel," *Variety*, July 7, 2014, *http://variety.com/2014/tv/news/cosmos-draws-biggest-global-audience-ever-for-national-geographic-channel-1201257111/*.

7. David Lindberg and Ronald Numbers, *When Science and Christianity Meet* (Chicago: University of Chicago Press, 2003), 1.

8. For instance, historian of science David Lindberg writes, "A widespread myth that refuses to die . . . maintains that consistent opposition of the Christian church to rational thought in general and the natural sciences in particular, throughout the patristic and medieval periods, retarded the development of a viable scientific tradition, thereby delaying the Scientific Revolution and the ori-gins of modern science by more than a millennium. Historical scholarship of the past half-century demonstrates that the truth is otherwise." David C. Lindberg, "The Fate of Science in Patristic and Medieval Christendom," in *The Cambridge Companion to Science and Religion*, ed. Peter Harrison (Cambridge: Cambridge University Press, 2010), 21. See also David Lindberg, *The Beginnings of Western Science: The European Scientific Tradition in Philosophical, Religious, and Institutional Context, 600 B.C to A.D. 1450* (Chicago: University of Chicago Press, 1992).

9. For example, historian of science James Moore writes, "Darwin's theory of evolution by natural selection could be accepted in substance only by those whose theology was distinctly orthodox; that this was so because the theory itself presupposed a cosmology and a causality which, owing much to orthodox doctrines of creation and providence, could be made consonant *a priori* with orthodox theistic beliefs." James R. Moore, *The Post-Darwinian Controversies: A Study of the Protestant Struggle to Come to Terms with Darwin in Great Britain and America, 1870–1900* (Cambridge: Cambridge University Press, 1979), ix. See also David N. Livingstone, *Darwin's Forgotten Defenders: The Encoun-ter Between Evangelical Theology and Evolutionary Thought* (Grand Rapids: Eerdmans, 1987).

10. The author is indebted to physicist and theologian Robert John Russell for the phrase "cre-ative mutual interaction" as a description of the relationship between science and religion. See Robert John Russell, *Cosmology from Alpha to Omega: The Creative Mutual Interaction of Theology and Science* (Minneapolis: Fortress, 2008).

With Science and Religion One Size Does Not Fit All

Not all religions are the same. For instance, Buddhists believe the universe is eternal, with no beginning and no Creator, while Jews, Christians, and Muslims believe the cosmos was created by one God at the beginning of time. In Hinduism, the notion that the souls of humans transmigrate into animal bodies is commonplace, while in Judaism only human beings are said to be created in the image and likeness of God. The fact that religions are dissimilar means that each will have a different kind of relationship with science. In the same way that there is unbounded variety among religions, there is also great diversity within the natural sciences. The categories of mathematical beauty, symmetry, and elegance are more at home in the physical sciences than the biological sciences, which focus more on historical processes, contingency, and adaptive behavior. In a similar manner, discussions of conscious agency in the material world are commonplace in the writings of neuroscientists and psychologists, while the topic of free will is well outside the scientific domain of chemists and physicists. In this way, explains historian of science John Hedley Brooke, "the sciences of quantum mechanics and evolutionary biology might be correlated with religious concerns in quite different ways, and those concerns might vary considerably from one religion to another."[11] Rather than speaking of the relationship of "science and religion," then, says Brooke, "it is more helpful to speak of *sciences* and *religions*."[12]

Following Brooke's insight, this text will not take a "one-size-fits-all" approach to either religion or science. While some of the discussion in *Science and Religion: Beyond Warfare and Toward Understanding* will apply to all religions—more or less equally—many of the specific case studies and examples will not. For instance, scientific understandings of big bang cosmology have implications for Christian theological understandings of creation that do not apply to any similar religious concepts within Buddhism. Christians who struggle with Darwinism because of their convictions about the age of the Earth can hardly be equated with Buddhists who struggle with natural selection because it offers an explanation for the evolution of life that is an alternative to the law of karma.[13] Since it is important to treat the various religions and the different sciences on their own terms, this text will focus primarily on the theistic faiths in general (and the Christian faith in particular), while treating nontheistic religions in a more summary fashion. In the same way, the topics in the natural sciences

---

11. John Hedley Brooke, "The Changing Relations between Science and Religion," in *Interdisciplinary Perspectives on Cosmology and Biological Evolution*, eds. Hilary Regan, Mark Worthing, and Nancey Murphy (Adelaide: Australian Theological Forum, 2002), 3.

12. Ibid., 3, emphasis in original.

13. For example, because Darwinian evolution appears to replace karma, the Dalai Lama asserts, "the theory of natural selection is not something that Buddhism should easily accommodate." Donald Lopez, *Buddhism and Science: A Guide for the Perplexed* (Chicago: University of Chicago Press, 2008), 36, 142–43.

that are treated more in-depth will be those with the most relevance for theistic understandings of the cosmos, as it is affirmed as God's creation.

There are a number of reasons why this text will focus on the relationship between Christian theism and science. Christianity is the largest global faith, the most common faith in the English-speaking world, and the religion most represented within the most technologically and scientifically advanced societies. Christianity is consequently the religion that the majority of current, practicing scientists encounter most frequently. The history of Western science is deeply rooted within the late medieval and early modern Christian conceptual framework. As a result, the Christian religion has had a long encounter with modern science that has led to centuries of discussion that people today can evaluate and from which they can learn.[14] Beyond this, many of the philosophical assumptions of early scientists (and most scientists today) derive from a Christian theological context and culture.[15] Owing to these factors, a great deal of the conversation in the academic field of "science and religion" up to the present has been within a Christian context. Perhaps due to the same set of factors, the majority of popular misconceptions, misunderstandings, and myths about science and religion are likewise concerned with theological affirmations that are either specifically Christian or broadly theistic. At a popular level, Hinduism, Buddhism, and Islam are not typically perceived as being at war with science, but Christianity is.[16] As it concerns the Christian faith in particular, then, there is currently far more work to be done—especially at a popular level—in moving the conversation between science and religion beyond warfare and toward understanding.

Defining the Boundaries of Science and Religion

The first four chapters of *Science and Religion: Beyond Warfare and Toward Understanding* explore the much-disputed borderlands between science and religion. Chapter 1 investigates this boundary to see whether it has inevitably served as the frontlines of a never-ending conflict. Far from finding a perpetual

---

14. "Christianity has encountered modern science fully because of the roots of modern science in Europe." Alan Padgett, "Science and Religion in Western History: Models and Relationships," in *Science and Religion in Dialogue*, ed. Melville Y. Stewart (Chichester, UK: Wiley-Blackwell, 2010), 849.

15. As Brooke notes, "In the past, religious beliefs have served as a presupposition of the scientific enterprise. . . . A doctrine of creation could give coherence to scientific endeavor insofar as it implied a dependable order behind the flux of nature." Brooke, *Science and Religion*, 19. See also Christopher Kaiser, *Creational Theology and the History of Physical Science* (Leiden: Brill, 1997).

16. As historian of science Thomas Dixon writes, "A narrative of conflict between science and one religious tradition can simultaneously be reinforced by a story of harmony with another." Thomas Dixon, "Introduction," in *Science and Religion: New Historical Perspectives*, ed. Thomas Dixon, G. N. Cantor, and Stephen Pumfrey (Cambridge: Cambridge University Press, 2010), 6. For how Islam has served this function see Harun Küçük, "Islam, Christianity, and the Conflict Thesis," in *Science and Religion*, ed. Dixon, Cantor, and Pumfrey. For a discussion of Buddhism in this role, see Lopez, *Buddhism and Science*, 36–38.

state of warfare between science and religion, historians of science such as Lawrence Principe have discovered otherwise. "The 'conflict model,'" says Principe, "has been rejected by every modern historian of science; it does not portray the historical situation. . . . Popular tales of repression and conflict are at best oversimplified or exaggerated, and at worst folkloristic fabrications."[17] To illustrate Principe's point, chapter 1 investigates a number of the most popular war stories from the history of science and religion. It uncovers legends about Giordano Bruno and others (who, it is said, have been burned at the stake for practicing science), exposes the myth that medieval Christians believed the Earth was flat, and examines oversimplified accounts of the Galileo affair and fictions about the Scopes Monkey Trial. To further exemplify how science and religion have not been engaged in perpetual conflict throughout the ages, chapter 2 examines a number of historical cases where religious faith played a constructive role within the history of science. Chapter 2 highlights a number of overarching concepts within science, such as the laws of nature, and standard current scientific theories within geology, cosmology, and biology that were initially motivated and supported by religious interests and developed in light of theologically inspired philosophical assumptions.

If religious ideas often influence scientific understandings, what is the difference between religion and science? Chapter 3 takes up this question by looking at how philosophers of science have defined and demarcated the discipline of "science." Philosophers of science have found that discerning the precise boundaries between science, faith, and philosophy has proven a surprisingly difficult task. The practice of science appears to require a vital element of faith, and scientific theories are inevitably grounded in philosophical presuppositions—some of which originate from within a religious context. In addition to this, religions affirm a number of beliefs that directly concern the nature of physical reality. The discoveries of the natural sciences thus have a significant and immediate bearing on the content of religious faith.

Whether or not such domains might ever be adequately defined theoretically, religion and science, in everyday practice, do not stick to their separate spheres.[18] As physicist, philosopher, and theologian Ian G. Barbour writes, "If science and religion were totally independent, the possibility of conflict would be avoided, but the possibility of constructive dialogue and mutual enrichment

---

17. Lawrence Principe, *The Scientific Revolution: A Very Short Introduction* (Oxford: Oxford University Press, 2011), 37. Historian of science Frank M. Turner similarly says, "The relationship of science and religion, as numerous historians have argued, has not always been and is not one of essential conflict or warfare." Frank M. Turner, "The Late Victorian Conflict of Science and Religion as an Event in Nineteenth-Century Intellectual and Cultural History," in *Science and Religion*, ed. Dixon, Cantor, and Pumfrey, 88.

18. This is one of the problems with Stephen Jay Gould's NOMA (Non-Overlapping Magisteria of Authority) approach. See Joshua Moritz, "Rendering unto Science and God: Is NOMA Enough?" *Theology and Science* 7 (November 2009): 363–78.

would also be ruled out." The reality is, says Barbour, that "we do not experience life as neatly divided into separate compartments; we experience it in wholeness and interconnectedness before we develop particular disciplines to study different aspects of it."[19] While the fact that science and religion unavoidably influence each other can serve as a potential source of fruitful conversation, it is also often an occasion for genuine conflict. Chapter 4 maintains that much of the historical and current cases of contention between scientific theories and religious beliefs can be understood in terms of the misapplication of philosophical interpretations of science to ultimate reality, on the one hand, and the misapplication of philosophical interpretations of theological convictions about physical reality to science, on the other. In other words, when scientists make claims that go beyond the physically observable and testable universe, such claims cease to be scientific. And when religious believers turn a willfully blind eye to the data of the physical world—in order to insist on a given doctrine about the physical world— they exchange a properly theological faith that seeks understanding for an irrational faith-based skepticism that ultimately undermines itself. In cases where either religious faith or atheistic faith masquerades as science, conflict often arises.

Religions and Sciences in Conversation

Chapters 5 through 10 examine specific areas of interaction between religious beliefs and concepts on one hand and theories arising from the natural sciences on the other. Chapter 5 examines the question "Why is there something rather than nothing?" and brings religious affirmations about the nature of reality into conversation with contemporary scientific cosmology. The standard big bang theory has been interpreted by many as supporting theistic understandings of creation from nothing at the beginning of time. Beyond this, the initial conditions and laws of the universe appear "fine-tuned" for the existence of intelligent life, giving rise to the question of whether the universe exhibits evidence of transcendent design. Theorizing beyond the realm of what is observable, the notion of an infinite and eternal multiverse evades the question of cosmic fine-tuning and resounds more with Buddhist understandings of cosmic reality.

Chapter 6 transitions from contemplating the beginning of the universe, and considers the origin of the various forms of life. Religions differ widely on how they address the question of where the abundance of Earth's life comes from. As Donald Lopez explains, the Hindu and "Buddhist answer to why there are so many different species in the world—a question answered by science with the theory of natural selection—[is] the law of karma; the physical forms of the beings in the universe are the direct results of deeds done in the past."[20] Within

19. Ian G. Barbour, *When Science Meets Religion* (San Francisco: HarperSanFrancisco, 2000), 22.
20. Lopez, *Buddhism and Science*, 142–43.

the theistic traditions, biological life is acknowledged as being created by God. Focusing on Jewish and Christian understandings of the creation of life as found in the Bible, chapter 6 examines the language of the Hebrew Bible to illustrate how Jews and Christians may affirm an understanding of God's creating plants, animals, and even humans through noninstantaneous, developmental processes. In other words, there seems to be no reason, in principle, to suppose that the Bible is fundamentally opposed to the idea that God creates through evolution. Chapter 6 then goes on to survey both Darwinian and non-Darwinian understandings of evolution and raises the question of whether science can discern a clear direction or trend within the evolutionary history of life.

Chapter 7 discusses theological issues surrounding human nature, human uniqueness, and human destiny as related to the natural sciences. In the Eastern religious traditions, human beings are not claimed to be absolutely distinct from animals, but in the Jewish and Christian understanding humans are said to be uniquely in "the image and likeness of God." However, the Jewish and Christian scriptures do not directly equate any specific characteristics with the image of God in humans, and God's creation of humans in the Bible is not distinguished by any specific terms (such as "spirit" or "soul") that are not also used to describe the creation of animals. As studies of nonhuman animals increasingly reveal more similarities to humans than differences, a precise scientific description of human uniqueness remains elusive. This raises the question of whether human uniqueness resides in a nonphysical soul. While belief in an eternally existing, individual soul is a mainstay of popular religion, many faith traditions disallow this idea. In Hinduism, the soul is essentially one with the undifferentiated cosmic whole. Buddhists explicitly reject the notion of an immortal soul or a permanent self. Even among the Western theistic religions, in traditional Judaism and Christianity the human person is viewed as an undivided psychosomatic unity that depends on God for life, rather than as an amalgam of perishable body and immortal soul. The destiny of human beings in the theistic traditions is physical resurrection of the body rather than eternal life as disembodied souls. Science and numerous religious faiths are thus in harmony in terms of viewing the human person as a unified entity that needs physical existence to experience the fullness of life—either in this world or the next.

Chapter 8 examines the question of miracles and their relation to the natural sciences. Within the major religious traditions, there are numerous ways miracles are understood. Western theistic conceptions of miracles are not easily adapted to beliefs about wondrous events found in the religious traditions of Hinduism and Buddhism.[21] In the West, the notion that there are regular laws of nature has played a key part in how miracles have been defined. Perceptions of miracles and conceptions of the laws of nature have changed throughout the

---

21. Gavin Flood, "Miracles in Hinduism," in *The Cambridge Companion to Miracles*, ed. Graham H. Twelftree (Cambridge: Cambridge University Press, 2011), 184.

ages. While initially in the West no sharp divide was discerned between the natural and the supernatural, by the time of the European Enlightenment miracles came to be viewed as scientifically impossible violations of the laws of nature. With the dawn of quantum physics in the twentieth century, it has been shown that the Enlightenment concept of physical law is no longer *scientifically* valid. Consequently, arguments based on Enlightenment assumptions about natural law that reject the possibility of miracles are no longer sound. Beyond this, current scientific understandings have raised new possibilities for how God's interaction with the world of nature can be understood.

Chapter 9 takes up the problem that suffering poses for the various world religions and specifically examines how it relates to the natural sciences and the world of nature. Within Hinduism and Buddhism, "karma, the law of the cause and effect of actions, according to which virtuous actions create pleasure in the future and nonvirtuous actions create pain . . . accounts for all the happiness and suffering in the world."[22] Seeing karma as the cause of all suffering, the Eastern religions hold that no beings are innocent and that there is no all-powerful and all-loving creator God who can be held accountable. Within the theistic tradition, however, one might ask why an omnipotent and omnibenevolent God would permit suffering. For those who affirm belief in one Creator God, much of the suffering that occurs in the world can be understood in light of the conditions necessary to allow God to accomplish certain key goals within creation. The divine goals for creation are likewise inextricably intertwined with the questions of why God does not perform more miracles and why a loving God would choose to create life through evolution.

The final chapter of this volume addresses questions surrounding religious and scientific understandings of the end of the world. According to science, this present universe was not built to last forever, and—one way or another—all life in the cosmos will eventually end. Thus physicist Paul Davies observes, "If there is a purpose to the universe, and it achieves that purpose, then the universe must end, for its continued existence would be gratuitous and pointless."[23] At the point where the vision of science reaches its limits, it would seem that one needs the eyes of faith to discern any prospects of a future cosmic hope. The notion of an absolute end of time is absent from Hindu and Buddhist theological conceptions, and Eastern traditions focus on salvation that lies beyond the realm of the physical. In the West, however, the idea that there is an end to history has played a pivotal theological role because theistic understandings of redemption have traditionally focused on the resurrection and transformation of the physical body and the physical cosmos at the end of days.

---

22. Donald Lopez, *The Story of Buddhism: A Concise Guide to Its History and Teachings* (San Francisco: HarperSanFrancisco, 2001), 19.

23. Paul Davies, *The Last Three Minutes: Conjectures about the Ultimate Fate of the Universe* (New York: Basic Books, 1994), 155.

Resources for Discussion and Further Exploration

At the end of each chapter are resources to assist readers in their further exploration of the topic. The "Discussion Questions" at the end of each chapter are intended to be used in either a classroom or a small group setting and provide an occasion for readers to reflect on the chapter content together with their peers. The "Beyond the Classroom" section features additional discussion questions and activities that allow the reader to creatively engage others outside the class (who have not read this book) with the concepts and information here; these activities can also be used *within* the classroom as "ice-breakers" or conversation starters. The bibliographic and online materials included under the heading "Resources for Further Study" are recommended as additional course texts and readings to instructors and as trustworthy sources to students and readers who wish to learn more about the topic. In this section I have also included my own online lectures that introduce and discuss the material covered in the chapter (see "Internet Resources"). These lectures, which feature numerous illustrative images and examples, may be used in conjunction with the reading.

A Note on Science and Religion Typologies

One customary approach to presenting issues of science and religion is to introduce various *typologies* or frameworks that provide a conceptual structure defining how science and religion relate to one another.[24] This method of using typologies to discuss science and religion emphasizes that their relationship is complex and that it can take a variety of forms. Late physicist, philosopher, and theologian Ian Barbour, for example, offers a fourfold typology wherein the relationship between religion and science is understood under the categories of conflict, independence, dialogue, and integration.[25] *Conflict* is exemplified by persons, such as Richard Dawkins, who argue that science and religion are always at war.[26] The *independence* position (or *two languages* approach)—espoused by the late Harvard biologist Stephen Jay Gould (who referred to this position as NOMA [Non-Overlapping Magisteria of Authority]) and by biologist Francisco J. Ayala—holds that science and religion do not overlap at all

---

24. For example Arthur Peacocke developed an eightfold typology. See Arthur Peacocke, *The Sciences and Theology in the Twentieth Century* (Notre Dame, IN: University of Notre Dame Press, 1981), xiii–xv; and Arthur Peacocke, *Theology for a Scientific Age: Being and Becoming—Natural, Divine, and Human* (Minneapolis: Fortress, 1993), 20–21. See also John F. Haught, *Science and Religion: From Conflict to Conversation* (New York: Paulist Press, 1995); and Mikael Stenmark, *How to Relate Science and Religion: A Multidimensional Model* (Grand Rapids: Eerdmans, 2004).

25. Ian G. Barbour, *Religion and Science: Historical and Contemporary Issues* (San Francisco: HarperSanFrancisco, 1997); Ian G. Barbour, *When Science Meets Religion* (San Francisco: HarperSanFrancisco, 2000).

26. Richard Dawkins, *The God Delusion* (Boston: Houghton Mifflin, 2006).

because science speaks one language that exclusively deals with issues of fact, while the religion speaks another language that only relates to issues of value and meaning.[27] *Dialogue* focuses on how science and religion share boundary questions (e.g., why is there something rather than nothing?), have a number of methodological parallels—such as reliance on data (e.g., scripture in theology and the natural world in science), and how both make use of models, metaphors, and logic in their pursuit to understand reality. Barbour's fourth category, *integration*, highlights how some thinkers fully join or combine science and religion in such a way that scientific data, theories, and models are brought to bear *directly* on theological concepts and convictions. The discipline known as *natural theology* serves as an example of integration in that it endeavors to arrive at affirmative knowledge about God from scientific knowledge about nature.

The present work will depart from the typological approach to understanding science and religion for a number of reasons. First, any *historical* approach to "science" and "religion" will show that the notion that these two concepts can be clearly distinguished is a relatively recent one. As historian of science Peter Harrison explains, "To speak of the relationship between theology and science" before the mid-nineteenth century "is to ignore the categories that the historical actors themselves were operating with."[28] Second, contemporary definitions of science that de facto exclude religion, or definitions of religion that *automatically* exclude science are concerned more with philosophical *ideals* or social *constructions* than with the *actual* relationships of science and religion. The conflict position is thus historically untenable, and while the independence (or NOMA) approach might look promising in theory, in practice it is unworkable. This is why, explains physicist and theologian John Polkinghorne, "virtually all of us engaged in the [science and religion] dialogue reject the offer of a false truce, proffered by Stephen J. Gould (1999) through his concept of 'nonoverlapping magisteria' (NOMA)."[29] This book will not presume to demarcate the entities called "science" and "religion" by definitional fiat, but rather will explore how these two concepts emerged historically and how their contemporary interactions shed light on how their relationship is best understood. The examples discussed within this volume will show that in the majority of cases the relationship of science and religion both in the past and the present reflects some combination of Barbour's *dialogue* and *integration* categories. Where conflict *does* appear to be present, it will be argued that such apparent conflict is not typically

27. Stephen Jay Gould, *Rocks of Ages: Science and Religion in the Fullness of Life* (New York: Ballantine Books, 1999), 6; Francisco J. Ayala, *Darwin's Gift to Science and Religion* (Washington, DC: Joseph Henry Press, 2007).

28. Peter Harrison, "'Science' and 'Religion': Constructing the Boundaries," in *Science and Religion*, ed. Dixon, Cantor, and Pumfrey, 25.

29. John Polkinghorne, "The Continuing Interaction of Science and Religion," *Zygon: Journal of Religion and Science* 40, no. 1 (March 2005): 44.

between science and religion per se, but rather conflict emerges as a consequence of how the respective data of science and religion are interpreted and employed.

Conclusion

While war stories about science and religion have been greatly exaggerated, many tales of science and religion working together in concord are too frequently left untold. The true account of the relationship between science and faith is complex—including instances of both harmony and creative tension. Exploring how religious faith has engaged the natural sciences in the past and the present, this text endeavors to enter into the complex world of "science and religion" in an approachable and nontechnical manner. The search for understanding is fundamental to being human, and understanding is essential for wisdom. The aim of this text is that readers—be they lovers of wisdom or not—may develop a better understanding of two of the greatest forces that shape human culture and inform the human condition. Wisdom will come when it may, and when it does, if joined together with knowledge, it has the power to heal and bring warfare to an end.

Resources for Further Study

Brooke, John Hedley, and Ronald L. Numbers, eds. *Science and Religion around the World*. Oxford: Oxford University Press, 2011.

Harrison, Peter, ed. *The Cambridge Companion to Science and Religion*. Cambridge: Cambridge University Press, 2010.

Lopez, Donald. *Buddhism and Science: A Guide for the Perplexed*. Chicago: University of Chicago Press, 2008.

Polkinghorne, John. *Faith, Science, and Understanding*. New Haven: Yale University Press, 2000.

Richardson, W. Mark, Robert John Russell, Philip Clayton, and Kirk Wegter-McNelly, eds. *Science and the Spiritual Quest: New Essays by Leading Scientists*. London: Routledge, 2002.

Ruse, Michael. *Science and Spirituality: Making Room for Faith in the Age of Science*. Cambridge: Cambridge University Press, 2010.

Southgate, Christopher, ed. *God, Humanity and the Cosmos: A Text in Science and Religion*. 3rd ed. London: T&T Clark, 2011.

CHAPTER 1

Science versus Religion
The War That Never Was

Since the beginning of history, a deep rift has existed between science and religion.

—*Dan Brown, fiction writer,* Angels and Demons

Science began as an outgrowth of theology, and all scientists, whether atheists or theists . . . accept an essentially theological worldview.

—*Paul Davies, physicist,* Are We Alone?

In This Chapter

* Science and Religion at War: The Birth of a Modern Myth
* How Columbus *Didn't* Prove the World Was Round
* How Galileo *Never* Went to Jail
* How the Scopes Monkey Trial Was *Not* about Science versus Religion
* Discussion Questions
* Beyond the Classroom
* Resources for Further Study

Many think the relationship between science and religion—especially the Christian religion—has been one of conflict, debate, or even all-out warfare. Ask the average person on the street, and they will likely tell you the war between science and religion is as old as history. Everyone seems to know for a "fact" that religion and science have always had a hard time getting along. This common notion, that science and religion have experienced a long history of conflict or warfare is called the conflict thesis by historians of science and religion. This chapter first examines the historical roots and social context of the origin of the conflict thesis and then evaluates three historical cases that are often cited in support of the conflict thesis: (1) that Christopher Columbus was persecuted by the Roman Catholic Church for holding that the Earth is a globe and not flat; (2) that the Church hounded, tortured, and imprisoned Galileo Galilei (and Nicolaus Copernicus before him) for suggesting that the sun is the center of the solar system; and (3) that John T. Scopes—the defendant in the famous 1925 Scopes Monkey Trial—was a "martyr for science" who heroically taught evolution and paid the price by being thrown behind bars. Investigation of these three cases will demonstrate that the language of warfare falls far short of historical reality. A more accurate understanding of these events reveals a complexity of interactions characterized by both creative tension and constructive dialogue.[1]

Science and Religion at War: The Birth of a Modern Myth

In Dan Brown's best-selling novel *Angels and Demons* (also a 2009 movie), the hero of the story, Harvard professor Robert Langdon asserts that "early scientists were branded alive, on the chest, with the symbol of a cross," and "outspoken scientists like Copernicus were murdered by the church for revealing scientific truths." He also declares, "Since the beginning of history, a deep rift has existed between science and religion," and "religion has always persecuted science."[2] While Hollywood films are *not* typically viewed as authoritative sources for historical truth, high school and college textbooks generally *are*. And here one often finds the same theme—that the Christian church has resisted science and persecuted scientists from the beginning. Many textbooks include references to popes who banned the number zero or excommunicated Halley's Comet, bishops who opposed vaccination and human dissection, or how the Catholic Church burned at the stake the early scientist Giordano Bruno (1548–1600) for his scientific support of heliocentrism.[3] Students are often surprised to learn that these stories are false in a variety of ways. As a number of contemporary historians of science

---

1. Oxford historian John Hedley Brooke makes a case for what he labels the "complexity thesis" to describe the historical relationship between science and religion. See *Science and Religion: Some Historical Perspectives* (Cambridge: Cambridge University Press, 1991). Historian James Hannam describes the relationship as one of "creative tension." See James Hannam, *The Genesis of Science: How the Christian Middle Ages Launched the Scientific Revolution* (Washington, DC: Regnery Publishing, 2011).

2. Dan Brown, *Angels and Demons* (New York: Simon and Schuster, 2000), 31.

3. For a reference to popes banning vaccination and dissection, see the college textbook by Emily Jackson, *Medical Law: Text, Cases, and Materials* (Oxford: Oxford University Press, 2013), 7. For a reference to Bruno being burnt at the stake for his science, see the popular college textbook by Louis P. Pojman, *Philosophy of Religion* (New York: McGraw-Hill, 2001), 147. For a discussion on why these are all myths, see Ronald L. Numbers, ed., *Galileo Goes to Jail, and Other Myths about Science and Religion* (Cambridge, MA: Harvard University Press, 2009).

have pointed out, the truth is that the church never did any of these things. In fact, the Catholic Church encouraged the early practices of vaccination and supported human dissection. Moreover, there is not one clearly documented instance of the church ever burning *anyone* at the stake for scientific opinions.[4]

While professional historians of science try their best to set the record straight, a good story dies hard, and the notion of the perennial warfare between science and religion is a persistent myth. But from where does the myth of the ages-long warfare between religion and science derive? According to historian of science Thomas Dixon, the conflict thesis was invented by anti-church rationalists of the European Enlightenment in the late 1700s and then embellished and propagated by anti-Christian secular "free-thinkers" in the late 1800s.[5] The Enlightenment rationalists contrasted their own "Age of Reason" with what they called the "Dark Ages" of Christian Europe, and they promoted the story of the warfare between science and religion to make a case for social revolution. Among these Enlightenment rationalists were the French patriot Voltaire (1694–1778) and the American patriot Thomas Paine (1737–1809), both scientific thinkers who were opposed to Christianity and who viewed the institutional churches of France and England as the oppressive tentacles of the established monarchies. In his enormously popular book *The Age of Reason* (1794), Paine railed against "the continual persecution carried on by the Church, for several hundred years, against the sciences and against the professors of science." Paine contended that Christianity placed shackles on the mind and that no scientifically progressive person could ever embrace the central doctrines of the Christian faith. What Paine sought through his literary efforts, however, was not to end religion but to replace the Christian religion with a secularized "rational" religion based on science.[6]

In the 1800s, the rhetorical torch of the anti-religious Enlightenment thinkers was taken up by the "free-thinkers" of the Victorian Age who sought to stage a social revolution in the scientific establishment, which at that time was dominated by religiously devout practitioners.[7] Foremost among the free-thinkers were "Darwin's Bulldog," British naturalist Thomas Henry Huxley (1825–1895), along with the American promoters of science and secular education, John W. Draper (1811–1882) and Andrew Dickson White (1832–1918). Huxley, who resented the influence of the Anglican establishment within the scientific culture of his day, embellished a vision of Western history where "extinguished theologians lie about the cradle of every science as the strangled snakes

---

4. For an in-depth discussion of why such stories are unfounded see Hannam, *Genesis of Science*; and Numbers, ed., *Galileo Goes to Jail*.

5. Thomas Dixon, *Science and Religion: A Very Short Introduction* (Oxford: Oxford University Press, 2008), 9.

6. See ibid., 11–12.

7. See Peter Harrison, "Religion, the Royal Society, and the Rise of Science," *Theology and Science* 6, no. 3 (2008): 255–71.

beside the cradle of Hercules."[8] Coining the term "agnostic" to describe his own position on religion, Huxley enlisted Darwin's scientific theory to champion the cause of religious skepticism. He had no patience with scientific colleagues, such as Roman Catholic biologist St. George Mivart who accepted evolution and insisted that Darwinism was perfectly compatible with historic Christian teaching. Huxley, infuriated by Mivart's position, insisted that Mivart choose whether he wanted to be "a true son of the Church" or "a loyal soldier of science."[9] If Huxley was to create a proper war between science and religion, he could not afford to have soldiers fighting loyally for both sides.

To further the cause of secularizing the scientific establishment and help spread the message of the war between science and religion, Huxley also founded the X-Club—a group of like-minded, agnostically oriented, and scientifically influential friends, whose key aim was to reform the foremost British scientific organization, known as the Royal Society. (Draper and White were distinguished members.) The explicit mission of Huxley and his colleagues in the X-Club was to rid—with an evangelical fervor—the discipline of the natural sciences of women, amateurs, and Christian clergy, and to place secular science into the center of cultural life in Victorian England.[10] Between the time of its inception in 1864 and the end of the nineteenth century, the X-Club and its members gained much prominence within the scientific community, exerting considerable influence over scientific thought. "The enduring legacy of this group," explains historian of science Peter Harrison, "has been the perpetuation of the myth of a perennial warfare between science and religion."[11]

Draper (a prominent chemist, founder and first president of the American Chemical Society) and White (the first president of Cornell University) prosecuted the war of rhetoric against religion in the United States. From these authors come two books that have been in print for more than a century and are still among the most widely read books in the history of science and Christianity. Draper's book, *The History of the Conflict between Religion and Science* (1874), tells of "ferocious theologians" hounding the pioneers of science with a Bible in one hand and a flaming torch in the other. His book is primarily a tirade against the Roman Catholic Church, which he blames for almost everything he

---

8. Quoted in Richard G. Olson, *Science and Religion, 1450–1900: From Copernicus to Darwin* (Baltimore: Johns Hopkins University Press, 2006), 204.

9. Timothy Larsen, "'War Is Over, If You Want It': Beyond the Conflict between Faith and Science," *Perspectives on Science and Christian Faith* 60, no. 3 (September 2008): 149–50. As Larsen says, "Huxley and others who aspired to turn scientific pursuits into a profession . . . 'needed' a war between science and religion."

10. See Ruth Barton, "'An Influential Set of Chaps': The X-Club and Royal Society Politics 1864–85," *British Journal for the History of Science* 23, no. 1 (March 1990): 53–81.

11. Peter Harrison, "'Science' and 'Religion': Constructing the Boundaries," in *Science and Religion: New Historical Perspectives*, ed. Thomas Dixon, Geoffrey Cantor, and Stephen Pumfrey (Cambridge: Cambridge University Press, 2010), 27.

views as wrong in Western history (including encouraging the "evolutionarily unfit" to breed). Draper was reacting to the new wave of Catholic immigrants in America, to the first Vatican Council, and, in particular, to the doctrine of papal infallibility. On top of this, he was angry that his own sister had become a nun.

White's book, *A History of the Warfare of Science with Theology in Christendom* (1896), similarly speaks of the struggle between religion and science as "a war waged longer, with battles fiercer, with sieges more persistent, with strategy more shrewd than in any of the comparatively transient warfares of Caesar or Napoleon." Indeed, he tells the reader, "The coming of Christianity arrested the normal development of the physical sciences for over fifteen hundred years . . . imposing a tyranny of ignorance and superstition that perverted and crushed true science."[12] White, too, was annoyed with the Christian church, but for different reasons. He was provoked to write because of criticism he received for establishing Cornell University without a religious affiliation. Beyond this, White's Cornell was competing with religiously affiliated colleges to get money from Congress; thus he had to make a historical case to show why religion and the natural sciences shouldn't mix.

What do historians of science make of the conflict thesis that science and religion have been in a perpetual state of warfare? University of Wisconsin historians of science David Lindberg and Ronald Numbers explain that "recent scholarship has shown the warfare metaphor to be neither useful nor tenable in describing the relationship between science and religion."[13] Johns Hopkins University historian of science Lawrence Principe likewise says that the historical formulation of Draper and White "rests on very shaky (and sometimes fabricated) foundations and was contrived largely for quite specific political, professional, and racist purposes. . . . Serious modern historians of science have unanimously dismissed the warfare model as an adequate historical description."[14]

How Columbus *Didn't* Prove the World Was Round

Although professional historians of science have "unanimously dismissed" the rhetorical fictions of Draper and White as anti-religious propaganda, Draper and White's legacy lives on in the anecdotes of popular culture. One legend from White's work that remains ubiquitous today is the notion that Christians in the European Middle Ages thought the world was flat—an idea White

---

12. Quoted in David Lindberg and Ronald Numbers, eds., *God and Nature: Historical Essays on the Encounter between Christianity and Science* (Berkeley: University of California Press, 1986), 3.

13. David C. Lindberg and Ronald L. Numbers, "Beyond War and Peace: A Reappraisal of the Encounter between Christianity and Science," *Perspectives on Science and Christian Faith* 39, no. 3 (September 1987): 140–49, at 141.

14. Lawrence Principe, "The Warfare Thesis," *Science and Religion*, recorded lecture (Chantilly, VA: The Teaching Company, 2006).

picks up from Washington Irving's fictional *Life of Columbus* (1828) and then asserts as history. As the story goes, the Spanish explorer Christopher Columbus (1451–1506), pictured as an enlightened man of science, defies the dogmatic superstitions held by medieval Christian culture and boldly ventures to prove, by experiment, the error of the Church's ways. Yet, declares White, "even after he was triumphant, and after his voyage had greatly strengthened the theory of the earth's sphericity, the Church by its highest authority solemnly stumbled and persisted in going astray."[15]

This myth is still at work in many places. For example, a 2013 *Infinity* car commercial opens with a reference to Columbus: "If no one ever challenged the status quo, the earth would still be flat." A popular play from a few years earlier, titled *Christopher Columbus*, includes the following dialogue:

> COLUMBUS. The Earth is not flat, Father, it's round!
>
> ROMAN CATHOLIC PRIEST. Don't say that!
>
> COLUMBUS. It's the truth; it's not a mill pond strewn with islands, it's a sphere.
>
> ROMAN CATHOLIC PRIEST. Don't, don't say that; it's blasphemy.[16]

As part of elementary school and high school education, many Americans grew up with stories about Columbus proving the world was round and his crew begging him to turn back lest they sail off the edge of the earth. In the 1980s, the popular fifth-grade history textbook *America Past and Present* explained to elementary school pupils: "The European sailor of a thousand years ago believed . . . that a ship could sail out to sea just so far before it fell off the edge of the sea."[17] A widely used middle-school textbook at that time asserts, "Columbus felt he would eventually reach the Indies in the East. Many Europeans still believed that the world was flat. Columbus, they thought, would fall off the earth."[18] Thus, there remains the quite common notion that a flat earth—as opposed to a spherical earth—was generally assumed by the average person who lived in medieval Europe.

Is there any historical truth in this tale? In fact, there is no written record of *anyone* in medieval Europe believing in a flat earth. University of Santa Barbara historian Jeffrey B. Russell explains that "no educated person in the history of Western Civilization from the third century B.C. onward believed that the earth

---

15. Andrew Dickson White, *A History of the Warfare of Science with Theology in Christendom* (Buffalo, NY: Prometheus, 1993), 108.

16. Quoted in Edward Grant, *God and Reason in the Middle Ages* (Cambridge: Cambridge University Press, 2002), 345.

17. Joan E. Schreiber, *America Past and Present* (Glenview, IL: Scott Foresman, 1983), 98.

18. David Bidna, *We the People: A History of the United States of America* (Lexington, MA: Heath, 1982), 28–29.

was flat."[19] Lindberg observes, "The truth is that the sphericity of the earth was a central feature of theoretical dogma as it came down to the Middle Ages—so central that no amount of contrary theoretical or empirical argumentation could conceivably have dislodged it."[20] British historian of science James Hannam agrees: "We can state categorically that a flat Earth was at no time ever an element of Christian doctrine and that no one was ever persecuted or pressurized into believing it."[21]

De Agostini Picture Library / Bridgeman Images

Martin Behaim constructed this globe, or *Erdapfel* ("Earth-apple"), between 1491 and 1493. Its spherical shape represents the consensus of European scholarship at the time of Columbus's voyage.

Not only did medieval Christians know that the world is a sphere, they also possessed a fairly accurate sense of its size. During Columbus's day, the works of Roman naturalist and geographer Pliny the Elder (ca. 50 CE) were popular. Pliny recorded Eratosthenes's (250 BCE) measurement of the Earth's circumference as 23,000 miles—which is quite close to the true figure of 24,900 miles. Also known to medieval Europeans was the estimate of Strabo (15 CE) and Ptolemy (120 CE), two renowned Greek geographers who argued that the Earth's circumference is around 16,500 miles; Columbus argued for this smaller figure. The Spanish geographers wisely urged Columbus not to set sail—warning that he and his crew would most likely starve during the long ocean voyage across half the globe. Fortunately, at least for Columbus and his crew, the Americas lie between the Atlantic and Pacific Oceans. Thus, if Columbus proved anything about the shape of the Earth, he proved that the majority of medieval, geographical experts were correct about the size of its circumference and that he, in fact, was wrong.

---

19. Jeffrey Burton Russell, "The Myth of the Flat Earth," American Scientific Affiliation Conference, August 4, 1997, Westmont College, Santa Barbara, CA. See also Jeffrey Burton Russell, *Inventing the Flat Earth: Columbus and Modern Historians* (New York: Praeger, 1991).

20. Quoted in Russell, *Inventing the Flat Earth*, 2.

21. Hannam, *Genesis of Science*, 28.

How Galileo *Never* Went to Jail

A second myth regularly cited in popular discussions of science and religion is the story of how the famous astronomer Galileo Galilei (1564–1642) defied the dogmatism of the Catholic Church in the name of science and paid for it dearly. This myth generally asserts that Galileo, for holding certain scientific views, was persecuted by the church, tortured by the Catholic Inquisition, and thrown in a dungeon to rot for the rest of his life. In some versions of the myth, he is burned at the stake as a scientific heretic. In other words, the myth holds that Galileo essentially became "a martyr for science" at the hands of the Roman Catholic Church. Again, Andrew Dickson White is primarily responsible for the popularization of this myth. White says that, for his scientific heresies, "Galileo was tortured and humiliated as the worst of unbelievers."[22] The historical truth, however, is quite different. From the available evidence, it is clear Galileo was not burned at the stake and was neither persecuted for his scientific views nor tortured by the Church. He was *not* thrown in a dungeon to rot away; in fact, he never spent a single day in prison. Beyond this, the Galileo affair was not even a clear case of science versus religion. Indeed, much of the controversy was theological in nature and concerned with how to (and who may) properly interpret the Bible.

Because the events surrounding Galileo's trial are complex, a bit of background aids in understanding the theological and scientific situation in Galileo's day. Long before 1609 when Galileo began advocating the view of Nicholaus Copernicus (1473–1543) that the planets went around the sun (known as heliocentrism), several key religiously orthodox Christian thinkers had already discussed the possibility that the planet Earth was rotating. They had also debated whether the sun and planets were moving relative to the Earth or vice versa. The famous professor of the University of Paris John Buridan (1295–1362) and the fourteenth-century bishop Nicole Oresme (1320–1382) both discussed the issue of relative motion in the solar system and argued that the observable data of physics alone could not demonstrate whether the Earth was rotating or not. Cardinal Nicholas of Cusa (1401–1464) likewise freely discussed the possible motion of the Earth. In his well-known book *On Learned Ignorance*, Nicholas proposed that the Earth is a star like other stars, that it is not the center of the universe, and that it is not at rest.

By the time Copernicus came onto the scientific scene in the early sixteenth century, there was no reason to think that the reappearance of the idea of a moving Earth would cause a theological controversy.[23] When Copernicus published his famous *Revolutions of the Celestial Spheres* in 1543, it was after many high-ranking church officials had encouraged him in his astronomical work. For

---

22. Quoted in Numbers, ed., *Galileo Goes to Jail*, 2.
23. Lindberg and Numbers, "Beyond War and Peace," 141.

example, in 1515 Pope Leo X (1513–1521) and other church leaders sought the astronomical expertise of Copernicus to help reform the Julian calendar. In 1533, Pope Clement VII (1523–1534) was so fascinated by Copernicus's new model that he invited his personal secretary (and Copernicus's
disciple) Johann Widmannstetter
to the Vatican gardens to give a
public lecture on the subject, "to
the delight of Pope Clement
and several cardinals."[24] Then
on November 1, 1536, Cardinal
Nicolas von Schoenberg wrote
to Copernicus saying, "With the
utmost earnestness I entreat you,
most learned sir, unless I incon-
venience you, to communicate
this discovery of yours to scholars."[25] From this series of events,
it is clear that "if Copernicus had
any genuine fear of publication, it
was the reaction of scientists, *not*
clerics, that worried him."[26] And

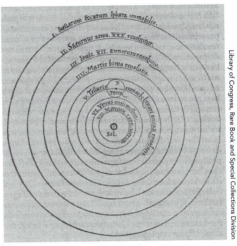

Copernicus first published his heliocentric theory in 1543, some seventy-two years before
Galileo's trial. Copernicus's book included this
diagram of the solar system.

there was a good reason for this: Copernicus, in fact, had no new empirical evidence to justify his theory. Rather, he thought that his view had more internal
coherence and greater explanatory power than Ptolemy's, and that it was more
theologically satisfying.[27]

Living in the 1600s, Galileo was researching and writing in the wake of the
Protestant Reformation—a time when more conservative theological and scientific views were on the rise within Roman Catholic culture. One of the central
tenets of the Protestant Reformers was that each individual Christian had the
right to interpret Scripture and read the Bible in his or her own language, rather
than encountering the teaching of Scripture only through the mediation of professional Bible scholars and priests. To discourage further schism in the Church,

---

24. Lawrence Principe, *The Scientific Revolution: A Very Short Introduction* (Oxford: Oxford University Press, 2011), 49.

25. Jack Repcheck, *Copernicus' Secret: How the Scientific Revolution Began* (New York: Simon and
Schuster, 2007), 79.

26. Lindberg and Numbers, "Beyond War and Peace," 142, emphasis in original.

27. Richard J. Blackwell, "Galileo Galilei," in *The History of Science and Religion in the Western
Tradition: An Encyclopedia,* ed. Gary B. Ferngren (New York: Garland, 2000), 98; see also John Hedley Brooke, "Religious Belief and the Content of the Sciences," in *Science in Theistic Contexts: Cognitive Dimensions,* ed. John Hedley Brooke, Margaret J. Osler, and Jitse M. van der Meer (Chicago:
University of Chicago Press, 2001), 15.

the Roman Catholic Council of Trent (1545–1563) countered this individual-istic Protestant notion of reading the Bible and forbade any reinterpretation of Scripture "contrary to the consensus" of the patristic writers. In Galileo's day, the dominant understanding of Scripture held by the Catholic Church favored a *geostatic* (i.e., a nonmoving or stationary Earth) and *geocentric* (i.e., Earth as the center of the solar system) view of the solar system over that of Copernicus. Galileo, for his part, attempted as a layman to make a scriptural case to the con-trary. In doing this he, in essence, "violated 'intellectual turf' by claiming that his biblical interpretations were superior to those of theologians, especially while he told theologians to stay out of natural philosophy."[28]

In 1615, Galileo went to Rome to defend the Copernican theory, cer-tain that he possessed the empirical truth. However, at this time—and even to the end of his life—a conclusive proof of the Copernican system still had not been found. Galileo believed that he had such a proof in his argument that the motion of the Earth causes the tides, but many other astronomers and physicists remained unconvinced (and sci-entists now know, in hindsight, that Galileo's theory of the tides was wrong). Beyond this, there were other models of the solar system that could explain the observational data just as well—including that of Dan-ish astronomer Tycho Brahe (1546–1601), which was partly heliocentric and partly geo-centric. As a result, Galileo's case was empirically undecid-able, and there was sufficient doubt about the relative mer-its of Copernicanism and the alternatives "that an objective observer would have pronounced the scientific question an open one."[29] Many influential Catholic Church officials believed that Galileo might be right, but they had to wait for more scientific proof.[30]

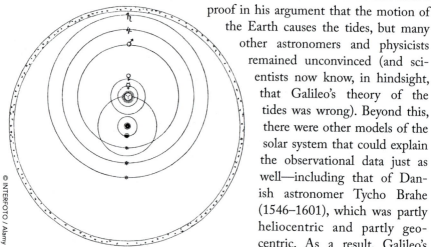

© INTERFOTO / Alamy

The Copernican model's chief rival was the "geo-heliocentric" model of Tycho Brahe (1546–1601), shown here. Since both models fit the data avail-able at the time, there was no clear, scientific basis for preferring one over the other.

28. Lawrence Principe, "Galileo's Trial," *Science and Religion*, recorded lecture (Chantilly, VA: The Teaching Company, 2006).

29. Dixon, *Science and Religion*, 31.

30. Jerome J. Langford, *Galileo, Science, and the Church* (Ann Arbor, MI: University of Michigan Press, 1992), 69.

In 1616, a committee was asked to report on the question of Copernican-ism and concluded that it was at that time both unfounded as scientific theory and contrary to the teachings of Scripture. However, "the decree was issued in a reformable manner by a fallible authority . . . without any special endorsement of the Pope."[31] In light of the committee's decision, Cardinal Robert Bellarmine asked Galileo not to present Copernicanism as *literally true* and as a *scientifically proven fact*. Galileo agreed to comply with Bellarmine's request. Bellarmine per-mitted Galileo to continue to research and write, with the understanding that he should treat his scientific theories tentatively until he had conclusive evidence. "Prove your theory," said Bellarimine, "and we will change our exegesis, other-wise teach it as a hypothesis."[32] Bellarmine conceded that a sound demonstra-tion of the Earth's motion would lead to reinterpretation of Scripture, but, as of yet, Galileo had no such proof.

Then in 1623, Galileo was exceedingly encouraged when his friend Car-dinal Maffeo Barberini was elected as Pope Urban VIII. Barberini had been an admirer and active supporter of Galileo's work since 1611; he even composed a poem celebrating Galileo's scientific discoveries. Galileo, now a scientific celeb-rity and feeling that he could do no wrong, embarked for Rome to speak with the new pope. Urban VIII warmly received Galileo, "granted him no less than six audiences; gave him a painting, two medals. . . . and the promise of a pen-sion for his son; and, last but not least, agreed that he could write about the motion of the earth provided he represented it not as reality but as a scientific hypothesis."[33] In other words, Galileo was granted permission from the pope to write about the Copernican system as long as he treated it as a *theory* and *not* as an *established fact* that was proven beyond all doubt.

Galileo, however, was not entirely satisfied with these conditions. Instead of abiding by the pope's request, Galileo published his *Dialogue Concerning the Two Chief World Systems* (1632), where he not only defended Copernicanism as a *proven fact* and as *physically true*, but also placed the Pope's own arguments about its *hypothetical* character in the mouth of the dim-witted, bumbling Aristotelian fool, Simplicio; Galileo claimed the name was meant to refer to Simplicius of Cilicia, a sixth-century commentator on Aristotle, but many believed the name was intended as a pun on the Italian word for "fool" (*simplice*). Galileo also made various arguments against the theologians and biblical scholars about the correct way to interpret Scripture. In addition, the pope learned for the first time of Galileo's 1616 legally binding agreement with Bellarmine where he promised not to present the Copernican theory as an established fact—something Gal-ileo failed to mention when he met with the pope. The combination of these

---

31. Ibid., 101.

32. Ibid., 69.

33. William R. Shea, "Galileo and the Church," in *God and Nature*, ed. Lindberg and Numbers, 128.

actions alienated Galileo from the pope, who up to that point had been Galileo's enthusiastic supporter and friend. As a result, Galileo fell prey to his scientific rivals who wanted him silenced (largely due to personal jealousies and insults they had received from his pen). Beyond this, Galileo found himself caught in a power struggle between rival *scientific* schools of thought roughly corresponding to the views of the Dominicans and Jesuits. While all of Galileo's accusers were Dominicans, Galileo was on good terms with the Jesuits, who had confirmed his telescopic discoveries and supported his work. Indeed, the Jesuit astronomers were quite eager for further scientific proof so they could come out solidly in favor of Copernicus and abandon Brahe's system.

It was for breaking his agreement with high-ranking officials of the Church, rather than for seeking to understand the natural world through observation and reasoning, that Galileo was tried and convicted in June 1633. It was not Galileo's scientific opinions that led to his trial, but *how he conducted himself* as he promoted them. When he was tried, Galileo was neither charged nor convicted of scientific heresy. He was charged with promoting Copernicanism as a *fact* and, by doing so, breaching his legally binding agreement. Guilty as charged, Galileo was not a hapless victim.[34] And even at the end of the proceedings, several cardinals did not sign the conviction—a signal that Galileo still had the support of Church leaders and that the trial was intended to be something of a slap on the wrist.[35]

As far as the part of the myth that says Galileo went to jail, it is a point of historical fact that "Galileo was never held in prison, either during the trial (as was universal custom) or afterward." Throughout all the events surrounding Galileo's trial, explains historian Maurice Finocchiaro, he received "unprecedentedly benign treatment."[36] When he was summoned to Rome, he was permitted

---

34. In 1979 Pope John Paul II initiated an interdisciplinary commission to re-investigate the Galileo case in order to expose the "wrongs from whatever side they come." The investigation took 13 years. In its final report in 1992 the commission emphasized that Galileo did not possess solid scientific proof for the Copernican hypothesis. Thus, explained the report, Galileo, "had not succeeded in proving irrefutably the double motion of the earth" as Cardinal Bellarmine had challenged him to do. When, however, an "optical proof" of the Earth's motion around the Sun became available in the following century, Pope Benedict XIV had the Holy Office grant the official stamp of approval to Galileo's works in 1741 ("Galileo: Report on Papal Commission Findings," *Origins: Catholic News Service*, November 12, 1992, 22, 375–6). While reaffirming that the scientists at the time of Galileo were objective in their request for more evidence, the Pope censured the theologians of the time as shortsighted. In this respect, says John Paul II, "Galileo as a sincere believer, showed himself to be more perceptive in this regard than the theologians who opposed him." According to the pope the key lesson to be learned from the Galileo affair is the fundamental harmony between science and religion. "The myth of Galileo's case had encouraged the erroneous idea that science and Christian faith were in opposition," but, declares John Paul II, "this sad misunderstanding now belongs to the past" (Pope John Paul address to the Plenary session on "Emergence of Complexity in Mathematics, Physics, Chemistry and Biology" October 31, 1992); see also Maurice A. Finocchiaro, *Retrying Galileo, 1633–1992* (Berkeley: University of California Press, 2005), 354–55.

35. Principe, "Galileo's Trial."

36. Maurice A. Finocchiaro, "Myth 8: That Galileo Was Imprisoned and Tortured for Advocating Copernicanism," in Numbers, ed., *Galileo Goes to Jail*, 74.

Following his trial, Galileo was ordered to return to his villa in Arcetri, shown here. He was free to leave the grounds to visit his children, and he was permitted to continue to publish his scientific research.

to lodge at the Tuscan embassy. For eighteen days of his trial, he was housed in a six-room apartment, together with a servant who brought him meals from the Tuscan embassy. Later Galileo moved to the Villa Medici in Rome, a luxurious palace owned by the grand duke of Tuscany. After his trial, Galileo was allowed to leave for Siena, where he was hosted at the palace of the archbishop (a good friend of Galileo's); later, he moved back home to Arcetri near Florence where, under "house arrest," he was restricted to the confines of his spacious villa and country estate. He was permitted to visit his children who lived nearby and to continue publishing scientific papers.

In conclusion, the Galileo affair was neither about the Church's persecution of Galileo nor a matter of Christianity waging war on science. All participants called themselves Christians, and all acknowledged biblical authority. On all sides of the Galileo case, there was agreement that it was proper and rational to seek accurate knowledge of the world through observation of nature and to base one's beliefs on the study of Scripture. The dispute was not between the empirical sciences and dogmatic religious faith. Rather, it was a disagreement—complicated by personal rivalries—between differing views *within* the Catholic Church about how to interpret both nature and Scripture when they seem to disagree.[37]

---

37. Dixon, *Science and Religion*, 18.

How the Scopes Monkey Trial Was *Not* about Science Versus Religion

A third frequently cited case of "science versus religion" is the *Inherit the Wind* story—named after the popular 1955 play and 1960 film starring Spencer Tracy, Frederic March, and Gene Kelly—that purports to accurately dramatize the events surrounding the famous Scopes Monkey Trial in Dayton, Tennessee, in 1925. According to the popular version of this story, John T. Scopes (1900–1970) is portrayed as a "heroic evolutionist standing up against a repressive Christian establishment in 1920s Tennessee."[38] Scopes is pictured as a champion of learning and of human rights who merely wanted to bring a little scientific light into a dogmatically dark place but instead ended up a victim of religious bigotry and anti-scientific fundamentalism. The movie version has the free-thinking, science-loving Scopes passionately introduce his students to the evolutionist ideas of Charles Darwin (1809–1882), only to be violently denounced by the religious town leaders. Scopes is thrown into prison and there awaits his fate as his sweetheart—the preacher's daughter—begs him to renounce his belief in Darwin's theory. To the rescue comes defense lawyer Clarence Darrow (1857–1938), who is portrayed as the defender of the "little man," champion of the underdog, and advocate of science, truth, reason, learning, and humanity. Darrow's counterpoint, the prosecuting attorney William Jennings Bryan (1860–1925), is revealed as an ill-mannered ignorant bigot, a young Earth creationist, and a Christian Fundamentalist who opposes science and freedom of thought.[39] As the script reads:

> DARROW. Darwin took us forward to a hilltop from where we could look back and see the way from which we came; but for this insight and for this knowledge, we must abandon our faith in the pleasant poetry of Genesis.
>
> BRYAN, interrupting. We must not abandon faith! Faith is the most important thing![40]

Thanks to the *Inherit the Wind* version of the Scopes Monkey Trial, it is often interpreted in the popular mind as a classic case of science versus religion. What, however, is the historical truth? The true story of the Scopes Monkey Trial starts with the American Civil Liberties Union (ACLU) placing an

---

38. Ibid., 13.

39. In *Inherit the Wind* (directed by Stanley Kramer [Beverly Hills, CA: United Artists, 1960]), Bryan declares: "A fine Biblical scholar, Bishop Ussher, has determined for us the exact date and hour of the Creation. It occurred in the year 4004 BC. . . . It is not an opinion. It is literal fact, which the good Bishop arrived at through careful computation of the ages of the prophets as set down in the Old Testament. In fact, he determined that the Lord began the Creation on the twenty-third of October in the Year 4004 BC at—uh, at 9 a.m.!"

40. Ibid.

advertisement in the *Chattanooga Times*, offering legal support to any teacher prepared to stand trial for teaching evolutionist ideas (in order to oppose Tennessee's Butler Act of 1925, which prohibited the teaching of evolution in public schools). Local business leaders in Dayton, led by mining engineer and manager George Rappleyea and drugstore owner Frank Robinson, thought this trial—if held in Dayton—might be a good opportunity to publicize the town and boost the economy. Finding this plan agreeable, they recruited Scopes as the "sacrificial lamb." Scopes was not a biology teacher and never actually taught evolution. He was a part-time football coach and a general science instructor in the areas of physics and math. He did, however, fill in for the regular biology teacher from time to time. Thus Scopes agreed to be tried for teaching evolution, and the "Drugstore Conspirators"—as they were later called—sent a telegram to the ACLU to say they had found their man. Scopes volunteered to be arrested knowing that his fees and fines would be covered. He was charged with violating the Butler Act, and then immediately released on bail. At no time was Scopes held in jail on this charge.

Historian of science Edward Larson explains that for many Americans at this time the application of Darwinian natural selection to humans was associated "with a survival-of-the-fittest mentality that justified laissez-faire capitalism, imperialism, and militarism."[41] In the previous generation, industrialists such as Andrew Carnegie and John D. Rockefeller claimed Darwinism and the survival of the fittest as justification for their cutthroat business practices. During the years immediately preceding the Scopes trial, a scientific-sounding form of such social teachings aimed at culling the "evolutionarily unfit" gained widespread public attention under the name eugenics. In one of the popular biology textbooks of the day, George Hunter defined this term as "the science of improving the human race by better heredity."[42] One of Hunter's other textbooks, *A Civic Biology*, was the textbook from which John Scopes taught. As such it was the centerpiece of the trial. The evolution chapter in Hunter's *Civic Biology* explained, with regard to the mentally ill, mentally disabled, habitual criminals, and epileptics:

> If such people were lower animals, we would probably kill them off to prevent them from spreading. Humanity will not allow this, but we do have the remedy of separating the sexes in asylums or other places and in various ways preventing intermarriage and the possibility of perpetuating such a low and degenerate race.[43]

---

41. Edward J. Larson, *Summer for the Gods: The Scopes Trial and America's Continuing Debate over Science and Religion* (New York: Basic Books, 1997), 27.

42. George Hunter and Walter Whitman, *Civic Science in the Community* (New York: American Book Company, 1922), 422.

43. George Hunter, *A Civic Biology: Presented in Problems* (New York: American Book Company, 1914), 263.

William Jennings Bryan was no fan of eugenics. Bryan—a three-time Democratic Party nominee for the US presidency—had "built his political career on denouncing the excesses of capitalism and militarism," and in light of eugenics opposed the social application of Darwinism as "the merciless law by which the strong crowd out and kill off the weak."[44] Bryan was uneasy about the social implications of the theory of natural selection. He believed the militarism, racism, and eugenics programs of German society could be linked to its use of natural selection in social policy, and he saw America moving in the same direction. By the time of the Scopes trial, "24 states had passed laws permitting eugenic sterilizations, and about 12,000 sterilizations had been performed." The popular public support for eugenics "reflected both prejudice against recent immigrants and the growing faith in science of American intellectuals, who saw eugenics as a means of applying their scientific knowledge to social problems."[45]

Bryan's objection to the teaching of Darwinian evolution in public schools was not so much to the *scientific* theory as it was to the *social application* of the theory to US public policy. Bryan had read and understood Darwin's *Origin of Species* and *The Descent of Man* and was able to quote from them—and frequently did so during the trial. Contrary to myth within *Inherit the Wind*, Bryan publicly accepted the testimony of geologists regarding the great antiquity of the Earth, thought that the "days" of Genesis represented long eons of time, and had no objection to biological evolution up to the point of human beings.[46] As historian of science Ted Davis explains, "The real Bryan was a populist reformer, not a reactionary."[47]

For Clarence Darrow, the renowned attorney and outspoken atheist from Chicago, the Scopes trial was first and foremost a chance to attack Bryan's Christian views—and the Christian faith in general. When the Scopes trial arose, explains Larson, "Darrow volunteered his service for the defense—the only time he ever offered free legal aid—seeing a chance to grab the limelight and debunk Christianity."[48] Rather than defending the underdog—as the

44. Edward Davis, "Science and Religious Fundamentalism in the 1920s," *American Scientist* 93 (May–June 2005): 254–55.

45. Ibid., 255.

46. Ronald L. Numbers, "Creationism in 20th-Century America," *Science* 218 (1982): 538–44. See also Edward J. Larson, *Trial and Error: The American Controversy over Creation and Evolution* (New York: Oxford University Press, 1985). It must be stressed that, at this time, even many chief scientific supporters of Darwinian evolution resisted applying natural selection to the origin of human beings. Many prominent scientists at the time who had no affection for the Christian religion likewise "doubted whether the development of the human mind could be reduced to the action of natural selection." John Hedley Brooke, "Darwin and Victorian Christianity," in *The Cambridge Companion to Darwin*, ed. Jonathan Hodge (Cambridge: Cambridge University Press, 2003), 205. Even Thomas H. Huxley insisted that the human mind "could not be explained in mechanistic terms." Peter Bowler, *Evolution: The History of an Idea*, 3rd ed. (Berkeley: University of California Press, 2003), 219.

47. Davis, "Science and Religious Fundamentalism," 254.

48. Larson, *Summer for the Gods*, 73.

popular movie indicates—Darrow had a reputation for defending the rich and notoriously corrupt. Only months before the Scopes trial, he defended Nathan Leopold and Richard Loeb, the sons of two of the richest families in Chicago, when they gratuitously murdered fourteen-year-old Bobby Franks for apparently no other reason than to see if they could get away with it. Here, "Darrow used arguments of psychological determinism to save two wealthy and intelligent Chicago teenagers from execution for their cold-blooded murder of an unpopular former schoolmate."[49]

While the Scopes Monkey Trial myth holds up Darrow as a staunch defender of Darwin's science (and of scientific truth in general), in historical actuality Darrow "mixed up Darwinian, Lamarckian, and mutation-theory concepts in his arguments, utilizing whichever best served his immediate rhetorical purposes." Darrow's social views shaped his scientific ideas, rather than vice versa; and he embraced the most atheistic versions of Darwin's theory for the sake of its rhetorical expedience. Though Darrow spoke of "science as an objective arbitrator of truth," he nevertheless "would only present scientific evidence that supported his position." In short, says Larson, "he was a lawyer."[50]

Ironically, Darrow's personal lifelong quest to destroy the Christian religion was driven by the very myth of which he would become a central part. As a child in Kinsman, Ohio, Darrow imbibed the warfare model of science and religion as his fiercely anti-clerical father eagerly read Huxley, Draper, and White, "and made sure that his son did too." As a Chicago lawyer and politician, "Darrow quoted Draper and White in his public addresses and denounced Christianity."[51] Darrow saw Bryan's popular anti-evolution movement as one more chapter in the age-long war of religion against science. Enlisting himself in the militant ranks opposing religion, Darrow—inspired by the rhetoric of Draper and White—took up the banner of Scopes and Hunter's *Civic Biology* and tragically, perhaps unwittingly, came to the defense of "the scientific racism of the day."[52]

To summarize, then, a closer look at the historical and social context of the Scopes Monkey Trial shows that the main conflict was not between "science and religion" as such. Rather, the debate was chiefly between those who, like Darrow, utilized science to attack religion, a view called scientism, and those who, like Bryan, accepted scientific geology and even many of the scientific components of evolutionary theory, but, in the name of the values of the Christian religion, objected to the social application of Darwin's theory in eugenics. As for Scopes himself, far from being a martyr for science at the hands of religion, he was, instead, a willing party in a community-wide publicity stunt aimed at putting Dayton, Tennessee, on the map.

49. Ibid., 71.

50. Ibid., 72.

51. Ibid., 22.

52. Ibid., 23. Darrow was not generally a supporter of eugenics.

Conclusion

The culturally widespread notion that science and religion have experienced a long history of warfare is called the conflict thesis. This chapter has examined the historical roots of the conflict thesis and how it originated primarily in the late nineteenth-century anti-religious propaganda of Thomas H. Huxley's X-club and in the best-selling books of the American promoters of secularism, John Draper and Andrew Dickson White. Three cases from the history of science, that are often enlisted to support the conflict thesis, were then evaluated: (1) that Christopher Columbus was persecuted by the Church for holding, against Roman Catholic doctrine, that the Earth is a globe and not flat; (2) that the Church hounded, tortured, and imprisoned Galileo (and Copernicus before him) for suggesting that the sun is the center of the solar system; and (3) that John T. Scopes—the defendant in the famous 1925 Scopes Monkey Trial—was a "martyr for science" who taught evolution in defiance of angry, anti-science fundamentalist mobs led by William Jennings Bryan. Investigating these three cases shows that the popularly held versions of these stories are baseless myths and that the language of warfare falls far short of a historically accurate picture of the much more complex, rich, and creative interaction of religion and science during these historical events.

Discussion Questions

1. Today, no professional medieval historian would argue that medieval Europeans believed the Earth was flat. Yet this myth persists, in spite of all available documentary evidence—owing largely to Andrew Dickson White's invention and propagation of the story. Do you think John Draper and White were justified in fabricating myths about religion to promote science and secularism in education? Why or why not?

2. Why do you think the myth of the historical war between science and religion persists, despite the unanimous agreement of professional historians of science that science and religion were never at war?

3. What do you think such lessons from history can teach us about the present philosophical and theological search for truth?

4. Do you think striving for historical accuracy plays an important part in arriving at philosophical and theological truth? Explain why or why not.

Beyond the Classroom

Together with others who have not read this chapter, watch the short video "The World Was Never Flat," accessible at *http://vimeo.com/39912829* or *http://www .youtube.com/watch?v=a8HFDiVzWsM* (time 0:03:21). Lead a discussion on the film. Some suggested discussion questions are: "Does any of this information presented in this video surprise you? Why or Why not?" "Why do you think such myths were constructed? Whose interests do you think they serve?"

Resources for Further Study

Books

Bowler, Peter J. *Gorilla Trials and Monkey Sermons: Evolution and Christianity from Darwin to Intelligent Design.* Cambridge, MA: Harvard University Press, 2007.

Dixon, Thomas, Geoffrey Cantor, and Stephen Pumfrey, eds. *Science and Religion: New Historical Perspectives.* Cambridge: Cambridge University Press, 2010.

Ferngren, Gary B., ed. *Science and Religion: A Historical Introduction.* Baltimore: Johns Hopkins University Press, 2002.

Grant, Edward. *The Foundations of Modern Science in the Middle Ages: Their Religious, Institutional and Intellectual Contexts.* Cambridge: Cambridge University Press, 1996.

Hannam, James. *The Genesis of Science: How the Christian Middle Ages Launched the Scientific Revolution.* Washington, DC: Regnery, 2011.

Larson, Edward J. *Summer for the Gods: The Scopes Trial and America's Continuing Debate Over Science and Religion.* New York: Basic Books, 1997.

Lindberg, David. *The Beginnings of Western Science: The European Scientific Tradition in Philosophical, Religious, and Institutional Context, 600 B.C. to A.D. 1450.* Chicago: University of Chicago Press, 2007.

Lindberg, David, and Ronald Numbers. *God and Nature: Historical Essays on the Encounter between Christianity and Science.* Berkeley: University of California Press, 1986.

Numbers, Ronald L., ed. *Galileo Goes to Jail, and Other Myths about Science and Religion.* Cambridge, MA: Harvard University Press, 2009.

Olson, Richard. *Science and Religion, 1450–1900: From Copernicus to Darwin.* Westport, CT: Greenwood, 2004.

Principe, Lawrence M. *The Scientific Revolution: A Very Short Introduction.* Oxford: Oxford University Press, 2011.

Internet Resources

"Bede's Library: The Mythical Conflict between Science and Religion." Accessible at *http://www.bede.org.uk/conflict.htm.*

Davis, Ted. "Christianity and Science in Historical Perspective." Test of Faith (website). Accessible at *http://www.testoffaith.com/resources/resource.aspx?id=623.*

Davis, Ted. "An Obituary for the 'Warfare' View of Science and Religion." BioLogos Forum website, August 28, 2009. Accessible at *http://biologos.org/blog /an-obituary-for-the-warfare-view-of-science-and-religion.*

Moritz, Joshua. "The War that Never Was: Exploding the Myth of the Historical Conflict between Christianity and Science." Voice of Light Productions. Accessible at *http://vimeo.com/41224717* (time: 01:02:24).

Stanford Encyclopedia of Philosophy. "Religion and Science." Revised May 27, 2010. Accessible at *http://plato.stanford.edu/entries/religion-science/.*

CHAPTER 2

The Role of Faith in the History of Science

Science is free of the main vice of religion, which is faith.

—*Richard Dawkins, evolutionary biologist, Oxford University*[1]

Anybody who has been seriously engaged in scientific work of any kind realizes that over the entrance to the gates of the temple of science are written the words: *Ye must have faith.* It is a quality which the scientist cannot dispense with.

—*Max Planck, Nobel laureate in physics*[2]

In This Chapter

- The Religious Roots of the Laws of Nature
- Religion and Earth History in Eighteenth-Century Geology
- Darwin's Sacred Cause: The Unity of Humanity
- The Beginning of the Big Bang: The Cosmic Quest of Faith
- Discussion Questions
- Beyond the Classroom
- Resources for Further Study

Is modern science free of faith, as evolutionary biologist Richard Dawkins claims, or is faith a necessary component of science, as Nobel Laureate and pioneer of quantum physics Max Planck affirms? This chapter examines a number of instances in the history of science where faith in general—and religious

1. Richard Dawkins, "Is Science a Religion?" *The Humanist* 57, no. 1 (January/February 1997): 26.

2. Max Planck, *Where Is Science Going?*, trans. James Vincent Murphy (New York: W. W. Norton, 1932), 214.

faith in particular—have provided both the philosophical foundations for key scientific concepts and the motivation for pursuing specific scientific theories and lines of research. The first part of chapter 2 illustrates how a fundamental concept within science—the idea that there are "laws of nature"—is essentially a philosophical assumption (or metaphysical presupposition) that has very deep theological roots in the Jewish and Christian religious traditions. While the concept of laws of nature is a *general* philosophical presupposition underlying the *entire* project of the natural sciences and serving as a necessary condition of the *whole* scientific enterprise,[3] there are also contextually specific or *particular* philosophical presuppositions (or faith assumptions) that motivate *specific* research programs within science and guide *distinct* avenues of scientific investigation. For example, certain scientific theories addressing the questions "Why are we here?" and "Where did we come from?" were once hotly debated. Before the current scientific theories concerning cosmic and human origins were finally established through empirical discoveries (discoveries based on observation and experiment), philosophical assumptions grounded in faith commitments played a key role in motivating, shaping, and guiding the development of these theories. This chapter singles out three areas of modern science—historical geology, evolutionary biology, and cosmology—in order to examine some of the contextually specific presuppositions that have motivated and guided research in these areas.

The Religious Roots of the Laws of Nature

Scientists are in the business of discovering and describing the laws of nature. Many would even see this as the primary task of science. The idea that laws of nature exist is indeed so central to science that it is hard to envision what the scientific endeavor would look like without this concept. The idea that regular laws govern nature was not always obvious, however. Centuries before the Scientific Revolution took shape in the 1600s, the idea that nature is governed by regular laws was an affirmation of faith grounded in fundamentally religious convictions.

Where Did the "Laws of Nature" Originate?

According to historian of science Christopher Kaiser, the idea that nature is governed by its own laws of operation can be traced to the ancient Jewish belief that God created the natural world to possess a significant degree of relative autonomy or independence.[4] Many cultures in the ancient Near East viewed the

---

3. Mariano Artigas, *The Mind of the Universe: Understanding Science and Religion* (London: Templeton Foundation Press, 2000), 21.

4. Christopher Kaiser, "Early Christian Belief and Science," in *Blackwell Companion to Science and Christianity*, ed. J. B. Stump and Alan G. Padgett (Malden, MA: Blackwell, 2012), 7.

world of nature as a realm of chaos and capriciousness reflecting the whims and wars of various deities. In contrast, the monotheistic Hebrews focused on the oneness of the Creator, whose will or law for creation reigned supreme, without rival. The natural inference from this belief was a unity of creation, all of which operated under the same laws and principles. Theologian Lydia Jaeger notes, "From the very beginning, the Bible presents an objective order in nature."[5] As God commands the cosmos into existence by the power of his word in Genesis 1, it is clear that day and night follow each other automatically and that new generations of plants and animals succeed each other without interference, through the normal processes of reproduction (vv. 5, 11, 21, 24). Elsewhere in the Bible, the regular courses of the sun, moon, and stars; the regularity of the seasons and the tides; and even meteorological phenomena like wind, rain, and lightning are seen as exemplifying the laws of the one Creator God.[6]

Developing the biblical understanding of the cosmos, the early Jewish philosopher Aristobulus of Paneas (ca. 200 BCE), argued that God established laws for nature at the beginning of time and that the natural world would observe these laws without ceasing. Another influential early Jewish thinker, Yeshua ben Sirach (ca. 200 BCE), similarly reflected on the ceaseless regularity and law-like order of nature:

> When the Lord created his works from the beginning, and, in making them determined their boundaries, he arranged his works in an eternal order, and their dominion for all generations. They neither hunger nor grow weary, and they do not abandon their tasks. They do not crowd one another, and they never disobey his word. (Sir. 16:26–28)

For Aristobulus, Ben Sirach, and many other early Jews, the regularity of natural law was a clear sign of God's active presence within creation and a testimony to the Creator's sovereignty over the cosmos.[7]

Early Christian Understandings of the Lawfulness of Nature

The first Christians inherited the Hebrew conception of the lawfulness and unity of nature as ordained by the one Creator God. Basil of Caesarea (329–379 CE),

---

5. Lydia Jaeger, "The Idea of Law in Science and Religion," *Science and Christian Belief* 20, no. 2 (2008): 135. Jaeger explains, "The act of creation encounters no obstacles, in stark contrast with other creation accounts of the time: whereas, in the Babylonian story, the world exists as result of a battle between the gods, the monotheism of Genesis shows us a creative work that doesn't meet with the least resistance" (136).

6. Job 38:33; Prov. 8:29; Ps. 148:1–12; Jer. 31:35–36, 33:20–21. See Christopher Kaiser, *Creation and the History of Science* (Grand Rapids: Eerdmans, 1991), 15–16.

7. Kaiser, *Creation and the History of Science*, 17.

an influential theologian in the early church, describes how the natural world, once created and put into motion, evolves in accordance with the laws God assigned it, without interruption or diminishment. Arguing against the Aristotelian philosophers of his day, who denied the concept of inertia, Basil compares the regular laws and cycles of nature to a spinning top that continues in motion after the initial twist. Reflecting on the decree of God in Genesis 1:11, "Let the earth put forth vegetation," Basil comments that the Earth adheres to this divine command even to this day and will continue to do so for all time: "For the voice that was then heard and this command were as a natural and permanent law for it; it gave fertility and the power to produce fruit for all ages to come."[8] Another key early Christian thinker, Ambrose of Milan, used the Latin phrase *lex naturae* ("law of nature") to describe the created world's obedience to the decrees of the Creator. As a result of the reflections of such early church fathers, the concept of the laws of nature "became commonplace in Western discourse long before its more specialized use in modern science."[9]

How the Religious Conception of the Lawfulness of Nature Entered Early Modern Science

Basil's image of the conservation of momentum in a spinning top as an exemplification of nature's orderly obedience to God's laws was passed down by Christian philosopher, scientist, and theologian John Philoponus (490–570 CE) and then introduced to the Middle Ages through various Syriac Christian and Arabic commentators. John Buridan (1300–1362), a theologian and philosopher at the University of Paris, further developed Basil's idea of momentum while still understanding such continuous motion within the context of nature's obedience to God's initial creative decrees. Buridan's work was foundational to the thought of Galileo, Descartes, Newton, Boyle, and other early modern scientists as they continued the Christian critique of Aristotelian physics and formulated the momentum conservation principle and other laws of nature in mathematical terms.[10] There was no doubt in the minds of these early modern scientists, who worked to mathematically express such laws of nature, that these were, as Descartes declared, "laws marvelously established by God."[11]

---

8. Basil, *Hexaemeron* 5.1, quoted in Kaiser, "Early Christian Belief and Science," 7.

9. Ibid., 7.

10. See Michael Foster, "The Christian Doctrine of Creation and the Rise of Modern Natural Science," *Mind* 43 (1934): 446–68, at 448.

11. Jaeger, "Idea of Law," 134–35.

The Laws of Nature as an "Unsolved Mystery" in Current Science

Today, the phrase "laws of nature" is practically synonymous with the natural sciences, and yet many scientists, upon deeper reflection, have found the laws of nature to be a somewhat mysterious concept that invites a philosophical or even religious interpretation. Consider, for example, physicist and Nobel laureate Eugene Wigner's assessment that the existence of mathematically describable laws of nature "is something bordering on the mysterious and there is no rational explanation for it,"[12] or Nobel Laureate Richard Feynman's estimation that the fact that there are laws of nature at all "is a kind of miracle."[13] For Albert Einstein, the mysterious aspect of the laws of nature evoked a religious interpretation: "Everyone who is seriously involved in the pursuit of science becomes convinced that a spirit is manifest in the Laws of the Universe—a Spirit vastly superior to that of man."[14] In the same vein, physicist Steven Hawking has remarked, "One could define God as the embodiment of the laws of nature."[15]

While many current scientists have embraced the mysterious aspect of the laws of nature, for some contemporary philosophers of science, such as Nancy Cartwright, the implicitly theological ramifications of the concept of laws of nature has led them to reject the notion of nature's laws altogether: "I think that in the concept of law there is a little too much of God. . . . In the end the concept of a law does not make sense without the supposition of a law-giver."[16] One of Cartwright's predominant reasons for opposing the concept of laws of nature is "the difficulty of incorporating the laws of nature in an atheist world-view." This difficulty, explains Cartwright "is why I have been combating laws of nature all these years." Since, according to Cartwright, "we cannot understand natural law without resorting to God," she argues that scientists must endeavor "to take into account modern science, without bringing the idea of law into play."[17] One way to accomplish this, argues Cartwright, is to move

12. Eugene Wigner, "The Unreasonable Effectiveness of Mathematics in the Natural Sciences," in *Mathematics*, ed. Douglas Campbell and John Higgins (Belmont, CA: Wadsworth, 1984), 3:117.

13. Richard Feynman, *The Meaning of It All: Thoughts of a Citizen-Scientist* (New York: Basic Books, 1998), 43.

14. Albert Einstein, quoted in *Albert Einstein, The Human Side: New Glimpses from His Archives*, ed. Helen Dukas and Banesh Hoffman (Princeton: Princeton University Press, 1979), 32.

15. Stephen Hawking, interview by Ki Mae Heussner, "Stephen Hawking on Religion: 'Science Will Win,'" ABC News, June 7, 2010, accessible at *http://abcnews.go.com/WN/Technology/stephen-hawking-religion-science-win/story?id=10830164*.

16. Nancy Cartwright, "Is Natural Science 'Natural' Enough? A Reply to Philip Allport," *Synthese* 94 (1993): 291–301, at 299.

17. Lydia Jaeger paraphrasing Cartwright's thesis given at a conference in Varenna, Italy, in October 2004. Lydia Jaeger, "Nancy Cartwright's Rejection of the Laws of Nature and the Divine Lawgiver," *Science and Christian Belief* 22, no. 1 (2010): 85.

away from the Judeo-Christian, law-oriented understanding of the cosmos and return to an Aristotelian understanding of the natural world that focuses on "natural powers."[18]

Religion and Earth History in Eighteenth-Century Geology

In addition to *general* philosophical (or metaphysical) presuppositions—such as the laws of nature—that are foundational to the entire scientific enterprise there are also *particular* presuppositions that correspond to specific historical frameworks and worldviews (known as research paradigms) within which scientific theorizing takes place.[19] Particular presuppositions play an important but more limited role within scientific theorizing than general presuppositions and are often related to certain key stages in the historical development of a given scientific theory. For instance, when the geological sciences were first developing in seventeenth- and eighteenth-century Europe, one important particular presupposition, which at that time was a matter of considerable debate between geologists, was related to the question of whether the planet Earth had a beginning and changed progressively through time or, alternatively, whether Earth was infinitely old (without beginning or end) and characterized by nonprogressive cyclical geological processes.[20] The first view is known as historical geology and the second view—an idea that had been promoted by Aristotle and other ancient thinkers—is Aristotelian eternalism (or geologic eternalism). Before the relevant empirical evidence was available to decide between the two alternative theories of time, history, and progressive change as it related to Earth's processes, discussions among early geologists about the timescale of the world was deeply colored by a "clash of theologies." As historian of geology Martin Rudwick explains, this "was not a case of 'Religion versus Science,' but of one religious view of the world against another."[21] At that point in time, there was not conclusive empirical evidence to demonstrate whether the planet Earth had a physical beginning or whether it was, in fact, eternal.

---

18. Ibid., 86.

19. Scientific research paradigms are "standard examples of scientific work that embody a set of conceptual and methodological assumptions." See Ian Barbour, *Religion in an Age of Science* (San Francisco: Harper and Row, 1990), 51.

20. Alan H. Cutler, "Nicolaus Steno and the Problem of Deep Time," in *The Revolution in Geology from the Renaissance to the Enlightenment*, ed. Gary D. Rosenberg (Boulder, CO: Geological Society of America, 2009), 143–48, at 143.

21. Martin Rudwick, *Bursting the Limits of Time: The Reconstruction of Geohistory in the Age of Revolution* (Chicago: University of Chicago Press, 2005), 118.

The Enlightenment Eternalists' Rejection of Earth's Geological History

Among the most influential advocates for the perspective of geologic eternalism was James Hutton (1726–1797). Investigating the phenomena of erosion and sedimentation and assuming that present geologic processes were the key to those in the past, Hutton argued that planet Earth persisted in a perpetual state of dynamic equilibrium, an ongoing state of balance. According to Hutton, both the Earth itself and the cyclical processes that constantly transform the surface of the planet revealed "no vestige of a beginning, no prospect of an end."[22] In every part of Hutton's system "an assumption of eternalism was implicit," and he maintained that this assumption was supported by the available evidence. "With respect to human observation," said Hutton, "this world has neither a beginning nor an end."[23] Hutton's system was profoundly ahistorical, and it left no room for any specific and unrepeated historical events or for any unique or distinctive periods in the still deeper past. Consequently, explains Rudwick, "Hutton showed no interest in plotting the particularities of geohistory; indeed, he explicitly rejected that kind of project."[24]

Hutton was a deist and his concept of time as eternal and belief in the cyclical nature of Earth's processes was commonplace among fellow Enlightenment deists and atheists as well. The radically ahistorical eternalist vision of the Earth held great appeal for those who "rejected the biblical account of the recent origin of humanity," discarded the notion from Scripture that Earth had a physical beginning, and "denied that the cosmos had an ultimately divine foundation."[25] For deists and atheists, explains Rudwick, "an eternal cosmos could seem the best guarantee of the absence of a creative deity of any kind. . . . Both breeds of 'skeptic' took the eternity of the cosmos to include the uncreated eternity of the human race, or at least of some such rational beings."[26] The eternalist framework assumed that there had never been a time when the world was without humans, or at least some sort of rational beings, and allowed for no conception of a prehuman or radically nonhuman world. By assuming that human history had been coextensive with the history of nature for all eternity, eternalism evaded the question of origins, and "by denying that any periods in the deep past

---

22. James Hutton, "Theory of the Earth," *Transactions of the Royal Society of Edinburgh* 1 (1788): 304. Quoted in Nicolaas Rupke, "Geology and Paleontology," in *Science and Religion: A Historical Introduction*, ed. Gary B. Frengren (London: Johns Hopkins University Press, 2002), 181, 189.

23. "Even though," says Hutton, "it was beyond human capacities to demonstrate it conclusively." Hutton, "Theory of the Earth," 304.

24. Rudwick, *Bursting the Limits of Time*, 172.

25. Ibid., 118, 169.

26. Ibid., 283, 334.

had been distinctive in their organisms or anything else," eternalism "denied that the earth and its life could have had any true *history*."[27]

The Theistic Faith Foundations of Historical Geology

While many deist and atheist geologists felt they had a "stake in the doctrine of the uncreated eternity of the world," many geologists who were "Christian (and Jewish) theists believed they had a stake in the short timescale, because it helped guarantee the doctrine of creation."[28] According to historian of science Alan Cutler, Aristotelian eternalism, which held that the world was infinitely old and cycles of time repeated eternally, "had been almost uniformly denounced by Christian theologians because, among other things, it appeared to deny the existence of a Creator (if Earth was eternal, it had not been created)."[29] The alternative historical view of geology that was proposed by Christian geologists strongly "countered the eternalism of Enlightenment deism and, in particular, the theory of an 'eternal present.'"[30] Deriving from a traditional Christian metaphysical framework, historical geology assumed the cosmos and the planet Earth to be both temporally linear (having a distinct beginning in time) and genuinely historical (progressively changing over time).

While there persists a popular misconception that Christians during the seventeenth and eighteenth centuries were constrained in their geological speculation by an "official" date of creation (said to be 4004 BCE), historical evidence reveals that the chronological estimates of early geologists, who were also devout Christians, were in no way concerned "about exceeding biblical time limits from either a religious or scientific standpoint."[31] As Rudwick explains, "Contrary to the historical myth that persists today both among historians (who ought to know better) and among scientists," Christian geologists in the eighteenth century "were not constrained in their theorizing by having to squeeze the whole story of the earth into a few thousand years."[32] The reason for this is because well before this point in history it was widely accepted among both theological authorities and the common faithful that "the seven 'days' of creation were not necessarily to be understood as ordinary days."[33] In fact, the interpretations of Genesis viewing the "days" as ages, or as following an indefinitely long period

27. Ibid., 456, 390.

28. Ibid., 118.

29. Cutler, "Nicolaus Steno and the Problem of Deep Time," 147. See also Martin Rudwick, *The Meaning of Fossils: Episodes in the History of Palaeontology*, 2nd ed. (Chicago: University of Chicago Press, 1985).

30. Rupke, "Geology and Paleontology."

31. Cutler, "Nicolaus Steno and the Problem of Deep Time," 148.

32. Rudwick, *Bursting the Limits of Time*, 116.

33. Ibid., 117.

of history that preceded them, were the majority views long before any geological evidence emerged to support such perspectives. Indeed, because theological arguments for accepting a long chronology for Earth preceded rather than followed geological findings, "the way was open for a longer time-scale" well before any serious geological evidence was to be considered.[34] Historian Michael Roberts thus explains that by the 1700s "only a handful of theologians adopted a strict six twenty-four hour day chronology for Genesis chapter 1," and for English-speaking Christians of all denominational backgrounds, "by 1700 the age of the earth was reckoned to be well in excess of 6,000 years and by 1800 to be numbered in millions."[35]

Initially, the data from the geologic (or stratigraphic) record could be interpreted in light of either eternalism or historical geology and could be understood to support both research paradigms equally. As evidence for a linear progression of life forms through time accumulated, though, it "strengthened the biblical Christian notion of time as a directional phenomenon, against the cyclical notion of time found in Enlightenment eternalism" and "undercut the uniformitarian, steady-state model of earth history."[36] The progression of life forms in the fossil record was seen as being qualitatively similar to the Genesis 1 account where various stages of animal life precede the emergence of human beings. The perception of the progress of life in Earth history was seen as going hand-in-hand with the biblical notion of history as a directional process.

This progressive dimension to life history in the fossil record was noted as early as Nicolaus Steno (1638–1686), one of the founding fathers of geology and, later, a Roman Catholic bishop. Steno emphasized the "agreement between nature and scripture" because the oldest sequence in the geological strata he studied lacked fossils—and thus "must have been deposited before the creation of animals."[37] One important consequence of Steno's argument was "that the history of Earth had a direction and an identifiable beginning."[38] "In this sense, the geological record" was interpreted as a "strong vindication of religious doctrine."[39] Had the oldest layers of sediment in Steno's research "been as abundantly fossiliferous as the youngest strata, the record could have been used to support

---

34. Michael Roberts, "Genesis Chapter 1 and Geological Time from Hugo Grotius and Marin Mersenne to William Conybeare and Thomas Chalmers (1620–1825)," in *Myth and Geology*, ed. L. Piccardi and W. B. Masse (London: Geological Society, 2007), 47. Additionally, by the mid 1800s "the view of the Flood as partial or limited had emerged as dominant among most English-speaking Christians, including evangelicals." See Rodney Stiling, "The Genesis Flood," in *History of Science and Religion in the Western Tradition: An Encyclopedia*, ed. Gary B. Ferngren, Edward J. Larsen, and Darrel W. Amundsen (New York: Garland, 2000), 479.

35. Roberts, "Genesis Chapter 1 and Geological Time," 42.

36. Rupke, "Geology and Paleontology,"189.

37. Cutler, "Nicolaus Steno and the Problem of Deep Time," 147.

38. Ibid.

39. Ibid.

an eternally cycling Earth in the fashion of Aristotle."[40] A few generations after Steno, the Oxford University geologist William Buckland (1784–1856) similarly contended that "evidence for a period before life itself existed—that is, in the Primary rocks, with no trace of fossils" and that this "was enough to indicate an origin within time, and hence to refute 'the hypothesis of an eternal succession of causes.'" In this way, Buckland argued "that geology, no less than older branches of natural history, gave evidence of divine providence."[41] Thus, in the minds of the historical geologists, the evidence from "geology served to refute not only atheists, but also deists."[42] However, those geologists who were philosophically committed to eternalism, such as Charles Lyell (1797–1875), "persisted in their denial that the stratigraphic record showed a progressive trend."[43] Historian of science Nicolaas Rupke notes, "Ironically, some of the anti-progressionist arguments used by Lyell [and other eternalists] have become part of the armamentarium of modern-day [young Earth] creationists in their opposition to the Darwinian theory."[44]

Darwin's Sacred Cause: The Unity of Humanity

From the prominence given by the current media to debates between creationists and evolutionists, one might be tempted to think the historical foundations of evolutionary biology must have been one hundred percent faith-free. Indeed, today many assume that Charles Darwin (1809–1882) changed the world precisely because he was a tough-minded scientist doing good empirical science without any philosophical or religious trappings to cloud his objectivity. In this popular view, it was Darwin's single-minded pursuit of science and unhindered objective zeal for scientific knowledge that kept him on target to dispense with God and place humanity among the beasts. Atheists subsequently tend to laud Darwin for his purely secular scientific endeavor, and creationists chastise him for abandoning the faith. But according to Darwin biographers Adrian Desmond and James Moore, this popular portrayal of a philosophically dispassionate Darwin pursuing science free of faith "isn't just simplistic; most of it is plain wrong."[45] At the core of Darwin's scientific quest was a religiously inspired conviction that drove his research agenda. "Rather than seeing 'the facts' force evolution on Darwin," explain Desmond and Moore, "we find a

---

40. Ibid.

41. Rudwick, *Bursting the Limits of Time*, 610.

42. Rupke, "Geology and Paleontology," 188.

43. Ibid., 189.

44. Ibid.

45. Adrian Desmond and James Moore, *Darwin's Sacred Cause: How a Hatred of Slavery Shaped Darwin's Views on Human Evolution* (Boston: Houghton Mifflin Harcourt, 2009), xvi.

moral passion firing his evolutionary work. He was quite unlike the modern 'disinterested' scientist who is supposed (supposed, mark you) to derive theories from 'the facts' and only then allow the moral consequences to be drawn."[46]

The Abolitionist Faith in the Adamic Unity of Humanity and the Roots of Darwinian Evolution

The central faith assumption and philosophical presupposition that inspired and motivated Darwin's scientific work was the concept of the unity of humanity. This view, called monogenism, affirmed that all present human diversity stemmed from a common source and that all races were historically united in a single "brotherhood of man."[47] From the start, Darwin was transfixed by the idea of human unity as it related to the question of human origins. From where did Darwin's unwavering belief in the unity of humanity derive? The notion of human unity—along with the corresponding rejection of slavery—was a key element of Darwin's family heritage. Darwin grew up within a family that was deeply committed to abolitionism, the movement to abolish slavery, which was led by evangelical Christians such as William Wilberforce and Thomas Clarkson.

Library of Congress, Rare Book and Special Collections Division

In particular, Darwin's grandfather, Josiah Wedgwood, supported Clarkson's work.[48] Indeed, Wedgwood designed the official seal of the abolitionist movement himself: an image depicting an African slave on one knee, shackled hand and foot, with eyes and hands pointing heavenward, pleading, "Am I not a Man and a Brother?" To help promote the abolitionist cause, Wedgwood produced thousands of copies of this seal on pottery and on

Josiah Wedgwood, Darwin's grandfather, produced copies of this seal on his famous pottery to promote the abolitionist cause. Darwin shared his grandfather's conviction that all people shared a common ancestor and were "brothers."

---

46. Ibid., xviii.

47. Ibid., 54, xvii.

48. "Darwin's childhood religion had a distinctly evangelical cast." Ibid., 58.

ceramic medallions at his own expense for distribution throughout British and American society. "Belief in Adam as the father of mankind was solid and the theological premise of anti-slavery," and this central, faith-inspired conviction was firmly anchored in the worldview of young Charles. "Adamic unity and the brotherhood of man were axiomatic in the anti-slavery tracts that he and his family devoured and distributed. It implied a single origin for black and white, a shared ancestry."[49] When Darwin began his evolutionary quest in search of human origins, his "starting point was the abolitionist belief in blood kinship, a 'common descent'" for all human beings. And this deep conviction and faith in the unity of the human race "was *the* unique feature of Darwin's peculiar brand of evolution."[50]

Darwin's Faith in Human Unity against the Scientific Tide

At the time that Darwin was conducting his research, the notion of monogenism was almost as scientifically controversial as the concept of evolution.[51] Monogenists were typically religiously devout abolitionists and evangelical Christians who upheld a single origin for all known races of humanity for the sake of "preserving the integrity of scripture."[52] In the opinion of the scientific establishment of the day, monogenesis was tainted as antiquated religious dogma. Consequently, the anthropological authorities of the mid-nineteenth century caricatured the notion of human unity in a common ancestor and commonly dismissed it as myth.[53] The alternative to monogenism that was in vogue among anthropologists and biologists at the time was a view called polygenism. Polygenists held that various human races were, in reality, different species with separate origins that never converged upon a common ancestor and perhaps even went back eternally. In Darwin's day, it was broadly understood that "modern science supported Polygenesis" and that an empirically objective, "dispassionate and fearless exegesis of the rocks and tombs" ultimately "pointed to a separate black and white ancestry."[54]

When Darwin thus enlisted his keen scientific mind to the aid of the monogenist cause, he was going deeply against the scientific tide of his day. Darwin's understanding of human unity flew in the face of the world's scientific

---

49. Ibid., 54, xvii.

50. Ibid., xvii.

51. "Unity was almost as controversial as transmutation." Ibid., 329.

52. David Livingstone, *Adam's Ancestors: Race, Religion and the Politics of Human Origins* (Baltimore: Johns Hopkins Press, 2008), 20–23.

53. Desmond and Moore, *Darwin's Sacred Cause*, 289.

54. Ibid. Desmond and Moore, quoting Darwin, state, "If 'Unity versus Plurality' were to be settled by properly qualified anthropologists, 'the decision would' go to 'the polygenists,'" (353).

authorities.[55] As Desmond and Moore explain, "The 'unity hypothesis' was 'an article of faith' for Darwinites, a dogma as unfounded as the parsons' belief in Adam and Eve."[56] As Darwin developed his views on evolution from a common ancestor, he offered traditional scriptural monogenists "a deeper unity, a 'more humble' theology and more spectacular evolutionary 'grandeur.'"[57] And as a result, many scriptural monogenists enthusiastically embraced Darwin's scientific work. Natural selection permitted scientifically minded theologians, such as Benjamin B. Warfield, to welcome the fact that "both Bible and science taught the organic solidarity of the human species."[58]

The Beginning of the Big Bang: The Cosmic Quest of Faith

A further example of the vital role of religiously inspired faith assumptions (or particular philosophical presuppositions) in scientific theorizing comes from the history of twentieth-century physics. The current scientific understanding of the large-scale structure of the universe, a field of study known as cosmology, goes back to Albert Einstein's (1879–1955) theory of general relativity, which he proposed in 1915. Einstein's theory revolutionized the way the structure of the universe was understood by re-envisioning Newton's concept of gravity. Instead of seeing gravity as a mysterious force, as Newton did, Einstein described it as a function of the way massive objects curve the fabric of space-time—known as the space-time continuum.[59] When Einstein published his theory of general relativity, there were a number of different ways his equations could be legitimately interpreted, and there was not enough empirical evidence to decide definitively which of these interpretations was right. In this situation, where the data did not determine which scientific interpretation was correct (known as theory underdetermination), faith played a key part.

How Faith in a Static Universe Misled Einstein

At the beginning of the twentieth century, the predominant understanding of physicists was that the universe was static, unchanging, infinite, and eternal. This view of cosmology had been authoritatively passed down since the time of Isaac

---

55. "The unity-of-race thesis, secretly extended by Darwin to a unity-of-life thesis, was wading increasingly against the tide of new scientific thought." Ibid., 188, 352.

56. Ibid., 353.

57. Ibid., 316.

58. David Livingstone, *Darwin's Forgotten Defenders: The Encounter between Evangelical Theology and Evolutionary Thought* (Grand Rapids: Eerdmans, 1987), 120.

59. To picture Einstein's understanding of gravity, imagine how a bowling ball resting in the middle of a large trampoline would draw smaller objects toward it.

Newton (1642–1727), and all the empirical evidence available in the early 1900s appeared to support it. When Einstein began to work on applying his theory of gravity to the universe as a whole in 1917, these Newtonian assumptions about the cosmos "appeared unavoidable," and he "thought that one would get into bottomless speculation if one departed from [them]."[60] Einstein's philosophical beliefs (or faith assumptions) about the nature of the universe did not allow for an expanding universe with a beginning.[61] Einstein was surprised, then, when he realized his equations predicted that the universe was nonstatic and that it was either expanding or contracting. Neither of these alternatives were an acceptable option for him, and thus, he added a mathematical "fudge factor" called the *cosmological constant* to "prop up" the universe and keep it from changing. In effect, he "assigned a particular value to the cosmological constant so as to yield a static universe."[62] Einstein later reflected that the cosmological constant "was not required by the theory as such nor did it seem natural from a theoretical point of view" but, instead, was introduced to safeguard his initial assumptions about the nature of the cosmos.[63]

A Vision of the Cosmic Beginning Facilitated by Faith

In 1922, Russian physicist Alexander Friedmann (1888–1925) presented a solution to Einstein's equations that indicated the expansion of the universe. While Einstein "disliked the idea that the universe had a beginning," Friedmann's faith assumptions favorably disposed him toward a scientific interpretation Einstein would not consider. "Friedmann was not only a brilliant physicist," explains historian of science Jean-Pierre Luminet, "he was also a fervent Orthodox Christian," and "for him, general relativity suggested [the] creation of the world by God (although he did not formulate this statement in a published work)."[64] Against the prevailing view of the times, Friedmann's philosophical presuppositions enabled him to entertain the notion of an expanding universe as he worked

---

60. Albert Einstein, *Relativity: The Special and General Theory: A Popular Exposition*, 2nd ed. (New York: Crown, 1961), 196.

61. As Helge Kragh explains, Einstein's "belief that the universe was essentially stable and timeless . . . shaped his cosmological field equations of 1917." See Helge Kragh, *Conceptions of the Cosmos: From Myths to the Accelerating Universe: A History of Cosmology* (Oxford: Oxford University Press, 2007), 125. See Robert J. Russell, *Cosmology from Alpha to Omega: The Creative Mutual Interaction of Theology and Science* (Minneapolis: Fortress, 2008), 44–45.

62. Rodney Holder and Simon Mitton, "Georges Lemaître: A Brief Introduction to His Science, His Theology, and His Impact," in *Georges Lemaître: Life, Science and Legacy*, ed. Rodney Holder and Simon Mitton (New York: Springer, 2013), 40.

63. Einstein, *Relativity*, 152. Kragh explains, "In order to secure a universe static in time, Einstein was led to an important change in his field equations of 1915." *Conceptions of the Cosmos*, 132.

64. Jean-Pierre Luminet, "The Rise of Big Bang Models, from Myth to Theory and Observations," in *Antropogenesi, Dall' Energia al Fenomeno Umano*, ed. A. Pavan and E. Magno (Bologna: Il Mulino, 2008), 5.

out Einstein's equations. Thus, in his 1922 paper, he discussed a cosmos with a finite age and a beginning. Mathematically describing the origin of the cosmos in what is known as a space-time singularity, Friedmann clearly alluded to "the creation of the world."[65]

Like Friedmann, astrophysicist and Belgian Roman Catholic priest Georges Lemaître (1894–1966) held philosophical presuppositions that facilitated his openness to an expanding-universe interpretation of Einstein's equations, and Lemaître proposed such a theory, now known as the big bang theory, in a 1927 paper published in the journal *Nature*. Projecting the expansion of the cosmos back in time, Lemaître concluded that an initial "creation-like" event must have occurred where and when the fabric of time and space came into existence, a point that he called the "primeval atom." Lemaître welcomed the idea of a cosmic beginning, unlike the majority of cosmologists at the time who found the idea abhorrent. Indeed, in 1931, the well-known physicist Arthur Eddington considered Lemaître's theory and remarked, "Philosophically, the notion of a beginning of the present order of Nature is repugnant to me" because this is merely a confusion between physics and a theology of creation.[66] Einstein was repulsed by Lemaître's theory as well. At a conference near Brussels, Lemaître drew Einstein's attention to his results. Einstein abruptly responded, "Your calculations are correct, but your physical insight is abominable."[67] Reflecting on these events, historian of science Helge Kragh writes, "It is most remarkable that neither Friedmann's nor Lemaître's works made any impact at all. The reasons for the neglect are not entirely clear, but ingrained belief in the static nature of the universe was undoubtedly an important sociopsychological factor."[68]

While Lemaître's reasons for proposing an expanding universe with a finite beginning were solidly empirical, his faith assumptions prepared him to seriously consider the theory while the faith assumptions of Einstein and most of his contemporaries led them to dismiss it offhand. As historian of science John North explains, "His [Lemaître's] science had a strong theological relevance for him. An initial singularity was not something to be avoided, but a positive merit,

---

65. Kragh explains, "In his paper of 1922, Friedmann discussed finite-age models originating from a space-time singularity and wrote about 'the creation of the world.'" See Kragh, "Cosmologies and Cosmogonies of Space and Time," in *Cambridge History of Science, Modern Physical and Mathematical Sciences*, ed. M. J. Nye (Cambridge: Cambridge University Press, 2003), 528.

66. Eddington continues, "As a scientist I simply do not believe the Universe began with a bang. . . . It leaves me cold." Quoted in Simon Singh, *Big Bang* (New York: HarperCollins, 2004), 280; original source uncited. See also Dominique Lambert, "Georges Lemaître: The Priest Who Invented the Big Bang," in *Georges Lemaître: Life, Science and Legacy*, ed. Rodney Holder and Simon Mitton (New York: Springer, 2013), 12.

67. Odon Godart, "Contributions of Lemaître to General Relativity (1922–1934)," in *Studies in the History of General Relativity: Based on the Proceedings of the Second International Conference on the History of General Relativity*, ed. Jean Eisenstaedt and A. J. Kox, Einstein Studies (Luminy, France: Birkhäuser, 1988), 442.

68. Kragh, "Cosmologies and Cosmogonies of Space and Time," 527.

a token of God's creation of the world."[69] Even Lemaitre's paper in *Nature* originally had references to God in it as he concluded: "I think that everyone who believes in a supreme being supporting every being and every acting, believes also that God is essentially hidden and may be glad to see how present physics provides a veil hiding the creation."[70] However, deciding that such religious language might negatively bias other physicists against his interpretation, Lemaitre decided to remove all references to God in the final draft.

While Friedmann's and Lemaître's faith assumptions opened the way for them to consider an expanding universe with a beginning, Einstein, holding a metaphysical framework that would not allow this, rejected solutions to his own equations that eventually turned out to be correct. After the empirical confirmation of Friedmann's and Lemaître's interpretation, Einstein referred to his own inability to see beyond the received philosophical understanding of the universe as "the biggest blunder of my life," and in a 1947 letter to Lemaître, admitted, "Since I introduced this term [the cosmological constant] I had always had a bad conscience."[71] Later in life, as he described his efforts in 1919 to safeguard his Newtonian philosophical assumptions about the cosmos, Einstein said that even though the introduction of the cosmological constant was "gravely detrimental to the formal beauty of the theory," he could not, at that time, see any alternative.[72]

Atheistic Faith Assumptions and Resistance to the Big Bang

While many passively dismissed Friedmann's and Lemaître's interpretations of Einstein's equations, some cosmologists actively opposed the theory of a cosmic beginning on explicitly metaphysical grounds. The greatest opponent to Lemaître's big bang theory, who in fact gave it that name as a way of poking fun at it, was Cambridge cosmologist Sir Fred Hoyle (1915–2001). Hoyle

---

69. John North and Roy Porter, *The Norton History of Astronomy and Cosmology* (New York: Norton, 1994), 526. In a manuscript from about 1922 Lemaitre states that the universe began with light just as Genesis had suggested. However, Odon Godart notes that "Lemaitre was too careful a scientist to build his theory on what was no more than an intuitive opinion; a scientific basis was necessary." See Rodney Holder, "Georges Lemaitre and Fred Hoyle: Contrasting Characters in Science and Religion," in *Georges Lemaitre: Life, Science and Legacy*, ed. Rodney Holder and Simon Mitton (New York: Springer, 2013), 49. According to Kragh, Lemaitre's theology may have influenced his preference for a spatially finite universe (positive curvature) over an infinite one. See Helge Kragh, *Cosmology and Controversy: The Historical Development of Two Theories of the Universe* (Princeton: Princeton University Press, 1999), 198.

70. Lambert, "Georges Lemaître," 16.

71. Kristine M. Larsen, *Cosmology 101* (Westport, CT: Greenwood, 2007), 63.

72. Albert Einstein, *The Principle of Relativity: A Collection of Original Memoirs on the Special and General Theory of Relativity* (New York: Dover, 1952), 193. See Kragh, *Cosmology and Controversy*, 10.

despised organized religion. Annoyed by the theistic implications of Lemaître's theory, he developed a rival theory and even popularized it in a series on BBC radio.[73] Hoyle's alternative steady-state theory envisioned an unchanging universe with neither beginning nor end. Hoyle's atheism was a key motivator in the development of this alternative theory and his lifelong refusal to accept the big bang theory. As historian and physicist Rodney Holder explains, "Hoyle disliked the notion of an initial cause beyond the realms of science, which is what seems to be implied by the Big Bang, and he certainly associated the steady-state theory with atheism."[74] In other words, says historian of science Edward Davis, "Precisely because he did not believe in God, and because he did not like the implications of Lemaître's theory, Hoyle ridiculed" it and with "two other English astronomers proposed the 'steady-state' theory, to provide an alternative explanation without the implication that the universe had a beginning."[75] On the other hand, Lemaître "could not take the steady-state theory seriously, mainly because it differed so radically from his own view but possibly also because he thought it incompatible with his theology."[76] For Friedmann, Lemaître, Einstein, Hoyle, and others, faith assumptions—both religious and atheistic—played a vital role as they developed various conceptions of the cosmos throughout the twentieth century.

Conclusion

Today, it is commonly believed that faith—especially religious faith—only plays a negative role in science. The history of science, however, shows this has generally not been the case. Historians of science have described numerous instances of scientific inspiration and motivation driven by key philosophical assumptions initially grounded in faith. This chapter examined the important role that faith assumptions (or particular presuppositions) played in eighteenth-century geology, nineteenth-century biology, and twentieth-century cosmology. These faith assumptions—that Earth has a history, that all humans come from a common ancestor, and that the cosmos has a beginning—eventually ceased to be *assumptions* because they were increasingly supported, and thus justified, by the empirical data. Other faith assumptions within science, called general presuppositions, serve as the continuous foundation of the entire scientific enterprise, both past and present, and are "basic necessary conditions for science to exist and develop."[77] Because general presuppositions are philosophical they are *in*

---

73. Holder, "Georges Lemaître and Fred Hoyle," 39.

74. Ibid., 46.

75. Edward Davis, "Is the Big Bang Theory Irreligious?," *Harrisburg Patriot-News*, July 25, 2002, A-13. See also Kragh, *Cosmology and Controversy*, 192–93.

76. Holder, "Georges Lemaître and Fred Hoyle," 50.

77. Artigas, *Mind of the Universe*, 52.

principle beyond the scope of the practice of science to empirically establish or evaluate. One example of a general presupposition—with deep theological roots—that was examined in this chapter is the concept of laws of nature. As historian of science Lydia Jaeger remarks, "Without any doubt, European civilisation received the idea of created laws of nature from the biblical Scriptures."[78] Even though this was once a purely religious idea, the laws of nature came to occupy a central place in modern science, even to the point that some would now define science as the discovery and study of the laws of nature. Others, however, motivated by atheistic faith assumptions, have in recent decades become suspicious of the idea of such laws, owing to the concept's inescapably theological roots. As this debate continues, it remains to be determined whether science can ultimately survive without the laws of nature.

Discussion Questions

1. Considering the role that religiously inspired "faith assumptions" have played within certain scientific theories (e.g., historical geology, evolution, and big bang cosmology), do you think there is a clear dividing line between religion and science? Why or why not?

2. Do you think the eventual justification of initial religious assumptions through scientific discovery provides evidence for the religious views that provided those assumptions? For example, steady state theory was motivated by Hoyle's atheistic assumption that there was no cosmic beginning. If his theory were found to be correct, would this be seen as support for atheism? Why or why not?

3. Do you think the assumption that there are "laws of nature" is necessary for science? Explain why or why not.

Beyond the Classroom

As an informal activity with a small group of friends or as a facilitator in a classroom setting, have each person think of something he or she holds as true (a knowledge claim) beyond what is immediately evident to the senses at this moment. Have them consider why they hold it as true, and then have each person reflect on the following questions:

1. What is your evidence for the knowledge claim above?

2. How far back can the chain of evidence be traced?

3. At what point or points does trust or faith enter into the chain of evidence?

---

78. Jaeger, "Idea of Law," 135; or as C. S. Lewis reflects, "Men became scientific because they expected Law in Nature, and they expected Law in Nature because they believed in a Legislator." See C. S. Lewis, *Miracles* (New York: Macmillan, 1974), 169.

Resources for Further Study

Books

Artigas, Mariano. *Knowing Things for Sure: Science and Truth.* Lanham, MD: University Press of America, 2006.

Barbour, Ian. *Religion in an Age of Science,* Gifford Lectures 1989-1991. Vol. 1. New York: HarperCollins, 1990.

Barbour, Ian. *When Science Meets Religion: Enemies, Strangers, or Partners?* London: SPCK, 2000.

Jaeger, Lydia. *Einstein, Polanyi, and the Laws of Nature.* West Conshohocken, PA: Templeton Press, 2012.

Kaiser, Christopher. *Creation and the History of Science.* Grand Rapids: Eerdmans, 1991.

Kragh, Helge. *Cosmology and Controversy: The Historical Development of Two Theories of the Universe.* Princeton: Princeton University Press, 1999.

Richardson, Mark, and Gordy Slack. *Faith in Science: Scientists Search for Truth.* London: Routledge, 2001.

Roberts, Michael. *Evangelicals and Science.* Westport, CT: Greenwood, 2008.

Russell, Robert J. *Cosmology from Alpha to Omega: The Creative Mutual Interaction of Theology and Science.* Minneapolis: Fortress, 2008.

Articles

Jaeger, Lydia. "Laws of Nature." In *Blackwell Companion to Science and Christianity,* edited by J. B. Stump and Alan G. Padgett, 453–63. Oxford: Wiley-Blackwell, 2012.

Kaiser, Christopher. "Early Christian Belief and Science." In *Blackwell Companion to Science and Christianity,* edited by J. B. Stump and Alan G. Padgett, 3–13. Oxford: Wiley-Blackwell, 2012.

Internet Resources

Artigas, Mariano. "Articulating Science and Theology: Presuppositions and Implications of Science." Presented at the Sixth European Conference on Science and Theology (ESSSAT VI), Cracovia, Poland, March 26–31, 1996. Accessible at *http://www.unav.es/cryf/articulatingsciencieandtheology.html.*

Moritz, Joshua. "The Metaphysical Foundations of Science and the Role of Science in Faith." Voice of Light Productions. Accessible at *http://vimeo.com/38669457* (time: 0:50:50).

CHAPTER 3

The Boundaries and Limits of Science and Faith

Without the belief that it is possible to grasp the reality with our theoretical constructions, without the belief in the inner harmony of our world, there could be no science. This belief is and always will remain the fundamental motive for all scientific creation.

—*Albert Einstein, physicist*[1]

The scientist and the theologian both work by faith, a realist trust in the rational reliability of our understanding of experience.

—*John Polkinghorne, physicist and theologian*[2]

In This Chapter

- What Is Science?
- Why Science Needs Faith
- Why Religious Faith Needs Science
- Discussion Questions
- Beyond the Classroom
- Resources for Further Study

Are there fundamental limits to the scientific enterprise and the types of questions science can answer? Where should one draw the boundary line between religion and science? To adequately address these questions, one first needs some understanding of precisely what science is. This chapter considers how to define

---

1. Albert Einstein and Leopold Infeld, *The Evolution of Physics: The Growth of Ideas from Early Concepts to Relativity and Quanta* (New York: Simon and Schuster, 1966), 296.

2. John Polkinghorne, *Belief in God in an Age of Science* (New Haven: Yale University Press, 1998), 124.

"science" by examining in what way the term has been understood by historians and philosophers of science. The broad consensus of contemporary philosophers of science is that any proper understanding of science entails that there are essential limits to the scientific endeavor. The limits of science are both internal (or empirical) and external (or metaphysical). Empirical limits arise when science discovers fundamental boundaries beyond which science can never hope to see.[3] External or metaphysical boundaries of science are related to the foundational assumptions of science that lie *outside* of empirical science yet play a key role *within* science as principles that shape scientific theory and practice. These shaping principles of science include presuppositions underwriting science, sanctions and motives for doing science, and guides for regulating scientific methodology and for selecting acceptable theories.[4] While some of science's shaping principles are aesthetic, ethical, and philosophical, many are broadly theological in their essence and historical origin. Since theologically derived shaping principles historically served as the metaphysical foundation of science as it began to take shape in the European Middle Ages, and because these principles continue to play a vital and necessary role within science today, science appears to require a good degree of faith. Yet it also seems that religious faith—and theistic faith in particular—needs science as well. This is because the Jewish and Christian scriptures affirm that the world of nature is God's creation. As the Jewish Bible (the Christian Old Testament) encourages the faithful to consider God's created works (Ps. 111), the practice of science consequently becomes a theological imperative. The Christian Bible even teaches that "God's invisible qualities—his eternal power and divine nature" cannot be "clearly seen or understood" without some reference to the created, finite, material reality that is unveiled through the scientific investigation of nature (Rom. 1:20). Thus if the Christian is to truly understand God the Creator, he or she must strive to understand the realm of God's creation.

What Is Science?

In the current global culture, the authority and power of science is unrivaled. However, what kind of knowledge can be properly classified as "scientific"

---

3. In the current scientific understanding there are empirical or observational limitations that arise from the discovery of the big bang and in the standard interpretation of quantum physics. Because all of space and time and matter and energy begin at the big bang, it is not possible to see "before" or "beyond" the big bang. In quantum physics, which studies matter at the minutest level, there are fundamental limits in principle to how accurate a given measurement can be. These limits in measurement are related to Heisenberg's uncertainty principle. Empirical limits related to both the big bang and Heisenberg's uncertainty principle will be discussed in more detail in the next chapter.

4. John Hedley Brooke, *Science and Religion: Some Historical Perspectives* (Cambridge: Cambridge University Press, 1991), 18–33; and Edward B. Davis, "Christianity and Early Modern Science: The Foster Thesis Reconsidered," in *Evangelicals and Science in Historical Perspective*, ed. David N. Livingstone, D. G. Hart, and Mark A. Noll (Oxford: Oxford University Press, 1999), 77.

knowledge? Within the philosophy of science, the question of how to adequately define science is known as the demarcation problem. The demarcation question essentially asks how to draw a boundary between what can be counted as science and what cannot. It seeks to determine "what science is, how it works, and what makes science different from other ways of investigating the world."[5] Attempts to address this question have been diverse and complex, and straightforward answers have been elusive. Philosopher of science Thomas Nickles explains, "The conclusion of the last two generations of philosophers of science, reinforced by modern science studies" is that "there is no one simple distinction that marks off science (and its potential technological applications) from pseudoscience, or good science from bad."[6] To gain a better sense of the meaning of "science," then, it is helpful to have some understanding of both the history of how science has been understood and current areas of consensus among contemporary philosophers of science.

The Classical and Inductive Understandings of Science

The word "science" comes from the Latin term *scientia*, meaning "knowledge." In the ancient, medieval, and early modern periods, "science" referred to any body of reliable knowledge that could be logically and rationally explained. This included not only the natural sciences, then known as "natural philosophy," which sought to gain knowledge of physical reality and the material causes of things, but also to the results of logical, geometrical, and mathematical demonstrations that revealed general and necessary truths. Scientific knowledge, in this classical sense, could be gained in a number of different disciplines besides the natural sciences.

From the 1500s through the 1700s, during a period known as the Scientific Revolution, medieval natural philosophy was transformed into early modern science. Increasingly, "science" referred to the use of careful observation and the experimental method as the primary way to attain knowledge of the natural world. The "scientific method," as it came to be known, was developed and popularized by Francis Bacon (1561–1626) who contended that science should proceed through inductive reasoning. According to Baconian inductivism, the practice of science involves gathering experimental and observational facts about nature so that one can infer general patterns or universal laws that describe the particular phenomena that are observed. In this way, the scientific method was seen as enabling one to discern "a universal truth from the outcome of a single

5. Peter Godfrey-Smith, *Theory and Reality: An Introduction to the Philosophy of Science* (Chicago: University of Chicago Press, 2003), 1.

6. Thomas Nickles, "The Demarcation Problem," in *The Philosophy of Science: An Encyclopedia*, ed. S. Sarkar and J. Pfeifer (New York: Routledge, 2005), 196.

experimental procedure."[7] According to Bacon's vision, science is a wholly objective endeavor involving the dispassionate collection of observational data and the rigorous application of pure reason to this data.

Problem of Induction and the Quest for the Scientific Verification

While the inductive approach successfully launched the scientific enterprise, beginning in the 1700s philosophers such as David Hume (1711–1776) realized there was a serious problem with it. Pointing out the weaknesses of this approach to science, Hume enquired, "What reason do we have for expecting patterns observed in our past experience to hold also in the future?" He also asked, "What justification do we have for using past observations as a basis for generalization about things we have not yet observed?"[8] Hume argued that no finite number of observations could ever justify a universal generalization, and he likewise concluded that there is no reason to expect the future to resemble the past. In other words, even if a scientist has observed thousands of swans and all of them are white, it does not logically follow, therefore, that *all* swans are white.

While today there is general agreement among philosophers of science that Hume's argument against induction is "unanswerable,"[9] from the 1930s to the 1970s a school of thought known as logical empiricism (or logical positivism) aspired to develop an understanding of science that would allow one to speak of the verification or confirmation of certain items of empirical knowledge.[10] Logical empiricists admitted that, owing to the problem of induction, scientific theories could never be proven. However, they believed that experimental and observational evidence could still be viewed as providing direct support for the confirmation of a given scientific theory.[11] For example, the influential logical positivist philosopher Carl Hempel suggested that, as a matter of logic, each observation of a black raven works to confirm the generalization that all ravens are black.[12]

---

7. Peter Dear, "The Meanings of Experience," in *Cambridge History of Science*, vol. 3, *Early Modern Science*, ed. Katharine Park and Lorraine Daston (Cambridge: Cambridge University Press, 2006), 129.

8. Godfrey-Smith, *Theory and Reality*, 39.

9. Peter Lipton, *Inference to the Best Explanation*, 2nd ed. (New York: Routledge, 2004), xi.

10. Here I use the terms "logical empiricism" and "logical positivism" synonymously. As Hardcastle explains, "The notion that 'logical empiricism' suggests an identifiable, discrete, and conscious departure from something called logical positivism is tantamount to historical falsehood." Gary Hardcastle, "Logical Empiricism," in *The Philosophy of Science: An Encyclopedia*, ed. S. Sarkar and J. Pfeifer (New York: Routledge, 2005), 458.

11. Godfrey-Smith, *Theory and Reality*, 40.

12. Ibid., 46.

Within the logical empiricist framework, scientific theories were viewed as having the potential to be verified through evidence. Scientific knowledge was believed to be cumulative and progressive. Viewing physics as the most ideal science, logical empiricists held a firm conviction in the unity of scientific knowledge, believing that "all sciences, including psychological and social sciences, might one day be unified and reduced to common, fundamental physical terms."[13] Logical empiricists maintained that science—when practiced rightly—was value-free, purely objective, and isolated from the influences of broader culture. Science was considered an autonomous and self-justifying enterprise without the need to seek concepts from outside of science for use in scientific theorizing. Above all, the logical positivists envisioned science as a project that stood on its own feet philosophically—free from all metaphysical concepts or content. In other words, they envisioned science as entirely faith-free.[14]

While the logical positivist vision of science is still quite common in popular perceptions of science (and even among many practicing scientists), among professional philosophers of science it is no longer considered a viable perspective. Philosopher of science Alan Richardson explains, "By 1976 logical empiricism was taken to be a thing of the past even within the professional organization of philosophers of science in North America, the Philosophy of Science Association (PSA)."[15]

Falsification as the Hallmark of True Science

The demise of the logical empiricist conception of science began with the work of the influential twentieth-century philosopher Sir Karl Popper (1902–1994).[16] Popper agrees with Hume that it is logically impossible to make inductive inferences that move from particular experiments or observations to universally valid laws. Against the logical positivists, Popper argues that confirmation is a myth; scientific knowledge and scientific theories can never be verified or confirmed by empirical data.[17] In fact, he contends, one "can never give positive reasons

---

13. Christopher Ray, "Logical Positivism," in *A Companion to the Philosophy of Science*, ed. William H. Newton-Smith (Oxford: Blackwell, 2000), 243.

14. Thomas Mormann, "The Structure of Scientific Theories in Logical Empiricism," in *The Cambridge Companion to Logical Empiricism*, ed. Alan Richardson and Thomas Uebel (Cambridge: Cambridge University Press, 2007), 136–54.

15. Alan Richardson, "'That Sort of Everyday Image of Logical Positivism': Thomas Kuhn and the Decline of Logical Empiricist Philosophy of Science," in *The Cambridge Companion to Logical Empiricism*, ed. Alan Richardson and Thomas Uebel (Cambridge: Cambridge University Press, 2007), 351.

16. In his autobiography Karl Popper takes the credit for sounding the death knell of logical positivism as early as 1934. See Karl Popper, *Unended Quest: An Intellectual Autobiography* (London: Routledge, 1993).

17. Godfrey-Smith, *Theory and Reality*, 58.

which justify the belief that a theory is true."[18] This is because there are always an infinite number of experimental tests that remain to be performed in order to confirm a theory. Consequently, "it is never possible to confirm a theory, not even slightly, and no matter how many observations the theory predicts successfully."[19] According to Popper, "Science can never claim to have attained truth or even a substitute for it, such as probability."[20] Because there are always an infinite number of experimental tests that remain to be performed, Popper argues that no amount of empirical data can ever raise the probability of a given scientific theory above zero.

Rather than focusing on induction, verification, or probability as the hallmark of science, Popper focuses on the central role of *falsification*. Scientific theories can never be confirmed, but they can be falsified. For instance, it takes only one black swan to falsify the hypothesis that all swans are white. If a given hypothesis is to be counted as truly scientific, it must make testable predictions about the world that may be potentially refuted by later experimentation or possible observation. In other words, "to be scientific, a hypothesis has to take a risk, has to 'stick its neck out.' If a theory takes no risks at all, because it is compatible with every possible observation, then it is not scientific."[21] Unfalsifiable theories (such as astrology, Freudian psychology, and Marxism) are not genuine science but rather what Popper calls *pseudoscience*. Because scientific knowledge makes progress through falsifying theories rather than through verifying them, the highest truth status that any scientific theory can reach is: "not yet falsified, despite our best efforts."[22]

In contrast with logical empiricism, Popper held that there is no clear way to separate the practice of science from the individual scientist and from wider individual human and cultural concerns. What many might consider to be *extra-scientific* factors such as imagination, interpretation, and creativity, in reality play a central role *within science* and are "present in every step of the scientific method," including the formulation of new hypotheses, the formulation and acceptance of the empirical statements that serve to test those hypotheses, and "the evaluation of the hypotheses under the light of the available evidence."[23] Popper likewise parted ways with logical positivism in his assessment of the role of metaphysics within science. Unlike the logical positivists, Popper "clearly acknowledged the

18. Karl Popper, *Conjectures and Refutation: The Growth of Scientific Knowledge* (London: Routledge, 2014), 310.

19. Godfrey-Smith, *Theory and Reality*, 59.

20. Karl Popper, *Logic of Scientific Discovery* (London: Routledge, 2002), 278.

21. Godfrey-Smith, *Theory and Reality*, 58.

22. Philip Clayton, "Philosophy of Science: What One Needs to Know," *Zygon* 32 (1997): 99–108, at 102.

23. Mariano Artigas, *The Mind of the Universe: Understanding Science and Religion* (Radnor, PA: Templeton Foundation Press, 1999), 167.

meaningfulness of metaphysical ideas" and even stressed that the very rationality underlying the scientific enterprise is rooted in a kind of metaphysical "faith in reason."[24] According to Popper's understanding of science, then, certain kinds of faith play a vital and necessary role.

Paradigms and Metaphysical Worldviews in Science

While Popper acknowledged that individual values, cultural concepts, and metaphysical ideas do have a key part to play within the scientific endeavor, Thomas Kuhn (1922–1996), the most influential historian and philosopher of science of the twentieth century, went beyond this to show that it is not possible—even in principle—to separate the everyday practice of science from the metaphysical frameworks and worldviews within which the community of scientists is embedded.[25] Examining how science has operated throughout history, Kuhn points out that scientific activity and theory is always embedded in a larger cultural context or worldview. This cultural context or worldview affects the basic assumptions, metaphysical commitments, values, questions, and problems of science as well as the possible interpretations of data within science. This larger cultural and metaphysical context within which science is nested, Kuhn calls a paradigm. In Kuhn's theory, a paradigm is "a whole way of doing science, in some particular field. It is a package of claims about the world, methods for gathering and analyzing data, and habits of scientific thought and action." A paradigm is the interpretive lens through which the scientist sees reality, determining "what there is in the world," and telling the scientist what he or she is seeing when doing experiments or recording observations.[26]

Kuhn calls the everyday practice of science within the framework provided by a given paradigm "normal science." Kuhn describes normal science as "puzzle solving," where the scientist uses the tools and concepts provided by the paradigm to describe and model what they are observing in order to get a new "riddle" to fit smoothly into the interpretive framework provided by the paradigm. During periods of normal science, "scientific education is a kind of 'indoctrination,' which results in scientists having a deep 'faith' in their paradigm."[27] Consequently, Kuhn contends, scientists cannot typically "see" beyond their current paradigm and into another. In this respect, different scientific paradigms are like different "worlds," with no logic or overarching perspective that allows one to compare it to another, a situation Kuhn calls "incommensurable." Experimental

---

24. Ibid., 167–69.

25. "Thomas S. Kuhn was the most widely read, and most influential, philosopher and historian of science of the twentieth century." Richard Grandy, "Thomas Kuhn," in *The Philosophy of Science: An Encyclopedia*, ed. S. Sarkar and J. Pfeifer (New York: Routledge, 2005), 419.

26. Godfrey-Smith, *Theory and Reality*, 75.

27. Ibid., 81–84.

evidence, "observational data and logic alone cannot force scientists to move from one paradigm to another, because different paradigms often include within them different rules for treating data and assessing theories."[28]

Rather than seeing scientific progress as a steady, cumulative, and gradual development within an enduring framework of understanding the world, Kuhn argues that scientific progress over the long term shows more a pattern of occasional, dramatic, and total transformations in our understanding of the world—what he refers to as paradigm shifts. As normal science proceeds, anomalies arise that do not fit nicely into the interpretive framework of a given paradigm. Typically, such anomalies are bracketed or ignored as puzzles that have resisted solution. As long as there are not too many anomalies, normal science proceeds as usual, and "normal scientists" will tolerate a good deal of temporary trouble without abandoning a paradigm as falsified. However, says Kuhn, when a critical mass of significant anomalies is reached, "the scientists start to lose faith in their paradigm," and the scientific community enters

Christos Georghiou/Shutterstock.com

A Gestalt image; do you see the human faces? A "paradigm shift" is similar in that it involves a new, alternative interpretation of scientific data, a new way of "seeing" what the data describe.

a state of crisis.[29] For Kuhn, a crisis period is when "an existing paradigm has lost the ability to inspire and guide scientists, but when no new paradigm has emerged to get the field back on track."[30] Science during a crisis period is more open to novel understandings, imaginative inspiration, and metaphysical ideas. When an attractive alternative paradigm appears, a radical shift—called a scientific revolution—may take place where the new paradigm replaces the old one. Kuhn describes the shift to a new paradigm as a type of "conversion" or a phenomenon akin to a gestalt switch (see figure of gestalt image). As Kuhn explains:

> The competition between paradigms is not the sort of battle that can be resolved by proofs. . . . The proponents of competing paradigms will often disagree about the list of problems that any candidate for paradigm must resolve. Their standards or their definitions of science are not the same. . . . Before they can hope to communicate fully, one

---

28. Ibid., 75.
29. Ibid., 82.
30. Ibid., 83.

group or the other must experience the conversion that we have been calling a paradigm shift. Just because it is a transition between incommensurables, the transition between competing paradigms cannot be made a step at a time, forced by logic and neutral experience.[31]

Kuhn answers the question "What is science?" by pointing to the dynamic nature of the scientific endeavor and the historical complexities involved in the process of scientific discovery. He demonstrates that the scientific process is anything but faith-free. According to Kuhn, leading scientists throughout history are "motivated by metaphysical doctrine" and employ such doctrine to both find and justify the theoretic claims they make. Kuhn clearly illustrates "the historical productivity of metaphysical doctrine in scientific research" and makes a compelling case that "such metaphysical doctrine continues to have a role to play in scientific research even today."[32] In addition to the centrality of experimental data and explanatory theories, then, another key element of science is the essential role played by metaphysical commitments and philosophical assumptions. Such beliefs and convictions are not irrelevant to science; on the contrary, they are foundational and help to shape science both in the past and present. As a working definition of science, then, one can say that science consists of essentially three basic components: (1) empirical data, (2) explanatory theories, and (3) nonempirical shaping principles.

Why Science Needs Faith

If nonempirical shaping principles are a key part of what science *is*—as Kuhn and many other historians and philosophers of science have shown—then science really does need faith. Such faith *within* science takes a number of different forms, including ethical values, aesthetic principles, philosophical commitments, metaphysical presuppositions, and theological motivations. Philosopher of science Del Ratzsch explains, "Doing science requires use of presuppositions involving criteria for theory construction, theory evaluation, and boundaries of concept legitimacy, plausibility structures, and a host of other matters." Since such factors both precede and inform the practice of science, "science itself cannot provide the rational justification for them." For instance, it is *in principle* not possible for one to "set up a scientific experiment to demonstrate that science or a particular scientific method gives an exhaustive account of reality."[33] There are also no properly scientific means or rules that allow one to choose between competing research

---

31. Thomas Kuhn, *The Structure of Scientific Revolutions* (Chicago: University of Chicago Press, 1962), 147–50; Godfrey-Smith, *Theory and Reality*, 89.

32. Richardson, "That Sort of Everyday Image," 349–50.

33. Del Ratzsch, quoted in Mikael Stenmark, *Scientism: Science, Ethics and Religion* (Aldershot, UK: Ashgate, 2001), 22.

paradigms in an absolutely logical or *purely scientific* way.[34] Science, then, appears to critically depend upon values and presuppositions that are not the result of scientific discovery or testing. Since they "lie somewhere beyond the borders of science," they cannot be directly evaluated through empirical investigation.[35]

Aesthetic and Moral Principles within Science

Consider, for example, the role of Ockham's Razor within science. Attributed to the logician and Franciscan friar William of Ockham (1287–1347), Ockham's Razor is a principle of parsimony or simplicity that affirms that the simplest explanation for a given phenomenon is most likely true. Both in the past and present, most scientists have believed that, all things being equal, simpler theories are better. The well-known physicist Isaac Newton (1643–1727) includes Ockham's Razor as one of his three "rules of reasoning in philosophy" in his *Principia Mathematica*: "Rule I: We are to admit no more causes of natural things than such as are both true and sufficient to explain their appearances."[36] Albert Einstein, writing more than two hundred years later, agrees: "The grand aim of all science . . . is to cover the greatest possible number of empirical facts by logical deductions from the smallest possible number of hypotheses or axioms."[37] But why should scientists favor simpler theories over more complex ones? In the end, it would seem that this is essentially an *aesthetic* value that has played and continues to play a central role in scientific explanation and theory choice.

As a second example, consider the place of "mathematical beauty" within physics. Many physicists have long taken the beauty of an equation as a sure guide to its physical truth. Kuhn points out that such beauty was so central to the Copernican astronomer Johannes Kepler that his "entire astronomical program is based in a metaphysical faith in mathematically expressed harmonies in nature."[38] A few centuries later, Einstein affirms that for physicists "the only

---

34. See George Ellis, "The Myth of a Purely Rational Life," *Theology and Science* 5, no. 1 (2007). The emphasis here on the lack of a *purely scientific* means to choose between competing paradigms does not intend to negate the idea that progress can be made in science. For example, the philosopher of science Imre Lakatos suggests that within science there are both *progressive research programs* (which make novel predictions that anticipate scientific findings) and *degenerative research programs* (which are forced to invoke ad hoc alterations to their central theories in the face of conflicting data). Within this Lakatosian framework, progressive research programs are discerned as a more genuine reflection of empirical reality. See Imre Lakatos, *Philosophical Papers* (Cambridge: Cambridge University Press, 1978).

35. Del Ratzsch, "The Nature of Science," in *Science and Religion in Dialogue*, ed. M. Y. Stewart (Oxford: Wiley-Blackwell, 2010), 47.

36. Isaac Newton, *Principia Mathematica* (London, 1687), 41:1.

37. Albert Einstein, *Ideas and Opinions* (New York: Crown, 1954), 282. Quoted in Leonard Kollender Nash, *The Nature of the Natural Sciences* (Boston: Little, Brown, 1963), 173.

38. Roger Trigg, *Rationality and Science: Can Science Explain Everything?* (Oxford: Blackwell, 1993), 224.

physical theories that we are willing to accept are the beautiful ones."[39] The Nobel Prize–winning atomic physicist Paul Dirac even goes so far as to say that "it is more important to have beauty in one's equations than to have them fit experiment."[40] More recently, the physicist Steven Weinberg reflects, "It is precisely in the application of pure mathematics to physics that the effectiveness of aesthetic judgments is most amazing. . . . Mathematical structures that confessedly are developed by mathematicians because they seek a sort of beauty are often found later to be extraordinarily valuable by physicists."[41] But why should physicists assume that beauty will point to truth? There is no purely empirical reason or justification for affirming this aesthetic criterion and, as the Nobel laureate Eugene Wigner remarks, the reason for the effectiveness of mathematical beauty in physics "is something bordering on the mysterious and there is no rational explanation for it."[42]

In addition to aesthetic principles, which shape the practice and content of science, there is also a central role for ethical or moral principles within science. One ethical principle that serves as a necessary foundation for science is the moral conviction that any knowledge gained should be freely and truthfully reported and shared. For science to make progress, scientists need to trust that the experimental results of other scientists are genuine and not falsified.[43] Other moral principles that shape science include ethical guidelines for conducting research on human and animal subjects, cultural norms and social values that determine the appropriateness of research topics (e.g., conservation biology, nuclear weapons research, genetic enhancement research), and the values of the individual scientist.[44]

---

39. Albert Einstein, quoted in Graham Farmelo, *It Must Be Beautiful: Great Equations of Modern Science* (London: Granta Books, 2002), xii. Original source uncited.

40. Paul Dirac, "The Evolution of the Physicist's Picture of Nature," *Scientific American* 208, no. 5 (1963).

41. Steven Weinberg, *Dreams of a Final Theory* (New York: Pantheon, 1992), 153.

42. Eugene Wigner, "The Unreasonable Effectiveness of Mathematics in the Natural Sciences," *Communications in Pure and Applied Mathematics* 13, no. 1 (February 1960): 1–14. Other scientists, chiefly non-physicists, have argued that beauty can sometimes be misleading. Thomas Huxley, for example, wrote that many a beautiful theory has been killed by an ugly fact. "President's Address to the British Association for the Advancement of Science," Liverpool, UK, September 14, 1870. *The Scientific Memoirs of Thomas Henry Huxley* (London: Macmillan, 1901), 3:580.

43. Peter Hodgson, *Theology and Modern Physics* (Burlington, VT: Ashgate, 2005), 20. Regarding the justification of this presupposition, see Meredith Wadman, "One in Three Scientists Confesses to Having Sinned," *Nature* 435, no. 7043 (June 9, 2005): 718–19. Wadman says that such "misconduct ranges from faking results outright to dropping suspect data points" (718–19).

44. Steven Shapin and Simon Schaffer, *Leviathan and the Air Pump* (Princeton: Princeton University Press, 1985). Other types of presuppositions enter into science as well. For example philosopher Mikael Stenmark explains, "Scientific knowledge presupposes introspective knowledge and knowledge based on memory, then one first must know these things to be able to do science." Stenmark, *Scientism*, 119.

The Metaphysical Presuppositions of Science

In addition to the moral values that shape science and the aesthetic principles that guide scientific discovery and theory choice, there are also general metaphysical presuppositions that serve as the deeper philosophical foundations of the entire scientific enterprise. These are a few of the metaphysical presuppositions that provide the necessary conditions for science:

1. *A belief that the world is, in some sense, good and therefore worthy of careful study.* This first necessary condition for the existence of science affirms that one must consider the goals of science as valuable and worth pursuing before one pursues the study and practice of it.[45]

2. *A belief that the world is orderly and rational.* If physical reality was assumed to be unstructured, disorderly, or fundamentally chaotic, science would be impossible.[46] The presupposition that order exists in nature is thus a necessary condition of scientific inquiry because if one did not believe that order existed at all in nature, then searching for it scientifically would be pointless.[47]

3. *A belief that the order of the world is open to the human mind.* Without a firm conviction that "the form of things is intelligible, and therefore definable," there would be no point in embarking on the scientific quest to make sense of the world.[48] One would not scientifically seek to understand the world unless one already believed that the world could be understood. As physicist and theologian John Polkinghorne elaborates,

> We are so familiar with the fact that we can understand the world that most of the time we take it for granted. It is what makes science possible. Yet it could have been otherwise. The universe might have been a disorderly chaos rather than an orderly cosmos. Or it might have had a rationality which was inaccessible to us. . . . There is a congruence between our minds and the universe, between the rationality experienced within and the rationality observed without. This extends not only to the mathematical articulation of fundamental theory but also to all those tacit acts of judgment, exercised with intuitive skill, which are equally indispensable to the scientific endeavour.[49]

---

45. Peter Hodgson, "Presuppositions and Limits of Science," in *The Structure and Development of Science*, ed. G. Radnitzky and G. Andersson, Boston Studies in the Philosophy and History of Science (Dordrecht: Reidel, 1979), 136.

46. Trigg, *Rationality and Science*, 224.

47. Artigas, *Mind of the Universe*, 44.

48. Michael Foster, "The Christian Doctrine of Creation and the Rise of Modern Natural Science," *Mind* 43 (1934): 446–68, at 455.

49. John Polkinghorne, *Science and Creation: The Search for Understanding* (London: SPCK, 1988), 20–21.

4. *A belief that the order of the world is contingent rather than necessary.* While *necessary* order could be discerned through pure introspective thought (like the truths of mathematics, geometry, or logic), *contingent* or dependent order can be discovered only by making experiments and through investigating what the world is really like. That which is contingent is knowable only by sense experience. There could have been a number of different ways that the universe was put together, but the only way to find out how it actually was put together is to examine it in its details and dynamics. The concept of contingency "is essential to science because contingency demands an empirical method."[50]

5. *A belief in metaphysical realism.* To engage in scientific theorizing means presupposing that there is a real world of objective physical reality and that one can, at least to some extent, obtain information about that world that exists independent of the mind. In other words, the attempt to gain knowledge about the world must first presuppose the existence of the world and that the world is not an illusion or virtual reality.[51] Philosopher of science Roger Trigg explains, "Science has to assume that it is investigating a world that has an independent existence. Otherwise it is a mere social construction reflecting the conditions of particular societies at a particular time."[52] The reality of the material world places crucial constraints on scientific theorizing, so true theories must match up with the structures and relationships already existing in nature. For science to make progress, reality as it concretely exists must be permitted to change one's previous abstract conceptions of that reality. This is why "scientific discoveries are often quite unexpected."[53]

6. *A belief in the unity and uniformity of the physical universe.* The assumption that physical reality at some deep level is consistent, and that nature

---

50. Artigas, *Mind of the Universe*, 44.

51. Nicholas Rescher, *Scientific Realism: A Critical Reappraisal* (Dordrecht: Reidel, 1987), 126. "Metaphysical realism," says Rescher, is not the result of an inductive inference, but is rather "a regulative presupposition that makes science possible in the first place," "a precondition for empirical inquiry," and "a presupposition for the usability of observational data as sources of objective information. . . . We do not learn or discover that there is a mind-independent physical reality, we presume or postulate it."

52. Roger Trigg, "Realism," in *Encyclopedia of Science and Religion*, ed. J. Wentzel Van Huyssteen (New York: Macmillan Reference, 2003), 714. Physicist Deborah Haarsma points out, "A scientist *could* do their work with an antirealist or instrumentalist view of science, not believing that their models say anything about the truth of physical reality, but I have never met a scientist with this view." Debora Haarsmah, "Science and Religion in Harmony," in *Science and Religion in Dialogue*, ed. M. Y. Stewart (Oxford: Wiley-Blackwell, 2010), 115. Biologist and theologian Alister McGrath writes, "There can be little doubt that most natural scientists espouse a range of opinions which are recognizably 'realist' in their core affirmations, reflecting a common commitment to the ontological finality of the natural order. Realism works." Alister McGrath, *A Scientific Theology*, vol. 2, *Reality* (London: T & T Clark, 2006), 123.

53. Ian Barbour, *Religion in an Age of Science* (San Francisco: Harper & Row, 1990), 44.

functions uniformly, is a fundamental presupposition of all scientific activity. Scientists assume that the speed of light as it has been measured in Lawrence Berkeley National Laboratory is the same as the speed of light on Jupiter, where it has not been measured. The assumption that the laws of nature are the same everywhere throughout the cosmos is what allows scientists to extrapolate from presently available knowledge to distant times (e.g., the past in geology and the past and future in cosmology) and to distant parts of the cosmos (e.g., in astronomy and cosmology). Without this postulated uniformity of the cosmos scientists could not make any inductive inferences or predictions.[54]

These general presuppositions about the nature of reality—the orderliness and regularity of reality, the ontological *reality* of reality, the intelligibility and contingency of existent structures and entities, and the unity and uniformity of the physical universe—necessarily precede and underpin all scientific experimentation and reasoning. Modern science presupposes these beliefs "as the condition of its own possibility."[55] Such presuppositions (and others) are a priori (independently of observation) "conditions that are necessary for the possibility of scientific activity as such, although they can be ignored by particular scientists."[56] As preconditions, they are absolutely required for science to take place and are not open to experimental confirmation or falsification by scientific experimentation. "For science to develop," says the late Oxford physicist and philosopher Peter Hodgson, "these beliefs must be held, at least implicitly, by society as a whole and by scientists themselves."[57] These philosophical presuppositions, explains physicist and philosopher of science Mariano Artigas, "continue to be present, not as a kind of philosophical ornament, but as a real part of science itself." When we study the presuppositions of science, says Artigas, "we are studying science itself in a strict sense."[58] And such presuppositions continue to significantly impact science today. Philosopher of science Ernan McMullin says that, while "one might be tempted to think that regulative principles of a broadly metaphysical kind no longer play a role in the natural sciences . . . even a moment of reflection about the current debates in elementary-particle theory, in quantum-field theory, and in cosmology ought to warn that this is far from the case."[59]

---

54. Ratzsch, "Nature of Science," 49.

55. Foster, "Christian Doctrine of Creation," 447

56. Mariano Artigas, "Three Levels of Interaction between Science and Philosophy," in *Intelligibility in Science*, ed C. Dilworth (Amsterdam: Rodopi, 1992), 123.

57. Hodgson, *Theology and Modern Physics*, 16. See also Hodgson, "Presuppositions and Limits of Science," 133–46.

58. Artigas, *Mind of the Universe*, 25.

59. Ernan McMullin, *Newton on Matter and Activity* (Notre Dame, IN: University of Notre Dame Press, 1978), 127.

The Role of Religious Faith in the Philosophical Foundations of Science

All the metaphysical presuppositions listed above, which continue to play a vital role within current science, require a certain degree of faith. Today, scientists take these philosophical assumptions for granted, and their implicit faith in them need not necessarily be considered religious. Historically, however, each of these presuppositions developed within a specific religious context, and all were supported by particular religious concepts within a particular religious culture. The specific religious context within which early modern science developed was the Christian faith as it was passed down from the European Middle Ages. Historian of science John Hedley Brooke explains, "Prominent natural philosophers of the early modern period did not distinguish what we would call the scientific aspects of their work from what we would call theology. Their study of the natural world was conceived as a study of God's creation, disclosing something of the nature of God."[60] Within this cultural matrix, a number of specifically Christian theological understandings of the natural world and the human mind encouraged the development of the foundational presuppositions of science. In other words, "Christian theology provided several of the beliefs on which science is based."[61]

The notion of the world's "goodness" is rooted in the foundational creation narrative of both Judaism and Christianity. In Genesis, God beholds the cosmos he created and asserts that "all that he had made" was indeed "good" (Gen. 1:31). The Hebrew word translated as "good" also means "beautiful." The created world here has an intrinsic value and the creatures therein "manifest in the most varied ways the power, wisdom, and goodness of God."[62] In the early Christian understanding, nature was seen as a type of "book" authored by God, and one could come to know God through reading and studying this book. The church father Augustine (354–430 CE) reflects, "Some people, in order to discover God, read books. But there is a great book: the very appearance of created things. Look above you! Look below you! Note it; read it. God, whom you want to discover, never wrote that book with ink; instead He set before your eyes the things that He had made. Can you ask for a louder voice than that?"[63] Continuing in this Augustinian train of thought, medieval theologian Hugh of St. Victor (1096–1141) develops specific techniques for the interpretation of the "text of nature." Hugh advocates the systematic investigation of the natural

---

60. John Hedley Brooke, Margaret Osler, and Jitse van der Meer, eds., *Science in Theistic Contexts: Cognitive Dimensions* (Chicago: University of Chicago Press, 2001), ix.

61. Hodgson, *Theology and Modern Physics*, 17.

62. Artigas, *Mind of the Universe*, 330.

63. Augustine, *City of God*, book 16. Quoted in Clarence Glacken, *Traces on the Rhodian Shore: Nature and Culture in Western Thought from Ancient Times to the End of the Eighteenth Century* (Berkeley: University of California Press, 1967), 203–4.

world "based on the general assumption that living things can be read as signs variously of God's power, wisdom and goodness." Discerning the power of God in the immensity of the created cosmos, Hugh likewise sees God's goodness and wisdom in the elegance and beauty of creatures.[64]

The idea that the world of nature is worth studying, as it entered into the practice of early modern science, is likewise historically rooted in the Jewish and Christian Genesis text. One particularly influential passage that deeply impacted the conceptual foundations of science was Genesis 2:19–20, in which Adam names the animals according to their own identities. Adam's naming of the different creatures had long been understood as his giving names to them in accordance with their particular natures and characteristics. Jews and Christians believed humans before the Fall had a deep knowledge of nature and that it was Adam's "encyclopedic knowledge that had made possible the naming" of the various animals.[65] In the 1600s, when Francis Bacon inaugurated the modern scientific endeavor, he drew upon this understanding of Adam's knowledge of the natural world. Bacon envisioned the natural sciences as a way of "restoring, or at least repairing, the losses to knowledge that had resulted from the Fall."[66] Historian of science Peter Harrison explains, "Francis Bacon's project to reform philosophy was motivated by an attempt to determine whether the human mind 'might by any means be restored to its perfect and original condition, or if that may not be, yet reduced to a better condition than that in which it now is.'"[67] As the disobedience of the first humans caused the human mind to fall into error and lose knowledge, the scientific method was, for Bacon and other early modern practitioners of science, a technique that could work to heal the cognitive damage wrought by human sin. During the scientific revolution, says Harrison, "the methodological strictures of particular programs of natural philosophy—experimental method being perhaps the best example—were understood as applying necessary external constraints to fallen minds which, left to their own devices, would simply fail to accumulate any useful knowledge of the natural world."[68]

The orderliness, rationality, and intelligibility of the natural world were similarly assumed by early modern scientists on the basis of the Christian doctrine of creation that was part of their cultural matrix.[69] Historian of science Christopher Kaiser explains, "The creation of all things by God, the consequent order

---

64. Peter Harrison, *The Bible, Protestantism, and the Rise of Natural Science* (Cambridge: Cambridge University Press, 1998), 57; Hugh of St Victor, *Didascalicon* 6.5; *De tribus diebus* 1.

65. Peter Harrison, *The Fall of Man and the Foundations of Science* (Cambridge: Cambridge University Press, 2007), 26.

66. Ibid., 4.

67. Ibid., 1.

68. Ibid., 15.

69. Though anachronistic, the word "scientists" is used here for clarity's sake.

and rationality of the cosmos, and the ability of human reason to comprehend this order all stem from the Judeo-Christian belief in creation, dating back at least to the second century BCE."[70] The concept of God's creation of all material reality out of nothing (Latin: *creatio ex nihilo*) "allowed the scientist to approach nature with the expectation that the divine rationality would be reflected in its structures and workings."[71] As a fellow creature of God, nature was given its own laws to follow, and unlike humans, nature had not disobeyed the laws that God ordained. The behavior of nature, therefore, was not irrational, as human behavior often is. Consequently, it was believed that the ways of nature were comprehensible and that "even those aspects of nature that threatened human safety were not lawless in themselves. They served God's purposes and had laws of their own, even if unknown to humans (Job 28:25–27). Hence, they were open to human comprehension, at least in principle."[72] Firmly believing that the natural world could be comprehended, "early Christian scientists sought intelligible order in nature, regarding it as an indication of God's rational plan for the universe."[73]

The belief that the order of the world is contingent rather than necessary is grounded in the Christian conception of the freedom of God.[74] Inherent in the Christian doctrine of *creatio ex nihilo*, which provided the conceptual matrix for early modern science, is the belief that God was free to choose how to create the universe. God "was not in any way constrained either to create or not to create it in the way that He did. It is therefore not a necessary universe in the sense that it had to be created or could not have been created otherwise."[75] Given this understanding of nature, one can never say a priori how God *must have* acted, and thus one can never say a priori how God's creation must behave. To obtain true knowledge about God's creation, one must proceed in an a posteriori manner— by studying the material creation and by conducting experiments.[76]

Related to the contingency of the order in the physical world is the notion of metaphysical realism. A philosophical faith in the existence of the external

70. Christopher B. Kaiser, "Early Christian Belief in Creation and the Beliefs Sustaining the Modern Scientific Endeavor," in *The Blackwell Companion to Science and Christianity*, ed. J. B. Stump and Alan G. Padgett (Malden, MA: Blackwell, 2012), 10.

71. Alister McGrath, *A Scientific Theology* (Edinburgh: T & T Clark, 2003), 1:140.

72. Kaiser, "Early Christian Belief in Creation," 6.

73. Paul Davies, "The Intelligibility of Nature," in *Scientific Perspectives on Divine Action: Quantum Cosmology and the Laws of Nature*, ed. Robert J. Russell, Nancey Murphy, and C. J. Isham (Berkeley, CA: CTNS and Vatican Observatory Publications, 1999), 149–64.

74. Kaiser, "Early Christian Belief in Creation," 5. McGrath writes, "The creator is to be regarded as free of limitations imposed by the 'inertia of a prior reality.'" McGrath, *Scientific Theology*, 1:195.

75. Hodgson, *Theology and Modern Physics*, 26. See also Margaret J. Osler, *Divine Will and the Mechanical Philosophy: Gassendi and Descartes on Contingency and Necessity in the Created World* (Cambridge: Cambridge University Press, 1994).

76. Michael Foster, "Greek and Christian Ideas of Nature," *The Free University Quarterly* 6 (1959): 125; McGrath, *Scientific Theology*, 2:139.

world that has a structure independent from the mind is clearly presupposed and applied by the Christian theological tradition.[77] In the Christian understanding, the material creation exists independent of the observer because God the creator exists and bestowed existence on both the human observer and the created objects being observed. The reality of both the external world and the human observer are affirmed because they are the creation of the same God.[78] The material world is understood as having its own reality owing to the fact that creation is independent or distinct from the Creator.[79] "On the Christian conception . . . nature is made by God, but *is not God.* There is an abrupt break between nature and God. Divine worship is to be paid to God alone, who is *wholly other than nature.* Nature is not divine."[80]

The affirmation of the unity and uniformity of the physical universe was likewise a core belief emerging from a Judeo-Christian understanding of the unity of creation as the product of a single Creator. While many ancient schools of thought "drew a sharp line between the starry heavens and the terrestrial realm," the Christian tradition insisted on "a single physics for both heaven and earth."[81] This conception of the cosmos had become well established in the early church and was passed down to later Islamic and medieval Christian thinkers. It was then handed on from the leading natural philosophers of the Middle Ages to the practitioners of early modern science. When early modern scientists, such as Isaac Newton, argued for the universality of the laws of nature, they justified this principle in theistic terms. Newton says, "If there be an universal life and all space be the sensorium of a thinking being [God] who by immediate presence perceives all things in it [then] the laws of motion arising from life or will may be of universal extent."[82] Even as late as the nineteenth century, the "quest for a unification of electricity, magnetism, and optics, culminating in the work of James Clerk Maxwell, was still inspired by this theological ideal."[83]

---

77. McGrath, *Scientific Theology*, 2:199.

78. Ibid., 2:172, 228.

79. "The reality of God and the derived and contingent reality of the creation can thus be seen as distinct." Ibid., 2:228.

80. Foster, "Greek and Christian Ideas of Nature," 123–24. Barbour refers to this as belief in the desacralization of nature. Barbour, *Religion in an Age of Science*; see also Artigas, *Mind of the Universe*, 22, emphasis in original.

81. Christopher Kaiser, "The Creationist Tradition in the History of Science," *Perspectives on Science and Christian Faith* 45 (June 1993): 80–89.

82. Isaac Newton quoted in Ratzsch, "Nature of Science," 65, original source uncited. A *sensorium* is the sum of an organism's perception, the "seat of sensation" where it experiences and interprets the environment it lives within.

83. Kaiser, "Creationist Tradition," 80. McGrath observes, "Since the uniformity of nature is an unjustified (indeed, circular) assumption within any non-theistic world-view, it could be argued that there is no firm basis upon which to engage in scientific activities, other than the belief that the regularities observed locally prove universal." McGrath, *Scientific Theology*, 2:153.

As they became embodied within philosophical presuppositions, these theological convictions worked together to form many of the key conceptual underpinnings of modern science. Rather than religion acting as a stumbling block to the rise of science, religion was, in fact, a cornerstone. As historian of science Edward Grant has shown, "in the Latin Middle Ages of Western Europe an intellectual environment was established that proved conducive to the emergence of early modern science." During this formative medieval period, a combination of cultural attitudes, institutions such as universities, and beliefs critically coalesced into what may be called the "the foundations of modern science."[84]

Why Religious Faith Needs Science

"Science," as contemporary philosophers of science understand it, consists of empirical data, theories that explain the data, and nonempirical shaping principles. Because, as shown in this chapter, many of the shaping principles of science come in the form of philosophical presuppositions or assumptions, science needs faith. But does religious faith need science? While this might not be the situation with all religions, this would certainly appear to be the case for the Jewish and Christian faiths. From the very beginning, Jews and Christians have affirmed a belief that God created everything that exists, both seen and unseen. The Hebrew Bible and Christian Old Testament encourage believers to consider God's works (Ps. 111), and the Christian New Testament proclaims that "God's invisible qualities—his eternal power and divine nature"—cannot be "clearly seen or understood" without understanding the created reality that is discovered through scientific investigation (Rom. 1:20). This Jewish and Christian imperative to investigate material creation has historically been expressed in the doctrine of "the unity of truth" and the doctrine of "God's two books."

The Unity of Truth

The Jewish and Christian doctrine of the unity of truth holds that *all* truth—wherever it may be found—is God's truth. There is not one truth for theological knowledge and another for knowledge gained from reason or natural philosophy or science. Since God is Creator of the whole universe, true knowledge from philosophy or the natural world will not contradict revealed knowledge from Scripture. If there are apparent contradictions between the various sources of truth, such inconsistencies cannot be ignored but must be resolved by the use of reason.

The notion that there exists but one reality or one cosmos, and that truth, as truth, must correspond to this reality, claims a very ancient philosophical and

---

84. Edward Grant, *The Nature of Natural Philosophy in the Late Middle Ages* (Washington, DC: Catholic University of America Press, 2010), ix.

theological pedigree. The Jewish historian Artapanus of Alexandria (ca. 250 BCE) contended that knowledge from the biblical revelations of the prophet Moses was one and the same with the knowledge of the natural world revealed through the investigations of the Egyptians. Both the Egyptians and the Jews held one truth in common, and Artapanus even believed that ancient Egyptians must have learned their science from Moses. Writing a hundred years later, the Jewish historian Eupolemus lauded the Jewish patriarch Abraham's knowledge of astronomy and speculated that Abraham taught astronomy to the Egyptians, Phoenicians, and Greeks. Like Artapanus, Eupolemus was keen to affirm the unity of truth since he viewed such knowledge about the stars as the common heritage of both Jews and Greeks. The Jewish philosopher Aristobulus of Paneas (150 BCE) and his successor Philo of Alexandria (20 BCE–50 CE) similarly spoke of Jewish and Greek knowledge as one and the same, pointing to the commonalities between Jewish philosophical concepts and those of Socrates, Plato, and Pythagoras. For both Aristobulus and Philo, Greek philosophy and science were natural developments of the teachings of Moses known through revelation.[85] One particular concept, which Philo borrowed from the Greek philosophical understanding of the cosmos to better understand and explain the Hebrew Scriptures, was the idea of the *Logos*, a term used by most schools of Greek philosophy to designate a rational, intelligent, and life-giving principle of the universe. For Philo and other Jews who engaged with Greek philosophy, the *Logos* was an expression of the wisdom or logic of God in creation, and as such, both Jews and Greeks who engaged in a careful investigation of the cosmos could discern this wisdom. For all these early Jewish thinkers, both Scripture and natural philosophy were seen as pointing to the same reality. Kaiser notes, "What we find in these early sources is not only a courageous affirmation of the value of Greek science (or natural philosophy) and technology, but an underlying belief in the essential unity of all knowledge."[86]

The first Christians inherited their theological and scientific worldview from early Judaism and continued to develop the Jewish idea of the unity of truth. As Christians proclaimed that the *Logos* of Philo and the Greeks took on flesh in Jesus of Nazareth, they continued to understand the truth of the Greeks and the truth of Scripture as one. The first-century Christian theologian Justin Martyr, for example, used the cosmic *Logos* concept to explain why Christians may embrace all truth as God's truth. "When Christians speak of Christ," explained Justin, they speak of "the cosmic *logos* known to the Greeks."[87] Because the wisdom of God through Christ the *Logos* is manifested throughout all of

---

85. See Christopher Kaiser, *Creational Theology and the History of Physical Science: The Creationist Tradition from Basil to Bohr* (Leiden: Brill, 1997), 36.

86. Ibid., 14.

87. Roger E. Olson, *The Story of Christian Theology: Twenty Centuries of Tradition and Reform* (Downers Grove, IL: InterVarsity, 1999), 61.

physical reality, Christians should embrace truth regardless of the source and use it without hesitation. "Whatever things were rightly said among all men," says Justin, "are the property of us Christians."[88] Many other Christian philosophers and theologians continued in this tradition, which became the standard by the time of Augustine.[89] Augustine taught that God is the teacher of truth, no matter where it is discovered. Thus he says, "If those who are called philosophers . . . have said things which are indeed true and are well accommodated to our faith, they should not be feared; rather, what they have said should be taken" and converted to Christian use.[90] Speaking to his fellow Christians, Augustine affirms that "all truth is ultimately God's truth, even if found in the books of pagan authors; we should seize it and use it without hesitation."[91]

God's Two Books

Closely related to the concept of the essential unity of all truth was the Jewish and Christian doctrine of God's two books. According to this understanding, God has "written" two books through which God can be known: the book of Scripture and the book of nature. The two books are complementary ways God reveals himself to humans. The idea that nature is a type of book is rooted in the Hebrew Scriptures. Psalm 19:1 declares, "The heavens declare the glory of God, and the sky above proclaims his handiwork." In a similar way, the early Jewish *Book of Wisdom* (first century BCE) teaches that God may be known through his created works, even by those who have not received the revelation of Scripture.[92]

Early Christians embraced this Jewish notion that both Scripture and nature are "books" where knowledge of God can be found. The Apostle Paul affirms, "What can be known about God is plain to" even those who do not have the revealed Scriptures "because God has shown it to them. Ever since the creation of the world, God's invisible nature, namely, his eternal power and deity, has been clearly perceived in the things that have been made" (Rom. 1:19–20).

---

88. Justin Martyr, *Second Apology* 13.4.

89. Even Tertullian, who is often portrayed as pitting faith against philosophy (rhetorically establishing a divide between "Athens and Jerusalem"), "took a reasoned approach to the classical tradition, going so far as to identify Christianity as the offspring of Greek philosophy and Judaism." Peter Harrison and David Lindberg, "Early Christianity," in *Science and Religion around the World*, ed. John Hedley Brooke and Ronald Numbers (New York: Oxford University Press, 2011), 69. According to Henry Chadwick, Tertullian was merely concerned "to preserve the distinctiveness of faith to prevent it from becoming absorbed within a suffocating system of metaphysical speculation where it has no room to breathe." Henry Chadwick, *Early Christian Thought and the Classical Tradition* (Oxford: Clarendon, 1966), 2.

90. Augustine, *On Christian Doctrine*, trans. D. W. Robertson Jr. (1958; repr., Indianapolis: Bobbs-Merrill, 1976), 40, 75.

91. Ibid. David Lindberg, "Early Christian Attitudes toward Nature," in *Science and Religion: A Historical Introduction*, ed. Gary Ferngren (Baltimore: Johns Hopkins University Press, 2002), 53.

92. Wis. 11:6–9; see also Sir. 17:8.

Justin Martyr spoke of the cosmos as being permeated by "seeds" of the divine word (*Logos*) that could be discerned without special revelation. The early church theologian Irenaeus of Lyons (130–202 CE) likewise avowed that theology was the discipline of interpreting God's words, while natural philosophy was the discipline of interpreting God's works. Even Tertullian (160–220 CE), who is often portrayed as rejecting Greek knowledge, "regarded the works of God as an important revelatory counterpart to the Bible."[93] The early Eastern Orthodox Church theologian and bishop John Chrysostom describes how the world of nature serves the function of a book of revelation for those of all walks of life: "Both the man of great wisdom and the unlearned man can look upon this text, and wherever their gaze may fall, there looking upwards towards the heavens, he will receive a lesson that is adequate to his understanding."[94] In the Asian East, the Syriac church father Ephrem similarly discusses nature and Scripture as God's two books. "Scripture and Nature (*ktaba* and *kyana*)," explains Ephrem, "constitute God's two witnesses, as required by Jewish law." They are, he says, "the witnesses which reach everywhere, are found at all times," and "are present at every moment."[95] And Augustine in the Latin West likewise explicitly endorses the idea of the two books.[96] According to Augustine, while knowledge of the natural world reveals the character of God, it is also necessary for discerning the correct interpretation of Scripture. Ignorance of mathematics, astronomy, biology, and natural history, explains Augustine, "renders us incapable of grasping the literal sense of Scripture."[97] For example, asks Augustine, how will we grasp the meaning of the biblical admonition to "be as wise as serpents and as innocent as doves" (Matt. 10:16)? Only if we are familiar with the natures of serpents and doves.[98] These early Christian thinkers stressed that both books require careful interpretation and that the correct interpretation of either Scripture or nature requires the rigorous exercise of reason. Within the early Christian understanding, "interpretations of biblical passages must be informed by the current state of sure scientific and other knowledge."[99] For Christians to properly understand the content of their faith, then, the natural sciences would seem absolutely necessary.

---

93. Peter Hess, "Two Books," in *Encyclopedia of Science and Religion*, ed. J. Wentzel Van Huyssteen (New York: Macmillan Reference, 2003), 905; Tertullian, *Adversus Marcionem* 2.3.

94. John Chrysostom, *Homilies to the People of Antioch* 9.5.162–63.

95. Sebastian Brock, *The Luminous Eye: The Spiritual World Vision of Saint Ephrem* (Kalamazoo, MI: Cistercian Publications, 1992), 41–42.

96. Augustine, *City of God* 11.22.

97. Augustine, *On Christian Doctrine* 74. Quoted in Lindberg, "Early Christian Attitudes toward Nature," 52.

98. Augustine, quoted in Lindberg, "Christian Attitudes toward Nature," 52.

99. They argued this, explains Lawrence Principe, "because it is often easier conclusively to prove natural and philosophical propositions than interpretations of specific biblical passages." Lawrence Principe, *Science and Religion*, The Great Courses (Chantilly, VA: Teaching Co., 2006), 8.

Why Faith Still Needs Science

While the doctrines of the unity of truth and the two books remained influential throughout much of Christian history, these understandings are not as popular in much of the contemporary Christian church. Yet a moment's reflection will show that the Christian faith still needs science to better understand and talk about who God is and what God does in the world. For example, when Christians confess that God is "eternal," one might reflect on how God's eternity is defined in relation to time. Furthermore, whose concept of time is being employed? Is it Aristotle's or Augustine's subjective view of time; Newton's notion of objective or absolute time, which exists independently of motion or change; Einstein's relativistic understanding of time as another dimension of space; or, perhaps, the concept of two-dimensional time from contemporary string theory? When Christians declare that God is "omnipresent," one might similarly wonder what understanding of space is being assumed—that of ancient Greek philosophy, classical Newtonian physics, general relativity theory, or the hyper-dimensional space of string theory. When Christians describe the miraculous acts of God, how do they understand how such acts relate to the regular course of the natural world? Are they invoking the eighteenth-century European Enlightenment's concept of immutable and deterministic laws of nature that can never be broken or the statistical and indeterministic laws of contemporary quantum physics? The content of the Christian faith, as it fundamentally involves descriptions of God and of God's relationship to the world and interaction with the world, inescapably uses scientific language and concepts—whether the believer is aware or not. Consequently, the Christian need to engage with contemporary science is, in essence, directly related to the Christian desire and vocation to better know the God of the Bible.

Conclusion

This chapter began by examining ways in which historians and philosophers of science addressed the question, "What is science?" Rather than seeing science as consisting simply of inductive inferences generalized from observational data to universal theories, philosophers of science view science as a complex phenomenon that may be understood as "a sequence of research projects, structured by accepted presuppositions which determine what observations are to be made, how they are to be interpreted, what phenomena are problematic, and how these problems are to be dealt with."[100] This chapter has discussed how the shaping principles and presuppositions underlying science methodologically precede scientific practice, and in so doing are by their very nature beyond the limits of

---

100. Harold Brown, *Perception, Theory, and Commitment: The New Philosophy of Science* (Chicago: University of Chicago Press, 1979), 166.

scientific enquiry. Such principles and presuppositions are a priori "conditions that are necessary for the possibility of scientific activity as such, although they can be ignored by particular scientists."[101] As preconditions, they are absolutely required for science to take place and are not open to experimental confirmation or falsification by scientific experimentation. Scientific enquiry is consequently limited not only by its particular subject matter but also by its historical, social, and metaphysical context. This chapter explored how part of the cultural context in which modern science emerged was the religious matrix of medieval Christian Europe. Considering the historical roots of modern science as it developed within the context of medieval Europe, historians and philosophers of science have acknowledged numerous "ways in which religious beliefs have influenced science."[102] Because theological concepts and values have provided (and continue to provide) the "foundational assumptions for certain key scientists and scientific discoveries," there are many significant ways in which science needs faith.[103] At the same time, a close examination of Jewish and Christian Scriptures reveals that faith also needs science. Since the Bible itself points to the natural world as one of the ways to know God, Jews and Christians have spoken of God as having authored two books of revelation—nature and scripture—which point to one truth.

Discussion Questions

1. Do you think atheists have an advantage over theists (or other religious believers) in doing science? In other words, do you think atheists make better scientists? Why or why not?

2. How do you think the transition in thinking about the truth value of scientific theories—from the positivist focus on verification to Popper's focus on falsification—affects the authority of science where it concerns what we can know for sure about objective reality?

3. Consider the role of religious beliefs in the philosophical presuppositions of science. What role do you think these can or should play in science today? Do you think scientists should be up front about their religious beliefs or don't they matter? Why or why not?

4. Consider the Jewish and Christian doctrines of the two books and the doctrine of unity of truth. From your own experience, are these approaches to understanding the relationship between Scripture and science similar to or different from the ways Jews and Christians approach science today? In what ways?

---

101. Artigas, "Three Levels of Interaction," 123.

102. Brooke, *Science and Religion*, 18–33.

103. Alan G. Padgett, "Science and Theology," in *The Encyclopedia of Christianity*, ed. Erwin Fahlbusch, et al. (Grand Rapids: Eerdmans, 2005), 4:873.

Beyond the Classroom

Discuss the following situation with others. Imagine two scientific research groups that perform an experiment yielding the following data plot.

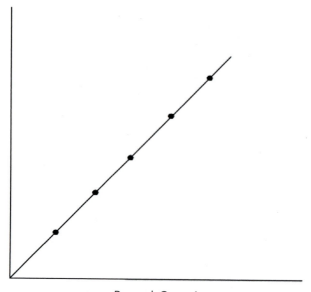

Research Group 1

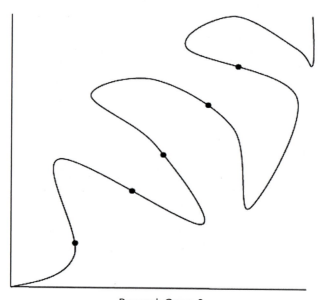

Research Group 2

Research Group 1 explains the relationship between the data by connecting the data points as shown in the first graph. Research Group 2 explains the relationship between the data by connecting the data points as shown in the second graph. Which explanation do you think is more likely to be correct and why? What role did Ockham's Razor play in your decision?

Resources for Further Study

Books

Artigas, Mariano. *The Mind of the Universe: Understanding Science and Religion.* Radnor, PA: Templeton Foundation Press, 1999.

Brooke, John Hedley. *Science and Religion: Some Historical Perspectives.* Cambridge: Cambridge University Press, 1991.

Godfrey-Smith, Peter. *Theory and Reality: An Introduction to the Philosophy of Science.* Chicago: University of Chicago Press, 2003.

Grant, Edward. *The Foundations of Modern Science in the Middle Ages: Their Religious, Institutional and Intellectual Contexts.* Cambridge: Cambridge University Press, 1996.

Articles

Harrison, Peter. "'Science' and 'Religion': Constructing the Boundaries." In *Science and Religion: New Historical Perspectives*, edited by Thomas Dixon, Geoffrey Cantor, and Stephen Pumfrey, 23–49. Cambridge: Cambridge University Press, 2010.

Padgett, Alan G. "Science and Theology." In *The Encyclopedia of Christianity*, edited by Erwin Fahlbusch et al., 4:873–79. Grand Rapids: Eerdmans, 2005.

Internet Resources

Harrison, Peter. "The Territories of Science and Religion." February 14, 2011. Accessible at *http://www.youtube.com/watch?feature=player_embedded&v=SSzN2 t5mAzM* (time: 1:13:28).

Moritz, Joshua. "What Is Science? Perspectives from the Philosophy of Science." Voice of Light Productions. Accessible at *http://vimeo.com/37045077* (time: 0:48:52).

Trigg, Roger. "Does Science Need Religion?" *The Faraday Papers*, April 2007. Accessible at *https://www.faraday.st-edmunds.cam.ac.uk/resources/Faraday Papers/ Faraday Paper 2 Trigg_EN.pdf.*

CHAPTER 4

Where the Conflict Really Lies
Science and Faith without Limits

There is no reason to suppose that science cannot deal with every aspect of existence. Only the religious—among whom I include not merely the prejudiced but also the underinformed—hope that there is a dark corner of the physical universe, or of the universe of experience, that science can never hope to illuminate.

—*Peter Atkins, chemist, Oxford University*[1]

Trouble arises when either science or religion claims universal jurisdiction, when either religious dogma or scientific dogma claims to be infallible. Religious creationists and scientific materialists are equally dogmatic and insensitive. By their arrogance they bring both science and religion into disrepute.

—*Freeman Dyson, physicist, Princeton University*[2]

In This Chapter

- Scientism: Denying That Science Has Limits
- Fideism: Denying That Faith Has Limits
- The Role of Interpretation in Science and Scripture
- Discussion Questions
- Beyond the Classroom
- Resources for Further Study

---

1. Peter Atkins, "The Limitless Power of Science," in *Nature's Imagination*, ed. John Cornwell (Oxford: Oxford University Press, 1995), 125.

2. Freeman Dyson, "Statement upon Receipt of Templeton Prize," at the Templeton Prize News Conference, March 22, 2000.

Every week the media seem to report some new story regarding the conflict between science and religion. For instance, as this sentence is written, NBC news reports a recent poll indicating that most Americans—around 51 percent— cite their religion as the reason why they "have trouble believing a Big Bang created the universe."[3] Chapter 1 showed that historical evidence poorly supports the idea that science and religion have always been at war. Chapters 2 and 3 pointed to the constructive role that faith—even religious faith—has played and continues to play within science. If this is indeed the case, why do so many people today perceive a fundamental conflict between science and religion? This chapter explores the essence of the conflict and contends that tension between science and religion emerges when either religious faith or scientific speculation proceeds as if it had no proper limits. The denial that science has limits is called *scientism*, and the denial that religious faith has limits is called *fideism*. Scientism denies that there is a legitimate place for faith within the practice of science, and fideism denies that there is a legitimate place for science and reason within the content of religious faith. As this chapter shows, the factors behind situations of discord between science and religion are not as simple or straightforward as the mere pitting of "facts against faith."[4] Because the boundaries of science and religion are in reality quite fuzzy, such territorial disputes are bound to occur from time to time. If science and religion were completely separate entities, there would never be such disputes. Perhaps ironically, border disputes do not prove that science and religion are opposites; rather, they reveal a good degree of common ground between the two. This chapter shows that such boundary disputes often arise not directly from the uncontested content of sacred scriptures or from the unmediated data of scientific theories but, rather, from the philosophical or theological interpretations given to science and scripture.

Scientism: Denying That Science Has Limits

The enormous success of the scientific enterprise since the 1700s has instilled in the minds of many an unyielding confidence that empirical methods will eventually address any and all questions worth asking. The logical empiricist philosopher Rudolph Carnap maintained, "There is no question whose answer is in principle unattainable by science."[5] This assertion well expresses the position of scientism, the idea "that any question that can be answered at all can best be answered by science."[6]

---

3. Seth Borenstein and Jennifer Agiesta, "Poll: Religion Trumps Belief in Big Bang Theory for Most Americans," NBC News website, April 21, 2014, *http://www.nbcnews.com/science/science-news /poll-religion-trumps-belief-big-bang-theory-most-americans-n85806*.

4. Ibid.

5. Rudolph Carnap, *The Logical Structure of the World* (London: Routledge and Kegan Paul, 1967), 290.

6. John Dupré, *Human Nature and the Limits of Science* (Oxford: Oxford University Press, 2001), 2.

The Unlimited Horizon of Science

Philosopher Mikael Stenmark describes scientism as the belief that "there are no real limits to the competence of science, no limits to what can be achieved in the name of science. There is nothing outside the domain of science, nor is there any area of human life to which science cannot successfully be applied. A scientific account of anything and everything constitutes the full story of the universe and its inhabitants."[7] Scientism is an overarching perspective that is quite common among atheist and agnostic scientists, philosophers, and promoters of science. For example, Richard Dawkins, evolutionary biologist and public advocate of both science and atheism, believes that the natural sciences—and in particular modern biology—will deliver answers to all of life's big questions. Dawkins holds that progress in science will, in time, lead to a place where people have "no longer . . . to resort to superstition when faced with the deep problems: Is there a meaning to life? What are we for? What is man?"[8]

Another atheist biologist, the late Stephen Jay Gould, affirms that even now science can provide a clear answer to the perennial question "Why are we here?" Gould responds that humans "are here because one odd group of fishes had a peculiar fin anatomy that could transform into legs for terrestrial creatures; because the earth never froze entirely during an ice age; because a small and tenuous species, arising in Africa a quarter of a million years ago, has managed, so far, to survive by hook and by crook." Although, says Gould, "we may yearn for a higher answer . . . none exists."[9] This is because, advocates of scientism argue, any knowledge that is not ultimately reducible to empirical testing is essentially meaningless. All knowledge that is true knowledge, biologist E. O. Wilson confidently contends, and every enterprise of culture—even the humanities and creative arts—will eventually be "subsumed by the natural sciences."[10] As science expands to encompass all domains of knowledge, affirms atheist philosopher Daniel Dennett, the ultimate reasons lying behind "everything we value—from sugar and sex and money to music and love and religion" will be revealed as "evolutionary reasons, free-floating rationales that have been endorsed by natural selection."[11] There are no things science won't eventually know. There are no limits to the scientific enterprise, and nothing is, in principle, beyond the reach of scientific understanding.

---

7. Mikael Stenmark, "Science and the Limits of Knowledge," in *Clashes of Knowledge: Orthodoxies and Heterodoxies in Science and Religion*, ed. Peter Meusburger, Michael Welker, and Edgar Wunder (New York: Springer, 2008), 111.

8. Richard Dawkins, *The Selfish Gene* (Oxford: Oxford University Press, 1989), 1.

9. Stephen Jay Gould, "The Meaning of Life," *Life Magazine*, December 1988, 84; quoted in Michael Ruse, *Science and Spirituality: Making Room for Faith in the Age of Science* (Cambridge: Cambridge University Press, 2010), 6.

10. Edward O. Wilson, *Consilience: The Unity of Knowledge* (New York: Knopf, 1999), 12.

11. Daniel Dennett, *Breaking the Spell: Religion as a Natural Phenomenon* (New York: Viking, 2006), 93.

Is Scientism Scientific?

In evaluating the perspective of scientism, one might ask if such unswerving confidence in the power of science is, itself, strictly scientific. E. O. Wilson admits that it is not and that the belief that all knowledge will one day be unified under the natural sciences is "a metaphysical world view" with "its best support" being "no more than an extrapolation of the consistent past success of the natural sciences."[12] In other words, scientism is based on a faith in the future success of science. One might also ask if proponents of scientism are justified in claiming that *all* legitimate questions about the meaning and purpose of life will in time be answered by the natural sciences. The empirically-minded rationalist philosopher Peter Medawar believes not: "That there is indeed a limit upon science is made very likely by the existence of questions that science cannot answer, and that no conceivable advance of science would empower it to answer." Questions such as "What are we all here for?" or "What is the point of living?" Medawar believes, are forever beyond the purview of science.[13] Nor does it seem reasonable—or scientific—to declare that all answers that are not scientific are consequently meaningless. Indeed, the claim that all nonscientific explanations are meaningless is a logically self-defeating claim. As philosopher of science Mariano Artigas explains, "The claim that there is no valuable knowledge *outside* science certainly cannot be supported from *within* science. This is an extremely simple philosophical error, akin to a child claiming that because all the people he knows are in his house, that there cannot be any people outside his house." According to Artigas, the epistemology (or theory of knowledge) that scientism offers is "not the consequence of any scientific investigation but rather reaches outside itself into the very realm that it claims does not exist."[14] Consequently, says biologist and theologian Alister McGrath, "It is clear that there are many questions that, by their very nature, have to be recognized as lying beyond the legitimate scope of the scientific method."[15]

The Empirical Limits of Science

Another problem with scientism is that it implicitly rejects scientific knowledge, pointing to areas where empirical research has discovered limits to what can be known through observation and experiment. Consider, for example, big bang

---

12. Wilson, *Consilience*, 9.

13. Alister E. McGrath, "The Ideological Uses of Evolutionary Biology in Recent Atheist Apologetics," in *Biology and Ideology from Descartes to Dawkins*, ed. Denis R. Alexander and Ronald L. Numbers (Chicago: University of Chicago Press, 2010), 340.

14. Mariano Artigas and Karl Giberson, *Oracles of Science: Celebrity Scientists versus God and Religion* (Oxford: Oxford University Press, 2007), 40.

15. McGrath, "Ideological Uses of Evolutionary Biology," 340.

cosmology—the leading scientific theory that describes the origin, structure, and development of the universe.[16] According to the standard big bang model, which is derived both from Einstein's theory of general relativity and observational data, the universe began 13.7 billion years ago in a *singularity*—an infinitely small point in which matter was infinitely compressed. Everything that physically exists, including matter, energy, space, and time, came into existence at the big bang singularity, and thus it makes no sense to speak of physical reality or even a "time before" this point. The existence of an initial singularity of this sort represents a fundamental limit to observational powers of science.[17] Within a fraction of a second after the initial singularity began to expand, the unimaginably small early universe entered a state called the Planck era, a period where the conditions were "so extreme that our current physics is completely unable to describe it."[18] The late physicist William Stoeger explains that, like the initial singularity, the Planck era represents "a limit falling outside the reliability" of the best current scientific model, and that "a new physics is needed" to understand it.[19] To assert that science will someday be able to adequately describe the extreme conditions of the Planck era or see "before" or "beyond" the initial singularity is not a statement that is grounded in current science but, rather, in a philosophical faith that all things can and will ultimately be understood and that all current physical mysteries are, in principle, comprehensible to the human mind.

A second fundamental empirical limit within cosmology concerns how far astronomers can ever hope to see. Given that the universe is expanding and that the speed of light is finite, one can never see further than the distance light has travelled since the big bang. Mathematical physicist John Barrow explains, "Astronomy can only tell us about the structure of the *visible* universe. . . . [W]e can know nothing of what lies beyond our horizon." Thus, while one may be able to say confidently that the observable universe has certain properties and characteristics, "we can say nothing about the properties of the Universe *as a whole* unless we smuggle in an assumption that the Universe beyond our horizon is the same, or approximately the same, in nature as the visible universe within our horizon."[20] This fundamental limit to human powers of observation—a limit that is imposed by the very nature of light and structure of the cosmos—"prevents us from making any testable statements about the initial structure, or the origin, of

---

16. This standard physical-mathematical model of the cosmos is called the Friedmann–Lemaître–Robertson–Walker (FLRW) model.

17. For a discussion, see Michael Heller, "The Initial Singularity and the Creation of the World," in *Ultimate Explanations of the Universe* (London: Springer, 2009).

18. William Stoeger, "God, Physics, and the Big Bang," in *The Cambridge Companion to Science and Religion*, ed. Peter Harrison (Cambridge: Cambridge University Press, 2010), 173.

19. Ibid., 176.

20. John Barrow, *Impossibility: The Limits of Science and the Science of Limits* (Oxford: Oxford University Press, 1998), 160.

the whole Universe."[21] Considering such cases, Barrow consequently concludes, "There are limits to what we can know about the Universe" and "those limits cut across all the major unsolved problems of cosmology."[22]

While cosmology reveals that there are limits to what scientists can know when studying the largest known phenomenon (the whole universe), quantum physics has revealed that there are also limits to what scientists can know when they study the smallest conceivable objects (atoms and their constituent parts). Classical physics, which was the standard view of physics before 1900, said that it was possible simultaneously to know both the position and motion of a given particle with complete accuracy. While the precision of a classical physicist might in practice be limited only by the available technology, there was no reason in principle to expect that better technology would not eventually overcome such limits. According to the standard view of current quantum physics, however, "even with perfect instruments it is impossible to measure the location and velocity of a body simultaneously" with perfect precision. This fundamental limit on the accuracy of measurement is known as Heisenberg's uncertainty principle.[23] "The quantum picture of reality," explains Barrow, "introduces a new form of impossibility into our picture of the world. This impossibility replaces a past belief in unrestricted experimental investigation of Nature which was based upon a misconception of what existed to be measured."[24] With quantum physics, says philosopher of science Michael Ruse, "we seem to have reached an outer point of what we can know. This is not a 'science stopper' in the sense of an appeal to miracles . . . but it is a recognition that there are areas where we cannot go."[25]

Fideism: Denying That Faith Has Limits

Fideism is the belief that faith is in some sense independent of or even adversarial toward reason. Philosopher of religion Alvin Plantinga describes fideism as an "exclusive or basic reliance upon faith alone, accompanied by a consequent disparagement of reason and utilized especially in the pursuit of philosophical or religious truth."[26] Fideism attempts to squeeze the data from science into

---

21. Ibid., 160.

22. Ibid., 159.

23. Ibid., 22–23.

24. Ibid.

25. Ruse, *Science and Spirituality*, 178. Ruse likewise argues, "We cannot—and never will—solve the body-mind problem," 180.

26. Alvin Plantinga, "Reason and Belief in God," in *Faith and Rationality: Reason and Belief in God*, ed. Alvin Plantinga and Nicholas Wolterstorff (Notre Dame, IN: University of Notre Dame Press, 1983), 87. What C. Stephen Evans terms *irrational fideism* denies that one can or should think rationally or logically about matters of faith. See C. Stephen Evans, *Faith Beyond Reason: A Kierkegaardian Account* (Grand Rapids: Eerdmans, 1998), 52, 55.

prefabricated concepts that are designed with the particular specifications dictated by religious faith. A fideistic approach to science is extremely selective, taking on board those parts that agree with religious ideas and casually dismissing those that do not. While Christian versions of fideism are well known in the West, fideism is found, to some degree, in every major world religious tradition. For example, while many Hindus and Buddhists embrace a positive attitude toward the findings of science, some contemporary Hindus and Buddhists have—for religious reasons—rejected the standard big bang theory that there was an initial singularity from which the universe came into existence. These believers reject the big bang theory because the notion of an absolute beginning to space and time appears to conflict with the traditional Hindu and Buddhist belief in "beginningless time"—that the Universe has existed forever and will continue to exist for all eternity. As the Tibetan Buddhist Dalai Lama explains,

> From the [traditional] Buddhist perspective, the idea that there is a single definite beginning is highly problematic. If there were such an absolute beginning, logically speaking, this leaves only two options. One is theism, which proposes that the universe is created by an intelligence that is totally transcendent, and therefore outside the laws of cause and effect. The second option is that the universe came into being from no cause at all. Buddhism rejects both these options.[27]

Within Hinduism and Buddhism one also finds a wide variety of responses to Darwinian evolution. In the same way that there is a spectrum of Christian perspectives on evolution, explains C. Mackenzie Brown, within the Hindu tradition "there is an array of often conflicting responses to Darwinian evolution—from vedic creationism to vedantic (advaitic) evolutionism."[28] Thus, while the majority of American Hindus embrace evolution as the best explanation for the origin of human life on earth,[29] a number of traditional Hindus—of the fideist variety—have rejected current understandings of human evolution on the grounds that certain Hindu sacred scriptures (the Vedas) seem to teach that the human race has existed for billions of years or even for all eternity. Leading proponents of this view, Michael Cremo and Richard Thomson, explain how "from the Vedic literature, we derive the idea that the human race is of great antiquity" and that modern

27. Dalai Lama, *The Universe in A Single Atom: The Convergence of Science and Spirituality* (New York: Morgan Road Books, 2005), 82.

28. C. Mackenzie Brown, *Hindu Perspectives on Evolution: Darwin, Dharma, and Design* (New York: Routledge, 2012), 1.

29. According to a recent Pew study (conducted in 2007), 80 percent of Hindus in the United States agree that evolution is the best explanation for the origin of human life on earth. "Religious Differences on the Question of Evolution," Pew Forum, February 4, 2009, *http://www.pewforum .org/2009/02/04/religious-differences-on-the-question-of-evolution/*. For a discussion on Hinduism and evolution, see David L. Gosling, *Darwin, Science and the Indian Tradition* (Delhi: ISPCK, 2011).

human beings have existed for hundreds of millions of years.[30] Such Hindu traditionalists also reject the linear aspect of Darwinian evolution because "the traditional Hindu view of the cyclical nature of the universe contrasts with the linear view generally assumed by modern science and by Darwinism in particular with its notion of a unique and largely unrepeatable history of life's evolution."[31]

The most well-known version of fideism that is found in the Christian West is young Earth creationism (also called scientific creationism). This view opposes the evolutionary origin of species and holds that the universe and the planet Earth were created within six, twenty-four-hour days less than ten thousand years ago. Ken Ham, a leading proponent of young Earth creationism, explains that when engaging questions of science, his "starting point is that God is the ultimate authority." Seeing his particular reading of the Bible as the lens through which science must be interpreted, Ham believes that in the struggle between creationism and evolution "the debate is ultimately not about facts." Rather, Ham asserts, the conflict has to do with "deeply held beliefs" that "we choose to hold, for whatever reason, and refuse to change regardless of contrary evidence." Thus, in a 2014 debate between Ham and Bill Nye (also known as "the Science Guy"), Ham, when asked by the CNN moderator, "What, if anything, would ever change your mind?" responded by saying, in essence, "Nothing would."[32]

Era	Period
Post Flood	Quaternary

Flood Sediment

Era	Period
Cenozoic *recent life*	Quaternary
	Tertiary
Mesozoic *middle life*	Cretaceous
	Jurassic
	Triassic
Paleozoic *ancient life*	Permian
	Carboniferous
	Devonian
	Silurian
	Ordovician
	Cambrian

The right diagram shows the scientific understanding of geological eras found in the Earth's strata. The left diagram shows the young Earth creationist view, which understands these strata as deposits from Noah's flood.

---

30. Michael A. Cremo and Richard L. Thompson, *Forbidden Archaeology: The Hidden History of the Human Race* (San Diego: Govardhan Hill, 1993), xxxvi.

31. Brown, *Hindu Perspectives on Evolution*, 7.

32. Mike Matthews, "The Debate Has Changed," *Answers*, April–June, 2014, 31–32; *http://www.answersingenesis.org/articles/am/v9/n2/debate-has-changed.*

Is Fideism Faithful to Religious Faith?

It is beyond the scope of this text to explore the alternatives to fideism within all the various world religions, but suffice it to say that in the major global religious traditions, the majority of believers have generally not been strict fideists. For example, Indian historian of science B. V. Subbarayappa notes, "The peaceful coexistence of traditional religious practices with new forms of science has been a particular feature of Indian culture, at least among intellectuals." "Among contemporary Indian scientists" as well, Subbarayappa detects "a willingness to regard literacy in the sciences and spiritual awareness as complementary rather than oppositional."[33] The Buddhist faithful have similarly been generally receptive to scientific findings, "with some suggesting that the essential teachings of Buddhism (variously identified) are in no way contradicted by the findings of science (variously enumerated), while others suggest the Buddha anticipated many of the key discoveries of science—that the Buddha knew more than two millennia in the past what scientists would only discover more than two millennia in the future."[34]

Is fideism a viable theological option for the faithful Christian? The vast majority of past and present Christian thinkers have thought not. From the very beginning, Christians have affirmed a deep connection between the rational structure or logic of the cosmos (*Logos*) and the word of God as known in and through Jesus Christ (John 1:1). In the Christian Gospels, McGrath explains, "true rationality of any kind is by definition already illumination by the Logos of God, precisely because God is both the source of being and the form of truth. While revelation is to be regarded as a higher measure of such illumination, it is not in any way discontinuous with it."[35] Continuing this understanding of faith and reason given in the Gospels, the Apostle Paul strives to make vital connections between the content of the Christian faith and Greek philosophy—to the point of citing key Greek philosophers as authorities (Acts 17). Paul even argues in Romans 1:20 that "anyone can attain to the truth of God's existence merely from using his or her reason to reflect on the natural world."[36] The view that reason was essential to a proper understanding of the Christian faith persisted throughout the early church period. Indeed, for many of the early church fathers, "heresy" consisted "precisely in refusing to admit the basic principles of scriptural rationality: the principle of non-contradiction, the principles of deductive logic, etc."[37]

---

33. See John Hedley Brooke and Ronald Numbers, *Science and Religion around the World* (Oxford: Oxford University Press, 2011), 8.

34. Donald Lopez, *Buddhism and Science: A Guide for the Perplexed* (Chicago: University of Chicago Press, 2008), 2.

35. Alister McGrath, *A Scientific Theology* (London: T&T Clark, 2006), 2:108.

36. James Swindal, "Faith and Reason," *Internet Encyclopedia of Philosophy*, 2001, *http://www.iep.utm.edu/faith-re/*.

37. Charles Kannengiesser, *Handbook of Patristic Exegesis: The Bible in Ancient Christianity* (Leiden: Brill, 2004), 634.

Throughout the Middle Ages, Christian theology continued to be defined as "faith seeking understanding" through reason. For influential medieval thinkers, such as Anselm of Canterbury (1033–1109) and Thomas Aquinas (1225–1274), "God is understood very much as supreme *rationality*, and his reflection in the order of things construed in terms of the logical relations which shape the structure of things."[38] Thus, concludes philosopher Michael Ruse, "traditional Christian thinking is that faith cannot be unreasonable, in the sense of illogical. It might push you beyond reason, certainly beyond empirical evidence, but it cannot make you believe the contradictory."[39] Fideism, then, would seem to be precluded by any traditional understanding of the Christian faith.

The Role of Interpretation in Science and Scripture

The endeavor to properly interpret and understand religious scripture, known as hermeneutics, emerges time and again in every area where religion engages contemporary culture. When science and religion appear to collide, religious persons often ask whether a different interpretation of sacred scripture is possible. The focus is less frequently on whether scientific theories and data are being adequately interpreted and presented. When faith and facts appear to clash, however, concerns regarding the correct interpretation of science should be no less important than concerns over the correct interpretation of scripture. Much interpreting of science is done through journalism, in order to present key scientific findings to the public and win funding for future scientific projects. It is well known among marketers of science that "science sells better if it is shown to conquer realms traditionally controlled by theology."[40] Persons who have no interest in either science or religion as separate subjects are often interested in their pairing, and stories of conflict are generally more attention-grabbing then those of concord.[41] Because headlines telling of conflict between science and religion sell newspapers, boost television ratings, and generate web traffic, journalists and marketers tend to weave stories of discord, even if the evidence of discord is scant. Journalist Barbara Hagerty, religion correspondent for National Public Radio, comments on this tendency as she acknowledges that her profession is "partly responsible for a perceived 'vicious conflict between religion and science.' Journalists like stories with conflict," explains Hagerty, "as do some

---

38. Colin Gunton, *The Triune Creator: A Historical and Systematic Study* (Edinburgh: Edinburgh University Press, 1998), 117.

39. Ruse, *Science and Spirituality*, 186.

40. Michael Heller, *Creative Tension: Essays on Science and Religion* (Philadelphia: Templeton Foundation Press, 2003), 82.

41. Lawrence Principe, *Science and Religion*, The Great Courses (Chantilly, VA: Teaching Co., 2006), lecture 1.

scientists who have taken a very aggressive stance in opposition to religion." However, in her reporting work, Hagerty has found that, contrary to popular perceptions, "religious believers tend to be fans of science."[42]

On a more philosophical level, when asking how to correctly interpret the claims of either science or religion, it is often helpful to acknowledge that the two areas are often seeking different kinds of answers. Frequently, religion is concerned with *ultimate* (or final) questions and causes, while science is interested in *proximate* (or immediate) causes. For example, imagine a tea kettle is boiling on the stove and someone asks, "Why is the kettle boiling?" One valid answer is that the kettle is boiling because gas has heated the water until the vapor pressure equaled the pressure of surrounding air. This scientific explanation of why the kettle is boiling is concerned with proximate causes. Another valid answer, though, is that the kettle is boiling because someone desires to make a cup of tea. The second explanation is concerned with ultimate causes that involve purpose. Both answers and explanations are correct. "We do not have to choose between these two accounts," explains physicist and theologian John Polkinghorne, "for both are true. Without taking the two of them together, the event of the boiling kettle would only be partially understood."[43]

Interpreting the Big Bang

Consider the NBC news headline mentioned at the beginning of this chapter reporting that most Americans "have trouble believing a Big Bang created the universe." Here, a scientific theory concerning proximate causes (the big bang) is invoked to fulfill the role of an ultimate cause within traditional theology (the creation of the universe). It is at such points that a proper *interpretation* of both science and theology becomes crucial. Since the majority of Americans are theists, one might ask if, within a theistic context, there are any good strictly theological or scientific reasons to juxtapose the big bang of physics with God's creation of the universe out of nothing? On the scientific side, neither Georges Lemaître, the priest and physicist who predicted the discovery of the big bang, nor the theory's greatest scientific opponent, the outspoken atheist Fred Hoyle, believed that the theory of the big bang contradicted the Christian doctrine of God's creation of the universe out of nothing. In fact, as was shown in the last chapter, "atheist cosmologists and physicists" were generally "hostile to the Big Bang for its perceived benefits to Christian belief."[44]

---

42. Earl Lane, "A Sociologist and a Journalist Assess How Science and Religion Get Along," *AAAS*, December 23, 2010, *http://www.aaas.org/news/sociologist-and-journalist-assess-how-science-and-religion-get-along-0*.

43. John Polkinghorne, *Science and Religion in the Quest for Truth* (New Haven: Yale University Press, 2011), 20.

44. Peter Hess and Paul Allen, *Catholicism and Science* (Westport, CT: Greenwood, 2008), 106.

On the religious side, many Jewish and Christian believers from a number of different traditions have viewed the big bang as supporting the biblical notion of God's creation of the universe from nothing (called *creatio ex nihilo*). Pope Pius XII, who was a contemporary of Lemaître, declared the big bang to be the very way that God created the universe.[45] A similar view has more recently been espoused by the Jewish physicist Gerard Schroeder,[46] and the evangelical Christian astronomer Hugh Ross.[47] Both Schroeder and Ross have interpreted the creation accounts in Scripture as referring to God's progressive creation of the universe over billions of years, starting with the creation of space and time at the big bang. In the view of these progressive creationists, Kate Boisvert explains, "since both the cosmos and the Bible are revelations from God, they will never conflict, when properly understood."[48]

Others, however, reject the interpretation that the Bible is in harmonious agreement with big bang cosmology. The most outspoken religious opponents of the big bang theory are young Earth creationists who believe that the creation of the universe by the big bang is a secular alternative to the creation account found in the biblical book of Genesis. The website for the leading young Earth creationist organization, Answers in Genesis, makes their position clear: "It is a great pity that many Christians are willing to 're-interpret' the infallible Word of God to fit a fallible, man-made theory like the big bang. Such ideas are ultimately devised to counter the biblical record, which is firmly against cosmic evolution over billions of years."[49] The young Earth creationist interpretation of the Bible leaves no room for a scientific version of *creatio ex nihilo* 13.7 billion years ago. In their view, God directly acts as both the ultimate cause *and* the proximate cause of the creation of the cosmos.

A more nuanced interpretation of the big bang is offered by scholars such as physicist and Protestant theologian Robert John Russell and Vatican Observatory astronomer and Catholic priest William Stoeger. Exploring how big bang cosmology relates to the question of whether God created the universe, Russell explains that the science behind the big bang can be interpreted in a number of ways. Under any scientific interpretation, though, says Russell, the big bang does lend indirect support to the theological idea of *creatio ex nihilo* since it points to the finitude of the universe as it relates to a definite beginning in

---

45. Ibid., 105.

46. Gerald Schroeder, *Genesis and the Big Bang: The Discovery of Harmony between Modern Science and the Bible* (New York: Bantam, 1990).

47. Hugh Ross, *The Fingerprint of God* (New Kensington, PA: Whitaker House, 2000); and Hugh Ross, *The Creator and the Cosmos: How the Greatest Scientific Discoveries of the Century Reveal God* (Colorado Springs, CO: NavPress, 1993).

48. Kate Grayson Boisvert, *Religion and the Physical Sciences* (Westport, CT: Greenwood, 2008), 165.

49. Werner Gitt, "What about the Big Bang?," *Creation* 20, no. 3 (1998): 42–44; *http://www.answersingenesis.org/articles/cm/v20/n3/big-bang*.

time. "Finitude," explains Russell, "is a form of contingency," which means that the universe depends upon something else (or someone else) for its existence.[50] While the question of exactly what that "something else" or "someone else" is remains open-ended, it certainly does not rule out a theological understanding. Stoeger agrees with Russell that the influence of cosmology and theology on one another is "indirect, but very important."[51] According to Stoeger, the big bang theory is consistent with the sort of theology of creation that "is primarily concerned with the *ultimate* source of the existence," rather than with its proximate causes. In the final assessment, says Stoeger, cosmology and theology are complementary: "What physics and cosmology discover and what theology legitimately asserts can never be in essential conflict. If conflict or incompatibility appear then that is a sure sign that there has been misinterpretation."[52]

Interpreting Evolution

Another current area of seeming discord between science and religion concerns the theory of evolution. If a Christian were given the choice between affirming that "humans evolved" or that "God created humans," the response would not be surprising. But does a Christian have to choose between God and evolution? When Charles Darwin's theory of evolution by natural selection was first proposed, there were a number of different responses, each hinging upon the proper interpretation of both the science and the Scriptures.

Scientists who were also devout Christians were among Darwin's most intimate confidants and staunchest supporters. Consider the case of Harvard botanist and evangelical Christian Asa Gray (1810–1888). During the late 1850s, Gray was the leading botanist in the United States, and his work was known worldwide.[53] Before Darwin's theory had been introduced, Gray was already interested in questions dealing with the evolution of species, and Gray's "uncompromising scientific approach to the study of nature brought him to the attention of Charles Darwin."[54] Darwin invited Gray into his inner circle of confidants where he discussed and worked out the details of his theory of natural selection before making it public. After Darwin published his theory, Gray referred to himself as "one who is scientifically, and in his own fashion,

50. Robert John Russell, "Did God Create Our Universe? Theological Reflections on the Big Bang, Inflation and Quantum Cosmologies," *Annals of the New York Academy of Sciences* 950 (December 2001): 108–27, at 118.

51. Stoeger, "God, Physics, and the Big Bang," 186.

52. Ibid. See also William Carroll, "Big Bang Cosmology, Quantum Tunneling from Nothing, and Creation," *Laval Theologique et Philosophique* 44, no. 1 (February 1998): 59–75.

53. David N. Livingstone, *Darwin's Forgotten Defenders: The Encounter between Evangelical Theology and Evolutionary Thought* (Vancouver, BC: Regent College Publishing, 1984), 50.

54. Ibid., 62.

a Darwinian."[55] As "Darwin's preeminent American disciple during the first decades," explains historian Ronald Numbers, Gray "labored mightily to ensure that Darwin received 'fair play' in North America." The early success of Darwin's theory in the United States was due largely to Gray's support.[56]

Gray saw much that was of scientific value in Darwin's theory and, as a Christian renowned for his orthodoxy, he also recognized the positive moral value of the theory in that one could use it to argue against the evil institution of slavery.[57] Gray welcomed Darwinian evolution as lending empirical support to the biblical notion of the common ancestry and unity of humanity. Moreover, Gray saw no reason why God should not create both humans and animals by means of the law of natural selection. Darwin, in fact, agreed with Gray on this point, writing,

> I had no intention to write atheistically. . . . I can see no reason, why a man, or other animal, may not have been aboriginally [or from the earliest times] produced by other laws; and that all these laws may have been expressly designed by an omniscient Creator, who foresaw every future event & consequence.[58]

Another Harvard biologist, Louis Agassiz (1807–1873), had no issues with the evolution of life in general, but preferred what is known as Lamarckian evolution to Darwin's theory. Agassiz "remained committed to the idea of divine creation" and didn't see evolution as contrasting with this religious view.[59] As historian of science Peter Bowler explains, "For Agassiz, the parallel between the development of the human embryo and the progressive sequence in the history of life on earth was a sign that both were governed by the same underlying pattern, a pattern emanating from the mind of God."[60] Where Agassiz did see conflict, however, was with the central role that Darwin assigned to random processes or chance throughout the history of the evolutionary creation of life. Agassiz argued that nature "exhibits a coherent pattern, more regular than anything permitted by natural selection," and that such patterns, while evolved over time, could not be due primarily to mere combination of chance, adaptation, and survival.[61]

---

55. Ronald L. Numbers, *Darwinism Comes to America* (Cambridge, MA: Harvard University Press, 1998), 27; See also John Hedley Brooke, *Science and Religion: Some Historical Perspectives* (Cambridge: Cambridge University Press, 1991), 316.

56. Numbers, *Darwinism Comes to America*, 27.

57. Ibid., 63.

58. John H. Brooke, "Darwin and Religion: Correcting the Caricatures," in *Science and Education* 19, nos. 4–5 (April–May 2010), 391–405, at 394.

59. Peter Bowler, *Monkey Trials and Gorilla Sermons: Evolution and Christianity from Darwin to Intelligent Design* (Cambridge, MA: Harvard University Press, 2007), 143.

60. Ibid., 145.

61. Ibid., 144.

On the other side of the Atlantic, both scientific and theological interpretations of Darwinian evolution were similarly mixed. For example, the biologist Alfred Russel Wallace (1823–1913), who co-discovered evolution by natural selection, "was a religious man who apparently saw no incongruity in the idea that evolution, even if driven solely by natural selection, could be accepted as God's mechanism of creation." Yet Wallace, like Agassiz, was doubtful that natural selection accomplished certain feats of creation without a higher guiding force. Wallace thus "could not follow Darwin" and "finally came out openly in favor of the view that some form of supernatural guidance had shaped the later stages of human evolution."[62]

The leading British anatomist Sir Richard Owen (1804–1892) and biologist St. George Mivart (1827–1900) were similarly theistic evolutionists who ultimately parted ways with Darwinian evolution where it concerned the central role of randomness within life's evolutionary history.[63] "Owen and Mivart opposed Darwin because they saw the development of life as something based on a coherent divine plan, not an endless sequence of local adaptations" driven by chance.[64] Mivart, a devout Roman Catholic, had originally been an ardent supporter of Darwin's theory of natural selection and "claimed that Darwinism was perfectly compatible with historic Christian teaching."[65] Thomas Henry Huxley (1825–1895), however, who interpreted Darwin's theory atheistically and popularized it as such, insisted that a theistic interpretation of Darwin's theory was not an option. He consequently informed theistic evolutionists like Mivart that they had to choose whether "to be 'a true son of the Church' or 'a loyal soldier of science.'"[66] Interestingly, explains Bowler, Huxley "was not opposed to Owen's [or Mivart's] view that something imposed a degree of unity on the development of life. But where Owen [and Mivart] wanted to see this 'something' as the expression of a divine plan, Huxley preferred to think in terms of natural forces limiting the pathways available to evolution." Huxley agreed with Mivart and Owen that "variation was not random, as Darwin supposed" but "was *directed* along certain lines" or trajectories of development. Where Huxley disagreed was in his interpretation of what directed or guided evolution. While Mivart and Owen saw a divine hand at work in the evolutionary development of life, Huxley invoked "purely natural forces."[67]

---

62. Ibid., 131.

63. Ibid., 129.

64. Ibid., 113.

65. Timothy Larsen, "War Is Over, If You Want It: Beyond the Conflict between Faith and Science," *Perspectives on Science and Christian Faith* 60, no. 3 (September 2008): 150.

66. Ibid. Bowler adds, "Wallace remained on good terms with the Darwinians, while Mivart was ostracized by the group for expressing views that were in some respects very similar. The difference was that Mivart campaigned actively against any purely natural explanation of evolution and did so as a member of a Church." Bowler, *Monkey Trials and Gorilla Sermons*, 131.

67. Bowler, *Monkey Trials and Gorilla Sermons*, 114.

Today, the debate among scientists over how to correctly interpret evolution continues along similar lines. Atheist evolutionists, such as Richard Dawkins and Stephen J. Gould, see no ultimate explanation for why life's historical development takes the path it does. Stressing the role of blind forces and chance in their interpretation of evolution, Dawkins and Gould view Darwin's theory as the philosophical precondition for atheism. "Although atheism might have been *logically* tenable before Darwin," says Dawkins, "Darwin made it possible to be an intellectually fulfilled atheist."[68] Other evolutionary biologists, however, do not see Darwin's theory as posing any threat to religious belief. For example, Roman Catholic evolutionary geneticist Francisco J. Ayala offers an interpretation of evolution more in line with that of Asa Gray. According to Ayala, Darwinian natural selection is simply how God creates life. Whereas natural selection is the *proximate* explanation for the creation of the various forms of life, God is the *ultimate* explanation. Neither explanation, "contradicts the other . . . if we understand the two narratives as conveying the same message, that the world was created by God and that humans are His creatures."[69] Cambridge University evolutionary biologist and evangelical Christian Simon Conway Morris agrees with Ayala and goes beyond him to observe that broader patterns may indicate that the actual course of evolution might not have been as random as once thought. According to Conway Morris, the history of life has "an innate tendency to evolve in a specific direction."[70] In other words, the chance events and "contingencies of biological history . . . make no long-term difference to the outcome."[71] While none of these scientific findings presuppose or prove the activity of God in creating life, says Conway Morris, they are certainly congruent with such an interpretation.[72]

What about theologians and church leaders? How have they understood Scripture and theology in light of evolution? Looking at responses when Darwin's theory was first published, one finds both theologians and "respectable Christian clerics who encouraged Darwin with their support" and accepted his understanding of human and animal evolution.[73] For instance, Christian clergyman and Cambridge professor Charles Kingsley (1819–1875), who had been sent

---

68. Richard Dawkins, *The Blind Watchmaker: Why the Evidence of Evolution Reveals a Universe without Design* (New York: Norton, 1986), 6.

69. Francisco J. Ayala, *Darwin's Gift to Science and Religion* (Washington, DC: Joseph Henry Press, 2007), 166.

70. Simon Conway Morris, "Evolution and the Inevitability of Intelligent Life," in *The Cambridge Companion to Science and Religion*, ed. Peter Harrison (Cambridge: Cambridge University Press, 2010), 150.

71. Simon Conway Morris, *Life's Solution: Inevitable Humans in a Lonely Universe* (Cambridge: Cambridge University Press, 2003), 328.

72. Ibid., 330.

73. John Hedley Brooke, "Darwin and Victorian Christianity," in *Cambridge Companion to Darwin*, ed. J. Hodges and Gregory Radick (Cambridge: Cambridge University Press, 2003), 206.

an advance review copy of Darwin's *Origin*, praised the work and wrote that he had "long since, from watching the crossing of domesticated animals and plants, learnt to disbelieve the dogma of the permanence of species."[74] Grateful for his high opinion, Darwin included some of Kingsley's comments in the second edition of the *Origin*, stating, "A celebrated author and divine has written to me that 'he has gradually learnt to see that it is just as noble a conception of the Deity to believe that He created a few original forms capable of self-development into other and needful forms, as to believe that He required a fresh act of creation to supply the voids caused by the action of His laws.'"[75] In a similar way, Frederick Temple (1821–1902), the future Archbishop of Canterbury, embraced Darwin's theory wholeheartedly. In sermons espousing Darwin's ideas, Temple strongly rebuked "those theologians who had so often built on the shifting sand of what science could not yet explain." Temple, for his own part, energetically welcomed natural selection as an extension of natural law "because this made it more probable that the world was also governed by moral law."[76]

Perhaps even more surprising to those who envision a state of perpetual warfare between Darwinism and Christianity is that in late nineteenth century "the foremost modern defender of the theologically conservative doctrine of the inerrancy of the Bible, was also an evolutionist."[77] Princeton professor of theology Benjamin Breckinridge Warfield (1851–1921) was "one of the chief theological architects of *The Fundamentals*,"[78] and "the ablest modern defender of the theologically conservative belief in the inerrancy of the Bible."[79] Warfield was also an unashamed supporter of Darwin's theory of evolution and was, in his own words, "a Darwinian of the purest water."[80] Like Gray, Warfield argued that God's creative purpose in the world is in "no way inconsistent with—[but] rather necessarily involved in—a complete system of natural causation. Every teleological system implies a complete 'causo-mechanical' explanation as its instrument."[81] Warfield maintained that evolution by natural selection is a viable

---

74. Charles Kingsley, quoted in *The Correspondence of Charles Darwin*, vol. 7, *1858–1859*, ed. Frederick Burkhardt and Duncan M. Porter (Cambridge: Cambridge University Press, 2004), 379.

75. Charles Darwin, *The Origin of Species by Means of Natural Selection*, 6th ed. (London: John Murray, 1873), 422.

76. Brooke, "Darwin and Victorian Christianity," 206.

77. David N. Livingstone and Mark A. Noll, "B. B. Warfield (1851–1921): A Biblical Inerrantist as Evolutionist," *Isis* 91, no. 2 (June 2000): 283.

78. David N. Livingstone, "B. B. Warfield, the Theory of Evolution and Early Fundamentalism," *Evangelical Quarterly* 58, no. 1 (January 1986): 69.

79. Mark Noll, "Charles Hodge and B. B. Warfield on Science, the Bible, Evolution, and Darwinism," *Modern Reformation* (May/June 1998): 7.

80. Joseph E. Illick, "The Reception of Darwinism at the Theological Seminary and the College at Princeton, New Jersey, Part 2, The College," *Journal of the Presbyterian Historical Society* 38 (December 1960): 115.

81. David N. Livingstone, "The Idea of Design: The Vicissitudes of a Key Concept in the Princeton Response to Darwin," *Scottish Journal of Theology* 37, no. 3 (1984): 347.

scientific working hypothesis that describes *how* different species originated. Consequently, he explains, Darwin's "form of the theory is not made to *account* for anything more than other second causes account for" and therefore is not only consistent with theism, but "implies and presupposes theism."[82]

Warfield even finds a theological basis for Darwin's theory of evolution in the works of John Calvin (1509–1564). According to Warfield, Calvin insisted that the term "creation" be used only when referring to the initial creative act.[83] All that has arisen since then "except the souls of men alone—has arisen as a modification of this original world-stuff by means of the interaction of its intrinsic forces. . . . [These modifications] find their account proximately in secondary causes; and this is not only evolutionism," says Warfield, "but pure evolutionism."[84] This understanding of evolution as the development of matter through intrinsic forces, which God had initially instilled, was seen to be consistent with both the Christian conception of the creation of animals as well as the biblical understandings of the construction of the human body.[85] Warfield saw no theological dilemma "if under the directing hand of God a human body [was] formed at a leap by propagation by brutish parents"—an evolutionary position which, minus the hand of God, differed little from Huxley's own views.[86] In fact, Warfield declared, "I am free to say, for myself, that I do not think that there is any general statement in the Bible or any part of the account of creation, either as given in Gen 1 and 2 or elsewhere alluded to, that need be opposed to evolution."[87] Even the Creator's forming of human beings into "the image of God was in itself no 'denial of the interaction of an evolutionary process in the production of man.'"[88]

In Darwin's day, then, there were very few Christians who rejected evolution based on a literal interpretation of Scripture, and even fewer who believed that the Bible taught that the Earth was less than ten thousand years old.[89] As historian Ronald Numbers explains, "Even the most literalistic Bible believers accepted the antiquity of life on Earth as revealed in the paleontological record."[90] Historian Edward Davis likewise writes that even "the fundamentalists

---

82. Bradley J. Gundlach, "McCosh and Hodge on Evolution: A Combined Legacy," *Journal of Presbyterian History* 75 (Summer 1997): 98.

83. Livingstone, "Idea of Design," 347.

84. Noll, "Charles Hodge and B. B. Warfield," 6–7.

85. Ibid., 8.

86. Livingstone, *Darwin's Forgotten Defenders*, 119.

87. Ibid., 118.

88. B. B. Warfield, "Editorial Note," *The Bible Student* 8 (1904): 243; quoted in ibid., 119.

89. Ronald L. Numbers, *Darwinism Comes to America* (Cambridge, MA: Harvard University Press, 1998), 2.

90. Ronald Numbers, "Darwinism, Creationism, and 'Intelligent Design,'" in *Scientists Confront Creationism: Intelligent Design and Beyond*, ed. Andrew Petto and Laurie Godfrey (New York: W. W. Norton, 2007), 32.

of the 1920s fully accepted the geological ages, to such an extent that" William Bell Riley, founder and president of the largest global Christian fundamentalist organization, "could not identify a single intelligent fundamentalist who claims that the earth was made six thousand years ago." Moreover, affirmed Riley, "the Bible never taught any such thing."[91] And, among Biblical literalists and fundamentalists, "none believed that evolution among the lower animals contradicted core Christian doctrines such as creation."[92] The one exception to this general theological rule was the Seventh Day Adventists, initially a small sect of charismatic Christians who had expected the immanent return of Christ on October 22, 1844. The post-1844 leader of the Adventists, Ellen G. White (1827–1915), claimed to receive messages and visions directly from God, and her church placed these supernaturally inspired pronouncements on par with the Bible.[93] In one important trancelike vision, White was "carried back to the creation" event by God himself, "and was shown that the first week, in which God performed the work of creation in six twenty-four-hour days and rested on the seventh day, was just like every other week."[94] Informed by her visions from God, "White also endorsed the largely discarded view of Noah's flood as a worldwide catastrophe that had buried the fossils and reshaped the Earth's surface." She was shown, by God, that during Noah's flood, God created all the various geological layers of sediment and fossils by burying the organic debris and causing "a powerful wind to pass over the Earth . . . in some instances carrying away the tops of mountains like mighty avalanches . . . burying the dead bodies with trees, stones, and earth."[95] White taught that Earth history extended into the past only about six thousand years.[96] Speaking on Darwinian evolution, White warned that such "science, so-called . . . cannot be passed on as of equal authority with revelation."[97] Inspired by the teachings and revelations of their visionary prophetess, Adventists rejected both the ancient age of the Earth given by geology and Darwin's theory of evolution as contrary to the correct interpretation of Scripture.[98]

The Adventist amateur geologist George McCready Price (1870–1963) was especially keen on promoting White's teachings on evolution and the role of Noah's flood in geology. Unhindered by the blinders of a formal scientific or theological education, Price "adamantly rejected the evidence of geological ages"

91. Edward Davis, "Science Falsely So Called," in *The Blackwell Companion to Science and Christianity*, ed. J. B. Stump and Alan Padgett (Malden, MA: Blackwell, 2012), 49.

92. Ibid., 49.

93. Michael B. Roberts, *Evangelicals and Science* (Westport, CT: Greenwood, 2008), 18–19.

94. Ronald L. Numbers, *The Creationists: The Evolution of Scientific Creationism* (Berkeley: University of California Press, 1992), 74.

95. Ibid., 74.

96. Gerhard Pfandl, "Ellen G. White and Earth Science," *Journal of the Adventist Theological Society* 14 (2004): 176–94, at 185.

97. Ibid., 184.

98. Bowler, *Monkey Trials and Gorilla Sermons*, 180.

and hence the interpretations of Scripture—which were standard even among literalists at the time—that easily accommodated an ancient Earth. Instead, "inspired by Ellen G. White's divine 'testimonies' . . . he squeezed Earth history into about six thousand years and collapsed virtually the entire geological column [i.e., all of Earth's geological history] into the year of Noah's flood."[99] In 1961, Southern Baptist civil engineer Henry Morris (1918–2006) and Grace Brethren theologian John Whitcomb revived the flood geology of Price in their immensely popular book *The Genesis Flood*. This book became the foundation for what is now known as young Earth creationism or scientific creationism.[100]

The Meaning of Biblical Literalism

The atheist molecular biologist Francis Crick wrote, "A knowledge of the true age of the earth and of the fossil record makes it impossible for any balanced intellect to believe in the literal truth of every part of the Bible in the way that fundamentalists do."[101] However, it is clear from the examples above that the meaning of the phrase "biblical literalism" is not at all that straightforward or simple. The views that are today equated with biblical literalism (i.e., anti-evolutionist young Earth creationism) were not the views of biblical literalists fifty years ago or even two thousand years ago.

Consider, for instance, the hermeneutical approach of Irenaeus of Lyons (ca. 115–202 CE)—a disciple of Polycarp (ca. 69–155 CE), who was in turn a disciple of the Apostle John (ca. 6–100 CE). Writing before the New Testament collection of Scriptures was finalized, Irenaeus contended with a heresy known as Gnosticism over what should be considered the correct literal understanding of the early chapters of Genesis. The gnostics believed that the Creator God described in the Old Testament was evil and ignorant. And they saw Genesis 2:17b to be the smoking gun within the Old Testament that proved the impotence and inferiority of the Creator God.[102] They reached this conclusion because, as the gnostics understood it, the serpent was telling the truth; Adam and Eve did not literally die "the very day" that they ate of the forbidden fruit. In response to the gnostic interpretation, Irenaeus argued that if one understands these early chapters of Genesis literally, then he or she will see that Adam did in fact die the very day that he ate the forbidden fruit since "the day of the Lord is a thousand years [2 Pet. 3:8] and Adam died at the age of 930"—just seventy years short of a day from God's perspective.[103] If God meant *literal* death,

---

99. Ronald Numbers, *Science and Christianity in Pulpit and Pew* (Oxford: Oxford University Press, 2007), 64.

100. Ibid., 64.

101. Francis Crick, *What Mad Pursuit: A Personal View of Scientific Discovery* (New York: Basic Books, 1988), 11.

102. "For in the day that you eat of it [i.e., the forbidden fruit] you will surely die."

103. Eric Osborn, *Irenaeus of Lyon* (Cambridge: Cambridge University Press, 2001), 70–71.

which appears to be the plain meaning of the text, and Adam *literally* died 930 years later, then—according to Irenaeus—a "day" in Genesis 1–3 must *literally* be understood as a thousand years and not twenty-four hours.

Or consider the literalist interpretation of Basil of Caesarea (329–379 CE). In a number of Bible passages regarding the relationship between humans and animals, Basil understands the text to emphasize the earthiness of human existence and our common bond with animals since both were created from soil. In Basil's interpretation, Scripture teaches that humans, like the other animals, are composed of a "mundane perishable substance" and are "nothing special at the level of material composition."[104] Because this is the clear meaning of Scripture, explains Basil, "one should not fear or resent the reality of the 'soil' in one's makeup" and "one should retain what he calls a 'natural attachment' to the earth." This is because the Earth, as it creates both humans and animals, is acting as the faithful and obedient servant of God's command. When, says Basil, the Creator commanded, "Let the Earth bring forth living beings" (Gen. 1:24), God literally empowered the very Earth with the creative ability to produce such animals. This God-bestowed capacity of the Earth to create creatures continues even unto this day as, explains Basil, "some creatures . . . are produced spontaneously from soil."[105] For Basil, it is not that the Earth is conscious or that it has a soul or the power to create of its own will. But, rather, he sees Genesis as literally teaching that God gives the Earth the power to create or "bring forth" in the same way that animals and humans are given the power to be fruitful and multiply. The Earth "did not [merely] produce the seeds contained within it," says Basil, "but God who gave the command at the same time gifted the earth with the grace and power to bring forth." Thus, declares Basil, "I, for my part, look upon the Earth as an ancient mother, so that I do not take it as an insult to be born of a servant" to God's word.[106]

Conclusion

Are science and religion necessarily on a collision course, or do conflicts between them arise only from specific interpretations of how science and religion should relate to one another? This chapter contends that science and religion collide

---

104. Philip Rousseau, "Human Nature and Its Material Setting in Basil of Caesarea's Sermons on the Creation," *The Heythrop Journal* 49 (2008): 228.

105. Basil, *Hexaemeron* 9.2. Lactantius (ca. 240–320) likewise did not discount the possibility that some animals could be generated spontaneously. And some medieval thinkers, such as William of Conches, believed that Earth's divinely bestowed creative power to spontaneously generate life was so strong that it required God's intervention to keep new species from being continuously produced by nature. See David Lindberg, *The Beginnings of Western Science: The European Scientific Tradition in Philosophical, Religious, and Institutional Context, 600 B.C. to A.D. 1450* (Chicago: University of Chicago Press, 1992), 200–201.

106. Basil quoted in Rousseau, "Human Nature," 229.

when either is interpreted as being without limits. Religion is not equipped to assess proximate causes and explanations, and "when it comes to 'ultimate questions' . . . science simply does not possess the intellectual resources necessary for answers."[107] There are serious philosophical and scientific problems with scientism and equally substantial philosophical and theological issues with fideism. Interpretations of Scripture frequently encounter interpretations of science, but the correct interpretation of either is not easily acquired. Until the 1960s, a literal reading of Scripture was not generally perceived as conflicting with biological evolution or the idea of the great antiquity of the Earth. And throughout the history of the Christian faith, an interpretation of Genesis 1 as a "strict six-day creation was *never* the dominant view, and was the official position of *no* church in Europe or America (until the late twentieth century)."[108] In a similar manner, most Christians have interpreted the big bang as being generally supportive of traditional theological understandings of God's creation of material reality from nothing. Scientifically, there are a number of ways to interpret the details of evolutionary biology and big bang cosmology, but in principle, there are no scientifically legitimate interpretations that can rule out God's creative activity as the ultimate explanation.

Discussion Questions

1. Do you think scientism is a type of religion? Why or why not?
2. Do you think one can ignore science and still present a reasonable account of religious belief? Why or why not?
3. In your own personal experience (as opposed to what is reported in the news) where have you witnessed areas of conflict or concord between science and religion?
4. Do you think evolutionary biology and big bang cosmology rule out a deeper theological or religious explanation for the creation of the cosmos and the various life forms that inhabit it? Explain your answer.

Beyond the Classroom

Discuss the meaning of biblical literalism in light of the examples given in this chapter. Consider the passage in Genesis 1:24: "Then God said, '*Let the Earth produce* every sort of animal, each producing offspring of the same kind—livestock, small animals that scurry along the ground,' and it was so" (emphasis

---

107. McGrath, "Ideological Uses of Evolutionary Biology," 340.

108. Michael B. Roberts, "Genesis Chapter 1 and Geological Time from Hugo Grotius and Marin Mersenne to William Conybeare and Thomas Chalmers (1620–1825)," in *Myth and Geology*, ed. Luigi Piccardi and W. Bruce Masse (London: Geological Society, 2007), 47–48.

added). In this verse, what is the proximate or immediate cause of the creation of the animals? What is the ultimate cause?

Resources for Further Study

Books

Artigas, Mariano, and Karl Giberson. *Oracles of Science: Celebrity Scientists versus God and Religion*. Oxford: Oxford University Press, 2006.

Bowler, Peter. *Monkey Trials and Gorilla Sermons: Evolution and Christianity from Darwin to Intelligent Design*. Cambridge, MA: Harvard University Press, 2009.

Hess, Peter, and Paul Allen. *Catholicism and Science*. Westport, CT: Greenwood, 2008.

Plantinga, Alvin. *Where the Conflict Really Lies: Science, Religion, and Naturalism*. Oxford: Oxford University Press, 2011.

Roberts, Michael B. *Evangelicals and Science*. Westport, CT: Greenwood, 2008.

Stenmark, Mikael. *Scientism: Science, Ethics and Religion*. Burlington, VT: Ashgate, 2001.

Articles

Rescher, Nicholas. "Authority." In *The Blackwell Companion to Science and Christianity*, edited by J. B. Stump and Alan G. Padgett, 74–81. Malden, MA: Wiley-Blackwell, 2012.

Stenmark, Mikael. "How to Relate Christian Faith and Science." In *The Blackwell Companion to Science and Christianity*, edited by J. B. Stump and Alan G. Padgett, 63–73. Malden, MA: Wiley-Blackwell, 2012.

Internet Resources

Burnett, Thomas. "What Is Scientism?" AAAS website, last updated November 6, 2014. Accessible at *http://www.aaas.org/page/what-scientism*.

Crawley, William. "Science and Religion: Duet or Duel?" BBC website, June 10, 2011. Accessible at *http://www.bbc.co.uk/blogs/legacy/ni/2011/06/science_and_religion_duet_or_d.html*.

Giberson, Karl. "Adventist Origins of Young Earth Creationism." Accessible at *http://biologos.org/uploads/static-content/Giberson-scholarly-essay-1.pdf*.

Stenmark, Mikael. "The Fallacy of Scientism as a Worldview." Faraday Institute for Science and Religion website, July 25, 2006. Accessible (audio and video) at *https://www.faraday.st-edmunds.cam.ac.uk/Multimedia.php?Mode=Add&ItemID=89* (time: 1:11:52).

CHAPTER 5

Creation and the Cosmos

People often ask: When did the big bang occur? The bang did not occur at a point in space at all. Space itself came into existence with the big bang. There is a similar difficulty over the question: What happened before the big bang? The answer is, there was no "before." Time itself began at the big bang. As we have seen, Saint Augustine long ago proclaimed that the world was made *with* time and not *in* time, and that is precisely the modern scientific position.

—Paul Davies, physicist[1]

As we look out into the universe and identify the many accidents of physics and astronomy that have worked together for our benefit, it almost seems as if the universe must in some sense have known that we were coming.

—Freeman Dyson, physicist[2]

In This Chapter

- Why Is There Something Rather Than Nothing?
- Scientific Views of the Cosmos: The Big Bang and Beyond
- Human Beings at Home in a Finely Tuned Universe
- Metaphysical Explanations for Cosmic Fine-Tuning
- Discussion Questions
- Beyond the Classroom
- Resources for Further Study

---

1. Paul Davies, *The Mind of God: The Scientific Basis for a Rational World* (New York: Simon & Schuster, 1992), 50.

2. Freeman Dyson, "Energy in the Universe," *Scientific American* 225, no. 3 (September 1971), 59. Quoted in Peter Hodgson, *Theology and Modern Physics* (Burlington, VT: Ashgate, 2005), 188.

Why is there something rather than nothing? This question, known as the *onto-logical* question (from the Greek *ontos*, meaning "being" or "existence"), is as old as human reflection itself. The ontological question has received a number of answers from various religious and philosophical traditions. An account of why the world exists or how the present world came into being is called a *cosmogony* (meaning "origin of the cosmos"). While the question of cosmic origins had long been within the purview of religion alone, more recently science has begun to address the question of cosmogony. In the twentieth century, the scientific study of the universe as an organized and structured entity (a discipline known as *cosmology*), revealed a number of surprising details about cosmic origins. The most surprising discovery was that the universe was not infinitely old (as had long been believed) but, in fact, had a distinct beginning in time—which came to be known as the big bang. While popularly portrayed as a cataclysmic and chaotic explosion that haphazardly threw matter and energy into the cosmos, upon closer inspection, cosmologists found that the big bang was an event so finely orchestrated that the slightest variation of the initial conditions from their actual values would have resulted in a universe entirely inhospitable to life. In this way, the fundamental structure of the universe appears to be balanced on a razor's edge for the existence of intelligent life. This chapter explores the interface between scientific and religious cosmogonies, focusing on Jewish and Christian theological understandings of creation as they relate to the scientific discipline of cosmology.

Why Is There Something Rather Than Nothing?

Three thousand years ago, most religions answered the ontological question by affirming that there was never a time when there was absolutely nothing. The majority of ancient religions believed the material world had always existed in some way, shape, or form, and that physical reality was as old as the gods or perhaps even older. The ancient world produced a variety of accounts of how the present order came into being. For example, according to one ancient Egyptian creation story, the gods arose from "a primordial mound or island that had emerged from the primeval ocean."[3] In another Egyptian account, the pre-existent watery abyss, personified as Nun ("the mother of gods"), gave rise to the sun god Atum (also known as Re), who then proceeded to create the other gods, who in turn mated to produce the next generation of gods. Within this third divine generation, the Earth god Geb and the sky goddess Nut defined the limits of the world inhabited by both gods and humans.

---

3. Rosalie David, "Ancient Egypt," *A Handbook of Ancient Religions* (Cambridge: Cambridge University Press, 2007), 59.

Ancient Mesopotamian creation accounts similarly envisioned a primeval watery chaos that preexisted the gods. For instance, "the Babylonian Epic of Creation refers to a time before the present generation of gods in which there were two waters, male and female, commingling with no distinct separation."[4] As the primordial waters—known as the god Apsu and the goddess Tiamat—combined, they yielded several pairs of male and female gods, who in turn produced successive generations of gods. Irritated by the younger gods, Apsu decided to act against them, but they learned of his plans and killed him. Desiring to avenge her consort, Tiamat took the form a giant monster to destroy her children. One of her offspring though, Marduk the god of storms, defeated the chaotic monster Tiamat, and cut her corpse in two halves, "like a shellfish into two parts," separating them into the Earth and the Sky.[5] Marduk then "established cosmic and earthly order making Tiamat's stomach the path of the sun" god Shamash, and "the blood and bones of Tiamat's lover were turned into human beings."[6]

Among current world religions, both Hinduism and Buddhism share with these ancient views a belief in an eternal cosmos with no definite beginning and no end. Traditional "Hindu thought," explains Hindu scholar Harold Coward, "sees the universe and time as having been going on beginninglessly" and "there

Public Domain

In Egyptian cosmology, the sky is Nut's body; Geb, the Earth, lies beneath her. Recent scholarship tends to emphasize the distinctiveness of Hebrew cosmology from that of Egypt and other ancient Near Eastern cultures.

---

4. Benjamin Foster, "Mesopotamia," in *The Penguin Handbook of Ancient Religions*, ed. John Hinnells (London: Penguin, 2009), 183.

5. David Leeming, *Creation Myths of the World* (Santa Barbara, CA: ABC-CLIO, 2010), 18.

6. Ibid., 18.

is no notion of an absolute first creation or beginning to time."[7] Instead, the universe is believed to go through an endless series of cycles, similar to the life cycle of a plant or animal. Traditional Buddhists have similarly upheld the reality of "beginningless time" with "innumerable universes going through successive phases of origination, abiding, and eventual destruction."[8] As in Hinduism, in Buddhist thought "the universe has no specific creator."[9]

In the Beginning: The Created Cosmos

In contrast to ancient polytheistic creation accounts and the cosmogonies of contemporary Hinduism and Buddhism, theistic religions have answered the ontological question by affirming the reality of a unique Creator God who brought the universe into being at the beginning of time. The common thread uniting all theistic cosmogonies is the idea that one God, who has existed from eternity, has created all that presently exists. The most ancient monotheistic creation account and the key source for Jewish and Christian theological understandings of the cosmos is found in the first two chapters of the biblical book of Genesis.

For some time biblical scholars have understood that Genesis 1 and 2 comprise two different and unrelated creation accounts—perhaps written by two or more independent authors. However, more recently it has been pointed out that the literary form of Genesis 1 and 2 as a unified or single account has key similarities to other ancient Near Eastern creation accounts that have a similar literary form. The structural similarity is related to the use of what is called a literary doublet or couplet—where the first element of the creation account serves as a general description (from a cosmic perspective), and the second element gives a more specific description (from the earthly perspective of a human observer). The use of a "general-detailed pattern" is a feature found in the creation accounts of ancient Ugaritic, Akkadian, and Egyptian literatures.[10] Like other ancient creation accounts, explains Bible scholar and linguist David Tsumura, the first two

---

7. Harold Coward, "Time in Hinduism," *Journal of Hindu-Christian Studies* 12, no. 8 (1999): 22.

8. Alan Wallace, *Buddhism and Science: Breaking New Ground* (New York: Columbia University Press, 2003), 386.

9. Rupert Gethin, "Cosmology," in *Encyclopedia of Buddhism*, ed. Robert Buswell (New York: Macmillan Reference, 2004), 183. According to Buddhist scholar Allan Wallace, "Buddhism considers that the world can only be beginningless and that an apparent beginning, such as the big bang of our present universe, can only be an episode in a vaster process." Wallace, *Buddhism and Science*, 275. While traditional Theravada Buddism is nontheistic, some versions of Mahayana Buddhism focus on the worship of Buddist deities known as bodhisattvas. Even in Mahayana Buddhism though, there is still a denial of a unique Creator or first cause.

10. David Tsumura, "Genesis and Ancient Near Eastern Stories of Creation and Flood: An Introduction," in *"I Studied Inscriptions from Before the Flood": Ancient Near Eastern, Literary, and Linguistic Approaches to Genesis 1–11*, ed. Richard Hess and David Tsumura (Winona Lake, IN: Eisenbrauns, 1994), 30. See also Richard Hess, "Genesis 1–2 in Its Literary Context," *Tyndale Bulletin* 41, no. 1 (1990): 145.

chapters of Genesis describe the act of creation by "zooming in from an overall perspective to a closeup, with a corresponding shift in reference." In this way, the two creation accounts of Genesis "have different scopes or viewpoints by which the author or narrator describes one and the same creation of mankind, first with relation to the cosmos, and then with a narrower focus on the man's relationship with the woman, the animals, and the environment in the second story."[11]

While there are some similarities between the biblical creation account and other ancient Near Eastern creation narratives, the Genesis account differs markedly from all other ancient cosmogonies in a number of key aspects. As ancient Near Eastern scholar Richard Hess observes, "There are more distinctions in form and content than similarities between the creation account of Genesis 1:1–2:4 and the many ancient Near Eastern stories."[12] For instance, in Genesis, the existence of the one and only Creator God is assumed, and there is no attempt to explain God's origins. Among all the ancient accounts of creation, says Hess, "only Genesis describes one God acting alone without reference to or acknowledgement of other deities."[13] While many other ancient accounts describe the act of creation as a violent struggle between rival gods, writes Old Testament scholar Gerhard Hasel, in the Genesis account there is "a complete absence of any suggestion that God accomplished the creation of the world after the conquest of hostile forces."[14] Here, says Bible scholar Gordon Wenham, "God is without peer and/or competitor. He does not have to establish his power in struggle with other members of a polytheistic pantheon. The sun and moon are his handiwork, not his rivals. His word is supreme: a simple fiat is sufficient. He speaks and it is done. Word and deed reveal his omnipotence."[15]

---

11. Tsumura, "Genesis and Ancient Near Eastern Stories," 30.

12. Richard S. Hess, "God and Origins: Interpreting the Early Chapters of Genesis," in *Darwin, Creation, and the Fall: Theological Challenges*, ed. R. J. Berry and Thomas Noble (Nottingham, UK: Apollos, 2009), 91. The differences may be due to independent origins or due to the Genesis author's deliberate intention to critique other accounts. On the former option, Tsumura says, "Genesis 1 and 'Enuma elish,' which was composed primarily to exalt Marduk in the pantheon of Babylon, have no direct relation to each other," (ibid., 31). Gerhard Hasel similarly writes, "In recent years a number of the leading Egyptologists point to decisive differences between the Egyptian cosmogonies and Genesis creation, so that one can really no longer say that 'the Egyptian view of creation was very similar to that of Israel.'" Gerhard Hasel, "The Polemic Nature of the Genesis Cosmology," *Evangelical Quarterly* 46 (1974): 84. On the latter option, Gordon Wenham writes, "The author of Genesis 1 . . . shows that he was aware of other cosmologies, and that he wrote not in dependence on them so much as in deliberate rejection of them." Gordon Wenham, *Genesis 1–15* (Waco, TX: Word Books, 1987), 9. Claus Westermann holds that the biblical author, in explaining the creation of the firmament (expanse), "does not reflect in this act of creation the contemporary world-view, rather he overcomes it." Claus Westermann, *Genesis 1–11: A Commentary* (Minneapolis: Augsburg, 1984), 160.

13. Hess, "God and Origins," 91.

14. Hasel, "Polemic Nature of the Genesis Cosmology," 85.

15. Wenham, *Genesis 1–15*, 38; Gerhard von Rad notes that the Hebrew verb *bara'* (create)—as it is used in this passage without a modifier—"contains the idea both of complete effortlessness and *creatio ex nihilo*, since it is never connected with any statement of the material." Gerhard Von Rad, *Genesis: A Commentary* (Philadelphia: Westminster, 1972), 49.

Tsumura adds, "Not only is the creation by divine fiat in Genesis unique in the ancient Near East, the creation of light as the first creating act appears only in Genesis."[16] While in other ancient accounts, the power to create new life through reproduction requires divine intervention and constant renewal through religious fertility rituals, in Genesis "the power of created life to replenish itself is a power given to each species at its creation," and "it is not dependent upon subsequent rites, that is to say, the fertility cult, for its effect."[17] In other words, says Hess, "the Genesis account alone describes how the plants and animals have the power within themselves to reproduce."[18] Beyond this, continues Hess, "only in the Genesis account is there a clear sequence of ordering the world and then filling it with life."[19]

A Cosmos Created Out of Nothing?

The first sentence of Genesis—"In the beginning, God created the heavens and the earth"—points to a key difference between the Jewish and Christian understanding of creation and other contemporary ancient Near Eastern accounts. Interpreters agree that the phrase "the heavens and the earth" connotes the totality of things that exist (both seen and unseen). These words are "clearly intended to be a way of saying 'everything.'"[20] This first verse of Genesis, comments Wenham, "could therefore be translated 'In the beginning God created everything.'"[21] For more than two thousand years, the majority of interpreters of this verse have understood it to mean that God created everything out of absolutely nothing (Latin: ex nihilo). Today, however, there are many theologians who deny that the doctrine of creatio ex nihilo is found in the Genesis accounts and, instead, claim that "creation 'out of nothing' is not a biblical concept."[22] In a recent analysis of this view, Tsumura notes that "these theologians all base their interpretation of Gen 1:2 on" the work of bible scholar Hermann Gunkel (1862–1932), "who saw in Gen 1:2 a pre-creation condition of watery chaos as in the Babylonian creation myth Enuma elish." According to Gunkel, the Hebrew word tehom (the deep waters) is "the mythological remnant from the

---

16. Tsumura, "Genesis and Ancient Near Eastern Stories," 31.

17. Ibid., 35.

18. Hess, "God and Origins," 91.

19. Ibid. There are a number of other distinctive features of Genesis as well. For instance, says Hess, "only Genesis has an emphasis on seven days," with one day (the Sabbath) set aside for rest.

20. Colin Gunton, The Triune Creator: A Historical and Systematic Study (Edinburgh: Edinburgh University Press, 1998), 16.

21. Wenham, Genesis 1–15, 15.

22. Ian Barbour, Religion in an Age of Science, Gifford Lectures 1989/1991 (San Francisco: Harper & Row, 1990), 1:144. See also Thomas Jay Oord, Defining Love: A Philosophical, Scientific, and Theological Engagement (Grand Rapids: Brazos, 2010), 157.

chaotic sea goddess Tiamat against whom the creator storm god Marduk had to battle before the creation of cosmos."[23]

Tsumura points out, however, that there have been a number of important developments in biblical scholarship since the time of Gunkel and that his view of Genesis 1:2, "which has been so influential among biblical scholars, is now under close scrutiny and needs to be drastically revised."[24] For instance, says Hess, it has been shown linguistically that the Hebrew word *tehom* "does not come from *Tiamat*," and "Genesis 1 contains no evidence for mythical remnants of a fight between God and chaos as may be found in Babylonia."[25]

Similarly, instead of interpreting *tohu wabohu* as "primeval chaos," Hess maintains that a better translation would be "empty and unproductive" or "invisible and unprepared."[26] Tsumura agrees, stating that "the phrase *tohu wabohu* has nothing to do with primeval chaos; it simply means 'emptiness.'"[27] Or, as Wenham says, it conveys a sense of "nothingness."[28] Since there was no word within the ancient Hebrew vocabulary to signify *absolutely nothing*, the notion of emptiness expressed in Genesis 1:2 is about as close to absolutely nothing as an ancient Semitic author could get. While the phrase *creatio ex nihilo* is not explicitly used in the text, the overall thrust and context of the Genesis 1:1–2 narrative implies that this is indeed how God initially creates the cosmos "in the beginning." The idea of God shaping or "modeling pre-existing matter," says Wenham, "is far removed from this account."[29] Consequently, asserts Wenham, while in all other ancient cosmogonies the physical universe is fashioned out of preexisting material, Genesis 1:1–2 is "a rejection of the common notion that matter preexisted the gods' work of creation" by asserting "that God created the whole universe, by implication out of nothing."[30]

The Christian Affirmation of *Creatio ex Nihilo*

Regardless of how Genesis 1:1–2 is translated, the idea that God created the universe *ex nihilo* was certainly how God's initial act of creation has been understood by the majority of thinkers throughout the Jewish and Christian theological

---

23. David Tsumura, "The Doctrine of *Creatio ex Nihilo* and the Translation of Tōhû Wābōhû," in *Pentateuchal Traditions in the Late Second Temple Period*, ed. Akio Moriya and Gōhei Hata (Leiden: Brill, 2012), 7.

24. Ibid., 7.

25. Hess, "Genesis 1–2 and Recent Studies of Ancient Texts," *Science and Christian Belief* 7 (1995): 141–49. Wenham concurs that "a direct borrowing is impossible." *Genesis 1–15*, 16.

26. Hess, "God and Origins," 94.

27. Tsumura, "Genesis and Ancient Near Eastern Stories," 33.

28. Wenham, *Genesis 1–15*, 15.

29. Ibid., 38.

30. Ibid., 37.

traditions.[31] As Christian theologian Robert Jenson explains, "According to Genesis, certainly as Judaism and the church have read it, before there is the creature, there is God and nothing. And this nothing is not the kind that can be the antecedent of something. God and only God is the creature's antecedent."[32] Over a century before the emergence of Christianity, one finds within early Judaism a clear confession of *creatio ex nihilo* in 2 Maccabees 7:28: "Look at the heavens and the earth and see everything that is in them, and recognize that God did not make them out of things that existed." In the New Testament, one also finds an affirmation of this doctrine: God "restores the dead to life and calls into existence those things that had not existed" (Rom. 4:17). Similarly Hebrews 11:3 teaches, "By faith we understand that the world was created by the word of God, so that what is seen was created out of things which were not seen." The *Shepherd of Hermas*, which was considered sacred scripture in parts of the early church, affirms the doctrine of *creatio ex nihilo* "as the first and foundational item of his rule of faith." *Hermas* declares, "First of all believe that there is one God who created the universe and made the universe to be from having not been."[33]

The doctrine of a creation out of nothing was likewise the consensus among the early church fathers. For instance, in the second century, Tatian the Assyrian (120–180 CE) and Bishop Theophilus of Antioch (120–190 CE) both confessed a strong doctrine of *creatio ex nihilo*. Tatian perceived this idea as intimately tied to the fundamental goodness of the created material realm.[34] And Theophilus likewise affirmed that "God has created everything out of nothing into being," proclaiming that "nothing was made evil by God, but all things good, yea, very good."[35] Theophilus expressly opposed Plato's idea that pre-existing matter was as eternal and uncreated as God.[36] Like Tatian and Theophilus, the second-century bishop Irenaeus of Lyons (130–203 CE) confidently acknowledges the doctrine of *creatio ex nihilo* and understands this doctrine as pointing to the essential goodness of the created cosmos. Irenaeus writes, "While humans, indeed, cannot make anything out of nothing, but only out of matter

---

31. Wolfhart Pannenberg writes, "OT statements about creation in, e.g., Ps 104:14–30; 139:13; 147:8f., refuse to limit the creative power of God by linking it with preexistent matter. Like the thought of creation by the Word in Gen 1, they imply the unrestricted freedom of God's creative action that the phrase 'creation out of nothing' would later express." Wolfhart Pannenberg, *Systematic Theology* (Grand Rapids: Eerdmans, 1994), 2:17.

32. Robert Jenson, "Aspects of a Doctrine of Creation," in *The Doctrine of Creation: Essays in Dogmatics, History and Philosophy*, ed. Colin Gunton (New York: T&T Clark, 2004), 22.

33. *The Shepherd of Hermas* 2:1, quoted in ibid.

34. Gerald F. Hawthorne, "Tatian and His Discourse to the Greeks," *Harvard Theological Review* 57, no. 3 (1964): 162.

35. Theophilus, *To Autolycus* 1.4, 2.4; translation from *The Ante-Nicene Fathers: The Writings of the Fathers Down to A.D. 325*, ed. Alexander Roberts and Sir James Donaldson (New York: Cosimo, 2007), 2:98.

36. Pannenberg, *Systematic Theology*, 2:14.

already existing . . . God is in this point preeminently superior to humans, that He Himself called into being the substance of his creation, when previously it had no existence."[37] The early Christian theologian Tertullian (160–220 CE) likewise argued that God created material reality out of nothing since "any reality co-eternal with God would undermine his sovereignty in creating."[38]A century and a half later, at the council of Nicaea in 325 CE, leading Christian representatives from three continents would gather together to affirm, "We believe in one God, the Father Almighty, Maker of heaven and earth, and of all that is, seen and unseen." In this way, says theologian Karl Barth, the affirmation of *creatio ex nihilo* was theologically so significant that "it became one of the firmest parts of the general teaching of the Church concerning creation."[39]

Preparing the Cosmos for Life

The "days" of creation in Genesis 1, denoted by the Hebrew word *yom*, have been the subject of much discussion, interpretation, and debate for over two thousand years. Within the history of interpretation, some have viewed the word *yom* as a twenty-four-hour day, while others have understood this term to mean an indefinite period of time. Among early Jewish and Christian thinkers, there was a general belief that the creation of the cosmos somehow took place *both* instantaneously *and* over a period time. One reason for this understanding is because all of the seven creation "days" in Genesis 1 are subsequently summarized by the same word for "day" (*yom*): "In the *day* that the Lord God made the earth and the heavens" (Gen. 2:4). Thus, seven "days" needed to somehow all fit into one "day."[40] Another feature of the Genesis creation account that led interpreters to reject a week of twenty-four-hour days was the fact that the sun is not made to appear until the fourth day. If literal days are determined by the movement of the sun, then how could literal days be measured before there was a sun? The early Jewish commentator Philo of Alexandria (20 BCE–50 CE) "wrestles with the problem that there was evening and morning but the heavenly bodies did not appear until the fourth day."[41] Reflecting on these hermeneutical puzzles he remarks,

> It is quite foolish to think that the world was created in six days or in a space of time at all. Why? Because every period of time is a series of

---

37. Irenaeus, *Against Heresies* 4.20.2, quoted in Gunton, *Triune Creator*, 53.

38. Tertullian, *Against Hermogenes* 34. See also Gunton, *Triune Creator*, 54.

39. Karl Barth, *Church Dogmatics: The Doctrine of Creation*, ed. Thomas Forsyth Torrance, trans. Harold Knight et al. (Edinburgh: T&T Clark, 1960), 3.2.153.

40. Jack P. Lewis, "The Days of Creation: An Historical Survey of Interpretation," *Journal of the Evangelical Theological Society* 32 (December 1989): 434. Lewis writes, "This exegesis made interpreters wrestle with how the whole could have been instantaneous and at the same time stretched over six days" (449).

41. Ibid., 435.

days and nights, and these can only be made such by the movement of the sun as it goes over and under the earth: but the sun is a part of heaven, so that time is confessedly more recent than the world. It would therefore be correct to say that the world was not made in time, but that time was formed by means of the world, for it was heaven's movement that was the index of the nature of time.[42]

Many key thinkers in the early Christian church, including Clement of Alexandria (150–215 CE), Origen (185–254 CE), and Augustine (354–430 CE), followed Philo in rejecting the notion that the days of Genesis 1 were normal twenty-four-hour days. Augustine affirms, "The creation days are so great, so majestic and so profound that we cannot consider them as mere sun-divided days but as God-divided days. They are creative days, not solar days."[43]

Other early church fathers brought passages such as Psalm 90:4 ("A thousand years in your sight are like a day") to bear on the meaning of the word "day" in Genesis 1 and 2. Consider the *Epistle of Barnabas*, a document written in the first century CE, which many early church fathers (including Clement of Alexandria, Origen, and Jerome) affirmed as authoritative scripture. *Barnabas* borrows from an idea found in the early Jewish *Book of Jubilees* (*Jub.* 4:29–30) to explain "how Adam could live to the age of 930 years and yet die 'in the day' he ate of the fruit." *Barnabas* utilizes Psalm 90:4 and 2 Peter 3:8 ("With the Lord a day is like a thousand years, and a thousand years are like a day") to derive the idea that the six days of creation stand for six thousand years.[44] Among early church fathers, Irenaeus and Justin Martyr (100–165 CE) similarly apply the days-as-ages interpretation of the text. As Justin Martyr explains, "For as Adam was told that in the day he ate of the tree he would die, we know that he did not complete a thousand years. We have perceived, moreover, that the expression, 'The day of the Lord is as a thousand years,' is connected with this subject."[45] Cyprian of Carthage (200–258 CE) likewise affirms, "The first seven days in the divine creation contained seven thousand years."[46]

Some modern biblical scholars, such as Terrence Fretheim, argue that the days of Genesis 1 are twenty-four-hour days,[47] while others, such as Jack Collins

---

42. Philo of Alexandria, *On the Creation of the Cosmos According to Moses* (London: William Heinemann, 1959), 13. Quoted in Lewis, "Days of Creation," 434–35.

43. Bernard Ramm, *The Christian View of Science and Scripture* (Grand Rapids: Eerdmans), 214–15. Original source uncited.

44. *Barn.* 1513–14. Cited in Lewis, "Days of Creation," 436.

45. Bryan Hodge, *Revisiting the Days of Genesis: A Study of the Use of Time in Genesis 1–11* (Eugene, OR: Wipf & Stock, 2011), 102.

46. Cyprian, *Treatises* 11:11.

47. Terence E. Fretheim, "Were the Days of Creation Twenty-Four Hours Long? Yes," in *The Genesis Debate*, ed. Ronald F. Youngblood (Grand Rapids: Baker, 1990), 19–20.

argue that they are not.[48] Hess maintains that the days of creation are best understood as "phases" where each phase sets the stage for the next. "Rather than a chronological order," explains Hess, "the result is a logical one in which each day prepares for the next and so anticipates it or 'begets' it."[49] Hess describes how "the pattern of the days in Genesis 1, with its recurrent formula, corresponds to the pattern of the generations in the genealogies" found in the subsequent chapters of Genesis. The central concern here is not with the amount of time as measured in days or millennia, but "the *forward movement* of God's creative work. Each day accomplishes something new, bringing about a greater completion of the work of creation. Each day 'begets' the next. . . . The events of the first three days are a necessary background for and correspond to what occurs in the fourth through to the sixth day."[50] This concern with the progressive linear movement of time—as opposed to a cyclical understanding—is yet another feature that distinguishes the Genesis creation account from others in the ancient world. "Such a forward sequence in the flow of events contrasts with any kind of a mythical or cyclical view of events, wherein the regular rehearsal of the events is necessary to ensure fertility or blessing." Indeed, says Hess, "it points to a perspective in which each day of creation, as each generation of humanity, progresses in the unfolding of a divine plan."[51]

Regardless of how one understands the word *yom*, it is clear the overall theme of the six "days" of creation in Genesis 1 is God's preparation of the universe so that it could sustain an abundance of life. The central emphasis of the creation days is that God creates the cosmos with the sustenance of life specifically in mind—forming "the contexts for life in the first half of the creation week" before creating "life itself in the second half." In this vision of the cosmic creation, explains Hess, "the first three days set the background" and situate the environments that will sustain the various forms of life that are brought into being in the next three days.[52] In Genesis 1 God creates through separation. God separates light from darkness, day and night, the dry land from the waters,

---

48. Jack Collins writes, "my own exegesis has convinced me of a view of the Genesis days as 'analogical days,' namely they are God's work days: they are analogous, and not identical, to ours, structured for the purpose of setting a pattern for the human rhythm of work and rest. According to this interpretation, the days are 'broadly consecutive' (allowing for the possibility that parts of the days may overlap, or that there may be logical rather than chronological criteria for grouping some events in a particular day)." Jack Collins, "Discourse Analysis and the Interpretation of Gen 2:4–7," *Westminster Theological Journal* 61 (1999): 269–76, at 271. Mark Futato says, "The arrangement of the six days of creation in Genesis 1 must be topical not chronological." Mark Futato, "Because It Had Not Rained: A Study of Gen 2:5–7 with Implications for Gen 2:4–25," *Westminster Theological Journal* 60 (1998): 1–21, at 1.

49. Hess, "God and Origins," 90.

50. Hess, "Genesis 1–2 in Its Literary Context," 152, emphasis in original.

51. Ibid., 151.

52. Hess, "God and Origins," 88.

and so on.[53] The process of creation occurs through God's separating and order-ing the various aspects of cosmic reality in such a way that life may eventually inhabit the world and flourish within it.

Scientific Views of the Cosmos: The Big Bang and Beyond

As was discussed in chapter 2, the scientist who initially predicted the expan-sion of the universe was the Catholic priest and physicist Georges Lemaître. Lemaître suggested that "since the universe is expanding, there must have been a time in the very distant past when everything in the universe—matter and radiation alike—was concentrated in a state of infinite density at a point."[54] Lemaître preferred to call this initial point the "primeval atom," but today it is commonly known as the big bang. The big bang was the emergence and sudden expansion or "explosion of space at the beginning of time." According to the big bang model of cosmic origins, both space and time began at a definite point in the finite past. In his bestselling book, *A Brief History of Time*, physicist Ste-phen Hawking observes that the discovery of the big bang "finally brought the question of the beginning of the universe into the realm of science."[55] In other words, as physicists unveiled evidence for a dynamic universe with a beginning, cosmogony became cosmology.

The Unfolding Cosmos through Time

According to standard big bang cosmology, known as the Friedmann–Lemaître–Robertson–Walker or FLRW model, the universe began in an unimaginably hot, dense state about 13.7 billion years ago. Matter, energy, space, and time came into existence at this point (often labeled as time=0, t=0).[56] The standard FLRW model predicts that the initial state of the universe was a *singularity*—described

53. Wehnham, *Genesis 1–15*, 18. Wenham adds, "Elsewhere separation almost becomes synony-mous with divine election."

54. Tai L. Chow, *Gravity, Black Holes, and the Very Early Universe: An Introduction to General Rel-ativity and Cosmology* (New York: Springer, 2008), 123.

55. Stephen Hawking, *A Brief History of Time* (New York: Bantam Books, 1988), 8.

56. According to Einstein's theory of general relativity, the universe does not expand *into* space but rather *space itself* expands as the universe expands. Physicist Tai Chow explains, "As time elapses, space itself expands. The expansion of the universe is the expansion of space. The universe has no center and no edge. If you take a balloon, blow it up, and mark a number of small dots on the surface, then blow it up some more. You will see all the dots move away from each other. This is rather like the expansion of the universe: the expansion of the universe is not by the galaxies moving through space, but rather it is that the space between the galaxies is expanding. The three spatial dimensions of our universe can be thought of as the two dimensions on the surface of the balloon. A creature can only crawl around the surface, never finding an edge or the center." Chow, *Gravity, Black Holes*, 123.

as a point of infinite density, infinite pressure, infinite temperature, and zero volume. "At this singularity," explain cosmologists John Barrow and Frank Tipler, "space and time came into existence; literally *nothing* existed before the singularity, so, if the Universe originated at such a singularity, we would truly have a creation *ex nihilo*."[57] In other words, says physicist Michael Heller, "all histories of photons and particles emerge from nothingness."[58] While the standard FLRW model of the cosmos predicts such a singularity, what actually happened in the beginning is beyond the observational limits of science. As physicists Stephen Hawking and George Ellis explain, "The results we have obtained support the idea that the universe began a finite time ago. However, the actual point of creation, the singularity, is outside the scope of presently known laws of physics."[59]

If there was a singularity from which the cosmos emerged from nothing, it is veiled by what is known as the Planck epoch, a phase of the universe that lasted only a fraction of a second (from $t=0$ to 10^{-43} seconds after the hypothesized singularity).[60] The Planck epoch was a period of extremely high temperatures (about 10^{32} degrees C, which is 10 followed by 31 zeros) where the physics of space-time as known today—along with the standard big bang model—breaks down. Before the Planck epoch, all four fundamental forces (gravity, electromagnetism, the strong nuclear force, and the weak nuclear force) were one unified superforce. Describing this superforce is beyond our current capacities and, explains astrophysicist Kristine Larsen, the details "await a successful theory of quantum gravity."[61] Because the universe was so small at this point, quantum physics would play a central role. In order to describe this period of cosmic history adequately, a new physics of quantum cosmology is needed, one that can provide a quantum treatment of space-time and gravity.[62] Very little is known about this very brief and mysterious period. Larsen notes, "We currently lack the information to trace the history of the universe all the way back to the absolute beginning."[63] Consequently, says cosmologist Alan Guth, "the true history of the universe, going back to '$t=0$', remains a mystery that we are probably still far from unraveling."[64]

57. John Barrow and Frank Tipler, *The Anthropic Cosmological Principle* (Oxford: Clarendon, 1986), 442.

58. Michael Heller, *Creative Tension: Essays on Religion and Science* (Philadelphia: Templeton Foundation Press, 2003), 83.

59. S. W. Hawking and G. F. R. Ellis, *The Large Scale Structure of Space-Time* (Cambridge: Cambridge University Press, 1973), 364.

60. 10^{-43} is scientific notion for the number 0.000000000000000000000000000000000000000000 0001.

61. Kristine Larsen, *Cosmology 101* (Westport, CT: Greenwood, 2007), 116.

62. William Stoeger, "God, Physics, and the Big Bang," in *The Cambridge Companion to Science and Religion*, ed. Peter Harrison (Cambridge: Cambridge University Press, 2010), 176.

63. Larsen, *Cosmology 101*, 116.

64. Alan Guth, *The Inflationary Universe: The Quest for a New Theory of Cosmic Origins* (Reading, MA: Addison-Wesley, 1997), 87.

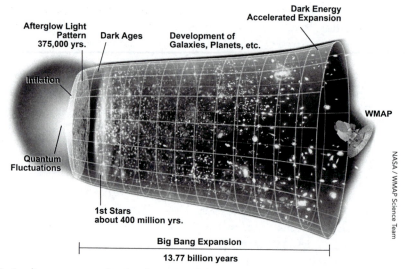

This timeline represents the development of the universe over 13.77 billion years, beginning with the big bang. The far left depicts the earliest moment science can probe, when a period of "inflation" produced a burst of exponential growth in the universe.

The Planck era was followed by the inflation phase, which lasted from 10^{-35} seconds to 10^{-32} seconds after $t=0$. "In this briefest of instants," explains astrophysicist Sandra Faber, "our entire visible Universe (now 30 billion light years across) inflated by a factor of 10^{60}, from an indescribably small speck to about the size of a grapefruit."[65] All of the space visible today was created out of virtually nothing during this brief flash of inflation. Immediately after inflation, the universe was a seething hot "soup" of energy (at 10^{27} degrees C) and fundamental particles (electrons, quarks, neutrinos, and less familiar types) with the four fundamental forces still unified as a superforce. Then, at 10^{-6} seconds—one millionth of a second after $t=0$—the cosmos began to expand "normally," becoming less dense and cooling as it expanded. At this point, the superforce separated into the four basic forces. First, gravity separated, then the strong nuclear force (which holds the nuclei of atoms together), followed by the weak nuclear force, and finally, the electromagnetic force. At the end of this period, the universe had cooled enough (to 10 billion degrees C) for fundamental particles to join together to form protons and neutrons. "With this phase completed," says Larsen, "the stage was finally set for the formation of the first elements."[66]

By three minutes after $t=0$, the universe had cooled to about 100 million degrees C, and the density of the universe was around that of water. At this

65. Sandra M. Faber, "The Big Bang as Scientific Fact," in *Cosmic Questions*, ed. James B Miller (New York: New York Academy of Sciences, 2001), 47.

66. Larsen, *Cosmology 101*, 117.

point, protons and neutrons joined together to form the nuclei of the two simplest elements, hydrogen and helium. It was still too hot, however, for electrons to be captured into orbits around these nuclei to form stable atoms. Although photons exited at this point, there was no light in the universe, due to charged electrons and protons that scattered the photons—preventing any light from shining. The universe was thus shrouded in a dense fog of thick darkness.

And Then There Was Light

About 300,000 years after the first instant of time, when the cosmos was about 10,000 degrees C, the cosmos underwent another key transition, as electrons began to orbit the nuclei of hydrogen and helium to form stable atoms. "With the electrons safely bound into atoms," clarifies Larsen, "there was nothing to scatter the photons, and they flew through the universe unimpeded."[67] The opaque cosmic darkness now became transparent, and light separated from the darkness to shine out in the universe for the first time. The photons from this first instant of light—known as the cosmic microwave background (CMB)—continue to flood the universe today. The CMB that originates from this period, which was first detected in 1964 and precisely measured in the mid-1990s, gives cosmologists a direct picture or "snapshot" of how matter was distributed at this early phase in cosmic history.

As time passed, the photons from the CMB lost energy, resulting in their having a longer wavelength. As the wavelength of this light shifted from the visible part of the light spectrum to the infrared part (a process known as redshifting), the universe was once again plunged into utter darkness. This period, known as the cosmic dark ages, lasted from a half million to about 200 million years after the beginning of the universe. Starting around 1 billion years after the beginning, when the universe had cooled to 200 degrees C, "regions of matter with slightly higher than average density tended to clump together under the influence of gravity."[68] As gravity amplified slight irregularities in the density of the primordial hydrogen and helium, creating increasingly denser pockets of gas, stars began to ignite. As the light of these first stars shone out in the universe, the cosmic dark ages finally came to an end.

Setting the Cosmic Stage for Life

Beyond providing light to the cosmos, this first generation of stars was also a crucial factor in setting the stage for the eventual emergence of life. As astrophysicist William Stoeger explains,

---

67. Ibid., 119.
68. Ibid.

The advent of stars was extremely important for our universe. Without them, the universe would have remained chemically impoverished—and therefore biologically sterile. Up until the formation of stars, the only elements present were hydrogen, helium, and a little lithium, the lightest metal. All the other elements—including carbon, oxygen, iron, etc.—were formed in stars or as the result of stellar explosions.[69]

In other words, almost all of the elements absolutely essential for the development of life were built up in the cores of the first stars, where temperatures reached hundreds of millions of degrees. Then, as the most massive of these stars exploded as supernovae, the heavier elements were dispersed throughout the universe.

This whole process of stellar birth and death occupied the first 9 billion or so years of cosmic history. After the first generation of stars produced all elements heavier than hydrogen and helium, subsequent generations of stars would be formed out of material enriched with these heavier elements. As a result, the later generations of stars could also have planets. And some of these planets could, in turn, possess the right combination of elements required for the production and sustenance of life. The chemical elements of which the planets, and everything on them, are made were built up inside the cores of earlier generations of stars. The combined events of this 10-billion-year history would enable one planet in particular—the planet Earth—to become a cosmic sanctuary for biological life.

Human Beings at Home in a Finely Tuned Universe

Do the order, beauty, and structure of the cosmos owe their existence to a series of chance events that started over 13 billion years ago with a chaotic explosion called the big bang? Some contemporary Christians, pointing to the impossibility of order emerging out of chaos, are doubtful. As Christian homeschooling textbook author Robin Sampson argues,

> The big bang scenario suggests that our ordered universe randomly resulted from a gigantic accidental explosion. Never in the history of human experience has a chaotic explosion been observed that has produced such an intricate order that operates purposefully. An explosion in a print shop does not produce an encyclopedia. . . . No building contractor dumps his materials on a vacant lot, attaches dynamite, and then waits for a completed home from the resulting "bang." The idea is absurd.[70]

---

69. Stoeger, "God, Physics, and the Big Bang," 177.

70. Robin Sampson, *The Heart of Wisdom Teaching Approach: Bible Based Homeschooling* (Merritt Island, FL: Heart of Wisdom Publishing, 2005), 109.

Do scientists really maintain that the big bang was a random and chaotic explosion of this sort? Recent investigations into the origins of the cosmos have revealed that the scenario described by Sampson is very far from accurate. As Nobel laureate in physics George Smoot explains, "The big bang, the most cataclysmic event we can imagine, on closer inspection appears finely orchestrated."[71] Beginning in the late twentieth century, cosmologists were increasingly struck by the fact that the initial conditions of the big bang, the laws of physics, and fundamental physical constants (such as the values for the speed of light and the strength of gravity) seem to be "fine-tuned" in such a way as to encourage the existence and development of complex life. To explain the present state of the universe, current scientific theories require that the physical constants of nature and the beginning state of the universe needed to have extremely precise values. The slightest variation of these fundamental constants or initial conditions from their actual values would have resulted in a universe entirely inhospitable to life.

The Fine-Tuning of the Initial Conditions of the Big Bang

Consider the precision of the initial conditions of the cosmos going back to the first moment of time after the Planck epoch. During the brief period of cosmic history called inflation, a very precise balance was needed between two components of an inflation-driving force known as the cosmological constant. If these two factors (called *Bare lambda* and *quantum lambda*) were *perfectly* balanced during this period, they would cancel each other out, and inflation would never have occurred. Philosopher of physics John Leslie writes, "A deity wishing to bring about life-permitting conditions would seemingly need to have made two components of an expansion-driving 'cosmological constant' cancel each other with an accuracy better than of one part in 10^{50}."[72]

Immediately after the inflation period, the expansion rate from the very first second of the universe's existence had to be precisely what it was if there was ever to be life within it. As Stephen Hawking explains, "If the rate of expansion one second after the big bang had been smaller by even one part in a hundred thousand million million, the universe would have re-collapsed before it ever reached its present state."[73] On the other hand, notes cosmologist Paul Davies, if the expansion rate was slightly greater, by even as little as one part in 10^{60} (10 followed by 59 zeros), this "would have had a serious inhibiting effect on the formation of galaxies."[74] Philosopher of science Robin Collins says that "an

71. George Smoot and Keay Davidson, *Wrinkles in Time: The Imprint of Creation* (London: Little, Brown, 1993), 135.

72. John Leslie, *Universes* (London: Routledge, 1989), 3–4.

73. Hawking, *Brief History of Time*, 126.

74. Paul Davies, *The Accidental Universe* (Cambridge: Cambridge University Press, 1982), 89.

accuracy of one part in 10^{60} can be compared to firing a bullet at a one-inch target on the other side of the observable universe, twenty billion light years away, and hitting the target." If the strength of the initial big bang explosion had differed by even the tiniest fraction, says Collins, "the universe would have either quickly collapsed back on itself, or expanded too rapidly for stars to form. In either case, life would be impossible."[75]

Another important instance of fine-tuning in the earliest second of the universe is related to the distribution of the mass-energy.[76] The initial mass-energy distribution—as measured by entropy (the entropy of a system refers to the system's tendency toward disorder)—had to be within an exceedingly narrow range to produce a universe that could eventually sustain life. The mass-energy of the universe had to have an extremely low entropy (i.e., be incredibly highly ordered) right at the beginning so that any kind of structure could emerge at all, rather than all of the matter collapsing into black holes. Discussing the initial distribution of mass-energy at the big bang, theoretical physicist and mathematician Roger Penrose considers the *phase space* (or possibility space) of this particular parameter.[77] Imaging a transcendent being who desired to create a particular low-entropy universe out of the whole possible range of universes, Penrose examines what sort of accuracy this hypothetical creator would require. Penrose writes that "in order to produce a universe resembling the one in which we live, the Creator would have to aim for an absurdly tiny volume of the phase space of possible universes—about $10^{10^{123}}$ of the entire volume." Commenting on the degree of precision this number indicates, Penrose exclaims,

> This is an extraordinary figure. One could not possibly even write the number down in full, in the ordinary denary [or decimal based] notation: it would be '1' followed by 10^{123} successive '0's! Even if we were to write a '0' on each separate proton and on each separate neutron in the entire universe and we could throw in all the other particles as well for good measure we should fall far short of writing down the figure needed.[78]

Collins puts the immensity of this number into further perspective: "According to Penrose's calculations, the precision of the Big Bang explosion must be much

75. Robin Collins, "A Scientific Argument for the Existence of God," in *Philosophy of Religion: An Anthology*, ed. Louis Pojman and Michael Rea (Boston: Wadsworth, 2012), 203.

76. Within physics, *mass–energy* refers to how the mass of an object or system is equivalent to its energy content. This equivalency relationship is given by Einstein's famous equation $E=mc^2$ where energy (E) equals mass (m) times the speed of light (c) squared.

77. In physics and mathematics, the term *phase space* refers to a space representing all possible states of a system, where each possible state of the system corresponds to a unique point in the phase space.

78. Roger Penrose, *The Emperor's New Mind: Concerning Computers, Minds, and the Laws of Physics* (Oxford: Oxford University Press, 1989), 344.

greater than that needed to blow up a pile of rubble and obtain a fully formed building replete with desks, tables, chairs, and computers!"[79]

The Fine-Tuning of the Fundamental Physical Constants

In addition to the precision required in the initial conditions of the universe, the fine-tuning of the cosmos for life is also perceived in the values of the constants of nature. "The laws of science, as we know them at present," explains Hawking, "contain many fundamental numbers, like the size of the electric charge of the electron [$1.602176565 \times 10^{-19}$ coulombs] and the ratio of the masses of the proton and the electron. . . . The remarkable fact is that the values of these numbers seem to have been finely adjusted to make possible the development of life."[80] Regarding the proton-electron mass ratio, physicist Rodney Holder explains that "the mass of the proton must be almost exactly 1,837 times the mass of the electron, as it is, for the possibility of interesting chemicals to be made and to be stable, certainly for complicated molecules such as DNA, which are the building blocks of life."[81] Similarly, Collins observes, "If the neutron were not about 1.001 times the mass of the proton, all protons would have decayed into neutrons or all neutrons would have decayed into protons, and thus life would not be possible."[82]

Or consider the fine-tuning of the values for the four fundamental forces. Reflecting on the electromagnetic force, Hawking says, "If the electric charge of the electron had been only slightly different, stars either would have been unable to burn hydrogen and helium, or else they would not have exploded."[83] Either scenario would have resulted in a biochemically impoverished universe lacking the necessary elements for the development of any conceivable form of life. Leslie adds, "With *electromagnetism* very slightly stronger, stellar luminescence would fall sharply. Main sequence stars would then all be red stars: stars probably too cold to encourage life's evolution and at any rate unable to explode as the supernovae one needs for creating elements heavier than iron. Were it very slightly *weaker* then all main sequence stars would be very hot and short-lived blue stars."[84] Collins similarly points to calculations that have shown that if the force of "gravity had been stronger or weaker by one part in 10^{40}, then life-sustaining stars like the sun could not exist. This would most likely make

---

79. Robin Collins, "Cosmology and Fine Tuning: Three Approaches," lecture given as part of the Lemaître Conference, April 10, 2011, Faraday Institute Lectures, *http://www.sms.cam.ac.uk/media/1140462* (time 01:00:29).

80. Hawking, *Brief History of Time*, 129.

81. Rodney Holder, *Big Bang, Big God: A Universe Designed for Life?* (Oxford: Lion, 2013), 90.

82. Collins, "Scientific Argument for the Existence of God," 203.

83. Hawking, *Brief History of Time*, 129.

84. Leslie, *Universes*, 4.

life impossible."[85] Reflecting on the current value of another fundamental force, physicist and philosopher of science Ernan McMullin explains, "If the strong nuclear force were to be just a little stronger, all of the hydrogen in the early universe would have been converted into helium."[86] This slight increase, explains physicist John Barrow, would result in disastrous consequences for life because "stars would rapidly exhaust their fuel and collapse to degenerate states or black holes."[87] On the other hand, adds McMullin, if the strong force "were to be slightly weaker in percentage terms, helium would not have formed, leaving an all-hydrogen universe."[88] The weak nuclear force (responsible for radioactive decay and other interactions) likewise has an extremely restricted range for life to be possible. If it were stronger, says Leslie, "then the Big Bang would have burned all hydrogen to helium. There could then be neither water nor long-lived stable stars." And making it weaker "would again have destroyed the hydrogen: the neutrons formed at early times would not have decayed into protons."[89] Both water and long-lived, steady-burning hydrogen stars are essential for the development of life. Thus even the smallest change to any of these values, says McMullin, "would lead to a universe in which life could not have developed."[90]

Another instance of fine-tuning concerns the two heavier elements that are more fundamental to life than any others: carbon and oxygen. These two elements, explains Collins, "are produced by the processes of nuclear synthesis in stars via a delicately arranged process." First, "a star burns hydrogen to form helium," and "when enough hydrogen is burnt, the star contracts, thereby increasing the core temperature of the star until helium ignition takes place." This, in turn, "results in helium being converted to carbon and oxygen."[91] In order for significant amounts of both oxygen and carbon to form, the rates of these two processes must be just right. In 1953, the astrophysicist Fred Hoyle was investigating a number of fortuitous coincidences that allowed for the balance of the carbon and oxygen synthesis rates. According to Barrow, Hoyle, to his surprise,

---

85. Collins, "Scientific Argument for the Existence of God," 203.

86. Ernan McMullin, "Tuning Fine Tuning," in *Fitness of the Cosmos for Life: Biochemistry and Fine-Tuning*, ed. John D. Barrow (Cambridge: Cambridge University Press, 2008), 75.

87. John Barrow, "Cosmology, Life, and the Anthropic Principle," *Annals of the New York Academy of Sciences* 950 (2001): 139–53, at 147.

88. McMullin, "Tuning Fine Tuning," 75.

89. Leslie, *Universes*, 4.

90. McMullin, "Tuning Fine Tuning," 75.

91. Robin Collins, "Evidence for Fine-Tuning," in *God and Design: The Teleological Argument and Modern Science*, ed. Neil Manson (London: Routledge, 2003), 184. Leslie adds, "For carbon to be created in quantity inside stars the nuclear strong force must be to within perhaps as little as 1 per cent neither stronger nor weaker than it is. Increasing its strength by maybe 2 per cent would block the formation of protons—so that there could be no atoms—or else bind them into diprotons so that stars would burn some billion billion times faster than our sun. On the other hand decreasing it by roughly 5 per cent would unbind the deuteron, making stellar burning impossible." Leslie, *Universes*, 4.

soon "recognized that the presence of a significant level of carbon in the universe hinges upon a fine coincidence of physical constants taking values that just allow the carbon nucleus to possess a resonance [or specific energy state] for the production of carbon from helium, yet just fails to possess a resonance for the reaction that would then burn it all away into oxygen."[92] Hoyle was stunned as he discovered the value for the carbon resonance and remarked that it appeared to be intentionally set with the production of life in mind. "A commonsense interpretation of the facts," wrote Hoyle, "suggests that a super-intellect has monkeyed with physics as well as with chemistry and biology, and that there are no blind forces worth speaking about in nature. The number one calculates from the facts seem to me so overwhelming as to put this conclusion almost beyond question."[93]

These are only a few examples of the many known instances of fine-tuning with regard to the physical constants.[94] These constants determine the properties of the elementary components of the natural world and the general size of almost all composite objects. The size and structure of stars and planets, for example, are not random, but rather are manifestations of the different strengths of various forces of nature that govern both the origin of the universe and the activity of the matter it contains.[95] Barrow explains, "The sizes of all the astronomical bodies from the scale of asteroids up to stars are determined by the relative values of the fine- and gravitational-structure constants alone."[96] The present order manifested throughout the universe is not merely due to the chance coincidences of an initial cataclysmic chaotic explosion, then, but rather the structure and harmony of the cosmos appears to have been written into the very laws of nature and the finely orchestrated conditions that were present in the beginning.

The Fine-Tuning of the Cosmic Timeline

The immensity of the observable universe, with its 100 billion galaxies, each with an average of 100 billion stars, can sometimes seem daunting to the inhabitants of Earth, which in comparative size is effectively a speck of cosmic dust. Physicist and theologian John Polkinghorne, however, says, "We should not be upset" about our relative insignificance, "because only a universe at least

---

92. Barrow, "Cosmology, Life, and the Anthropic Principle," 147.

93. Fred Hoyle, "The Universe: Past and Present Reflections," *Engineering and Science* (November 1981): 12.

94. For more examples of cosmic fine-tuning, see Barrow and Tipler, *Anthropic Cosmological Principle*.

95. Alister E. McGrath, *A Fine-Tuned Universe: The Quest for God in Science and Theology* (Louisville: Westminster John Knox, 2009), 115.

96. John D. Barrow, *New Theories of Everything* (Oxford: Oxford University Press, 2007), 127.

as big as ours could have lasted the fourteen billion years required to enable human beings to appear on its scene. Anything significantly smaller would have had too brief a history."[97] Scientifically speaking, the universe needs to be precisely the size it is, with a hundred thousand million galaxies in order for there to be life.

One key reason that a life-sustaining universe has to be over 10 billion years old, explains Barrow, is that life requires "chemical complexity," which "requires basic atomic building blocks which are heavier than the elements of hydrogen and helium that emerge from the hot early stages of the universe." Biochemistry requires and uses almost all of the chemically active and reasonably abundant elements in the rest of the periodic table. However, continues Barrow,

> Heavier elements, like carbon, nitrogen, and oxygen, are made in the stars as a result of nuclear reactions that take billions of years to complete. Then they are dispersed through space by supernovae, after which they find their way into grains, planets, and ultimately, into people. This process takes billions of years to complete and allows the expansion to produce a universe that is billions of light-years in size. Thus we see why it is inevitable that the universe is seen to be so large. A universe that is billions of years old and hence billions of light-years in size is a necessary prerequisite for observers, on the basis of chemical complexity.[98]

In addition to the amount of time it takes to manufacture the necessary chemistry for life, it also takes a minimum of billions of years to manufacture the types of long-burning stars and inhabitable Earth-like planets that can serve as a home for life. The cosmic events starting with the big bang set the stage for the birth of life on planet Earth around 10 billion years after the beginning. The first forms of life on Earth emerged within an atmosphere that would be deadly for the majority of life forms that exist today. During this early phase of Earth history, called the Proterozoic, explains astrobiologist Stephen Mojzsis, "the surface biosphere became transformed from a wholly microbial and anoxic world to an oxygenated domain poised for the emergence of diverse multicellular life."[99] The activities of these organisms (such as producing oxygen) influenced the composition of the atmosphere and shaped the surface of the planet Earth so as to prepare the way for later forms of life. Finally, after 3.8 billion years of preparation, the Earth was ready to become the home of human beings.

---

97. John Polkinghorne, "The Anthropic Principle and the Science and Religion Debate," *Faraday Papers*, no. 4 (April 2007), Faraday Institute for Science and Religion, 2.

98. Barrow, "Cosmology, Life, and the Anthropic Principle," 140–41.

99. Stephen J. Mojzsis, "Probing Early Atmospheres," *Nature* 425 (September 18, 2003), 249.

Metaphysical Explanations for Cosmic Fine-Tuning

According to Polkinghorne, "All scientists agree that the physical fabric of the universe had to take a very particular form if carbon-based life were to be able to evolve within its history. Where disagreements begin is in discussing what might be the significance of this remarkable fact."[100] Scientists and philosophers have interpreted the scientific fact of fine-tuning in a number of different ways in an attempt to provide an explanation for the occurrence of these remarkable cosmic coincidences.

Cosmic Fine-Tuning as a Lucky Accident

Some philosophers and scientists have viewed the types of coincidences discussed earlier as the consequence of a lucky accident. NASA astrophysicist Robert Naeye reflects this view: "On Earth, a long sequence of improbable events transpired in just the right way to bring forth our existence, as if we had won a million-dollar lottery a million times in a row. Contrary to the prevailing belief, maybe we are special."[101] The logic of the lucky accident approach says that because humans exist, the laws of nature and fundamental physical constants clearly must be the ones compatible with life. Otherwise, human beings simply wouldn't be here to notice the fact. Many cosmologists and philosophers have questioned whether this is an adequate explanation of cosmic fine-tuning— let alone a reasonable one. To illustrate the problem with this approach, Leslie invokes what he calls the firing squad analogy. Imagine fifty expert sharpshooters lined up for an execution. An officer gives them the order to fire—and then they all miss. The lucky accident explanation, in effect says, "Of course the fifty sharpshooters all missed me, if they hadn't all missed then I wouldn't be here to notice that I'm still alive."[102] Leslie argues that this "is not an adequate response" because the reason *why* they all missed has still not been given.

Or consider another example given by philosophers Michael Murray and Michael Rea. A group of four friends get together to play poker and one of the players, John, draws royal flushes for ten straight hands. Upon revealing his tenth straight royal flush, John's friends accuse him of cheating and threaten to take the money back and throw him out. But John replies, "I know it is improbable that I would get a straight flush of hearts on any given hand. . . . But what is the probability that I get a hand with two spades (a three and a six) and three hearts (a nine, a Jack, and an ace)? That hand is garbage. But the probability of getting it is the same. . . . I had to get some series of hands or other, so why do

---

100. Polkinghorne, "Anthropic Principle," 2.

101. Robert Naeye, "OK, Where Are They?" *Astronomy*, July 1996, 36.

102. Leslie, *Universes*, 13–14. See also Karl Giberson and Francis Collins, *The Language of Science and Faith: Straight Answers to Genuine Questions* (Downers Grove, IL: InterVarsity, 2011), 187.

you find one improbable series more surprising or in need of explanation than another? There is, of course, no good reason." Murray and Rea explain, "What needs an explanation in this case is not that he drew an 'improbable series of hands' but that he drew, against incredible odds, a series of unbeatable hands." The poker hands John drew were improbable in a very special way, and it is the specialness, rather than just the improbability, that needs explaining. The same can be said in the case of fine-tuning.[103]

Cosmic Fine-Tuning as an Inevitable Result of an Undiscovered Principle of Physics

A second response is to attempt to derive the various constants of physics from some more fundamental theory. The thinking here is that one day humans will discover a "theory of everything" (TOE) or a unique "grand unified theory" (GUT) that will determine the values of all the constants of nature and explain all other facts of physics. Such a theory, if discovered, will explain why the universal constants, physical laws, and initial conditions are not special, but must have such specific values. Once this theory is discovered, the finely tuned features of the universe will show themselves to have been inevitable. This theory of everything will even be able to explain its own existence. Einstein spent his later years in a search for such a theory. "What I am really interested in," reflected Einstein, "is whether God could have made the world in a different way."[104] Einstein's search, which assumed no essential contradiction with God being behind it all, came up empty-handed. Today, string theorists are still searching.

The main problem, however, with proposing the yet-to-be-discovered TOE or GUT as the explanation for fine-tuning (also known as anthropic coincidences) is that this unique Theory of Everything itself would be an extreme example of fine-tuning. "Besides being entirely speculative," explains Collins, "the problem with postulating such a law is that it simply moves the improbability of the fine-tuning up one level, to that of the postulated physical law itself."[105] Astrophysicists Bernard Carr and Martin Rees observe, "Even if all apparently anthropic coincidences [or coincidences which allowed for the development of life] could be explained [in terms of a theory of everything], it would still be remarkable that the relationships dictated by physical theory happened also to be those propitious for life."[106] Polkinghorne adds, "One would still have to explain why relativity and quantum theory are to be treated as givens" and why

---

103. Michael Murray and Michael Rea, *An Introduction to the Philosophy of Religion* (Cambridge: Cambridge University Press, 2008), 153.

104. Holder, *Big Bang, Big God*, 105.

105. Collins, "A Scientific Argument for the Existence of God," 215.

106. Bernard Carr and Martin Rees, "The Anthropic Cosmological Principle and the Structure of the Physical World," *Nature* 278 (April 12, 1979): 605–12 , at 612.

they should be logical necessities. These theories, he says, "certainly seem to be anthropic necessities, but they are by no means *logically inevitable*." Thus Polkinghorne concludes, "If there really were a unique GUT, the greatest anthropic coincidence of all would surely be that this theory, determined on grounds of logical consistency, also proved to be the basis for a world capable of evolving beings able to comprehend that consistency."[107]

Cosmic Fine-Tuning as the Inevitable Consequence of an Infinite Multiverse

A third and more popular approach that physicists use to explain cosmic fine-tuning is to postulate the existence of an unimaginably large (or even infinite) number of actual universes.[108] In one version of this view, each of the universes within this "multiverse" has different properties, laws of nature, and values of the basic constants of physics. In fact, this vast number of existing universes embraces the whole range of values of the constants and initial conditions. Given this countless number of universes, just by chance, there is *one* capable of developing carbon-based life. In other words, since the number of other universes is so extremely large, it is less surprising that one of them happens to provide the specific conditions for life. While the vast majority of these universes cannot sustain life, humans just happen to live in a universe with biologically friendly properties. According to this view, says Polkinghorne, "an anthropic cosmos is simply a rare winning ticket in a multiversal lottery."[109] Our own universe is not special, but rather it is a statistical inevitability. To return to the firing squad parable, the multiverse hypothesis says that perhaps there are many, many, many executions taking place today and given enough executions there will be one where all fifty marksmen miss their target.

This first understanding of the multiverse as containing a limited number of universes with only one of them containing life still leaves one with a sense that that one life-sustaining universe is special. A second version of the multiverse thus postulates an *infinite* number of actual universes that cover the whole range of values for the fundamental constants and initial conditions. Since there are an infinite number of universes, there are an infinite number of universes that contain life. Since there are no statistical limits where infinity is concerned, there are also an infinite amount of universes that contain Earths that are identical to the planet that humans inhabit. And there are an infinite number of identical copies of you. And there are also an infinite number of universes that contain infinite varieties of different versions of you (e.g., an infinite number of "you" who are

107. Polkinghorne, "Anthropic Principle," 3–4, emphasis in original.

108. See Bernard Carr, *Universe or Multiverse?* (Cambridge: Cambridge University Press, 2007).

109. Polkinghorne, "Anthropic Principle," 4.

wearing blue today and an infinite number of "you" who are wearing red today). Given the dynamics of infinity, there is nothing special about our own particular universe or planet Earth.

There are some serious problems with the various conceptions of the multiverse insofar as they are employed to explain cosmic fine-tuning. According to Polkinghorne, discussions of vast numbers of universes that can, in principle, never be observed, or an infinite amount of such universes, take "one into a realm of speculation beyond the scope of sober physical thinking."[110] For a theory to be considered scientific, it must be—at least in principle—testable. Holder explains that "experimental or observational verification is at the heart of scientific method," yet in the case of the multiverse, "this seems to be lacking in this case even in principle."[111] The trouble with the multiverse hypotheses as a *scientific* explanation, explains cosmologist George Ellis, "is that no possible astronomical observations can ever see those other universes. The arguments are indirect at best."[112] Consequently, says Holder, postulating "the existence of many universes provides, not a scientific, but a metaphysical explanation of the fine-tuning of this universe." The multiverse theory can never be supported by any direct observational evidence; nor can it be falsified, and thus it is not science.

A second problem with the infinite multiverse scenario is that it leads to some bizarre paradoxes and possibilities. Reflecting on the strange consequences of the multiverse, Holder says,

> It is worth contemplating for a moment what we are being asked to swallow if we are to believe in infinitely many universes. . . . There will be some in which an "I," virtually identical with me up to now, fell under a bus before completing this paper; some where there is even more unimaginable evil and suffering than in this one; some where conditions are benign and Edenlike; some in which gorgons or unicorns or wyverns actually exist; and so on, and so on. Just simply trying to contemplate the infinitely many universes makes us realize how bizarre the hypothesis is.[113]

While "scientists proposed the multiverse as a way of resolving deep issues about the nature of existence," says Ellis, "the proposal leaves the ultimate issues unresolved." The same deeper questions and issues "that arise in relation to the universe arise again in relation to the multiverse. If the multiverse exists, did it come into existence through necessity, chance, or purpose? That is a metaphysical

---

110. Polkinghorne, "Anthropic Principle," 4.

111. Rodney Holder, "Fine-Tuning, Many Universes, and Design," *Science and Christian Belief* 13, no. 1 (2001): 19.

112. George Ellis, "Does the Multiverse Exist?," *Scientific American*, August 2011, 39.

113. Holder, "Fine-Tuning, Many Universes, and Design," 20.

question that no physical theory can answer for either the universe or the multiverse."[114] In the final assessment, say cosmologists Ellis, Stoeger, and Kirchner, the multiverse theory "simply represents a regress of causation. Ultimate questions remain."[115]

Nor does the multiverse in any way rule out a Creator God. Astrophysicist and Evangelical Christian Don Page affirms that "God could well have designed the entire multiverse, choosing elegant laws of nature by which to create the entire thing."[116] The theological idea that God might have created a multiplicity of worlds beyond our own goes back to the early church fathers. For Origen and others, "the idea of a plurality of worlds came out of an investigation into the foundations of theology," rather than scientific understandings of cosmic fine-tuning. Rather than seeing this as contrary to the idea of a creator, though, these early Christians believed that "the idea of an ensemble of universes demonstrated the infinite power and eternal sovereignty of God."[117]

Cosmic Fine-Tuning as the Intentional Design of a Transcendent Being

A fourth explanation for the fine-tuning of the cosmos is that the special parameters were intentionally chosen by a Fine-Tuner who transcends the cosmos. To illustrate this line of argument, philosopher Robin Collins imagines a scenario where space explorers from Earth travel to a planet in a distant galaxy and "found a domed structure in which everything was set up just right for life to exist. The temperature, for example, was set around 70 degrees F and the humidity was at 50 percent; moreover, there was an oxygen recycling system, an energy gathering system, and a whole system for the production of food." This domed structure appeared to be a fully functioning biosphere that could sustain human life. Collins asks, "What conclusion would we draw from finding this structure? Would we draw the conclusion that it just happened to form by chance? Certainly not. Instead, we would unanimously conclude that it was designed by some intelligent being."[118] Or consider the firing squad scenario. According to the intentional design explanation, *someone* purposefully intended for the bullets to miss. Leslie asks, instead of concluding "that there may have been greatly many squads at work, making it quite likely that somewhere some lucky person

114. Ellis, "Does the Multiverse Exist?," 43.

115. George Ellis, William Stoeger, and U. Kirchner, "Multiverses and Physical Cosmology," *Monthly Notices of the Royal Astronomical Society* 347 (2004): 921–36, at 935.

116. Don Page, "Does God So Love the Multiverse?," in *The Blackwell Companion to Science and Christianity*, ed. J. B. Stump and Alan G. Padgett (Malden, MA: Blackwell, 2012), 205.

117. Christopher Kaiser, *Toward a Theology of Scientific Endeavour: The Descent of Science* (Burlington, VT: Ashgate, 2007), 35.

118. Collins, "Scientific Argument for the Existence of God," 47.

would be asking, 'How did they all manage to miss?' . . . [i]sn't there a more attractive hypothesis . . . that you are popular with the sharpshooters?"[119]

Many physicists have pondered the intentional design hypothesis as an explanation for cosmic fine-tuning.[120] Even Hoyle, who remained a lifelong atheist, observed, "I do not believe that any scientist who examined the evidence would fail to draw the inference that the laws of nuclear physics have been deliberately designed with regard to the consequences they produce inside the stars." Cosmologist Paul Davies goes beyond Hoyle to see intelligent life as part of the purpose behind fine-tuning. Davies comments, "The laws, which enable the universe to come into being spontaneously, seem themselves to be the product of exceedingly ingenious design. If physics is the product of design, the universe must have a purpose, and the evidence of modern physics suggests strongly to me that the purpose includes us."[121] Davies "prefers not to pursue the idea of an ensemble of many universes (a multiverse) as a way around this problem" of fine-tuning, but instead maintains "that it is simpler and easier to believe in a unique Designer than it is to believe in a potential infinity of unobservable universes."[122] Polkinghorne agrees and believes that it makes more sense to see the life-friendly (or anthropic) character of the cosmos as reflecting "the endowment of potentiality given it by its Creator in order that it should have a fruitful history."

Many cosmologists have acknowledged that belief in the multiverse requires just as much faith as belief in a transcendent Fine-Tuner. Ellis thus asks, "Is the degree of faith required to believe in a multiverse more or less than that required to believe in a creator God?" To this he answers, "I suggest that because of the lack of conclusive evidence in both cases, the degree of faith required to believe in either is the same." Both explanations can be argued on the basis of reasonable extrapolation from known data. And neither, he says, is in fact provable.[123] Hawking agrees and concludes that there are essentially two responses to fine-tuning. "A bottom-up approach to cosmology," Hawking explains, "either requires one to postulate an initial state of the Universe that is carefully

119. Leslie, *Universes*, 147.

120. The discussion here of intentional design at the level of cosmic fine-tuning should not be confused with the intelligent design movement that maintains evidence for a designer at the level of biological organisms. For a discussion of intelligent design in biology, see Michael Ruse, *Darwin and Design: Does Evolution Have a Purpose?* (Cambridge, MA: Harvard University Press, 2003); Robert Pennock, *Intelligent Design Creationism and Its Critics* (Cambridge, MA: MIT Press, 2001); William Dembski and Michael Ruse, *Debating Design: From Darwin to DNA* (Cambridge: Cambridge University Press, 2004); and Robert B. Stewart, *Intelligent Design: William A. Dembski & Michael Ruse in Dialogue* (Minneapolis: Fortress, 2007).

121. Paul Davies, *Superforce: The Search for a Grand Unified Theory of Nature* (New York: Simon and Schuster, 1984), 243.

122. Kaiser, *Toward a Theology of Scientific Endeavour*, 37.

123. George Ellis, "Multiverses and Ultimate Causation," in *Creation: Law and Probability*, ed. Fraser N. Watts (Minneapolis: Fortress, 2008), 77.

fine-tuned—as if prescribed by an outside agency—*or* it requires one to invoke the mighty speculative notion of the generation of many different Universes."[124] However, while the designer hypothesis "is a metaphysical guess," says Polkinghorne, "in contrast to the multiverse, it is one that does a number of other explanatory pieces of work in addition to addressing anthropic issues." For example, says Polkinghorne, "the intelligible and wonderful order of the world, so striking to the scientist, can be understood as being a reflection of the mind of its Creator."[125]

Conclusion

This chapter has explored theological and scientific conceptions of the origin and nature of the cosmos. The biblical vision of creation was examined and contrasted with cosmogonies from surrounding ancient Near Eastern cultures. Unlike other creation accounts in the ancient Near East, Genesis 1:1–27 describes a physical cosmos that, through the sole power of God's word, has progressively taken shape over time toward the ultimate goal of sustaining life. Among ancient creation accounts, the Bible is distinct in viewing the created cosmos as a historical entity and in describing how divine will has shaped creation from the time when everything was formless, void, and dark—before the stars, sun, Earth, or moon existed—to the time when the created world could be inhabited by plants, animals, and human beings. The central theme of the Genesis creation account is that God formed the cosmos in order that he might fill it with life. Included in these central affirmations unique to the biblical faith are the convictions that there is only one God and that God is the sole Creator; that God's creative activity is voluntary, rational, and effortless; that the world was created out of nothing; that the Creator is distinct from the created world; that creation is characterized by law-like order rather than chaos; and that creation is created to be creative.

When looking at the story of the universe as told by science, one can discern clear areas of consonance between the basic thrust of the biblical narrative and that of cosmic history. Like the Genesis account, the standard big bang model of cosmic history affirms that there was a time when everything was formless, void, and dark; that there was a time before there was light; that there was a time before the stars, sun, Earth, and moon existed; that there was a time before plants, before animals, and before human beings. Physicists agree that our universe had a beginning at the big bang, that it emerged suddenly from that which

---

124. S. W. Hawking and Thomas Hertog, "Populating the Landscape: A Top Down Approach," *Physical Review D* 73 (June 23, 2006). See also appendix A in John Polkinghorne and Nicholas Beale, *Questions of Truth* (Louisville: Westminster John Knox, 2009), 99–117.

125. Polkinghorne, "Anthropic Principle," 4.

is not seen, that it has changed—becoming progressively more complex—over time, that the course of cosmic history has been governed by law rather than chance, and that humans are latecomers on the cosmic scene. The initial singularity of the big bang, says cosmologist Michael Heller, "strongly resembles the theological concept of creation out of nothing (*creatio ex nihilo*)."[126] Beyond this, recent investigations into the origins of the universe have revealed that the big bang was an event so finely orchestrated that the slightest variation of the initial conditions from their actual values would have resulted in chaos rather than a cosmos. Setting the cosmic stage for the foundations of life, the fine-tuning of the initial conditions and fundamental physical constants of the cosmos determined the properties of the elementary components of the natural world and made the general size and structure of almost all of its composite objects inevitable. In this way, observes Collins, "the fundamental structure of the universe is balanced on a razor's edge for the existence of intelligent life."[127] While, explains Davies, "there is now broad agreement among physicists and cosmologists that the universe is in several respects 'fine-tuned' for life,"[128] a marked disagreement remains on how such fine-tuning is best explained. Some argue that a possible explanation is that our cosmos is a lucky outcome in a countless number of universes generated within an infinite multiverse. Others, such as philosopher Alvin Plantinga, believe that "it is extremely unlikely that this should happen by chance, but much more likely that this should happen, if there is such a person as God."[129]

Discussion Questions

1. Is the question, "Why is there something rather than nothing?" a meaningful question? If it is meaningful, do you think it points to a "person" or "agent" as a potential explanation of the universe? Explain your answer.

2. Do you think it is reasonable to ask what the reason, cause, or explanation for the existence of the universe is, or do you think that the existence of the universe requires no deeper explanation and that "it just is"? Explain your answer.

3. In your opinion, does the scientific discovery of a beginning of the universe (where both space and time come into existence from nothing) lend *rational* support to the *theistic* idea of a Creator God? Why or why not?

---

126. Heller, *Creative Tension*, 84.

127. Robin Collins, "The Teleological Argument: An Exploration of the Fine-Tuning of the Universe," in *The Blackwell Companion to Natural Theology*, ed. William Lane Craig and J. P. Moreland (Malden, MA: Wiley-Blackwell, 2009), 202.

128. Paul Davies, "How Bio-Friendly Is the Universe?" *International Journal of Astrobiology* 2, no. 2 (2003): 115.

129. Alvin Plantinga, "The Dawkins Confusion: Naturalism ad Absurdum," *Books and Culture* 13, no. 2 (March/April 2007): 21.

4. The interactions of the initial conditions, fundamental physical constants, and laws of nature give us a precise scientific description of how stars (and our own sun) come into being, develop through time, and eventually pass away. Do you think scientific knowledge about the origin of stars precludes the creative activity of God in their formation? Do you think it conflicts with Scripture to see God as directly creating the stars through the physical constants of nature? Can the physical constants of the cosmos be seen as a direct expression of God's sovereign will for the stars?

Beyond the Classroom

With a small group, watch the video link below and discuss the question that follows.

"In the Beginning . . . ," Voice of Light Productions, August 1, 2012, accessible at *http://vimeo.com/46550352* or *http://www.youtube.com/watch?v=4NvXIG SmQIM* (time 00:03:34).

The discovery of cosmic "fine-tuning" has lead many physicists and philosophers to a point where they have been rationally compelled to take "a leap of faith"—to either affirm the existence of a designer or the existence of an infinite multiverse. Which explanation of "fine-tuning" do you think is more compelling: an infinite multiverse (which entails identical copies of you) or a cosmic designer? Explain your answer.

Resources for Further Study

Books

Gunton, Colin. *The Triune Creator: A Historical and Systematic Study.* Edinburgh: Edinburgh University Press, 1998.

Heller, Michael. *Ultimate Explanations of the Universe.* London: Springer, 2009.

Hess, Richard S., and D. T. Tsumura, eds. *"I Studied Inscriptions from Before the Flood": Ancient Near Eastern, Literary, and Linguistic Approaches to Genesis 1–11.* Winona Lake, IN: Eisenbrauns, 1994 .

Hodgson, Peter. *Theology and Modern Physics.* Burlington, VT: Ashgate, 2005.

Holder, Rodney. *God, the Multiverse, and Everything: Modern Cosmology and the Argument from Design.* Burlington, VT: Ashgate, 2004.

McGrath, Alister E. *A Fine-Tuned Universe: The Quest for God in Science and Theology.* Louisville: Westminster John Knox, 2009.

Worthing, Mark. *God, Creation, and Contemporary Physics.* Minneapolis: Fortress, 1996.

Articles

Ellis, George F. R. "Does the Multiverse Really Exist?" *Scientific American* 305, no. 2 (August 2011): 38–43.

Hess, Richard. "Genesis 1–2 and Recent Studies of Ancient Texts." *Science and Christian Belief* 7 (1995): 141–49.

Holder, Rodney D. "Fine-Tuning, Many Universes, and Design." *Science and Christian Belief* 13, no. 1 (April 2001): 5–24.

Internet Resources

Collins, Robin. "Cosmology and Fine Tuning: Three Approaches." Lecture given as part of the Lemaître Conference, April 10, 2011, Faraday Institute Lectures. Accessible at *http://www.faraday.st-edmunds.cam.ac.uk/Multimedia .php?ItemID=Item_Multimedia_409&Mode=Add&Play=MP3&width=720 &height=460* (time: 01:00:16).

Ellis, George. "The Multiverse, Ultimate Causation and God." November 6, 2007. Accessible at *http://www.faraday.st-edmunds.cam.ac.uk/Multimedia.php ?ItemID=Item_Multimedia_190&Mode=Add&Play=MP3&width =720&height=460* (time: 01:00:33).

Hess, Richard. "God and Origins: Interpreting the Early Chapters of Genesis." November 5, 2008. Accessible at *http://www.faraday.st-edmunds.cam.ac.uk /Multimedia.php?ItemID=Item_Multimedia_272&Mode=Add&Play=MP3 &width=720&height=460* (time: 01:25:42).

Moritz, Joshua. "In the Beginning—Space, Time, the Cosmos, and the Creator: Part 1." Voice of Light Productions. Accessible at *http://vimeo.com/38687775* (time: 01:00:16).

Polkinghorne, John. "The Anthropic Principle and the Science and Religion Debate." *The Faraday Papers*, April 2007. Accessible at *www.faraday.st-edmunds. cam.ac.uk/resources/Faraday Papers/Faraday Paper 4 Polkinghorne_EN.pdf.*

CHAPTER 6

The Forming of Life
From Cosmic Dust to Consciousness

Nature proceeds little by little from inanimate things to living creatures, in such a way that we are unable, in the continuous sequence to determine the boundary line between them or to say to which side an immediate kind falls. Next after the inanimate things come the plants: and among the plants there are differences between one kind in the extent to which they seem to share in life, and the whole genus of plants appears to be alive when compared with other objects, but seems lifeless when compared with animals. The transition from them to animals is a continuous one.

—Aristotle (350 BCE)[1]

The only preachers and scientists who argue against each other are those who understand neither the God of Genesis nor the science of the universe. The preachers make God too small to make use of science, the scientists make science so big they think it can function without God's having given it life. Both are wrong, for they do not grasp how big God truly is. The true debate is not over evolution, but over the simple question: How big is God? Is he big enough to use any means he chooses?

—George MacDonald, theologian[2]

In This Chapter

- Does God Create through Natural Processes?
- Describing God's Creation of Life through Science
- Where Is the Evolutionary Process Going?

Continued

---

1. Aristotle, *History of Animals* 5888b4.

2. George MacDonald, *The Landlady's Master*, ed. Michael R. Phillips (Minnianapolis: Bethany House, 1989), 123–24. MacDonald (1824–1905) was a Scottish author, poet, theologian, and Christian minister.

In This Chapter Continued

* Discussion Questions
* Beyond the Classroom
* Resources for Further Study

Monotheistic religious traditions affirm that God is the creator of life. However, in the current cultural context, there is much debate over the question of how life was originally created. Some contemporary Christians hold that the Bible teaches that God created plants, animals, and especially humans through direct "special creation" without mediating such acts of creation through natural laws or natural causes. These "special creationist Christians" argue that seeing God as directly creating the various forms of life—as opposed to seeing God as "indirectly" creating life through natural processes—is the view that is most faithful to the witness of Scripture. Southern Baptist theologian Steve Lemke, for example, rejects any account of the creation of life that "removes God from being *directly* involved in much of creation by utilizing natural processes instead," because, he says, such understandings diverge from the "the biblical account [which] presents God as *directly* involved in the details of creation, both in the beginning and throughout history."[3] Other Christians, however, believe that God creates life through the processes of nature, and they embrace evolution as the way God creates life.[4] For instance, Christian philosopher Alvin Plantinga affirms, "The scientific theory of evolution . . . is entirely compatible with the thought that God has guided and orchestrated the course of evolution, planned and directed it, in such a way as to achieve the ends he intends."[5] In order to see whether the language of Scripture categorically rules out God's noninstantaneous creation of life by employing processes in nature, this chapter begins by examining the biblical understanding of how God creates. Looking closely at the Hebrew terms to describe God's creating activity, this chapter shows that the understanding of creation given in Scripture clearly entails a number of processes—such as the development of a human being in the womb—that were observed in a nonscientific manner in the days of the original author. This chapter then takes a

---

3. Steve Lemke, "Southern Baptist Voices: Evolution and Evil," *BioLogos Forum*, December 28, 2012, accessible at *http://biologos.org/blog/southern-baptist-series-evolution-and-the-problem-of-evil*, emphasis in original.

4. To get a sense of the number and variety of both scientific and religious organizations that have officially affirmed the reality of evolution see Molleen Matsumura, ed., *Voices for Evolution* (Berkeley, CA: National Center for Science Education, 1995).

5. Alvin Plantinga, *Where the Conflict Really Lies: Science, Religion, and Naturalism* (New York: Oxford University Press, 2011), 308.

close scientific look at the process of evolution to discern whether there is any essential conflict between the biblical understanding of God's creation of life and that given by contemporary science.

Does God Create Through Natural Processes?

Before investigating how God creates *life* according to Scripture, it is helpful to look at how Scripture says that God creates things in general. Does Scripture ever speak of God creating something that involves a scientifically well-known—or even an experimentally repeatable—natural process? In other words, are there any phenomena in nature that God is said to create for which there is also scientific knowledge concerning how these same phenomena physically (or naturally) come into being? A survey of Scripture reveals that it is full of examples of God *directly* creating phenomena that scientists now conclude occur through natural processes.

God's Creation of Meteorological Phenomena

In Scripture, God is said to directly create meteorological phenomena such as clouds, rain, wind, lightning, and snow. For example, Psalm 135:7 declares that the Creator "makes clouds rise from the ends of the earth; he creates [Hebrew '*asah*] lightning with the rain and brings forth the wind from his storehouses." Psalm 147:16 similarly affirms God's direct activity in creating: "He *makes* snow like wool" and "scatters the frost like ashes."[6] And Amos 4:13 speaks of God as the one who "*creates* [Hebrew *bara*'] the wind." The Bible clearly affirms that God directly creates certain types of weather, but it doesn't provide any details concerning *how* God makes it.

Scientists know a great deal about the processes through which wind, clouds, rain, lightning, and snow are made, and researchers can even simulate these processes within a number of contexts. Consider, for example, the process of snow formation. The idea that natural processes produce snowflakes is uncontroversial among Christians. As leading young Earth creationist spokesperson Ken Ham writes, "The properties of water—and the information that's already there in the molecule—cause snowflakes to form under the right conditions."[7] Snowflakes reflecting the variety of those found in nature are routinely grown in the lab, and the dynamics of the processes that create snowflakes have been precisely measured. Much is known about the process of snowflake formation,

---

6. See also Job 37:6 ("He says to the snow, 'Fall on the earth,' and to the downpour and the rain"); Job 37:10 ("The breath of God produces ice, and the broad waters become frozen"); and Ps. 148:8 ("lightning and hail, snow and clouds, stormy winds fulfilling ['*asah*] his word").

7. Ken Ham, *And God Saw That It Was Good: Reflections of God's Handiwork* (Green Forest, AR: Master Books, 1998), section 21.

and yet physicist and snowflake expert Kenneth Libbrecht concedes that scientists who study snow "still don't understand why ice does all of what it does."[8] Mathematical physicists Janko Gravner and David Griffeath agree, remarking, "To this day, snowflake growth from molecular scales, with its tension between disorder and pattern formation, remains mysterious in many respects."[9]

What scientists *do* know about snowflakes is that the process is not nearly as simple or straightforward as Ham conveys. The formation of each individual snowflake is a dynamic development that balances on the edge of deterministic order and random chaos. The process begins when the temperature within a cloud drops low enough for water vapor in the gaseous state to condense directly into the solid state without first becoming liquid. The condensation process starts "with some nucleus, typically a tiny dust grain, to which water molecules can easily attach" and leads to the formation of an "ice embryo." The growth of a maturing snow crystal from an ice embryo follows a fractal-like pattern that depends not only on "some sophisticated physics, mathematics, and chemistry" but also on the individual history and trajectory of each particular snowflake as it falls through the sky. Libbrecht explains, "Since no two crystals follow exactly the same path through the sky as they fall, each grows into a slightly different shape. So we end up with a myriad of complex, symmetric patterns, with no two alike." The growth or development of a unique snowflake is not just a result of the initial physical conditions but also is due to the pathway it takes as it develops and responds to the environment. "The final crystal shape," observes Libbrecht, "can be very complex, reflecting the complex path the crystal followed through the atmosphere."[10]

NOAA/National Weather Service Collection

The Psalms assert that God "makes" the snow (147:16), yet theologians generally agree that God does this by allowing natural processes to run their course.

---

8. Kenneth Libbrecht, "Morphogenesis on Ice: The Physics of Snow Crystals," *Engineering and Science* 64, no. 1 (2001): 16.

9. Janko Gravner and David Griffeath, "Modeling Snow Crystal Growth I: Rigorous Results for Packard's Digital Snowflakes," *Experimental Mathematics* 15, no. 4 (2006): 421–44.

10. Libbrecht, "Morphogenesis on Ice," 17.

There are few if any Christians today who argue that having scientific knowledge of the natural processes that bring snow, rain, or lightning into being means that the God of creation is no longer involved in *creating* these phenomena. There are, likewise, few if any who see the biblical affirmation that God creates these *meteorological phenomena* as implying that scientific knowledge about the origination of snow, rain, and lightning must be false. Instead, Christians from all traditions affirm that the same laws of nature that govern the formation of snow and lightning are in actuality physically observable expressions of the will of God for creation. Christians affirm that on seeing these natural laws and processes in action, one is, at the same time, witnessing the creative power of God.[11] Consequently, it appears that certain Hebrew words for "create" or "make" (*bara'* and *'asah*) can, at the same time, be used to describe what scientists see as noninstantaneous natural creative processes.

God's Creation of the Sun and the Stars

Scripture affirms that God created the sun and the other stars. Genesis 1:16 says, "God *made* the two great lights, the greater light to govern the day, and the lesser light to govern the night; He *made* the stars also" (emphasis added). The Hebrew word here for "made" or "created" is *'asah*—the same word that is often used to describe God's creation of various types of meteorological phenomena. Similarly Psalm 136:5–9 affirms that God "made [*'asah*] the heavens by his understanding" and "made [*'asah*] the great lights . . . the sun to rule by day" and "the moon and stars to rule by night." Isaiah 40:26 uses the Hebrew word *bara'* to describe God's formation of the stars: "Lift up your eyes on high and see who has *created* these stars" (emphasis added). Scripture is clear that God created the sun and stars, but it provides no details on *how* God accomplished this task.

One might thus ask what science knows about how the stars came into being. While stars cannot be produced in the laboratory in the same way as lightning or snowflakes, scientists can—thanks to certain unique properties of light—observe the various stages of stellar formation by looking deep into space. Since the particles of light (called photons) have a finite speed of 186,000 miles per second, when an astronomer looks at distant objects in space, he or she is observing photons that have been traveling through space for many years. In this way, looking up into the night sky is literally looking into the past (and the light that this moment reaches Earth from the sun, began its journey about eight minutes ago). Using telescopes, astronomers can look even deeper into the past, and larger telescopes allow astronomers to view galaxies that are more and more

---

11. For example, young Earth creationist author Jason Lisle writes, "The Bible tells us that there are laws of nature—'ordinances of heaven and earth' (Jer 33:25). These laws describe the way God normally accomplishes His will in the universe." Jason Lisle, "God and Natural Law," *Answers in Genesis*, August 28, 2006, accessible at *https://answersingenesis.org/is-god-real/god-natural-law/*.

distant in both space and time. Telescopes, in this way, are time machines that allow one to look back into the history of the universe.

Using the sky itself as a type of history book in which the story of the stars' creation can be read, astronomers have discovered that stellar birth is a complex and dynamic process involving a number of intricately interacting factors. Not only are the laws of physics and the fundamental physical constants (such as the force of gravity) important, but also the fine details of the structure of dense molecular clouds strewn with magnetic fields known as "stellar nurseries" and "the environment of a fledgling star." As astrophysicist Erick Young explains, "The final state of the new star depends not only on initial conditions in the core but also on the subsequent influences of its surroundings and its stellar neighbors. It is nature versus nurture on a cosmic scale."[12] Recently, observations from powerful telescopes such as the Spitzer Space Telescope have given scientists an increasingly precise understanding of how stars (and our own sun) come into being, develop through time, and eventually pass away.

Does scientific knowledge about the origin of stars preclude the creative activity of God in their formation? Does the Bible's affirmation that God directly creates stars preclude scientific descriptions of how such stars are born? In the case of lightning and snowflakes, young Earth creationists are content to hold that the laws of nature "describe the way God normally accomplishes His will in the universe," but in the case of stars, they assert that to embrace scientific descriptions is to rule out the creative activity of God.[13] Where the origin of stars is concerned, young Earth creationists "argue that the naturalistic origins theories accepted today are not adequate explanations of the process."[14] Other Christians, however, wonder why the laws and processes of nature should provide an adequate description of God's creation of snowflakes and lightning but not of God's creation of stars. Since the exact same Hebrew words are used to describe God's creative activity of both the weather and the stars, these Christians believe there is no contradiction in viewing God as directly creating stars through physical constants, natural laws, and dynamic processes of nature. According to this latter theological understanding of God's creating, one can view the laws of nature and physical constants of cosmos as a direct expression of God's sovereign will as it concerns the formation of the stars. Theologian and historian of science Christopher Kaiser observes, "In Scripture the relation between God and the world is conceived in terms of God's word. . . . The operation of nature is based on the decree of God. . . . And God's creatures are ever attentive to God's word." According to "this view of things," says Kaiser, "the course of nature is governed

---

12. Erick T. Young, "Mysteries of How a Star Is Born: Making a Star Is No Easy Thing," *Scientific American* 302, no. 2 (February 2010): 36.

13. Wayne Spencer, "Star Formation and Creation: Can We See Stars Forming?," *Answers in Genesis*, November 19, 2008, accessible at *https://answersingenesis.org/astronomy/stars/star-formation-and-creation/*.

14. Ibid.

by God in such a way that human investigation is possible, and the success of such investigation does not make God's agency redundant."[15]

God's Creation of Individual Human Beings

What about God's creative relation to the realm of organic things? Does the Bible provide any examples of God's directly creating living phenomena where scientists would now describe such origins through naturally occurring processes? One area where this is the case is human embryology and development. The Bible clearly describes God as directly orchestrating the events whereby each individual human being comes into existence. In Psalm 139:13–16, one reads: "You knit me together in my mother's womb. I will give thanks to you, for I am fearfully and wonderfully made ['asah]. . . . My bones were not hidden from you, when I was being made ['asah] in secret." Psalm 119:73 likewise affirms, "Thy hands have *made* ['asah] and fashioned me." Isaiah 44:2 declares, "Thus says the Lord who made ['asah] you and formed [yatsar] you from the womb." Isaiah 44:24 similarly says, "Thus says the Lord, your Redeemer, the one who formed [yatsar] you from the womb."[16] The Hebrew word for "made" ['asah] used in Isaiah and in Psalms to describe the noninstantaneous process of God directly creating or forming babies in the womb is the same word Scripture uses to describe God's creating or forming of meteorological phenomena, the sun, and the stars.

According to science, how are individual human beings made? The formation of a human being in the womb is an exquisitely intricate and delicately organized process of which scientists know many details. "From just one initial cell," explains researcher and science writer Heather Buschman, "an entire living, breathing body emerges, full of working cells and organs. . . . Embryonic development is a very carefully orchestrated process—everything has to fall into the right place at the right time."[17] Developmental geneticist Charles Boklage similarly observes that "the building of the human embryo is a biological process of transcendent complexity."[18] Developmental biologists have uncovered many of the extremely complicated particulars of this process (called *ontogeny*) through which two single cells first join to become one cell and then divide and develop to become an awesomely complex multicellular organism called a human being. The formation of a baby in the womb is a process that happens through time,

---

15. Christopher B. Kaiser, "The Laws of Nature and the Nature of God," in *Facets of Faith and Science*, vol. 4, *Interpreting God's Action in the World*, ed. Jitse van der Meer (Lanham, MD: University Press of America, 1996), 184–97, at 193.

16. See also Isaiah 49:5: "And now says the Lord, who formed [yatsar] me from the womb to be his servant."

17. Heather Buschman, "'Junk DNA' Drives Embryonic Development," *Science Daily*, December 3, 2012, accessible at *http://www.sciencedaily.com/releases/2012/12/121203091556.htm*.

18. Charles E. Boklage, "Human Embryogenesis," in *Embryogenesis*, ed. Ken-Ichi Sato (Croatia: InTech, 2012), 1.

not instantaneously. Fully developed human babies are not created out of nothing (*ex nihilo*) at the moment of conception.

If one accepts that the developmental process of ontogeny described by science is how each human comes into being, and if one also believes that God *directly* creates each human person, then it would seem that God *directly* creates each individual human person *through* the biological process of ontogeny. With the eyes of faith, Christians and Jews may affirm that God is at work in every detail of this process—even though they may use the language of science to describe *how* God creates people.[19]

God's Original Creation of Plant and Animal Life

Having explored the language that Scripture uses to describe the physical origins of phenomena that science has directly observed and knows many precise details about, one may go on to ask about the language Scripture uses to describe the origins of phenomena that took place without leaving directly observable records either in the present (e.g., ultrasounds of a developing embryo) or in the past (e.g., ancient light from distant galaxies). One phenomenon that scientists understand only through indirect evidence is the origin of life and the first emergence of life's various shapes and forms.

How does the Bible describe God's original creation of life in its various types? Interestingly, in both Genesis 1:11 ("Let the Earth produce vegetation") and in Genesis 1:24 ("Let the Earth bring forth living creatures"), God's command to create life is given to the Earth. Because Scripture says that Earth itself creates, in response to God's commands, some within the history of interpretation have understood this to imply that God literally empowered (and continues to empower) the Earth with the creative ability to produce certain types of life. Indeed, as was discussed in chapter 5, one of the unique features of the Genesis creation account that sets it apart from other ancient Near Eastern creation narratives is that God gives to created things the power to produce life themselves, as opposed to their requiring constant divine intervention to perpetuate life.[20] Affirming that God made creation to be creative, early church fathers such

---

19. The use of the word "directly" here to describe God's activity in the world is intentionally left vague to allow for a number of more nuanced metaphysical positions regarding the God-world relationship. Within a process metaphysical view, God's "direct" action could be conceived as God's luring or persuading entities within their interactions. See Joseph A. Bracken, SJ, *The World in the Trinity: Open-Ended Systems in Science and Religion* (Minneapolis: Fortress, 2014). In a neo-Thomistic view such action would be understood in terms of primary and secondary causation. See Michael Dodds, OP, *Unlocking Divine Action: Contemporary Science and Thomas Aquinas* (Washington, DC: Catholic University of America Press, 2012). It is beyond the scope of this introductory text to go into the details of such subtle and highly nuanced views of the God-world relationship.

20. See Richard S. Hess, "God and Origins: Interpreting the Early Chapters of Genesis," in *Darwin, Creation, and the Fall: Theological Challenges*, ed. R. J. Berry and Thomas Noble (Nottingham, UK: Apollos, 2009), 91.

as Augustine (354–430 CE), Basil of Caesarea (329–379 CE), and Lactantius (240–320 CE) understood Genesis 1:11 and 1:24 as saying God gave the Earth the power to create plant life and animal life. According to Basil, God bestowed the created realm with a good degree of creative autonomy. Interpreting Genesis 1:11 literally, Basil says, "It is this command which, still at this day, is imposed on the earth and, in the course of each year, displays all the strength of its power to produce herbs, seeds, and trees. Like tops, which after the first impulse continue their evolutions, turning upon themselves, when once fixed in their center; thus nature, receiving the impulse of this first command, follows without interruption the course of ages until the consummation of all things."[21] Basil reads Genesis 1:24 in a similarly literal way and even describes the spontaneous generation of life from Earth (an idea that was common in his day) as the continued response of Earth to God's initial command. "God who gave the command [to the Earth]," explains Basil, "at the same time gifted the Earth with the grace and power to bring forth. . . . Even unto this day, some creatures . . . are produced spontaneously from soil."[22]

Describing how God commanded the Earth to bring forth life, Genesis 1:25 says, "God made [*'asah*] the beasts of the earth after their kind, and the cattle after their kind, and everything that creeps on the ground after its kind." Genesis 2:19 similarly observes: "From the Earth the Lord God formed [*yatsar*] every beast of the field and every bird of the sky." And Genesis 3:1 refers to "the wild animals the Lord God had made [*'asah*]." In these passages, the same Hebrew words (*yatsar* and *'asah*) that describe the roughly nine-month-long process of development from a single cell to a fully formed human being is used to describe the Earth's "bringing forth" of the different types of animals in direct response to God's command. Since the same Hebrew words are used to describe both creative processes, it would thus seem that Scripture asserts a basic similarity between the way God originally created life and the way a human embryo develops in the womb.

Human Embryology and the Origins and Development of Life

Does a scientific survey of the evidence of Earth's past reveal any hint that the development of plant and animal life is analogous to the embryological

---

21. Basil, *Hexaemeron* 5.10, *Nicene and Post-Nicene Fathers*, ed. Philip Schaff, 14 vols. (New York: Christian Literature Publishing, 1886–1890), 8:81b.

22. Ibid. The spontaneous generation of life was a common belief in the ancient world and thus among the early church fathers, and remained so until the time of chemist and microbiologist Louis Pasteur (1822–1895) who devised experiments to disprove the hypothesis. The spontaneous generation of life is once again being debated among scientists, and it is ironic that many contemporary Christians now reject such a view in the name of Scripture.

development of an individual human being? On a broad level, the overall picture from the fossil record is that the emergence of plant and animal life happens through a sequence or a process where there is at first no sign of life; then single-celled organisms without nuclei appear; then eukaryotic organisms (cells with a nucleus) emerge; and, in time, these are followed by more complex multicellular creatures (plants and animals). In other words, in the emergence of plant and animal life through Earth history, one finds the same general trajectory of increasing complexity as in the formation of a human embryo in the womb: first single cells, then multicellularity, and then more complex organisms. Both the scientific picture of the development of life through time and the development of an individual human are likewise characterized by a seamless continuity that operates within the process. Under conditions that have existed on Earth for at least 3 billion years, all living organisms appear to have arisen from previously living organisms in such a way that the present complex living forms have developed by an unbroken and continuous process from the simplest living forms of the pre-Cambrian era (a period lasting from 4.6 billion years ago to 542 million years ago). The ontogeny of individual human beings directly connects with the development of life through time as "the sperm and the egg cell bring life forward from the parents, whose lives came from their parents, whose lives came from their parents, etc., etc., etc., all the way back to the very beginning of any form of life on Earth."[23] As a consequence, it seems that the Hebrew words *yatsar* and *'asah* are fittingly applied to *both* the embryological process of individual human development *and* the empirically observed emergence and development of complex plants and animals through time. If God's creative activity is responsible for the embryological process that gives rise to individual humans, then there is no scripturally-based reason not to see God as responsible for whatever processes might give rise to life in the first place and to the various forms of life.[24]

---

23. Boklage, "Human Embryogenesis," 14.

24. This chapter does not engage the various scientific discussions regarding how life might have originated in the first place. It will suffice to say that there is currently much scientific debate on this topic and very little consensus. Some researchers, such as geneticist Jacques Monod, argue "that life was pretty much the product of chance, a stupendous chemical fluke unique in the observable universe." Jacques Monod, *Chance and Necessity*, trans. A. Wainhouse (London: Collins, 1972). Others, such as Nobel Prize–winning cytologist and biochemist Christian de Duve, maintain that "life is a 'cosmic imperative,' more or less bound to occur wherever earthlike conditions prevail." Christian de Duve, *Vital Dust* (New York: Basic Books, 1995). See Paul Davies, "Physics and Life," in *The First Steps in the Origin of Life in the Universe*, ed. J. Chela-Flores, T. Owen, and F. Raulin (Dordrecht, Netherlands: Kluwer Academic, 2001), 14. In discussing the origin of life, one must not underestimate the remarkable complexity of the most primitive form of life as we know it. As microbiologist Lynn Margulis observed, "To go from a bacterium to people is *less* of a step than to go from a mixture of amino acids to a bacterium." Lynn Margulis, interviewed in *The End of Science*, by John Horgan (Boston: Addison-Wesley, 1996), 140–41.

Describing God's Creation of Life through Science

The Hebrew words in Scripture used to describe God's creation of life appear consistent with an interpretation that understands this creation as a God-directed developmental process that takes place through time, rather than an instantaneous creation of life out of nothing. Scientists commonly refer to any process that entails development or change over time as evolution (from the Latin, meaning "unfolding" or "unrolling"). Scientists use the word *evolution* to refer both to the straightforward *observation* that life has changed (and does change) over time and also as a way to describe *how* life changes or develops over time. The observation that the general shape of life has changed over time is often referred to as the *fact* of evolution. Theories that aim to explain how evolution occurred or what drives evolution are concerned not with the observed *fact* of change over time, but with the *mechanism* that is responsible for such changes.

The Fact of Evolution versus the Mechanisms of Evolution

The vast majority of scientists are in agreement about the *fact* of evolution—namely, that organisms have changed over time. Examining the fossil record, one can gather a general picture of the history of life on Earth. By employing the principle of superposition—the principle that, under typical geological circumstances, the layers of soil on top are younger than those beneath—scientists can reconstruct a basic understanding of the development of life on Earth as a whole. If one begins excavating the top or present layer of soil and then proceeds to examine deeper and older layers of soil and rock, one will eventually arrive at a level where no human artifacts or human fossils are found. If one continues to excavate deeper and thus more ancient layers of rock—each of which was at one time the top layer of soil—one eventually discloses layers in which no bird fossils are present. Continuing to dig deeper and deeper one successively discovers layers where there are no fossils of mammals, then no reptile fossils, then no fossils of four-footed animals, then no fish fossils, then no shells, and finally one comes to layers where there are no members of the animal kingdom represented, only single-celled organisms and the chemical signatures of their metabolic processes. Beyond these deepest layers of rock, one finds no evidence of life in any form. This observed fact that the types of fossilized plants and animals change through time is referred to as the law of fossil succession.

According to geneticist Richard Lewontin, biologists agree that "the facts of evolution are clear and are not disputed by any serious scientific worker."[25]

---

25. Richard C. Lewontin, "Introduction," in *Scientists Confront Creationism*, ed. Laurie R. Godfrey (New York: W. W. Norton, 1983), xxiii.

Period	Animals							Plants					
Quaternary							Humans						Flowering plants
Tertiary							Humans						Flowering plants
Cretaceous						Birds							Flowering plants
Jurassic					Mammals	Birds						Gingkos	
Triassic					Mammals							Gingkos	
Permian				Reptiles				Club mosses	Horsetail rushes		Pines		
Pennsylvanian			Amphibians	Reptiles				Club mosses	Horsetail rushes	Ferns	Pines		
Mississippian	Animals with shells		Amphibians					Club mosses	Horsetail rushes	Ferns			
Devonian	Animals with shells												
Silurian	Animals with shells	Fishes											
Ordovician		Fishes											
Cambrian													

The above chart correlates major types of plants and animals with the geological ages in which they first appeared. The geological record offers compelling evidence that life on Earth developed gradually, over billions of years.

These facts underpinning the reality of biological change over time are acknowledged even by scientists who disagree on the precise mechanisms or driving forces of evolutionary change. Because of this broad level of agreement among scientists, the National Academy of Sciences has affirmed that "compelling lines of evidence demonstrate beyond any reasonable doubt that evolution occurred as a historical process and continues today. . . . It is no longer possible to sustain scientifically the view that living things did not evolve from earlier forms or that the human species was not produced by the same evolutionary mechanisms that apply to the rest of the living world."[26]

The Darwinian Mechanism of Natural Selection

While there is broad acceptance among biologists regarding the reality or fact of evolution, there is currently much debate over the mechanism that has driven such changes through time. The most well-known mechanism of evolutionary change is natural selection—a concept advanced by Charles Darwin (1809–1882)[27] and then further developed by biologists in the first half of the twentieth century during what is known as the modern evolutionary synthesis

---

26. Kenneth R. Miller, *Finding Darwin's God: A Scientist's Search for Common Ground between God and Evolution* (New York: Harper Collins, 2002), 166.

27. Darwin was not the first to propose or publish the theory of natural selection. See Conway Zirkle, "Natural Selection before the 'Origin of Species,'" *Proceedings of the American Philosophical Society* 84, no. 1 (April 25, 1941): 71–123; Conway Zirkle, "Species before Darwin," *Proceedings of the American Philosophical Society* 103, no. 5 (October 15, 1959): 638.

(also known as neo-Darwinism). Today, most biologists allow a central role for natural selection in the evolution of life. For instance, even the molecular biologist Michael Behe, who is one of the founding fathers of the anti-Darwinian intelligent design movement, has come to acknowledge that natural selection is a key force in evolution.[28]

In his well-known work *On the Origin of Species* (1859), Darwin surveyed an immense amount of biological, geographical, and geological evidence that implied that the general shape of life had changed drastically over time. Based on his observations of selective breeding in dogs and pigeons, and the success of breeders in achieving a desired type (e.g., a Chihuahua or a Great Dane), Darwin proposed a mechanism through which similar kinds of changes could occur in nature, without human intervention:

> How do those groups of species, which constitute what are called distinct genera, and which differ from each other more than do the species of the same genus, arise? All these results . . . follow from the struggle for life. Owing to this struggle, variations, however slight and from whatever cause proceeding, if they be in any degree profitable to the individuals of a species . . . will tend to the preservation of such individuals, and will generally be inherited by the offspring. . . . I have called this principle, by which each slight variation, if useful, is preserved, by the term Natural Selection.[29]

Here one sees the three basic elements of Darwin's theory: (1) variation in traits, (2) inheritance of traits, and (3) the differential reproduction based on how well suited or useful a trait is in a given environment.[30] According to Darwin, variations occur randomly within a population of organisms. Heritable traits that help an animal survive until reproductive age are passed on and, as a result, succeeding generations become better adapted to their environment. Different combinations of useful traits (called adaptations) become increasingly represented in different populations. As such, differences accumulate over time, populations diverge, and new species emerge.

Darwin's scientific proposal went far in explaining how the process of evolution might have occurred, but several key questions remained unresolved. For instance, many wondered how variation occurs in the first place and what causes this variation. Others questioned whether such variation was really based on chance, as Darwin had argued. In addition to this, Darwin's mechanism lacked

28. Michael J. Behe, *The Edge of Evolution: The Search for the Limits of Darwinism* (New York: Free Press, 2007), 71–72. For a discussion, see *The Panda's Black Box: Opening Up the Intelligent Design Controversy*, ed. Nathaniel C. Comfort (Baltimore: Johns Hopkins University Press, 2007), 9.

29. Charles Darwin, *The Origin of Species* (New York: P. F. Collier & Son, 1909), 77.

30. Robert N. Brandon, *Concepts and Methods in Evolutionary Biology* (Cambridge: Cambridge University Press, 1995), 92.

a plausible theory of inheritance that could explain how nature remembers and transmits new variations to succeeding generations. In other words, what prevents the blending of traits and their subsequent dilution? For example, when a white flower is crossed with a red flower, why are the offspring not all pink?[31]

Even as Darwin unsuccessfully tried to win over skeptics of his theory by attempting to address these questions, the solution to Darwin's inheritance puzzle was being worked out in the experimental garden of the monastery school of Saint Thomas in Moravia by the Augustinian monk and biologist Gregor Mendel (1822–1884). As Darwin was writing his *Origin*, Mendel was busy discovering a type of hereditary unit (later called genes) that are passed on from parents to offspring in such a way that the blending of traits does not occur.[32] Mendelian genetics, as it came to be called, shed light on the relationship between genotype (an organism's hereditary information) and phenotype (an organism's observed properties or traits). Mendel's work was rediscovered at the turn of the twentieth century, and it was soon brought to bear on a number of the unresolved questions of Darwinian evolution. Starting in 1912 and continuing through the 1944, a scientific endeavor known as the modern evolutionary or neo-Darwinian synthesis sought to combine insights from Mendelian genetics with Darwin's understanding of evolution.

In addition to addressing the puzzle of inheritance through employing the concept of genes, geneticist Theodosius Dobzhansky and the biologists of the modern synthesis provided an explanation for what causes variation within a population of organisms.[33] In the 1930s, Dobzhansky showed that mutations within genes could introduce small amounts of variation within a species. He demonstrated that genetic mutations occur constantly, and while a few can be harmful and a few beneficial, the majority are neutral. As these mutations introduce small changes into populations, they create a significant amount of variability. Some of this variability confers an adaptive advantage. In the neo-Darwinian synthesis picture of evolution, then, "the environment imposes a set of adaptive demands on a population, and selection shapes that population so that it meets those demands increasingly well."[34] This understanding assumed that genetic

31. See Peter Bowler, *The Eclipse of Darwinism: Anti-Darwinian Evolution Theories in the Decades Around 1900* (Baltimore: Johns Hopkins University Press, 1983).

32. Although Mendel had done his research as a contemporary of Darwin and had even read a German translation of the second edition of Darwin's *Origin of Species* in 1862, Darwin never read Mendel's key 1866 paper, and Mendel's work on heredity remained in relative obscurity until the turn of the twentieth century.

33. See *The Cambridge History of Science*, vol. 6, *Modern Life and Earth Sciences*, ed. Peter J. Bowler and John V. Pickstone (Cambridge: Cambridge University Press, 2010), 261–62. Within the context of this book, it is also worth noting that Dobzhansky was a devout Christian. See *Science and Religion in Dialogue*, ed. Melville Y. Stewart (Malden, MA: Wiley-Blackwell, 2010), 253.

34. Kim Sterelny, "Development, Evolution, and Adaptation," *Philosophy of Science* 67, no. 3 (2000): 372–73.

mutation is the ground of all evolutionary variation as "evolution became re-defined as a change of gene frequencies in the gene pool of a population."[35]

Evolution beyond the Modern Darwinian Synthesis?

The Darwinian theory of evolution as it was reformulated and expressed in the modern synthesis dominated the scientific scene of the twentieth century, and "by the widely celebrated centenary of Darwin's Origin of Species in 1959, the modern synthesis had become virtual dogma within biology."[36] In its long reign as the scientific consensus, the modern synthesis view tended to over-shadow other understandings of evolution that both preceded and coexisted with neo-Darwinian notions. Beginning in the 1970s, though, a number of findings increasingly seemed to undermine certain mid-twentieth-century assumptions about how cells, organisms, and species work.[37] By the end of the twentieth century, new research in cellular biology, developmental biology, and molecular genetics began to raise a number of questions regarding the con-tinued adequacy of the synthetic view to serve as an overarching framework for understanding evolution. The picture of genetics that started to emerge in the 1990s challenged the modern synthesis view of the genome as a static, well-organized library of genetic information. At the same time the advent of evolutionary developmental biology ("evo-devo") in the mid-1990s supplied numerous instances of developmental constraints in evolution—which work to limit the degree and types of variation—and showed that there were ample sources of variation beyond those supplied by random genetic mutations. The discovery of novel evolutionary processes over the last few decades—such as hori-zontal gene transfer, symbiogenesis, and differential lineage sorting of genes—has greatly complicated the synthetic picture of the evolutionary tree of life.[38] More recently, observed instances of epigenetic inheritance have brought Lamarckian evolution back into the discussion.[39] Looking back, many contemporary biolo-gists and philosophers of biology have found that "the neo-Darwinian revolu-tion of the 1940s and 1950s was far from complete."[40] Thus, explains historian

---

35. Hans-Jörg Rheinberger and Staffan Müller-Wille, "Gene Concepts," in *A Companion to the Philosophy of Biology*, ed. Sahotra Sarkar and Anya Plutynski (Malden, MA: Blackwell, 2008), 6.

36. Edward Larson, *Evolution: The Remarkable History of a Scientific Theory* (New York: Modern Library, 2004), 237.

37. Michael Rose and Todd Oakley, "The New Biology: Beyond the Modern Synthesis," *Biology Direct* 2, no. 30 (2007).

38. While these processes have been shown to be drivers of evolution not accounted for by the modern evolutionary synthesis, they do not nullify the role of natural selection as a central driver in evolution or disprove natural selection.

39. Lamarckian evolution is named after biologist Jean-Baptiste Lamarck, 1744–1829, who pro-posed a theory of evolution through acquired characteristics.

40. Jan Sapp, *Genesis: The Evolution of Biology* (New York: Oxford University Press, 2003), 156.

of evolution Edward Larson, while "the modern synthesis stands at the heart of current evolutionary science . . . new discoveries have led many biologists to see this image as incomplete."[41]

Even as the work of new generations of biologists from several new specialties—molecular evolutionists, process structuralists, developmental evolutionists, and symbiologists—has been interpreted as challenging some of the central tenets of the modern Darwinian synthesis, the scientific defenders of the synthesis have continued to affirm its central assumptions. For instance, evolutionary biologists Hopi Hoekstra and Jerry Coyne have upheld the adequacy of neo-Darwinism to serve as the central framework for evolutionary biology, insisting that new insights from molecular and developmental biology can be seamlessly incorporated into the original structure of the modern synthesis.[42] While Hoekstra and her collaborators are open to the eventual development of an "extended evolutionary synthesis," they are currently holding out for more evidence that such a new synthesis is really necessary.[43]

Many others, however, have reached the conclusion that there is presently sufficient evidence to warrant a comprehensive reformulation of evolutionary theory—where Darwinian natural selection continues to play an important role, though not necessarily the lead act. Advocates of a revised or "extended evolutionary synthesis," including biologists Kevin Laland, Sean Carroll, Massimo Pigliucci, Scott Gilbert, Eva Jablonka, and Gerd Müller agree that "some of the assumptions underlying the 'Modern Synthesis' are based on an outmoded conception of the genome, and are significantly challenged by new developments in the molecular biosciences."[44] These scientists see Darwinian natural selection as one among *many* causes of evolution and "maintain that there are important

41. Larson wrote the first part of this quote in 2004 and the second part was added in an "Afterword" to the revised edition written in 2006. Larson, *Evolution*, 285 and 292.

42. Hopi Hoekstra and Jerry Coyne, "The Locus of Evolution: Evo Devo and the Genetics of Adaptation," *Evolution* 61 (2007): 995–1016. For a response to Hoekstra and Coyne, see Lindsay Craig, "Defending Evo-Devo: A Response to Hoekstra and Coyne," *Philosophy of Science* 76 (2009): 335–44.

43. Gregory Wray and Hopi Hoekstra, "Does Evolutionary Theory Need a Rethink?: No, All Is Well," *Nature* 514 (October 2014): 162.

44. Paul Griffiths and Karola Stotz, *Genetics and Philosophy: An Introduction* (Cambridge: Cambridge University Press, 2013), 7; Scott Gilbert, John Opitz, and Rudolf A. Raff, "Resynthesizing Evolutionary and Developmental Biology," *Developmental Biology* 173 (1996): 357–72 ; Massimo Pigliucci, "An Extended Synthesis for Evolutionary Biology," *Annals of the New York Academy of Sciences* 1168, no. 1 (2009): 218–28; A. M. Dean and J. W. Thornton, "Mechanistic Approaches to the Study of Evolution: The Functional Synthesis," *Nature Reviews: Genetics* 8 (2007): 1604–7; Sean Carroll, "Evo-devo and Expanding Evolutionary Synthesis: A Genetic Theory of Morphological Evolution," *Cell* 134 (2008): 25–36; Eva Jablonka, "Genes as Followers in Evolution: A Post-Synthesis Synthesis?," *Biology and Philosophy* 21 (2006): 143–54. See also Michael T. Ghiselin, "The Failure of Morphology to Assimilate Darwinism," in *The Evolutionary Synthesis: Perspectives on the Unification of Biology*, ed. Ernst Mayr and William Provine (Cambridge, MA: Harvard University Press, 1980), 180–93.

drivers of evolution that cannot be reduced to genes."[45] According to advocates of an extended synthesis, the current neo-Darwinian understanding is missing a number of key pieces to the evolutionary puzzle, including "how physical development influences the generation of variation (developmental bias); how the environment directly shapes organisms' traits (plasticity); how organisms modify environments (niche construction); and how organisms transmit more than genes across generations (extra-genetic inheritance)."[46] Summarizing the conclusions of those who advocate an extending or reworking of the evolutionary synthesis biologists and philosophers of science David Depew and Bruce Weber have reflected that "even in its current versions, [the modern synthesis] can no longer serve as a general framework for evolutionary theory. . . . Darwinism in its current scientific incarnation has pretty much reached the end of its rope."[47] While some of these scientists believe that revised Darwinian models of evolution could continue to play a central role in an extended evolutionary synthesis, others have their doubts. For example, integrative biologist and philosopher of science Sahotra Sarkar judges that "recent work in the evolution of genome architecture strongly suggests that selection may be largely irrelevant compared with other mechanisms of evolution."[48] In a similar way philosopher of biology Lindsay Craig deems that "the foundation of the Modern Synthesis framework, theoretical population genetics, faces significant, perhaps insurmountable challenges." Rather than seeing the extended synthesis as an elaboration of or addition to twentieth-century Darwinism, then, Craig believes that what is currently taking place within the biological sciences is "the development of a compatible evolutionary framework that addresses phenomena not accounted for by the framework developed during the Modern Synthesis."[49] Whether these scientists and philosophers believe that an *extended* synthesis is needed or whether a *new* evolutionary synthesis beyond Darwinism is needed, they all agree that there are now viable rival non-Darwinian understandings of evolution and that "any

---

45. Kevin Laland, "Does Evolutionary Theory Need a Rethink? Yes, Urgently," *Nature* 514 (October 2014): 161.

46. Ibid., 162.

47. David Depew and Bruce Weber write: "We are not saying . . . natural selection will not remain adequate for a range of problems. . . . The issue is whether the Darwinism of the Modern Synthesis and its successor programs, notably Selfish Gene Theory and its rival, the Hierarchically Expanded Modern Synthesis, can continue to present itself as a *general* theory of biological evolution. We are claiming that it cannot. Let us be clear, too, that in saying this we are not saying that Darwinism *as such* is on its deathbed. . . . We would be the last to suggest that Darwinism can't reform and reframe itself yet again." David Depew and Bruce Weber, "The Fate of Darwinism: Evolution after the Modern Synthesis," *Biological Theory* 6 (June 2011): 89–102.

48. Sahotra Sarkar, "Woese on the Received View of Evolution," *RNA Biology* 11, no. 3 (March 1, 2014): 220–24, at 221.

49. Lindsay Craig, "The So-Called Extended Synthesis and Population Genetics," *Biological Theory* 5 (2010): 117–23, at 117.

Darwinism of the future . . . will have to make itself empirically adequate and epistemologically secure by interacting with these rivals."[50]

Evolution through Association, Cooperation, and Community

Carl Woese and Nigel Goldenfeld are among the many scientists who in recent decades have been developing understandings of evolution that rival that of the modern synthesis. Arguing that the topic of evolution is much broader than just Darwinian natural selection, Woese and Goldenfeld "regard as rather regrettable the conventional concatenation [or equating] of Darwin's name with evolution, because there are other modalities [or mechanisms] that must be entertained," which are just as "mandatory during the course of evolutionary time."[51] One such non-Darwinian mechanism of evolutionary change is Horizontal Gene Transfer (HGT), also known as Lateral Gene Transfer. HGT involves "the non-genealogical transmission of genetic material from one organism to another."[52] According to evolutionary biologists Eugene Koonin and Yuri Wolf, the last decade of research in comparative genomics has demonstrated "the ubiquity and high frequency of HGT among prokaryotes, and a considerable level of HGT in unicellular eukaryotes as well."[53] More recently biologists have discovered that horizontally transferred genes are responsible for the acquisition of novel traits in eukaryotic—or multicellular—animals as well.[54] Through the mechanism of HGT, organisms may readily obtain and utilize DNA directly from their environment. While Darwin's evolutionary mechanism of natural selection relies on "traditional" gene transfer from parents to offspring via sexual or asexual reproduction (called *vertical gene transfer*), horizontal gene transfer involves the direct exchange of genes by organisms within the same generation, and such genetic exchanges are accompanied by an

---

50. David Depew and Bruce Weber, "Challenging Darwinism: Expanding, Extending, Replacing," in *The Cambridge Encyclopedia of Darwin and Evolutionary Thought*, ed. Michael Ruse (Cambridge: Cambridge University Press, 2013), 411.

51. Carl Woese and Nigel Goldenfeld, "Biology's Next Revolution," *Nature* 445 (2007): 369.

52. Ibid. As Sapp explains, "Lateral gene transfer between taxa [is] a decidedly non-Darwinian mechanism of evolution." Jan Sapp, *The New Foundations of Evolution: On the Tree of Life* (Oxford: Oxford University Press, 2009), 137.

53. Eugene Koonin and Yuri Wolf, "Is Evolution Darwinian or/and Lamarckian?," *Biology Direct* 4, no. 42 (2009). As Denis Noble and colleagues explain, "Lateral gene transfer is now recognized to be much more extensive and widespread than it was previously assumed to be; occurring in most orders and often among them. Recent examples include mechanisms of transfer from prokaryotes to eukaryotes generally and transfer from bacteria to insects." Denis Noble, Eva Jablonka, Michael Joyner, Gerd Müller, and Stig Omholt, "Evolution Evolves: Physiology Returns to Centre Stage," *Journal of Physiology* 592, no. 11 (June 1, 2014): 2237–44.

54. Luis Boto, "Horizontal Gene Transfer in the Acquisition of Novel Traits by Metazoans," *Proceedings of the Royal Society B: Biological Sciences* 22, no. 281 (February 2014): 1777.

immediate benefit. Genetic variation and evolution that occurs through HGT is not random or blind (as is evolution in the Darwinian mode) but, rather, is regulated and directed toward specific ends.[55]

Because the immediate acquisition of novel traits through HGT amounts to biological change over time that is driven by the inheritance of variations that are *directly* induced by environmental factors within a single generation, this phenomenon has been referred to as a type of Lamarckian evolution.[56] According to Koonin, HGT "shows obvious Lamarckian features: DNA is acquired from the environment, and naturally the likelihood of acquiring a gene that is abundant in the given habitat is much greater than the likelihood of obtaining a rare gene." Moreover, says Koonin, there is typically a "direct adaptive value of the acquired character" that has been gained through HGT.[57]

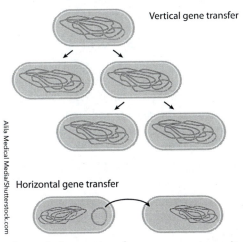

Vertical gene transfer

Horizontal gene transfer

Woese, Goldenfeld, Koonin, and other cellular biologists have shown that "early life must have evolved in an inherently Lamarckian way."[58] During the first three billion years of evolutionary history horizontal gene transfer was the ubiquitous evolutionary norm and during the first billion years of life Darwinian natural selection was nowhere to be found.[59] Moreover, explains Woese, "because of the high levels

In vertical gene transfer, genes are transmitted from the parental generation to offspring via sexual or asexual reproduction. In horizontal gene transfer, genes are transmitted between organisms in ways that do not involve reproduction.

Alila Medical Media/Shutterstock.com

---

55. As Eva Jablonka and Marion Lamb explain, "Contrary to long-accepted majority opinion, not all genetic variation is entirely random or blind; some of it may be regulated and partially directed." Eva Jablonka and Marion Lamb, *Evolution in Four Dimensions: Genetic, Epigenetic, Behavioral, and Symbolic Variation in the History of Life* (Cambridge, MA: MIT Press, 2014), 7.

56. Ibid. Although in the years after Darwin's death, Darwinian natural selection came to be contrasted with the "Lamarckian" idea of the inheritance of acquired characters, Darwin himself was a Lamarckian in the sense that he was "a firm believer that the effects of use and disuse could be inherited." Richard W. Burkhardt Jr., "Lamarck, Cuvier, and Darwin on Animal Behavior and Acquired Characters," in *Transformations of Lamarckism: From Subtle Fluids to Molecular Biology*, ed. Snait Gissis and Eva Jablonka (Cambridge, MA: MIT Press, 2011), 40.

57. Eugene Koonin, *The Logic of Chance: The Nature and Origin of Biological Evolution* (Upper Saddle River, NJ: FT Press Science, 2011), 267.

58. Woese and Goldenfeld, "Biology's Next Revolution," 369.

59. Carl Woese, "Default Taxonomy: Ernst Mayr's View of the Microbial World," *Proceedings of the National Academy of Sciences* 95 (September 1998): 11043.

of HGT, evolution at this stage [during the first billion or so years] would in essence be communal, not individual."[60] In other words the entire community of organisms would evolve together through the direct sharing of new genes with each other, and not through competition between individuals.

After the first billion years of life's history when vertical gene transfer emerged, Darwinian natural selection could begin to play a part in life's evolution—even as horizontal gene transfer continued to abound. Eventually, as more complex forms of life emerged, new forms of mutualism and cooperation also developed as key driving forces for biological change over time. One form of mutualism that was central in the early history of life and still serves as a major source of evolutionary variation and change is symbiotic relationships or *symbiosis*. According to biologist and historian of science Jan Sapp, "The view that symbiosis is a major source of evolutionary novelty paralleled the development of Darwinian theory."[61] However, says Sapp, the phenomenon of "symbiosis conflicted with the basic tenets of the evolutionary synthesis of the 1930s and 1940s based on natural selection acting on gradual transformations resulting from gene mutation and recombination between individuals of a species."[62] Although research on the role of symbiosis in evolution continued, the scientific focus through most of the twentieth century was on natural selection as the primary—if not sole—mechanism of evolutionary change. More recent understandings, however, have come to recognize "the universality of symbiosis in shaping eukaryotic life," that "multicellular organisms cannot exist in nature without their symbionts," and that symbiotic associations play a pivotal role in evolution.[63] Indeed, reflect evolutionary geneticists Robert Brucker and Seth Bordenstein, "the 20th century pioneers of evolutionary biology would have been astonished to see what roles microbiota play in eukaryotic evolution."[64]

While the possibility of speciation through symbiotic relationships was first suggested over a century ago, it wasn't until the later part of the twentieth century that biologists discovered how new types of cells and new species could form through cooperative synergism. Especially important is a type of symbiotic association known as *endosymbiosis* in which one or more organisms live inside another (such as bacteria in human intestines). Endosymbiotic relationships are often occasions for large-scale instances of horizontal gene transfer called endosymbiotic gene transfer (EGT). Recent research providing "examples of lateral gene transfers attending endosymbiosis clearly show that new species and even

---

60. Carl Woese, "A New Biology for a New Century," *Microbiology and Molecular Biology Reviews* 68, no. 2 (June 2004): 173–86, at 182.

61. Jan Sapp, *Evolution by Association: A History of Symbiosis* (New York: Oxford University Press, 1994), xiv.

62. Sapp, *The New Foundations of Evolution*, 119.

63. Robert Brucker and Seth Bordenstein, "Speciation by Symbiosis," *Trends in Ecology & Evolution* 27, no. 8 (2012): 443–51, at 443, 449.

64. Ibid., 449.

new clades [entire lineages of species] can evolve after genomic integration."[65] It is now clear that the endosymbiotic transfer of genes has been a major driving force in the evolution of both single cellular and multicellular organisms throughout the entire history of life.[66]

While at first glance it might seem that symbiotic relationships and EGT between cells might only play a role among single celled organisms, a moment's reflection reveals that such factors play a crucial role in the biology of more complex animals as well. The reason for this is because the bodies of all animals are essentially interactive communities of cells. "Every eukaryote is a superorganism," explains Sapp—a *symbiome* that includes its own genes, the genes of cellular organelles (mitochondria and/or chloroplasts), and the genes of symbiont bacteria and viruses living within the organism. "All plants and animals involve complex ecological communities of microbes."[67]

In the same way, each human being is an assemblage of microorganisms that perform a myriad of tasks so that a person may live and thrive. Recently, it has been shown that "humans carry more bacterial cells than human ones."[68] Microbiologist Jeffrey Gordon explains, "There are 10 times more microbial cells on and in our bodies than there are human cells. That means that we're 90 percent microbial and 10 percent human. There's also an estimated 100 times more microbial genes than the genes in our human genome. So we're really a compendium [and] an amalgamation of human and microbial parts."[69] These microbes, says Sapp, "form a sheath on our skin, and they cover the insides of our nose, throat, and gut. . . . Our mouths contain about eighty kinds of bacteria, and our stomach typically contains several hundred kinds. Although little is known about their interactions, if we did not have them in the proper relationship, we would not be able to function."[70] As a result, says Sapp,

---

65. Ulrich Kutschera and Karl Niklas, "Endosymbiosis, Cell Evolution and Speciation," *Theory in Biosciences* 124 (2005): 1–24, at 19.

66. As Kutschera and Niklas explain: "It gave rise to the first eukaryotic organisms during the Precambrian and it continued to give rise to numerous novel lineages of unicellular photosynthetic animals. . . . Today, primary, secondary (and tertiary) endosymbiosis is a well-established biological reality supported by a large body of empirical data." Karl Niklas and Ulrich Kutschera, "Macroevolution via Secondary Endosymbiosis: a Neo-Goldschmidtian View of Unicellular Hopeful Monsters and Darwin's Primordial *Intermediate Form*," *Theory in Biosciences* 127, no. 3 (July 2008): 277–89, at 286.

67. Sapp, *Genesis*, 235.

68. Melinda Wenner, "Humans Carry More Bacterial Cells than Human Ones," *Scientific American* 297, no. 5 (November 30, 2007); *http://www.scientificamerican.com/article/strange-but-true-humans-carry-more-bacterial-cells-than-human-ones/.*

69. Jeffrey Gordon, "Bacterial Bonanza: Microbes Keep Us Alive," *National Public Radio*, September 15, 2010, accessible at *http://www.npr.org/templates/story/story.php?storyId=129862107.* See Curtis Huttenhower et. al., "Structure, Function and Diversity of the Healthy Human Microbiome," *Nature* 486 (2012): 207–14.

70. Sapp, *Genesis*, 235. "Contemporary research indicates that our cells may be fashioned physiologically and morphologically by our bacterial community, which not only provides vitamins K and B12, but may regulate many of our own genes, and may be crucial in warding off pathogens" (236).

"symbiosis is at the very root of our being" and a central part of what it means to be human.[71]

Because symbiotic relationships are at the roots of life and are a key foundation underlying biological diversity, symbiosis is also a key factor in life's evolution. "Symbiogenesis," says biologist Francisco Carrapico, "must be considered as an evolutionary mechanism which implies that evolution should be understood in a broader context, where symbiosis plays an essential role in the organization and structuring of the biological world."[72] Evolutionary biologists Karl Niklas and Ulrich Kutschera agree, emphasizing that "the ecological and evolutionary importance of (endo)symbiosis, which was unknown to Darwin and ignored by the 'architects' of the synthetic theory, cannot be overstressed."[73]

Evolutionary Developmental Biology

At the same time that the neo-Darwinian synthesis was taking place in the early 1900s, significant research was also being done in the field of developmental biology (an area of research that studies the process—known as ontogeny—by which an organism grows and develops).[74] In 1922, developmental biologist Walter Garstang argued "that *ontogeny* (an individual's development) does not recapitulate [or repeat in summarized form] *phylogeny* (evolutionary history); rather, it *creates* phylogeny."[75] Developmental biologist Scott Gilbert explains that "this view of evolution as the result of hereditary changes affecting development was lost during the 1940s, when the Modern Synthesis of population genetics and evolutionary biology formed a new framework for research in evolutionary biology. The developmental approach to evolution was excluded from the Modern Synthesis."[76] According to philosopher and historian of biology Ron Amundson, the development of organisms was seen by neo-Darwinists to play little or no role in evolutionary theory and, thus, "for most of the twentieth century only a minority of evolutionary biologists believed that ontogenetic development had *any relevance at all* to evolution."[77]

---

71. Sapp, *Evolution by Association*, xiii.

72. Francisco Carrapico, "How Symbiogenic Is Evolution?," *Theory in Biosciences* 129 (2010): 135–39. "These ideas and concepts," says Carrapico, "should be integrated in a post-neodarwinian approach to evolution."

73. Kutschera and Niklas, "Macroevolution via Secondary Endosymbiosis," 286.

74. Scott Gilbert, *Developmental Biology*, 5th ed. (Sunderland, MA: Sinauer, 1997), 38–40.

75. Walter Garstang, "The Theory of Recapitulation: A Critical Restatement of the Biogenetic Law," *Proceedings of the Linnean Society of London (Zoology)* 35 (1922): 81; quoted in Jason Scott Robert, *Embryology, Epigenesis, and Evolution: Taking Development Seriously* (Cambridge: Cambridge University Press, 2004), 95.

76. Scott Gilbert, *Developmental Biology*, 6th ed. (Sunderland, MA: Sinauer, 2000), 634.

77. Ron Amundson, *The Changing Role of the Embryo in Evolutionary Thought: Structure and Synthesis* (Cambridge: Cambridge University Press, 2005), 1, emphasis in original.

It is now generally acknowledged, however, that the neo-Darwinian neglect of developmental biology was profoundly short-sighted. "Embryology," explains Gilbert, "was left out of the Modern Synthesis, as most evolutionary biologists and geneticists [at that time] felt it had nothing to contribute. However, we *know* now that it does."[78] Consequently, biologist and philosopher of science Jason Scott Robert writes, "The views of most contemporary evolutionary biologists have evolved significantly away from the Modern Synthesis."[79] The reason for this change, says Gilbert, is because "developmental biology and evolutionary biology are converging on a new synthesis for macroevolution, and this synthesis is very different from the Modern Synthesis of population genetics and evolutionary biology that accounted for microevolutionary processes." Because "the concept of the gene is very different between the two types of synthesis," it is not presently clear how or if the framework of the modern Darwinian synthesis will be able to integrate the perspective of the new developmental synthesis.[80]

According to current researchers who apply developmental biology to evolution (a field called evolutionary developmental biology or "evo-devo"), "while the Modern Synthesis could explain the *survival* of the fittest, it could not explain the *arrival* of the fittest."[81] In other words, evolutionary developmental biologists "agree that natural selection (random gene mutations and survival of the fittest) is not the true process of evolution causing the formation of novelties over time."[82] Evo-devo biologist Wallace Arthur explains that "since the emphasis in neo-Darwinian theory is on selection, it is also, inevitably, on destructive rather than creative forces. Selection can only retain, spread, or remove variants that are already in the population; it cannot itself create any new variants."[83] Moreover, the central neo-Darwinian idea of random mutation as the main vehicle for introducing variation into populations has been rendered increasingly problematic by new knowledge from the molecular biology regarding how proteins are constructed.

Gilbert explains that problems with mutation and the generation of evolutionary novelty "lay unsolved until evolutionary developmental biologists

---

78. Gilbert, *Developmental Biology*, 634, emphasis in original.

79. Robert, *Embryology, Epigenesis, and Evolution*, 97.

80. Scott Gilbert, "Genes Classical and Genes Developmental: The Different Use of Genes in Evolutionary Syntheses," in *The Concept of the Gene in Development and Evolution: Historical and Epistemological Perspectives*, ed. Peter Beurton, Raphael Falk, Hans-Jörg Rheinberger (Cambridge: Cambridge University Press, 2000) 178–79.

81. Scott Gilbert and David Epel, *Ecological Developmental Biology* (Sunderland, MA: Sinauer, 2009), 324. See also Gilbert, *Developmental Biology*, 683.

82. Eugene Balon, "Alternative Ontogenies and Evolution: A Farewell to Gradualism," in *Environment, Development, and Evolution: Toward a Synthesis*, ed. Brian Hall, Roy Pearson, Gerd B. Müller (Cambridge, MA: MIT Press, 2004), 39.

83. Wallace Arthur, "The Concept of Developmental Reprogramming," *Evolution and Development* 2, no. 1 (January/February 2000): 49–57, at 50.

demonstrated that large morphological changes could be made during development because of two conditions in the ways that organisms develop: *modularity* and *molecular parsimony*."[84] One of the most significant discoveries of evolutionary developmental biology, says Gilbert, "is that not only are the anatomical *units* modular (such that one part of the body can develop differently than the others), but that the DNA regions that form the *enhancers* of genes are modular."[85] Because the basic units of development are modular, certain sections of genes or parts of the body can be altered during development without interfering with the functions of other parts. In this way, observes Robert, "developmental reorganization functions by changing the design and construction of the organism while it develops, without sacrificing its survivability."[86] Through changes in the location—or the spatial alteration—of modular units, shift in the relative timing or growth rate of two or more developmental processes, or changes in the amount of a gene product or structure, the "stages of development can be altered to produce evolutionary novelties."[87] For example, investigations have revealed such regulatory changes associated with the initial evolution of butterfly eyespots, insect wings, tentacles, limbs and digits in land animals, bird feathers, and the turtle shell.[88]

The other developmental precondition for evolutionary change, molecular parsimony, refers to the fact that the molecular "toolkit" that is used by all of life is the same. "Although development differs enormously from lineage to lineage," explains Gilbert, "development within *all* lineages uses the same types of molecules. The transcription factors, paracrine factors, adhesion molecules, and signal transduction cascades are remarkably similar from one phylum to another."[89] For instance certain genetic transcription factors (proteins that control which genes are turned on or off in the genome), such as Pax and Hox gene complexes, "are found in *all* major animal groups [or phyla], including cnidarians [e.g., jellyfish, hydra, sea anemones, corals, etc.], insects, and primates." In fact, says Gilbert, "some 'toolkit genes' appear to play the same roles in all animal lineages. Thus, Pax6 appears to be involved in specifying light-sensing organs, irrespective of whether the eye is that of a mollusc, an insect, or a primate."[90] Even the basic toolkit or design for the central nervous system is shared by groups

---

84. Gilbert, *Developmental Biology*, 684.

85. Enhancers are sequences of DNA that have the ability to greatly increase the expression of genes in their vicinity. Gilbert, *Developmental Biology*, 684.

86. Robert, *Embryology, Epigenesis, and Evolution*, 86.

87. Gilbert, *Developmental Biology*, 684.

88. Gerd Müller, "Evo–Devo: Extending the Evolutionary Synthesis," *Nature Reviews Genetics* 8 (December 2007): 943–49, at 945.

89. Gilbert, *Developmental Biology*, 686. Paracrine factors are diffusible proteins used by embryos to induce particular cell types and to create boundaries between tissues.

90. Ibid.

as divergent as protostomes—which includes invertebrates such as arthropods (e.g., insects, crabs), mollusks (clams, snails), and annelid worms—and deuterostomes—which includes all vertebrates and the echinoderms (e.g., sea stars and sea urchins). Gilbert observes, "The protostome and deuterostome nervous systems, despite their obvious differences, seem to be formed by the same set of instructions. The plan for specifying the animal nervous system may have been laid down only once."[91]

Another ubiquitous kind of molecular developmental toolkit are sets of instructions called Hox genes or gene clusters, which, explains developmental biologist Günter Wagner, "are responsible for patterning the main body axis" in all animals and also for different types of patterns in the head, fins, limbs and other organs of vertebrates.[92] Because all multicellular organisms—animals, plants, and fungi—have Hox-like genes, developmental biologists believe "it is most likely that there was an ancestral Hox gene."[93] The origin of Hox gene clusters can be traced back to the origin of multicellular life about one billion years ago. Since then, major duplication events involving Hox genes have led to major transitions in the body plans of the various forms of life. For example, explains Wagner, "all invertebrate taxa extensively examined so far have only a single Hox cluster," and "the closest relative of vertebrates, *Amphioxus*, has a single Hox cluster," while "every major taxon of vertebrates has at least three if not up to eight such clusters."[94] The duplication of such modular gene clusters and their subsequent divergence, observes Gilbert, "are extremely important mechanisms for evolution. Duplication allows the formation of redundant structures, and divergence allows these structures to assume new roles." Consequently, he points out, "one of the most important differences between the genome of a fruit fly and that of a human is not that the human has new genes but that where the fly only has one gene, our species has multigene families."[95]

Where Is the Evolutionary Process Going?

One of the most theologically challenging aspects of the evolution of life is the Darwinian and neo-Darwinian focus on randomness and contingency. Evolution through natural selection has long been portrayed as a process that is, at

---

91. Ibid., 688.

92. Günter Wagner, Chris Amemiya, and Frank Ruddle, "Hox Cluster Duplications and the Opportunity for Evolutionary Novelties," *Proceedings of the National Academy of Sciences* 100, no. 25 (December 9, 2003): 14603–6, at 14603.

93. Gilbert, *Developmental Biology*, 687.

94. Wagner, Ameniya, and Ruddle, "Hox Cluster Duplications and the Opportunity for Evolutionary Novelties," 14603.

95. Gilbert, *Developmental Biology*, 688.

its very core, undirected and unguided. If it is really the case that random variations are the fuel of evolutionary change, then there appears to be no room for God's purposeful direction of the creation of life and, at the most, God the Creator "plays dice" with his creation.[96] For this reason when Princeton theologian Charles Hodge (1797–1878) asked "What is Darwinism?," his answer was, "It is atheism." For Hodge, and for many others since then, Darwin's theory seems to entail a God who has "abandoned the universe to itself to be controlled by chance and necessity, without any purpose on his part as to the result, or any intervention or guidance."[97] Darwin's focus on randomness and purposelessness in evolution appears to directly contrast with understandings of a creation that develops according to a discernible purpose. Consequently, the theory of natural selection, with its random variations, would seem more compatible with the relentlessly impersonal universe of Richard Dawkins than one governed by a compassionate, loving, and personal Creator.

Can "Chance" Mutations Be Guided?

Does natural selection, *in principle*, rule out the guiding activity of a transcendent creator God? The notion that the historical outcomes of natural selection are guided was commonplace at the time of Darwin. Even co-discoverer of natural selection, Alfred Russel Wallace, and agnostic promoter of Darwinism, T. H. Huxley, believed that the evolutionary process was in some sense directed.[98] Harvard biologist and devout Christian Asa Gray similarly saw variation as guided—though in the case of Gray it was assumed that the hand of God was ultimately doing the guiding. Gray made a case to Darwin "that variation has been led along certain beneficial lines," but Darwin had his doubts.[99] Still, Darwin never believed that the course of evolution was totally random and completely without purpose. Writing to Gray, Darwin confessed, "I am inclined to look at everything as resulting from designed laws, with the details, whether good or bad, left to the working out of what we may call chance. . . . I cannot

---

96. Hans Schwartz, *Theology in a Global Context: The Last Two Hundred Years* (Grand Rapids: Eerdmans, 2005), 219.

97. Charles Hodge, *What Is Darwinism?* See also Frederick Gregory, "The Impact of Darwinian Evolution on Protestant Theology," in *God and Nature: Historical Essays on the Encounter between Christianity and Science*, ed. David C. Lindberg and Ronald L. Numbers (Berkeley: University of California Press), 369–90, 370.

98. Peter Bowler, *The Eclipse of Darwinism: Anti-Darwinian Evolution Theories in the Decades around 1900* (Baltimore: Johns Hopkins University Press, 1983), 28.

99. Asa Gray quoted in Charles Darwin, *Variation of Plants and Animals under Domestication*, 2 vols. (New York: Orange, Judd, 1868), 2:516. See Anderson Hunter Dupree, "Christianity and the Scientific Community in the Age of Darwin," in *God and Nature: Historical Essays on the Encounter between Christianity and Science*, ed. David Lindberg and Ronald Numbers (Berkeley: University of California Press, 1986), 361.

think that the world as we see it is the result of chance; yet I cannot look at each separate thing as the result of Design."[100]

After the eclipse of Darwinism at the end of the nineteenth century, the legacy of the theory of natural selection was taken up by British geneticist and statistician Ronald Fisher (1890–1962) whose 1918 paper is considered the beginning of the modern evolutionary synthesis. As Fisher founded the population genetics that reworked Darwin's natural selection into a fundamentally statistical theory, at the same time he was also dedicated to "working out an expressly *Darwinian* Christianity, a faith that would triumph in history through struggle and toil."[101] Fisher held that the course of life's evolution revealed a clear direction and "believed absolutely and completely in biological progress" where "humans are right at the top."[102] According to Fisher's Christian vision of evolution, "creation was not all finished a long while ago, but is still in progress—in the language of Genesis, we are living in the sixth day."[103] Humans, says Fisher, are called to be created co-creators who work with God in establishing God's kingdom, and evolution is the chief means through which this is accomplished.

Theodosius Dobzhansky (1900–1975), the most influential founder of the second stage of the modern Darwinian synthesis, was similar to Fisher in discerning the metaphysical significance of evolution in terms of creaturely freedom and cosmic progress. In Dobzhansky's view organic evolution is developmental and progressive, culminating in the organism with the greatest adaptability or freedom: humankind. Dobzhansky's evolutionary worldview was profoundly influenced by his lifelong commitment to the Eastern Orthodox Christian faith. Indeed, says philosopher and historian of science Michael Ruse, "it was this faith which attracted Dobzhansky *to* evolutionism and which drove him on through all of his work."[104] For Dobzhansky the grand scheme of evolutionary history was ultimately meaningful because "evolution (cosmic and biological and human) is going towards something." In the same way, according to Dobzhansky, "Christianity is basically evolutionistic. It affirms that the meaning of history lies in the progression from Creation, through Redemption, to the City of God."[105] Dobzhansky's notion of redemptive progress through the course of evolutionary history resounded with that of paleontologist and Jesuit priest

---

100. Charles Darwin, letter to Asa Gray, May 22, 1860; *Darwin, F.* A888, 312; Charles Darwin, letter to Asa Gray, November 26, 1860; *Darwin, F.* A888, 378.

101. James Moore, "R. A. Fisher: A Faith Fit for Eugenics," *Studies in History and Philosophy of Science Part C* 38, no. 1 (2007): 110–35, at 118, emphasis in original.

102. Michael Ruse, *From Monad to Man: The Concept of Progress in Evolutionary Biology* (Cambridge: Harvard University Press, 2009), 296.

103. Fisher quoted in Moore, "R. A. Fisher," 130.

104. Ruse, *From Monad to Man*, 396.

105. Theodosius Dobzhansky, *The Biology of Ultimate Concern* (New York: New American Library, 1967), 112.

Pierre Teilhard de Chardin (1881–1955), who described the whole of cosmic reality as evolving first toward human consciousness and ultimately toward Jesus Christ as the "Omega Point." Dobzhansky admired Teilhard's "progressionism, rooted in a metaphysical synthesis of science and religion," and found this perspective akin to his own. Indeed, this was so much that case that Dobzhansky even became president of the American branch of the Teilhard society.[106]

In contrast to the progressive focus of Fisher and Dobzhansky, another pioneer of the neo-Darwinian synthesis, Sewall Wright (1889–1988), developed a theory of "genetic drift" that focused more on the role of chance as a central driving force of evolutionary change. In the late 1960s the Japanese population geneticist Motoo Kimura, seeing himself as a "latter-day champion of Sewall Wright," extended Wright's genetic drift theory into a theory of *neutral evolution* where chance was given an even more preeminent role in the dynamics of evolutionary history.[107] By the 1970s Fisher's and Dobzhansky's view of a goal-directed evolutionary process gave way to biochemist Jacques Monod's vision of life's evolution as primarily the product of chance. For Monod, "pure chance, absolutely free but blind, [is] at the very root of the stupendous edifice of evolution: this central concept of modern biology is no longer one among other possible or even conceivable hypotheses. It is today the sole hypothesis, the only one that squares with observed and tested fact."[108] In the 1980s biologist Stephen Jay Gould further developed Monod's emphasis on chance in evolution by pointing out that the pathway which evolution on Earth followed was riddled with contingency and historical happenstance. In light of this focus on evolutionary contingency Gould famously remarked, "Wind back the tape of life . . . let it play again from an identical starting point, and the chance becomes vanishingly small that anything like human intelligence would grace the replay."[109] Owing to the predominant role of chance in the evolutionary process, if one could rewind the tape of evolution and play it again and again, the same outcome would never happen twice.

Even as Gould was writing these words, though, a research group of philosophers, theologians, and scientists led by physicist and theologian Robert John Russell were endeavoring to make both a scientific and philosophical case that the "chance" within evolution is the very place where a transcendent Creator could act to bring about certain purposes within evolutionary history. According

---

106. Michael Ruse, "Dobzhansky and the Problem of Progress," In *The Evolution of Theodosius Dobzhansky: Essays on His Life and Thought in Russia and America*, ed. Mark Adams (Princeton: Princeton University Press, 2014), 233–46, at 233.

107. A. Berry, "Non-Darwinian Evolution," *Evolution* 50, no. 1 (February 1996): 462–66.

108. Jacques Monod, *Chance and Necessity: An Essay on the Natural Philosophy of Modern Biology* (New York: Vintage, 1972), 112.

109. Stephen Jay Gould, *Wonderful Life: The Burgess Shale and the Nature of History* (New York: Norton, 1989), 14.

to this view, called theistic evolution, "God creates through the whole process of law and chance, not by intervening in gaps in the process" but rather by working "in and through the processes of the natural world which science unveils."[110]

The random mutations in biology that give rise to variation are ultimately dependent on quantum events. Since quantum events—according to the standard Copenhagen interpretation of quantum physics—are physically *uncaused*, there is no scientific problem or philosophical contradiction in seeing God as the *hidden cause* of quantum events. Within the genetic "chance" mutations that crucially depend on uncaused quantum events, God could be seen as being secretly at work in the chance. In this view, explains philosopher of biology Elliott Sober, "God uses the evolutionary process [and] produces organisms *indirectly*."[111] As Russell explains, "The evolution of life on earth over the past 3.8 billion years depends in part on . . . the effects of quantum mechanics within genetic mutations," therefore one can truly see "God [as] both the absolute, transcendent source of the universe and the continuing, immanent creator of biological complexity."[112] In this way, says Russell, "God can be understood theologically as acting purposefully within the ongoing processes of biological evolution without disrupting them or violating the laws of nature."[113]

Sober judges that this quantum mechanical view of "theistic evolutionism is a logically consistent position."[114] Although neo-Darwinian biologists often refer to mutations as "unguided," such an assessment, says Sober, is technically not correct because evolutionary theory, according to the modern synthesis, is based on probability. In other words, Sober explains, "the theory does not tell you what must happen in the future, given a description of the population's present state. Rather, it tells you that different futures are possible and assigns

---

110. Ian G. Barbour, "Ways of Relating Science and Theology," in *Physics, Philosophy and Theology: A Common Quest for Understanding*, ed. Robert John Russell, William R. Stoeger, SJ, and George V. Coyne, SJ (South Bend, IN: University of Notre Dame Press, 1988), 42.

111. Elliot Sober, "Evolution without Naturalism," in *Oxford Studies in Philosophy of Religion* vol. 3, ed. Jonathan Kvanvig (Oxford: Oxford University Press, 2011), 189–90.

112. Robert John Russell, "Divine Action and Quantum Mechanics: A Fresh Assessment," in *Philosophy, Science and Divine Action*, ed. F. LeRon Shults, Nancey Murphy, and Robert John Russell (Leiden: Brill, 2009), 360. See also Robert John Russell, "Special Providence and Genetic Mutation: A New Defense of Theistic Evolution," in *Evolutionary Molecular Biology: Scientific Perspectives on Divine Action*, ed. Robert John Russell, Francisco J. Ayala, and William R. Stoeger, SJ, (Vatican City State: Vatican Observatory Publications; Berkeley, CA: CTNS, 1998), 193. For a critique of this view see Nicholas Saunders, *Divine Action and Modern Science* (New York: Cambridge University Press, 2002).

113. Russell, "Special Providence and Genetic Mutation," 193. Alvin Plantinga also argues that God guides single mutations (for instance, by choosing what happens at the quantum level): "In this way God can exercise providential guidance over cosmic history; he might in this way guide the course of evolutionary history by causing the right mutations to arise at the right time and preserving the forms of life that lead to the results he intends." Alvin Plantinga, *Where the Conflict Really Lies: Science, Religion, and Naturalism* (New York: Oxford University Press, 2011), 116.

114. Sober, "Evolution without Naturalism," 189.

a probability to each." Since evolution by natural selection is based on statistics, "the theory doesn't rule out the possibility that there are hidden variables. This means that it, like many other probability statements, doesn't rule out the possibility that there are *supernatural* hidden variables." Consequently, Sober argues, "Our scientific knowledge of mutation, properly understood, does not entail that God never guides mutations."[115]

Developmental Patterns that Inform Life and Constrain the Direction of Evolution

While neo-Darwinian understandings of evolution since the 1970s have tended to emphasize the role of chance and contingency in the historical process of life's development, beginning in the 1990s evolutionary developmental biologists have increasingly stressed the *directedness* of evolutionary processes. Evo-devo biologists Manfred Laubichler and Jane Maienschein, for instance, explain how "developmental mechanisms *per se* constrain variation in non-random ways." Even if mutations or other genomic changes might occur at random, developmental processes constrain such chance genetic events in ways "that will determine how random gene changes can be expressed in the phenotype in non-random ways."[116]

Evo-devo researchers have likewise shown that the variety and types of animal body plans are not random. Gilbert discusses how "all the different body plans seen in the animal kingdom" are encompassed in "only about three dozen major animal lineages." Gilbert asks, "Why don't we see more body plans among the living animals" even though "one can easily envision other body plans by imagining animals that do not exist?" The answer, he says, has to do with "the constraints that development imposes on evolution."[117] Gilbert and other developmental biologists point out, "the number and forms of possible phenotypes that can be created are limited by the interactions that are possible among molecules and between modules. These interactions also allow change to occur in certain directions more easily than in others." These limiting factors that

---

115. Elliott Sober, "Evolutionary Theory, Causal Completeness, and Theism: The Case of 'Guided' Mutation," in *Essays in Honor of Michael Ruse*, ed. D. Walsh and P. Thompson (Cambridge: Cambridge University Press, forthcoming). Sober argues "that evolutionary theory, properly understood, does not rule out God's causing some mutations." The idea that God's action is a priori ruled out, he says, "is a philosophical thesis, not a scientific theory at all." On the question of whether Russell and Sober's view represents a version of "God-in-the-Gaps," see Nicholas T. Saunders, "Does God Cheat at Dice? Divine Action and Quantum Possibilities," *Zygon* 35, no. 4 (September 2000): 517–44; and Keith Ward, "Divine Action in the World of Physics: Response to Nicholas Saunders," *Zygon* 35, no. 4 (September 2000): 901–6.

116. Manfred Laubichler and Jane Maienschein, *Form and Function in Developmental Evolution* (Cambridge: Cambridge University Press, 2009), 87.

117. Gilbert, *Developmental Biology*, 697.

influence the types and forms of life that can be produced are called "developmental constraints."[118]

Various kinds of developmental constraints channel the direction in which evolutionary novelty flows. For example, certain physical constraints on possible types of animal structures and forms emerge from "the laws of diffusion, hydraulics, and physical support."[119] There are also fundamental limits imposed by what are called morphogenetic constraints. For example, observations suggest that the construction of limbs must always follow certain physical, chemical, and mathematical sets of rules or guidelines.[120] "One set of rules constraining limb development," explains Gilbert, is "the mathematics of the reaction-diffusion mechanism, a model that can be extended throughout development."[121] The reaction-diffusion model for developmental patterning shows how substances interact to produce stable patterns during morphogenesis. The patterning process, explains Gilbert, "is analogous to the harmonics of vibrating strings, as in a guitar: only certain resonance vibrations are permitted, based on the boundaries of the string."[122] One dynamic patterning process known as the Mullins-Sekerka instability plays a vital role in a wide number of biological processes that involve branching. Interestingly, this same mathematical patterning process that comes into play during vertebrate limb branching, the development of lungs, veins, and other biological branching, is also responsible for the fractal branching of the arms of individual snow crystals.[123]

In addition to developmental constraints on evolution, there are also molecular or chemical constraints that direct evolution to choose certain pathways over others. Even within a purely neo-Darwinian framework, "it is now known," explains Daniel Weinreich and his colleagues, that "evolution can follow only very few mutational paths to fitter proteins" and "much protein evolution will be similarly constrained. This implies that the protein 'tape of life' may be largely reproducible and even predictable."[124] Another team of researchers, led

---

118. Ibid.

119. Ibid., 697–98.

120. See J. D. Murray, "Evolution, Morphogenetic Laws, Developmental Constraints and Teratologies," in *Mathematical Biology II: Spatial Models and Biomedical Applications* (New York: Springer, 2003), 396–415.

121. Gilbert, *Developmental Biology*, 698.

122. Ibid.

123. For an overview see *Branching in Nature: Dynamics and Morphogenesis of Branching Structures*, ed. Vincent Fleury, Jean-François Gouyet, and M. Léonetti (Berlin: Springer, 2001). For a survey of such processes in biology, see *Branching Processes in Biology*, ed. Marek Kimmel and David Axelrod (New York: Springer, 2002). For a detailed study on mathematical patterning in limb development, see Cornel Murea and H. G. E. Hentschel, "A Finite Element Method for Growth in Biological Development," *Mathematical Biosciences and Engineering* 4, no. 2 (2007): 339–53.

124. Daniel Weinreich et al., "Darwinian Evolution Can Follow Only Very Few Mutational Paths to Fitter Proteins," *Science* 312 (April 7, 2006): 111–14, at 111.

by molecular biologist Kourosh Salehi-Ashtiani, similarly reports, "Our results show that, despite the dominance of contingency (historical accident) in some recent discussions of evolutionary mechanisms (Gould 1989), purely chemical constraints (that is, the ability of only certain sequences to carry out particular functions) can lead to the repeated evolution of the same macromolecular structures."[125] As a consequence of physical, molecular, and developmental constraints and predispositions, then, it appears that the path of life's evolution is clearly directed toward certain ends.

Convergence and the Direction of Life's Evolution

The observation that the path of evolution is guided by deeper principles has likewise been highlighted by a number of biologists who study a phenomenon known as *evolutionary convergence* (also known as convergent evolution). Evolutionary convergence is when, in the course of evolutionary history, two or more lineages of organisms navigate to or arrive at the same biological outcome from very different starting points. In other words, evolutionary convergence is when biological traits and forms develop independently in two or more "unrelated" (or very distantly related) evolutionary lineages. Researchers have found instances of convergence to be ubiquitous. Biologist Patricia Willmer observes, "Convergent evolution is prevalent at all levels of organismal design—from cell chemistry and microstructure to cell types, organ systems, and whole body plans."[126]

A number of recent studies indicate "that evolution may be finding the same genetic solutions to a problem more often than previously thought."[127] Consider, for example, research on the characteristics of lizards of the genus *Anolis*, which have diversified independently across the islands of Cuba, Hispaniola, Jamaica, and Puerto Rico. A team of biologists led by Luke Mahler has discovered that despite the fact that the different lizard species evolved independently on different islands, the evolutionary outcomes were remarkable similar. "On each island in the Greater Antilles," explains Mahler, "anoles have independently evolved a similar set of habitat specialists termed 'ecomorphs' (such as 'twig' or 'grass-bush'). Each ecomorph is composed of morphologically and behaviorally similar species that occupy similar microhabitats." Moreover, the degree of similarity between various sets of lizards is much more than would be expected by chance.

125. Kourosh Salehi-Ashtiani and J. W. Szostak, "In Vitro Evolution Suggests Multiple Origins of the Hammerhead Ribozyme," *Nature* 414 (2001): 82–84, at 84.

126. Patricia Willmer, "Convergence and Homoplasy in the Evolution of Organismal Form," in *Origination of Organismal Form: Beyond the Gene in Developmental and Evolutionary Biology*, ed. Gerd B. Muller and Stuart A. Newman (Cambridge, MA: MIT Press, 2003), 33.

127. Erika Hayden, "Convergent Evolution Seen in Hundreds of Genes," *Nature News*, September 2013, accessible at *http://www.nature.com/news/convergent-evolution-seen-in-hundreds-of-genes-1.13679*; Joe Parker et. al., "Genome-Wide Signatures of Convergent Evolution in Echolocating Mammals," *Nature* 502 (October 10, 2013): 228–31.

Mahler thus concludes, "Gould famously argued that evolution over long time scales is 'utterly unpredictable and quite unrepeatable' due to historical contingency. Widespread convergence among entire faunas of Greater Antillean *Anolis* refutes Gould's claim and shows that adaptation can overcome the influence of chance events on the course of evolution."[128]

A second example comes from experiments led by biologist Richard Lenski, which have discovered evolutionary convergence even among single-celled organisms. To test Gould's hypothesis about rewinding the tape of life's evolution and never getting the same result, Lenski's research group devised an experiment to "replay the tape of evolution" under controlled conditions. Using twelve populations of *E. coli* bacteria founded from single cells of the same ancestral strain, they examined random mutational and changes in gene expression after 20,000 generations of evolution. Lenski discovered that the genetic "profiles showed strikingly parallel changes" and similarities even though they had evolved independently.[129] Evolution under a variety of different conditions took place in such a way that "populations that had evolved independently for 20,000 generations from a common ancestor were much more similar to one another in their overall expression patterns than they were to their ancestor."[130] As Lenksi's experiment with these bacterial lines continues, he has found that *both* contingency and convergence play a crucial role in the evolutionary process.[131] Reflecting on the experiment after 50,000 generations Lenski writes, "Although the lineages certainly diverged in many details, I was struck by the parallel trajectories of their evolution, with similar changes in so many phenotypic traits and even gene sequences that we examined."[132]

A third case of evolutionary convergence considers the evolution of different kinds of organs, such as the eye. Research has revealed that the same camera eye structure present in humans has evolved at least seven separate times in

---

128. D. Luke Mahler, Travis Ingram, Liam J. Revell, and Jonathan B. Losos, "Exceptional Convergence on the Macroevolutionary Landscape in Island Lizard Radiations," *Science* 341 (July 19, 2013): 292–95.

129. Tim Cooper, Daniel Rozen, and Richard Lenski, "Parallel Changes in Gene Expression after 20,000 Generations of Evolution in Escherichia Coli," *Proceedings of the National Academy of Sciences* 100, no. 3 (2003): 1072–107.

130. Richard E. Lenski, "Chance and Necessity in Evolution," in *The Deep Structure of Biology: Is Convergence Sufficiently Ubiquitous to Give a Directional Signal?*, ed. Simon Conway Morris (West Conshohocken, PA: Templeton Foundation Press, 2008), 11.

131. One line of bacteria even evolved to utilize a novel source of energy, a compound called citrate, which no other *E. coli* lines had done before. The citrate-using variant evolved in one population by 31,500 generations, causing an increase in population size and diversity. Zachary D. Blount, Christina Z. Borland, and Richard E. Lenski, "Historical Contingency and the Evolution of a Key Innovation in an Experimental Population of Escherichia Coli," *PNAS* 105, no. 23 (June 10, 2008): 7899–7906.

132. Richard Lenski, "Evolution in Action: A 50,000-Generation Salute to Charles Darwin" *Microbe* 6 (2011): 30–33.

unrelated groups—such as in cephalopods (e.g., squid), vertebrates (e.g., mammals), and the cnidarians (e.g., box jellies).[133] There is remarkable similarity of the structures of the various independently evolved camera-eye systems, despite the complexity of the organ, and despite the fact that the common ancestor between the vertebrates and the octopus lived about 580 million years ago in the Cambrian era before any types of eyes existed. Evolutionary paleobiologist Simon Conway Morris observes, "Beyond all reasonable doubt—and here we can draw on embryology, comparative anatomy, histology, molecular biology, phylogeny, and the fossil record—the common ancestor of the octopus and blue whale could not possibly have possessed a camera-eye."[134] Although their last common ancestor had, at most, a very simple photoreceptive spot, the ancestors of the octopus, and the ancestors of today's vertebrates independently developed the same eye structure. "Each group," says Conway Morris, "has independently navigated to the same evolutionary solution, and it is one that not only works very well but has arisen at least five more times, in animals as diverse as snails and, more extraordinarily, jellyfish."[135]

Scientific studies have revealed that there are even "striking convergences" between human, whale, bird, and insect *music* in terms of melody, harmony, structure, tone, timbre, and so on. Biologist and musicologist Patricia Gray observes, "The undersea songs of humpback whales are similar in structure to bird and human songs and prove that these marine mammals are inveterate composers. . . . Humpback whale songs are constructed according to laws that are strikingly similar to those adopted by human composers."[136] This leads Gray to wonder, "Is there a universal music [akin to mathematical Platonism] awaiting discovery, or is all music just a construct of whatever mind is making it, human, bird, whale? The similarities among human music, bird song, and whale song tempt one to speculate that the Platonic alternative may exist—that there is a universal music awaiting discovery."[137]

Reflecting upon numerous instances of the evolutionary convergence of biological form—where different historical evolutionary trajectories, which began from radically dissimilar starting places, have arrived at the same morphological destination—evolutionary biologist George McGhee concludes, "First, the view that the evolutionary process is nonrepeating . . . is demonstrably

---

133. Simon Conway Morris, "Lecture 2: Eyes to See, Brains to Think: The Inevitable Evolution of Intelligence," in *Darwin's Compass: How Evolution Discovers the Song of Creation*, Gifford Lectures, (Edinburgh: University of Edinburgh, 2007).

134. Conway Morris, ed., *Deep Structure of Biology: Is Convergence Sufficiently Ubiquitous to Give a Directional Signal?* (West Conshohocken, PA: Templeton Foundation Press, 2008), viii.

135. Ibid.

136. Patricia M. Gray, Bernie Krause, Jelle Atema, Roger Payne, Carol Krumhansl, and Luis Baptista, "The Music of Nature and the Nature of Music," *Science* 291 (January 5, 2001): 52–54, 52.

137. Ibid., 54.

false," and "second, the view that evolution is entirely historically contingent, and thus unpredictable (and nonrepeating), is demonstrably false."[138] Moreover, such examples of convergence appear to indicate that there are *stable points* in biological possibility space (known as *morphospace* or *biological hyperspace*) toward which evolution navigates.[139] On the level of biological form, Conway Morris maintains that most of the potential biological hyperspace is empty because there are a limited number of morphological destinations to which evolutionary pathways can lead. Conway Morris explains, "The phenomenon of evolutionary convergence indicates that . . . the number of alternatives is strictly limited, with the interesting implication that the vast bulk of any given 'hyperspace' not only never *will* be visited during evolutionary exploration but it never *can* be."[140]

Conway Morris holds that the available evidence from convergence points to "the existence of something analogous to 'attractors,' by which evolutionary trajectories are channeled towards stable nodes of functionality."[141] In this way, the emergence of different forms of life are similar to the emergence of different types of snowflakes and stars, where highly ordered patterns emerge according to predefined laws or rules, while at the same time reflecting a high degree of uniqueness that is related to the particular circumstances of their individuality, histories, and origins. Beyond this, Conway Morris believes the stable biological nodes within the hyperspace, where different forms can exist, have been ordained from the very beginning of the cosmos. "It is my suspicion," says Conway Morris that "the nodes of occupation are effectively predetermined from the Big Bang."[142] The designs for the various kinds of life were present at the first instant of the creation of the cosmos—plans that waited to be carried out through the unfolding course of cosmic history.

If the stable points along the trajectory of evolutionary history are written in the very constants and laws of the cosmos, then certain outcomes are not only predictable but also inevitable—"life navigates towards certain inevitable solutions."[143] Among these stable patterns or forms, "one such node," observes Conway Morris, "is that of the humanoid."[144] In other words, he says, "the constraints of evolution and the ubiquity of convergence make the emergence of

---

138. George McGhee, *Convergent Evolution: Limited Forms Most Beautiful* (Cambridge, MA: MIT Press, 2011), 271.

139. A *morphospace* is a representation of the possible form, shape, or structure of an organism where each point in the morphospace represents an individual organism.

140. Simon Conway Morris, *Life's Solution: Inevitable Humans in a Lonely Universe* (Cambridge: Cambridge University Press, 2003), 309.

141. Ibid.

142. Ibid., 310.

143. Simon Conway Morris, "The Navigation of Biological Hyperspace," *International Journal of Astrobiology* 2, no. 2 (2003), 152.

144. Conway Morris, *Life's Solution*, 310.

something like human beings a near-inevitability. . . . The contingencies of biological history will make no long-term difference to the outcome."[145]

Conclusion

How do both Scripture and science understand the origin and emergence of the various forms of life? To address this question, this chapter has examined the terms and metaphors the Bible uses when describing how God creates both life and nonlife. From the context and usage of various Hebrew terms describing God's creative activity, it is clear that Scripture affirms an understanding of God's creating of not only snowflakes and stars, but also plants and animals through noninstantaneous, developmental processes. Some of the same dynamic laws of nature that God uses to create individual snowflakes (such as Mullins-Sekerka instability) are also used to create trees, and hands, and feet. Given that the creation language of Scripture affirms the idea of God's creating life through processes, there is no theological reason to suppose that the Bible is fundamentally opposed to the idea that God creates through evolution. God commands the Earth to create, and the Earth creates. The details of *how* God creates are left for scientists to explore. How, then, does science describe God's creation of life? Scientists agree that life was created through evolution and that natural selection is a key component of this process. However, there are also a number of different evolutionary mechanisms that do not have Darwin's mechanism as their central core. One contemporary school of evolutionary thought, which focuses on symbiotic and cooperative relationships that form novel biological associations, understands natural selection to play a peripheral role (or none at all) in the actual origin of different species. Other evolutionary biologists—such as evolutionary developmental biology—envision the development of life through time as being fundamentally guided by general mathematically describable laws of biology. They maintain that the kinds or types of organisms we see, their molecular and genetic building blocks, key aspects of their body-plans, and even many of their traits are the result of natural laws rather than being merely the byproducts of historical contingency, environmental happenstance, and chance genetic mutations. A third group of evolutionary biologists who question the central role of chance in life's developmental history focus on a phenomenon known as evolutionary convergence—where several divergent lines of evolution converge to end up at the same endpoint or "solution." The numerous cases of convergence (such as the independent evolution of the "camera eye" at least seven different times) indicate that the number of potential forms that could evolve is strictly limited. Indeed, says Conway Morris, the roads of evolution are well defined, and evolution can

---

145. Ibid., 328.

go in only a very few directions. Consequently, "however many times we re-run the tape, we will still end up with much the same result."[146]

Discussion Questions

1. If, as the Bible says, God really creates individual human beings in the womb, what do you think this implies for how believers in God understand the biological development of a human embryo?
2. In your opinion, how is the creation of an individual person similar to or different from the evolutionary creation of life?
3. If a Christian or other theist believes that God creates *through* evolution, do you think that person can rationally appeal to God's *purposes* or *goals* for biological life? Why or why not?

Beyond the Classroom

With a small group, examine the examples of convergence described in Eric R. Pianka, "Convergent Evolution," *http://www.zo.utexas.edu/courses/THOC /Convergence.pdf*.

The evidence from evolutionary convergence indicates that the formation of camera-eyes, different types of lizards, music, and even human-like beings might be as inevitable as the formation of snowflakes and stars (because deeper laws govern both). This scientific evidence for *direction* in evolution certainly *contrasts* with the views of biologist Stephen Jay Gould (and Richard Dawkins in the 1980s), but do you think evolutionary convergence can be employed to support the idea that such direction is part of a Creator God's design? Why or why not?

Resources for Further Study

Books

Brandon, Robert N. *Concepts and Methods in Evolutionary Biology*. Cambridge: Cambridge University Press, 1996.

Conway Morris, Simon. *Life's Solution: Inevitable Humans in a Lonely Universe*. Cambridge: Cambridge University Press, 2003.

Conway Morris, Simon, ed. *The Deep Structure of Biology: Is Convergence Sufficiently Ubiquitous to Give a Directional Signal?* West Conshohocken, PA: Templeton Foundation Press, 2008.

---

146. Simon Conway Morris, "Evolution and the Inevitability of Intelligent Life," in *The Cambridge Companion to Science and Religion*, ed. Peter Harrison (Cambridge: Cambridge University Press 2010), 150.

Depew, David, and Bruce Webber. *Darwinism Evolving: Systems Dynamics and the Genealogy of Natural Selection*. Cambridge, MA: MIT Press, 1996.

Miller, Keith B. *Perspectives on an Evolving Creation*. Grand Rapids: Eerdmans, 2003.

Robert, Jason Scott. *Embryology, Epigenesis, and Evolution: Taking Development Seriously*. Cambridge: Cambridge University Press, 2004.

Articles

Conway Morris, Simon. "Creation and Evolutionary Convergence." In *The Blackwell Companion to Science and Christianity*, edited by J. B. Stump and Alan Padgett, 258–69. Malden, MA: Blackwell, 2012.

Gregersen, Niels Hanrik. "The Idea of Creation and the Theory of Autopoietic Processes." *Zygon* 33 (1998): 333–67.

Internet Resources

Conway Morris, Simon. "Eyes to See, Brains to Think: The Inevitable Evolution of Intelligence." Gifford Lectures, University of Edinburgh. Accessible at *http://www.ed.ac.uk/schools-departments/humanities-soc-sci/news-events/lectures/gifford-lectures/archive/archive-2006-2007/prof-conway/lecture-2-eyes-to-see* (time: 01:10:10).

Conway Morris, Simon. "What Would Happen If the Tape of Evolution Were Rerun?" Test of Faith, Faraday Institute for Science and Religion. Accessible at *http://www.testoffaith.com/resources/resource.aspx?id=350* (time: 0:02:36).

Moritz, Joshua. "'And the Earth Produced Living Beings': The Creation and Evolution of Life: Part 1." Voice of Light Productions. Accessible at *http://vimeo.com/38902718* (time: 01:04:08).

CHAPTER 7

From Consciousness to New Creation

The Nature and Destiny of Humanity

For the destiny of man and the destiny of animals is the same: As one dies, so dies the other; both have the same breath of life, and man has no preeminence over the animals. . . . All go to the same place; all come from dust, and to dust all shall return.

—Ecclesiastes 3:19–20

But ask the animals and they will teach you, or the birds of the air and they will tell you. . . . In his hand is the life of every creature and the breath of all humankind.

—Job 12:7–10

The difference in mind between humans and the higher animals, great as it is, certainly is one of degree and not of kind.

—Charles Darwin[1]

In This Chapter

* Human Nature and Human Uniqueness: Perspectives from Scripture
* Human Nature and Human Uniqueness: Perspectives from Science
* Humans as the Unique "Image and Likeness of God"
* The Destiny of Humanity
* Discussion Questions
* Beyond the Classroom
* Resources for Further Study

---

1. Charles Darwin, *The Descent of Man and Selection in Relation to Sex* (Princeton: Princeton University Press, 2002), 105.

What does it mean to be human? From the biblical psalmist pondering, "What is humanity, that you are mindful of them?" (Ps. 8:4) to the declaration of philosophers that "man is the measure of all things,"[2] many have reflected upon what fundamentally defines the core identity of human beings. One central question that emerges from considerations of human nature is, what makes humans unique? While numerous characteristics have historically been upheld as the traits that make human beings different than other creatures, many religious traditions seem unconcerned with defining human uniqueness in such a way. In Hinduism and Buddhism, human beings and animals exist along a continuum where movement is possible in either direction via reincarnation.[3] In an analogous way, the Scriptures of the Jewish and Christian faiths seem more intent on recognizing the many similarities between humans and other animals than on delineating their differences. Jewish and Christian Scripture does identify human beings as unique, however, in that they are designated "as the image and likeness of God" (Gen. 1:27). Some Jews and Christians have asserted that the "image and likeness of God" in humans is reflected in the unique biological and behavioral traits that distinguish humans from other creatures. Others, though, have seen the image of God in humans as a special type of relationship that humans share with God, or as a divine function the human species fulfills. Recent scientific work on evolutionary continuity between species has provided a plausible scientific explanation for the similarities between humans and animals, but a clear demarcation of the precise differences remains elusive. Complicating the scientific picture even more, discoveries of extinct nonhuman species (such as Neanderthals) who possessed language, culture, technology, and symbolic art have further emphasized the similarities between humans and other creatures.

Finally, there is the issue of human identity and continuity. Within the Hindu tradition the individual soul is identical with the undifferentiated universal soul, and all distinction is ultimately an illusion.[4] Traditional Buddhism explicitly rejects the doctrine of an eternal self or immortal soul, and "the hallmark of Buddhist thought is the doctrine of no-self."[5] Many persons affirming a theistic faith have sought out the essence of human personal identity and

---

2. Protagoras of Abdera (fifth century BCE), *Fragment 1*.

3. As Donald Lopez explains, in Buddhism, "the beings of the universe have been reborn without beginning in six realms, as gods, demigods, humans, animals, ghosts, and hell beings. Their actions create not only their individual experiences of pleasure and pain, but also the domains in which they dwell." Donald Lopez, *The Story of Buddhism: A Concise Guide to Its History and Teachings* (San Francisco: HarperSanFrancisco, 2001), 19. For a discussion on Hinduism and evolution, see David L. Gosling, *Darwin, Science and the Indian Tradition* (Delhi: ISPCK, 2011). See also C. Mackenzie Brown, *Hindu Perspectives on Evolution: Darwin, Dharma, and Design* (New York: Routledge, 2012).

4. David L. Gosling, "Embodiment and Rebirth in the Buddhist and Hindu Traditions" *Zygon* 48 (December 2013): 908–15. See also Philip Clayton, Roddam Narasimha, B. V. Sreekantan, and Sangeetha Menon, eds., *Science and Beyond: Cosmology, Consciousness and Technology in the Indic Traditions* (Bangalore, India: NIAS Publications, 2004)

5. Lopez, *Story of Buddhism*, 24.

continuity in an immaterial soul, even as scientific studies of the brain have shed light on the material foundations of human individuality and personality. For many Jews and Christians, scientific investigations of the human person may appear to undermine theological conceptions, but the authors of Scripture seem to embrace a physical foundation for human identity and continuity since they view the human person as an undivided unity. According to biblical anthropology, the human being is not a mixture of perishable physical body and immortal immaterial soul but an undivided unity of body and soul that depends on God for life. In the same way, Scripture asserts that the destiny of human beings is not the release or escape of the immaterial soul from the realm of the material but, rather, the physical resurrection of the body and the life everlasting.

Human Nature and Human Uniqueness: Perspectives from Scripture

The species *Homo sapiens* has often been captivated by reflections on its own uniqueness. The affirmation of the unique status of human beings among animals unites perspectives as diverse as that of anti-religious evolutionist Richard Dawkins and anti-evolutionist creationist Ken Ham.[6] Garnering the strong support of both Dawkins and Ham, one might suppose that both biology and the Bible agree on human uniqueness. However, a closer examination of science and Scripture reveals that the situation is neither that straightforward nor that simple. While everyone across the spectrum seems to agree that humans are unique, such concord quickly collapses when posed with the question of where exactly this uniqueness lies.

Is the Bible Concerned with Establishing Human Uniqueness?

Ask your average person on the street what the Bible says about the difference between humans and other creatures. If they feel they can answer at all, they will likely focus on some special quality or characteristic that humans have and that

---

6. For example, Ham and other prominent young Earth creationists argue that "there is no animal that is man's equal, and certainly none his ancestor. . . . God created man as the crown of His creation on Day Six." Thus they "conclude that the evidence points to the fact that man is a unique creation, made in the image of God." David N. Menton, "Did Humans Really Evolve from Ape-Like Creatures?," in *War of the Worldviews: Powerful Answers for an Evolutionized Culture*, ed. Ken Ham et al. (Green Forest, AK: New Leaf Press, 2006), 43. Dawkins sets humans apart from all other forms of biological life on the basis of the freedom through which they may defy the relentless drive of natural selection. "We are built as gene machines and cultured as meme machines," says Dawkins, "but we have the power to turn against our creators. We, alone on earth, can rebel against the tyranny of the selfish replicators." According to Dawkins humans alone can change the course of evolution. Richard Dawkins, *The Selfish Gene* (New York: Oxford University Press, 2006), 201.

animals lack. Many persons seem to assume that one can discern, from Scripture, a clear list of characteristics that make humans unique—traits like free will, self-awareness, language, awareness of mortality, art, morality, spirituality, or the soul.[7]

Bible scholars, however, give quite a different account of Scripture's teaching on the difference between humans and animals. Contrary to popular opinion, the Bible is not particularly concerned with listing characteristics that definitively establish the uniqueness of human beings over and against animals. Scripture never provides a list of exceptional capacities or traits that humans alone have. Indeed, explains Old Testament scholar Lawson Stone, assertions of human uniqueness based on certain characteristics and "claims for a 'special creation' of humanity in comparison with animals and the material world conflict with the strong assertion in Gen 2 that, physically (organically), Adam does not differ from the 'beasts of the field.'"[8] The language in Genesis 1 and 2, Stone says, "underscores Adam's *linkage* with the animal creation, not his *difference* from it."[9] Bible scholar Gordon Wenham similarly explains that in Genesis 2:7, which describes the human being as a living being or living soul (Hebrew: *nephesh*), "it is not man's possession of the 'breath of life' or his status as a 'living creature' that differentiates him from the animals—animals are described in exactly the same terms."[10] Hebrew scholar Dan Cohn-Sherbok similarly observes that in Scripture animals are "brought forth" from the earth, and humans are likewise shaped into existence by the hand of God from the very same soil.[11]

As the offspring of God's word and the Earth's fertile receptiveness to God's command, both animals and humans are described as "living souls" or "living beings" (*nephesh*).[12] Since the exact same term is used in Genesis to describe both kinds of creatures, this implies a profound kinship, making explicit a deep level of continuity between humans and animals. Bible scholar Iain Provan explains, "Human beings . . . are only one subset of God's 'living beings,' into

---

7. For examples of such unique characteristics that are attributed to the teachings of the Bible, see Kay Warren, "Puppies Aren't People: When Compassion for Animals Goes Too Far," *Christianity Today*, April 2009, accessible at *http://www.christianitytoday.com/women/2009/april/kay-warren-puppies-arent-people.html*. In this essay, Kay Warren cites the theological views of her husband—the evangelical megachurch leader and celebrity Rick Warren. See also Ann Coulter, *Godless: The Church of Liberalism* (New York: Crown Forum, 2006), 4; Peter Singer, *Animal Liberation* (New York: Harper Collins, 2002), 191.

8. Lawson G. Stone, "The Soul: Possession, Part, or Person? The Genesis of Human Nature in Genesis 2:7," in *What About the Soul? Neuroscience and Christian Anthropology*, ed. Joel B. Green (Nashville: Abingdon, 2004), 50.

9. Ibid., 57.

10. Gordon Wenham, *Genesis 1–15*, Word Biblical Commentary (Waco, TX: Word, 1987), 61.

11. "Adam is made from the dust of the ground—symbolizing his organic relationship to the earth." Dan Cohn-Sherbok and Andrew Linzey, *After Noah: Animals and the Liberation of Theology* (London: Mowbray, 1997), 20.

12. For animals see Gen. 1:20–24, 2:19, 9:10, 15. For humans see Gen. 2:7, 9:5.

whom God has breathed the breath of life" and established as "living souls."[13] According to the biblical understanding, then, writes Old Testament scholar Ray Anderson, "what is distinctive about human beings is *not* that they have a 'soul' which animals do not possess, nor that they have a 'spirit' which other creatures do not possess."[14] It is clear, says Joel Green, that "the possession of *nepheš* [breath of life or soul] is *not* a unique characteristic of the human person." Indeed, observes Green, "unless one is ready to grant that animals have 'souls' in the same way that humans are alleged to have, then we might better conclude that the Genesis account is referring to the divine gift of *life*."[15]

God, and Not Humans, as the Focal Point of Creation

Rather than being concerned with establishing the physical or biological uniqueness of humans among the animals, the Scriptures of the ancient Hebrews understand *all* life—plants, animals, and humans—as having its ultimate source in God's free creative decision. In this way, observes Cohn-Sherbok, "the orientation of scripture is *theocentric* as opposed to *anthropocentric*." It is exceptionally clear from the witness of Scripture, he says, that "humans are not God: they are not made gods in creation and they are not the goal of creation. . . . The world is not made just for human beings."[16] In both Genesis and the larger Hebrew conception of creation, it is unambiguous that human beings were meant to share the Earth and its resources with their fellow creatures. And indeed this is a distinctive focus of the Bible that sets it apart from other ancient accounts of the place of animals in creation. While other ancient religions viewed animals as "less than extras in the drama of reality," explains ancient Near Eastern religious scholar and archaeologist Ingvild Gilhus, the Hebrews presented the world with a vision of God who loves and cares for both humans and animals. "For the first time" within an ancient religion, he says, "animals are not only significant in

---

13. Iain Provan, "The Land Is Mine and You Are Only Tenants (Leviticus 25:23): Earth-Keeping and People-Keeping in the Old Testament," *CRUX* 42, no. 2 (Summer 2006): 5.

14. Ray Anderson, "Theological Anthropology," in *The Blackwell Companion to Modern Theology*, ed. Gareth Jones (Oxford: Blackwell, 2004), 85, emphasis added.

15. Joel B. Green, "Restoring the Human Person: New Testament Voices for a Holistic and Social Anthropology," in *Neuroscience and the Person: Scientific Perspectives on Divine Action*, ed. Robert John Russell, Nancey Murphy, Theo Meyering, and Michael Arbib (Berkeley, CA: CTNS; Vatican City State: Vatican Observatory, 1999), 5, emphasis in original. Other Hebrew biblical terminology reflects the unity or commonality of human and beast before God as well. For example, explains Elijah Judah Schochet, the phrase "spirit of life" (*ruach hayyim*) can indicate both animals and humans, as can the word "flesh" (*basar*), which refers to "life in general." In a similar manner, says Schochet, the expression "all flesh" (*kol basar*) means "all living creatures, animal as well as human." Elijah Judah Schochet, *Animal Life in Jewish Tradition: Attitudes and Relationships* (New York: Ktav Publishing, 1984), 53.

16. Cohn-Sherbok and Linzey, *After Noah*, 18.

themselves, belonging to Him and not to us; they are players . . . in the story of our own moral development."[17]

Genesis teaches that animals were here first, Earth is their God-given home, and God blesses their lives and activities and pronounces them "good." A bond of kinship or commonality between land animals and humans is revealed in the fact that these animals share the *same day* of creation with human beings. As theologian Andrew Linzey explains, the days of Genesis 1 represent concentric "circles of greater or lesser intimacy with God," and land animals together with humans "belong to the *innermost* circle of intimacy," having both been created on the sixth day.[18] The culmination and crown of creation—the seventh day Sabbath rest— also embraces both animals and humans.[19] God rests with the whole of creation on the Sabbath, which, says Cohn-Sherbok, is the enduring "symbol of the destiny of the *entire* created world—to be with God as God intended for all eternity."[20]

Do Humans Uniquely Need Redemption?

The Hebrew understanding of animals sees them as existing within the sphere of God's promises, and it is evident in the Bible that animals have a special morally responsible and redemptive relationship with God. This means that—according to Scripture—animals, like humans, are culpable and thus punishable for their actions and violations of God's commands. For instance, in Genesis 6:11–12 animals, having been given, along with humans, every green thing to eat, but having been forbidden to consume the flesh of fellow beasts, are held accountable by God for the violence that they (i.e., "all flesh" or "every living animal") have done upon the Earth, and for the corrupting of God's ways. In the flood account, God judges both humans and animals for their bloodthirsty behavior:

> Now the earth was corrupt in God's sight, and the earth was filled with violence. And God saw the earth, and behold, it was corrupt; for all animals and humans (*kol basar*) had corrupted their way upon the earth. And God said to Noah, "I have determined to make an end to all humans and animals (*kol basar*); for the earth is filled with violence through them. (Gen. 6:11–13)[21]

17. Ingvild Sælid Gilhus, *Animals, Gods and Humans: Changing Attitudes to Animals in Greek, Roman and Early Christian Ideas* (New York: Routledge, 2006), 78. See also Matthew Scully, *Dominion: The Power of Man, the Suffering of Animals, and the Call to Mercy* (New York: St. Martin's Griffin, 2002), 92.

18. Andrew Linzey, *Animal Theology* (Chicago: University of Illinois Press, 1995), 34, emphasis in original.

19. Jürgen Moltmann, *God in Creation: A New Theology of Creation and the Spirit of God* (Minneapolis: Fortress, 1993), 6. See also Lev. 25:6–7.

20. Cohn-Sherbok and Linzey, *After Noah*, 20. For two contemporary discussions on how the Sabbath includes the whole of creation, see Moltmann, *God in Creation*, 288; and Hans Schwarz, *Eschatology* (Grand Rapids: Eerdmans, 2000), 405, emphasis in original.

21. The Hebrew word *basar* refers to all living things besides plants, i.e., animals and humans.

The Flood in Genesis is thus as much a punishment for the wayward ways of animals as for humans. In a similar manner, explains Jewish Bible scholar Elijah Judah Schochet, "at Mount Sinai, animals as well as humans are threatened with punishment should they touch the mountain." While earlier Mesopotamian legal codes exact no such punishment, for the Hebrews, an ox that gores and kills a human is to be held guilty of a capital offense.[22] In a similar fashion, animals are called to fast and put on sackcloth and ashes with the rest of the repenting Ninevites in the book of Jonah, lest they be destroyed by God's judgment upon the city.[23] Throughout Scripture, sin is characterized as forgetting God's ways, and it is plain that as "non-human animals depart from the mode of flourishing God intended for them," they, like their human counterparts, are described as genuinely sinful.[24] The Hebrew Bible clearly reflects a theological zoology in which animals posses the capacity to stray from the will of God. "The doctrine of reward and punishment," and "retributive justice, is extended to beasts as well as to men . . . and scripture does not spare animals from responsibility for their deeds."[25] In the biblical vision, the phenomena of virtue and vice are found in both humans and animals, and the difference between their moral lives and choices, great as it is, certainly is one of degree and not kind.

Accountability, in the form of judgment, however, is merely the dark side of redemption. While in the book of Jonah God demands repentance from both the humans and animals of Nineveh (Jon. 3:7–8), God is likewise concerned with the redemption of both humans and animals. God counsels Jonah in his closing words, "And should I not have concern for the great city of Nineveh, in which there are a hundred and twenty thousand inhabitants who cannot tell their right hand from their left [i.e., children]—and also many animals?" (Jon. 4:11). Both accountability for sin and hope of redemption are grounded in God's covenantal relationship. In Genesis 9, God establishes a covenant not just with Noah and his family, but also with "every living creature." Thus in the Hebrew scriptural tradition, explains Cohn-Sherbok, "animals are included within the moral dealings of God with humankind."[26] God enters into covenantal community with both humans and animals and both partake in the curses and blessings.

The understanding of covenant in the Hebrew Scriptures as "God-given community with all living beings" demands a deep sense of responsibility toward animals and defines moral limits for human interactions with animals.[27]

---

22. Exod. 21:28. For a discussion see Schochet, *Animal Life in Jewish Tradition*, 54.

23. An interesting tradition within Judaism is that God spared Nineveh chiefly because he had compassion on the animals (Jon. 4:11). See Cohn-Sherbok and Linsey, *After Noah*, 26.

24. David L. Clough, *On Animals* (New York: T&T Clark, 2012), 1.

25. Schochet, *Animal Life in Jewish Tradition*, 54.

26. Cohn-Sherbok and Linzey, *After Noah*, 22.

27. Ibid., 23.

It is in the context of such care and concern for and kinship and covenanting with animals that one must understand the biblical concept of the dominion bestowed upon humans (Gen. 1:28). In the Bible, "dominion" is a term that is deeply linked to the biblical concept of kingship. Thus to understand dominion, one must ask how the ancient Hebrews viewed the office and calling of the king. The Hebrew king was to rule on behalf of God, explains ancient Near Eastern religious scholar Aubrey Johnson. The ruler who was granted dominion was required to "watch carefully over the rights of his subjects, and so ensure in particular that the weaker members of society may enjoy his protection and thus have justice done to them according to their need." From the beginning, says Johnson, the Hebrew understanding of kingship "makes it clear that the king is both dependent upon and responsible to Yahweh for the right to exercise his power; for his subjects, whatever their status in society, are one and all Yahweh's people."[28] Dominion, as it is ideally and rightly exercised in the Jewish scriptural tradition, is carried out on behalf of the poor, the oppressed, and the helpless.

As the king is called to live in concord with his subjects as their advocate and protector, the biblical ideal for the relationship between humans and animals is one of order, peace, and harmony. Within the garden of Eden, where God places the humans together with animals, there is no trace of violence or bloodshed between them or even among different species of animals. While violence does tragically enter into the picture at some point, Scripture anticipates a future when all bloodshed shall end, and nonviolent harmony between humanity and animals will be restored. In this coming age, which will be inaugurated through God's redemptive action, aggression between humans and animals will cease. As God declares in Hosea 2:18: "In that day, I will also make a covenant for them; with the beasts of the field, the birds of the sky and the creeping things of the ground. And I will abolish the bow, the sword and war from the earth; and will make them lie down in safety." Isaiah 11:6–9 foresees this future age of redemption as a fundamental transformation in the relationships between predator and prey.[29]

---

28. Aubrey R. Johnson, *Sacral Kingship in Ancient Israel* (Eugene, OR: Wipf & Stock, 1955), 7.

29. "And the wolf will dwell with the lamb,
   and the leopard will lie down with the young goat,
   and the calf and the young lion and the fatling together;
   and a little child will lead them.
Also the cow and the bear will graze,
   their young will lie down together,
   and the lion will eat straw like the ox.
The nursing child will play by the hole of the cobra,
   and the weaned child will put his hand on the viper's den.
They will not hurt or destroy in all my holy mountain,
for the earth will be full of the knowledge of the Lord,
   as the waters cover the sea." (Isa. 11:6–9)

The New Testament continues the ancient Jewish theme of animal redemption and future transformation. Theologian Denis Edwards points out "that there
is a real connection between Christ's life, death and resurrection and the whole
creation is made clear in the range of New Testament texts . . . which speak
of the creation and reconciliation of all things in Christ."[30] As Isaiah's vision is
reflected in the New Testament book of Revelation (5:13–14), Edwards explains
how "the animals, insects and fish of our planet are imagined as sharing in the
resurrection of the Lamb and joining in the great cosmic liturgy." Thus, says
Edwards, both animals and humans are part of the "redemption in Christ."[31]

Human Nature and Human Uniqueness: Perspectives from Science

While the Bible is silent on precisely which characteristics or qualities might
make humans unique and define the essence of human nature, the natural sciences have attempted to shed light on the matter. Throughout the years, scientists have suggested many characteristics that might serve as the scientifically
discernible location of human uniqueness. Traits such as self-awareness, empathy, morality, rationality, sexuality, language ability, use of tools, development of
technology, and attainment of culture have all, at one time or another, been put
forward as the one special quality that makes humans distinct. Over the past 150
years, however, scientific investigations have not found any of these criteria for
human uniqueness to be without exception, and studies showing the similarities between humans and animals have made the essence of human uniqueness
increasingly difficult to define.

Human Uniqueness in Culture, Tool Use, and Technology?

Which empirically observable physical characteristics or biological features
make humans unique—and unique in a nontrivial way—and distinguish them
from nonhuman creatures? The capacities for culture, tool use, and technology
were, at one time, held up as behaviors unique to human beings. Following the
lead of sociologist Emile Durkheim (1858–1917), sociologists and anthropologists have often singled out culture as "a uniquely human phenomenon uncon-
nected to the rest of the natural world, free from the constraints of biology."[32]

---

30. Denis Edwards, "The Redemption of Animals in an Incarnational Theology," in *Creaturely Theology: On God, Humans and Other Animals*, ed. Celia Deane-Drummond and David Clough (London: SCM, 2009), 81. See also John 1:1–14; Rom. 8:18–25; 1 Cor. 8:6; Eph. 1:9–10, 20–23; Col. 1:15–20; Heb. 1:2–3; 2 Pet. 3:13; Rev. 21:1–5, 22:13.

31. Edwards, "Redemption of Animals," 81.

32. Philip Pomper and David Gary Shaw, *The Return of Science: Evolution, History, and Theory* (Lanham, MD.: Rowman and Littlefield, 2002), 101.

Tool use and technological development have been regarded in a similar manner, and some have even suggested renaming the human species *Homo faber* ("man the toolmaker") in accordance with the supposedly exclusive human possession of technology.[33] In the wake of this longstanding intellectual tradition, many, such as philosopher Holmes Rolston III, have argued that animals do not possess technology and "do not form cumulative transmissible cultures."[34]

Empirical investigations of animal behavior in the last twenty years, however, have shown that neither technology nor culture is unique to human beings. Rather, both phenomena are exhibited in animals across the evolutionary spectrum. For instance, various nonhuman animals exhibit material culture or technology. Among the apes, explains primate researcher Tetsuro Matsuzawa, "chimpanzees in the wild use and manufacture a wide variety of tools, such as twigs to fish for termites or a pair of stones to crack open hard-shelled nuts." Not all chimpanzees use the same tools in the same way, however, and recent investigations "comparing different communities of chimpanzees have shown that each community develops its own unique set of cultural traditions."[35] For chimpanzees, primatologists were able to identify as many as thirty-nine different cultural traditions—both material and nonmaterial—"behavior patterns common in at least one community, yet absent in at least one other, with no simple environmental explanation."[36] Various levels of technological innovation have been found among nonhuman primates, and even the control and use of fire (along with the attempt to create fire) has been documented in chimpanzees.[37]

Culture, tool use, and technology have also been observed in crows. Captive New Caledonian crows in laboratory studies display insight and innovation by using unfamiliar materials to spontaneously construct novel tools for a specific

---

33. Hanna Arendt, *The Human Condition* (Chicago: University of Chicago Press, 1958); K. P. Oakley, *Man the Tool-Maker* (Chicago: University of Chicago Press, 1976).

34. Holmes Rolston III, *Science and Origins: Probing the Deeper Questions* (Kitchener, ON: Pandora, 2009), 43–44.

35. Tetsuro Matsuzawa, "Chimpanzee Ai and Her Son Ayumu: An Episode of Education by Master-Apprenticeship," in *The Cognitive Animal: Empirical and Theoretical Perspectives on Animal Cognition*, ed. Marc Bekoff, Colin Allen, and Gordon M. Burghardt (Cambridge, MA: MIT Press, 2002), 189.

36. Andrew Whiten and Carel P. van Schaik, "The Evolution of Animal 'Cultures' and Social Intelligence," *Philosophical Transactions of the Royal Society B* 362 (April 29, 2007): 607. The case is similar with orangutans, which exhibit at least nineteen different ecologically independent material and nonmaterial cultural traditions, with "each community displaying its own unique profile" (607).

37. See Elisabeth Townsend, "The Cooking Ape," *Gastronomica* 5, no. 1 (Winter 2005): 32; Jill Pruetz and Thomas LaDuke, "Reaction to Fire by Savanna Chimpanzees (*Pan troglodytes verus*) at Fongoli, Senegal: Conceptualization of 'Fire Behavior' and the Case for a Chimpanzee Model," *American Journal of Physical Anthropology* 141, no. 4 (April 2010). See also Anne Russon and B. Galdikas, "Imitation in Free-Ranging Rehabilitant Orangutans," *Journal of Comparative Psychology* 44 (1993): 147–61.

Thierry Van Baelinghem / Science Source

A carrion crow (Corvus corone) dislodges ants with a twig. Some crow species have been shown not only to use tools but also to make them—an ability formerly thought to be unique to humans.

task.[38] Rather than mechanically applying "a previously learned set of movements to the new situations," explain researchers Alex Weir and Alex Kacelnik, these crows "instead sought new solutions to each problem."[39] Research has shown that crows of this same species are also avid tool users in the wild. Moreover, the manufacture of tools among wild crows has been shown to demonstrate "cumulative technological evolution"—a phenomenon that has long been argued to be unique to humans.[40] In light of this research, observe Weir and Kacelnik, the birds of the corvid family have been shown to "rival nonhuman primates in tool-related cognitive capabilities."[41]

Human Uniqueness in Language?

Like culture and technology, the use of symbolic language has often been put forth as the mark distinguishing humans from animals. From the time of

38. Gavin R. Hunt and Russell D. Gray, "The Crafting of Hook Tools by Wild New Caledonian Crows," *Proceedings of the Royal Society of London B* 271 (2004): S88–90.

39. Alex A. S. Weir and Alex Kacelnik, "A New Caledonian Crow (*Corvus moneduloides*) Creatively Re-Designs Tools by Bending or Unbending Aluminium Strips," *Animal Cognition* 9 (2006): 317.

40. Gavin R. Hunt and Russell D. Gray, "Diversification and Cumulative Evolution in New Caledonian Crow Tool Manufacture," *Proceedings of the Royal Society of London B* 270 (2003): 867.

41. Alex A. S. Weir, Jackie Chappell, and Alex Kacelnik, "Shaping of Hooks in New Caledonian Crows," *Science* 297 (August 9, 2002): 981.

Darwin to the turn of the twenty-first century, many philosophers and scientists have agreed with the position of cognitive linguist Mohinish Shukla that "the faculty of language is unique to the human species."[42] In the past decade, however, there has arisen a considerable degree of debate over whether or not language can still be considered an exclusively human possession that sets humans apart from all other creatures.[43] While it is undeniable that humans are the most accomplished known users of language, many scientists have come to view the advanced linguistic ability of humans as a difference *in degree* rather than *in kind* from that of other animals.

Recent research has demonstrated that the linguistic abilities of nonhuman animals are more sophisticated than previously thought. For instance, linguist Noam Chomsky and biologist Tecumseh Fitch comment that many researchers who have assumed that human speech is qualitatively different from nonhuman communication have been engaged in a "vigorous research program studying animal speech perception and, more recently, speech production." To their surprise, though, say Chomsky and Fitch, "this research has turned up little evidence for uniquely human mechanisms special to speech, despite a persistent tendency to assume uniqueness even in the absence of relevant animal data."[44] It was once thought, for example, that the *categorical perception* of sounds (i.e., the ability to perceive sounds that belong to different categories) was an adaptation unique to humans because it is so specialized for processing the fine details of human speech. Over time though, it was discovered that numerous nonhuman animals also categorically perceive speech.[45] From such investigations, researchers eventually concluded that far from being unique to *Homo sapiens* categorical perception is, instead, a "primitive vertebrate characteristic."[46]

Cognitive scientist and linguist Chris Sinha explains that nonhuman creatures similarly have demonstrated "the capacity for communicative use of elements of the lexicons [i.e., the inventory of words], or elements corresponding to those of the lexicons, of human natural languages."[47] For example, experiments

---

42. Mohinish Shukla, "Language from a Biological Perspective," *Journal of Biosciences* 30, no. 1 (2005): 119.

43. See for example, Derek Bickerton, *Adam's Tongue: How Humans Made Language, How Language Made Humans* (New York: Hill and Wang, 2009). See also Noam Chomsky, *Knowledge of Language: Its Nature, Origin and Use* (New York: Praeger, 1986); and Philip Lieberman, *Uniquely Human: The Evolution of Speech, Thought, and Selfless Behavior* (Cambridge, MA: Harvard University Press, 1991).

44. Marc D. Hauser, Noam Chomsky, and W. Tecumseh Fitch, "The Faculty of Language: What Is It, Who Has It, and How Did It Evolve?," *Science* 298 (November 22, 2002): 1574.

45. P. K. Kuhl, "The Special Mechanisms Debate in Speech Research: Categorization Tests on Animals and Infants," in *Categorical Perception: The Groundwork of Cognition*, ed. S. Harnad (Cambridge: Cambridge University Press, 1987), 355–86.

46. Hauser, Chomsky, and Fitch, "Faculty of Language," 1572.

47. Chris Sinha, "The Evolution of Language: From Signals to Symbols to System," in *Evolution of Communication Systems: A Comparative Approach*, ed. D. Kimbrough Oller and Ulrike Griebel (Cambridge, MA: MIT Press, 2004), 217.

involving a nine-year-old Border Collie named Rico, observes psychologist and cognitive scientist Paul Bloom, provide evidence that domestic dogs "might well be capable of learning words" in a manner similar to young human children.[48] Domestic dogs are not alone in their ability to acquire key elements of human language. According to psychologists and primatologists Sue Savage-Rumbaugh and Karen Brakke, several species of primates have been trained to associate words with objects and "use symbols in many of the same ways as human beings," demonstrating a "cognizance of the significance of their utterances."[49] Studies involving bonobos which were reared within a research context where their mother was being taught lexical symbols showed that "it is not necessary to train language" for the experimental subjects to acquire it. By simply watching and hearing the caretakers training their mother, "as a child observes and listens to those around it," bonobos "began to use symbols appropriately" and eventually learned to respond appropriately to human speech.[50]

The most extensive investigations establishing linguistic capabilities among animals have been carried out with African grey parrots, a species whose longevity, large brain, and highly social nature resembles that of dolphins and primates.[51] Given these qualities, along with their remarkable vocal versatility, explains comparative psychologist Irene Pepperberg, these birds have shown that they can "solve various cognitive tasks and acquire and use English speech."[52] Grey parrots, says Pepperberg, exhibit "meaningful use" of the English language[53] and have the capacity to form abstract concepts.[54] The language use of these parrots extends to combining verbs with a variety of nouns and adjectives. For instance a parrot might say it wants an apple or wants to go to a chair. The trainers then grant such wishes "so that the birds experience the consequences of their utterances." Within this social communication context, the birds show

---

48. Paul Bloom, "Can a Dog Learn a Word?" *Science* 304 (June 11, 2004): 1605; Juliane Kaminski, Josep Call, and Julia Fischer, "Word Learning in a Domestic Dog: Evidence for 'Fast Mapping,'" *Science* 304 (June 11, 2004): 1682.

49. Sue Savage-Rumbaugh and Karen E. Brakke, "Animal Language: Methodological and Interpretive Issues," in *Readings in Animal Cognition*, ed. Marc Bekoff and Dale Jamieson (Cambridge, MA: MIT Press, 1996), 277.

50. Savage-Rumbaugh and Brakke, "Animal Language," 277. See also Sue Savage-Rumbaugh, et al., "Spontaneous Symbol Acquisition and Communicative Use by Pygmy Chimpanzees (*Pan paniscus*)," *Journal of Experimental Psychology* 115, no. 3 (1986): 211–35.

51. Irene Pepperberg, "Cognitive and Communicative Abilities of Grey Parrots," in *The Cognitive Animal: Empirical and Theoretical Perspectives on Animal Cognition* (Cambridge, MA: MIT Press, 2002), 247.

52. Irene Pepperberg, "Cognitive and Communicative Abilities of Grey Parrots," *Current Directions in Psychological Science* 11, no. 3 (2002): 83.

53. Ibid.

54. Irene Pepperberg, "Comparing the Complex Cognition of Birds and Primates," in *Comparative Vertebrate Cognition: Are Primates Superior to Non-Primates?*, ed. Lesley J. Rogers and Gisela Kaplan (New York: Kluwer Academic, 2004), 29.

that they *understand* what they are saying because they will use the word "no" and repeat their original request if given the wrong object or if brought to a place they did not ask to go. The grey parrots also will ask novel questions about their environment and even themselves. For instance, when a parrot named Alex "saw his reflection for the first time, he suddenly asked a trainer, 'What color?'" while pointing to himself in the mirror. In doing this, Alex had taken a question that was asked of him in relation to different objects and transferred it from the original setting to a new situation. According to science writer Christine Scholtyssek, "After the trainer overcame her initial surprise, she told him, 'Grey. You are a grey parrot.'"[55] To which Alex repeated "Alex is grey," and remembered ever since.

Human Uniqueness in Self-Awareness and Reflective Consciousness?

Alex's question to his trainer regarding his color raises the issue of whether self-awareness and reflective consciousness are qualities unique to human beings. Numerous studies in animal behavior have now led animal consciousness researchers, such as David DeGrazia, to the conclusion that a countless number of nonhuman creatures are clearly conscious and that "many animals are self-aware."[56] Mirror self-recognition has been clearly demonstrated in several primate species,[57] dolphins,[58] whales,[59] elephants,[60] and in birds of the corvid

---

55. Christine Scholtyssek, "Bird Brains? Hardly," *Scientific American Mind*, April/May 2006, 55.

56. David DeGrazia, "Self-Awareness in Animals," in *The Philosophy of Animal Minds*, ed. Robert W. Lurz (New York: Cambridge University Press, 2009), 201. For a detailed discussion on Darwin's views on animal consciousness and self-awareness, see Robert J. Richards, *Darwin and the Emergence of Evolutionary Theories of Mind and Behavior* (Chicago: University of Chicago Press, 1987), 195–212.

57. These include chimpanzees, orangutans, bonobos, gorillas, and capuchin monkeys. See D. Povinelli, A. Rulf, K. Landau, and D. Bierschwale, "Self-Recognition in Chimpanzees (*Pan troglodytes*): Distribution, Ontogeny, and Patterns of Emergence," *Journal of Comparative Psychology* 107 (1993): 347–72; J. Lethmate and G. Dücker, "Untersuchungen zum Selbsterkennen im Spiegel bei Orangutans und Einigen anderen Affenarten [Studies on Self-Recognition in a Mirror by Orangutans and Some Other Primate Species]," *Zeitschrift für Tierpsychologie* 33 (1973): 248–69; G. Gallup Jr., "Self-Awareness in Primates," *American Scientist* 67 (1979): 417–21; F. G. P. Patterson and R. Cohn, "Self-Recognition and Self-Awareness in Lowland Gorillas," in *Self-Awareness in Animals and Humans: Developmental Perspectives*, ed. S. T. Parker and R. W. Mitchell (New York: Cambridge University Press, 1994), 273–90; and P. G. Roma, A. Silberberg, M. E. Huntsberry, C. J. Christensen, A. M. Ruggiero, and S. J. Suomi, "Mark Tests for Mirror Self-Recognition in Capuchin Monkeys (*Cebus apella*) Trained to Touch Marks," *American Journal of Primatology* 69 (2007): 989–1000.

58. D. Reiss and L. Marino, "Mirror Self-Recognition in the Bottlenose Dolphin: A Case of Cognitive Convergence," *Proceedings of the National Academy of Sciences* 98 (2001): 5937–42.

59. F. Delfour and K. Marten, "Mirror Image Processing in Three Marine Mammal Species: Killer Whales (*Orcinus orca*), False Killer Whales (*Pseudorca crassidens*) and California Sea Lions (*Zalophus californianus*)," *Behavioural Processes* 53, no. 3 (April 26, 2001): 181–90.

60. J. M. Plotnik, F. B. M. de Waal, and D. Reiss, "Self-Recognition in an Asian Elephant," *Proceedings of the National Academy of Sciences* 103 (2006): 17053–57.

family.[61] Such self-recognition tests involve not only demonstrating the mere ability to perceive one's own image in a mirror, but also the capacity to recognize the reflection of one's own body as oneself.

Related to self-awareness are the capacities for *metacognition* and *mind-reading*. Metacognition refers to the ability to think about thinking and "to control and monitor one's own cognition."[62] The ability to mind-read or possess a theory of mind is when an organism is "capable of attributing mental states to others—when it understands that others see, feel, and know."[63] While in the past it was thought that humans alone possessed these higher reflective capacities, explains animal researcher Robert Lurz, "a number of recent studies of animal mind-reading and metacognition strongly indicate that apes, monkeys and dolphins are capable of higher order thoughts about their own minds and the minds of other animals."[64] Similar research points to metacognition, insight, and theory of mind in elephants.[65] Beyond the large-brained mammals, according to psychologists Allison Foote and Jonathon Crystal, recent studies indicate that even "rats are capable of metacognition."[66] Other researchers, such as cognitive psychologists Nathan Emery and Nicola Clayton, have shown that outside of mammals, there is also a good deal of "evidence [which] suggests that species of birds have cognitive abilities that are equal to or more sophisticated than have been demonstrated for primates."[67] Birds from the corvid family, in particular, have demonstrated numerous sophisticated cognitive abilities, including episodic memory, future planning, metacognition, and a theory of mind.[68]

---

61. In experiments involving the Eurasian magpie, *Pica pica* (from the Corvidae family), the birds spontaneously connected their reflections with their own bodies, thus illustrating "mirror-induced self-directed behavior." These findings "provide the first evidence of mirror self-recognition in a non-mammalian species" and entail that capacity for self-awareness has "evolved independently in different vertebrate classes with a separate evolutionary history." See H. Prior, A. Schwarz, and O. Güntürken, "Mirror-Induced Behavior in the Magpie (*Pica pica*): Evidence of Self-Recognition," *PLoS Biology* 6, no. 8 (August 2008): 1642.

62. Joelle Proust, "The Representational Basis of Brute Metacognition: A Proposal," in *The Philosophy of Animal Minds*, ed. Robert W. Lurz (New York: Cambridge University Press, 2009), 165.

63. Moti Nissani, "Theory of Mind and Insight in Chimpanzees, Elephants and Other Animals?," in *Comparative Vertebrate Cognition: Are Primates Superior to Non-Primates?*, ed. Lesley J. Rogers and Gisela T. Kaplan (New York: Kluwer Academic, 2004), 231.

64. Lurz, *Philosophy of Animal Minds*, 9.

65. See Nissani, "Theory of Mind?"; and Joyce H. Poole and Cynthia J. Moss, "Elephant Sociality and Complexity: The Scientific Evidence," in *Elephants and Ethics: Toward a Morality of Coexistence*, ed. Christen Wemmer and Catherine Ann Christen (Baltimore: Johns Hopkins University Press, 2008), 69–100.

66. The rats studied showed that they "know when they do not know the answer in a duration-discrimination test." Allison L. Foote and Jonathon D. Crystal, "Metacognition in the Rat," *Current Biology* 17 (March 20, 2007): 551.

67. Nathan J. Emery and Nicola S. Clayton, "Comparing the Complex Cognition of Birds and Primates," in *Comparative Vertebrate Cognition*, ed. Rogers and Kaplan, 36–37.

68. N. J. Emery and N. S. Clayton, "Effects of Experience and Social Context on Prospective Caching Strategies by Scrub Jays," *Nature* 414 (November 22, 2001): 443.

Human Uniqueness in Morality and Religion?

The capacity for morality has long been defended not only as a uniquely human characteristic but also as the supreme trait defining the very essence of human nature.[69] Over the last twenty years, however, moral philosophers and scientific researchers in the area of animal cognition have increasingly come to support the idea that some animals can act as moral agents and subjects. Scientific researchers in animal mentality, such as cognitive ethologist Marc Bekoff have argued that animals exhibit a broad repertoire of behaviors that can be regarded as moral—including displays of empathy,[70] conceptions of fairness, exhibiting trust, and acting reciprocally.[71] Recent experimental work on wolves, for instance, has documented that "social canids [dog family including wolves and foxes] refuse to play with individuals who violate social rules."[72] Other research, such as that by psychologist Sarah Brosnan, reveal that "ravens show third party intervention against norm violations," and that "capuchin monkeys and chimpanzees both respond negatively to distributional inequity."[73]

According to moral philosopher David DeGrazia, such examples, which describe "actions manifesting virtues—in cases in which the actions are not plausibly interpreted as instinctive or conditioned," support the attribution of moral agency to some nonhuman animals. Thus DeGrazia concludes, "On any reasonable understanding of moral agency, some animals are moral agents."[74] Moral philosopher Evelyn Pluhar likewise asks, "Is it really so clear . . . that the capacity for moral agency has no precedent in any other species?" Pluhar maintains

---

69. For a defense of this position, see Christian Smith, *Moral, Believing Animals: Human Personhood and Culture* (Oxford: Oxford University Press, 2003), 8.

70. Dale J. Langford et al., "Social Modulation of Pain as Evidence for Empathy in Mice," *Science* 312 (June 2006): 1967.

71. See for example, Janelle Weaver, "Monkeys Go Out on a Limb to Show Gratitude: Altruistic Behaviour in Primates Relies on Reciprocity," *Nature* (January 12, 2010); Gabriele Schino and Filippo Aureli, "The Relative Roles of Kinship and Reciprocity in Explaining Primate Altruism," *Ecology Letters* 13 (2010): 45–50. Other studies in nonprimates may have revealed key connections between gratitude, play, and joy. For instance, Jaak Panksepp and his research team have observed in their research on play and laughter within rats, "Young animals we have tickled become remarkably friendly toward us—apparently socially bonded. They actively chirp when we approach their cages. . . . Such sounds reflect a positive affective process which, in its most intense forms, can be emotionally characterized as a playful, social joy." Jaak Panksepp, "Affective Consciousness: Core Emotional Feelings in Animals and Humans," *Consciousness and Cognition* 14 (2005): 55. See also Robert A. Emmons and Michael E. McCullough, *The Psychology of Gratitude* (Oxford: Oxford University Press, 2004), 118, 225–28.

72. See Marc Bekoff, "Wild Justice, Cooperation, and Fair Play: Minding Manners, Being Nice, and Feeling Good," in *The Origins and Nature of Sociality*, ed. R. Sussman and A. Chapman (Chicago: Aldine de Gruyter, 2004), 53–79.

73. Sarah F. Brosnan, "Nonhuman Species' Reactions to Inequity and Their Implications for Fairness," *Social Justice Research* 19, no. 2 (June 2006): 153.

74. David DeGrazia, *Taking Animals Seriously* (New York: Cambridge University Press, 1996), 203.

that this is not the case and that "evidence has been gathered that indicates that nonhumans are capable of what we would call 'moral' or 'virtuous' behavior."[75]

More recently philosopher of mind Mark Rowlands has advanced a detailed scientific and philosophical case that "animals are capable of acting on the basis of moral reasons—as possessors of moral virtues (and vices) broadly understood."[76] Looking at both experimental and anecdotal evidence, Rowlands describes a number of remarkable cases in which animals seem to be motivated by concern for others. These actions appear to indicate emotions such as sympathy, empathy, compassion, grief, and courage. Coming from the moral perspective of virtue ethics, Rowlands maintains that an attitude that has "as its focus the welfare or fortunes of another is . . . the hallmark of a moral attitude." Consequently, if animals act on the basis of these moral attitudes, explains Rowlands, they are "motivated to act by moral considerations."[77] Because, as Rowlands argues, "the blanket dismissal of the possibility of moral action in animals cannot be sustained," it likewise cannot be sustained that the capacity for morality is a uniquely human characteristic.[78]

Recent research even suggests that animals also might share the phenomenon of religious awareness (understood as consciousness of transcendence). Such evidence for the awareness of transcendence in various groups of animals is gathered from funerary and mourning behavior in animals and from ritualized expressiveness in response to situations that inspire awe. Mourning and funerary behavior have been observed among animals both in captivity and in the wild. For instance, Bekoff describes an occasion where he and a colleague witnessed four magpies standing around a fifth who had been hit by a car and was lying lifeless on the side of the lane:

> One approached the corpse, gently pecked at it, just as an elephant would nose the carcass of another elephant, and stepped back. Another magpie did the same thing. Next, one of the magpies flew off, brought back some grass and laid it by the corpse. Another magpie did the same. Then all four stood vigil for a few seconds and one by one flew off.[79]

Philosopher and animal researcher Donovan Schaefer describes how, in similar a manner, "gorillas hold 'wakes' for their companions, a practice so well established

75. Evelyn Pluhar, *Beyond Prejudice: The Moral Significance of Human and Nonhuman Animals* (Durham, NC: Duke University Press, 1995), 2.

76. Mark J. Rowlands, "Virtue Ethics and Animals," in *Animal Ethics: Past and Present Perspectives*, ed. Evangelos D. Protopapadakis (Berlin: Logos, 2012), 35.

77. Mark Rowlands, *Can Animals Be Moral?* (Oxford: Oxford University Press, 2012), 8.

78. Ibid., xi.

79. Marc Bekoff, "Animal Emotions, Wild Justice and Why They Matter: Grieving Magpies, a Pissy Baboon, and Empathic Elephants," *Emotion, Space and Society* 2, no. 2 (December 2009): 82–85.

that zoos have formalized the process, inviting human onlookers to attend," and "elephants stage funeral gatherings and express special interest in the bones of deceased relatives."[80]

Researchers have also observed what appear to be ritualized reactions to experiences of religious awe within nonhuman animals. Consider for example the "waterfall dances" that have been witnessed among chimpanzees on occasions where they suddenly encounter a powerful and spectacular cascade hidden deep in the forest. As a chimpanzee approaches the waterfall, explains primatologist Jane Goodall,

> his hair bristles slightly, a sign of heightened arousal. As he gets closer, and the roar of falling water gets louder, his pace quickens, his hair becomes fully erect, and upon reaching the stream he may perform a magnificent display close to the foot of the falls. Standing upright, he sways rhythmically from foot to foot, stamping in the shallow, rushing water, picking up and hurling great rocks. Sometimes he climbs up the slender vines that hang down from the trees high above and swings out into the spray of the falling water.[81]

Such "dances" at the base of waterfalls, which last for ten or fifteen minutes and are also displayed in response to powerful electrical storms and violent gusts of wind, appear to be ritualized expressions of awe evoked by the experience of the transcendent in the beauty and power in nature.[82]

Human Uniqueness by Degree Rather Than by Kind?

Scientific research on nonhuman animal behavior and cognition has shown that there does not seem to be any one *qualitatively* distinguishing characteristic (or even combination of such characteristics) that all humans—and only humans—unambiguously possess. Some researchers have thus argued that it is not a difference in kind that makes *Homo sapiens* unique among the animals, but rather a difference in degree that stands as the foundation of human exceptionality. Making a case for human uniqueness by the degree of differences between *Homo sapiens* and their closest living relatives, biochemist and molecular geneticist James Sikela points out that "among the traits that distinguish humans from other primates are a *large* brain, *small* canine teeth, bipedalism, an

---

80. Donovan Schaefer, "Do Animals Have Religion? Interdisciplinary Perspectives on Religion and Embodiment," *Anthrozoos* 25 (July 2012): 182–83.

81. Jane Goodall, "Primate Spirituality," in *Encyclopedia of Religion and Nature*, ed. Bron Taylor (London: Continuum, 2005), 1304.

82. Marc Bekoff, *The Emotional Lives of Animals: A Leading Scientist Explores Animal Joy, Sorrow, and Empathy—and Why They Matter* (Novato, CA: New World Library, 2007), 62.

elaborate language, and *advanced* tool-making capabilities." In addition to this, "humans exhibit *reduced* hair cover, use sweating *more efficiently* as a means of thermoregulation, and are thought to be *more adept* long distance runners."[83] Sikela likewise points out that human cognitive abilities are more advanced. Psychologist Michael Corballis similarly argues that having more of a given trait is sufficient to establish human uniqueness over and against other animals that have the same trait, but to a lesser degree. Corballis says, "Chimpanzees may indeed have some capacity to discern what other individuals can feel, see, and perhaps know," but this is only "first-order recursion" or the first level of metacognition. "What they may lack though," continues Corballis, "is the extension to higher order recursion."[84] Even though chimpanzees and corvids might have relatively big brains, display self-awareness, exhibit metacognition, possess culture, use and make tools, display cumulative technological evolution, and so on, they still do not have the gratuitously large cranial capacity of humans, the high level of metacognition, the extensive variety of tools found in human society, or full-blown philosophical morality. While these are quantitative rather than qualitative distinctions, according to researchers such as Sikela and Corballis, it is precisely such differences in degree (rather than in kind) that make humans unique among the animals.

While the "uniqueness by degree" approach to human distinctiveness avoids certain pitfalls of approaches that focus on a singular unique trait, there are two key areas where this line of argument runs into problems. The first has to do with the question of human development and what it means to be a "normal" human. To put it simply, should children be considered less human than adults since children possess certain capacities to a lesser degree? And what about adult individuals who lack advanced metacognition (due to autism) or those who lack a developed capacity for language (due to Rett syndrome)? Are such individuals to be considered fully human? Developmental psychologist and cognitive scientist Justin Barrett has recently suggested that one gender may on average have a more advanced degree of metacognition than the other. If further research establishes this claim, does that mean that the other gender is less than fully human?[85]

The second area that renders the "human uniqueness by degree" approach problematic is contemporary research in paleoanthropology (an interdisciplinary branch of anthropology concerned with early humans and their ancestors).

---

83. James Sikela, "The Jewels of Our Genome: The Search for the Genomic Changes Underlying the Evolutionarily Unique Capacities of the Human Brain," *PLoS Genetics* 2, no. 5 (May 2006): e80, emphasis in original.

84. Michael C. Corballis, *The Recursive Mind: The Origins of Human Language, Thought, and Civilization* (Princeton: Princeton University Press, 2011), 150.

85. Justin Barrett, "The Evolution of Religious Brains," lecture, The Faraday Institute for Science and Religion, Cambridge, July 4, 2009. Others have made similar claims with regard to gender differences in rationality and empathy. See Simon Baron-Cohen, *The Essential Difference: Male and Female Brains and the Truth about Autism* (New York: Basic Books, 2004).

While it is clear that no presently living nonhuman animal possesses the advanced development of certain traits that would be necessary to seriously challenge human cultural and technological hegemony, the same cannot be said of the prehistoric human past when nonhuman humanoids (called hominins) shared these same traits with humans and apparently possessed them to the same degree. In other words, even if one were to attempt to contend for human uniqueness in light of the present state of biological life on Earth, such arguments ultimately fail when one considers the situation of the human species 100,000 years ago—when, as evolutionary geneticist Mark Thomas remarks, the situation looks more like "a *Lord of the Rings*-type world [with] many hominin populations."[86]

From the currently available evidence, it is clear that several nonhuman hominin species who existed at the same time as early humans had the capacity for complex language.[87] Reviewing the data, psycholinguistics researchers Dan Dediu and Stephen Levinson maintain that modern language and speech can be traced back to the last common ancestor humans shared with a number of nonhuman hominins roughly half a million years ago.[88] Genetic and archaeological research has revealed that the faculty for complex language was possessed by the Neanderthals, the Denisovans, the Flores hominins, and at least two other distinct hominin species (one in Asia and one in Africa).[89]

Advanced tool types, which indicate a high degree of metacognition, are also found among the nonhuman hominins. Investigations have even shown that nonhuman hominins were as technologically innovative as their human counterparts.

---

86. Ewen Callaway, "Mystery Humans Spiced Up Ancients' Sex Lives," *Nature News* (November 19, 2013), *http://www.nature.com/news/mystery-humans-spiced-up-ancients-sex-lives-1.14196.*

87. The language-related "mutations in FOXP2 . . . may actually have occurred some 1.8 million years ago, when *Homo habilis* and *Homo ergaster* were appearing in the fossil record, and as the human brain began gradually to triple in size from the 450 cc of chimpanzee and australopithecine brains to the 1,350 cc of modern human brains." Karl C. Diller and Rebecca L. Cann, "Evidence against a Genetic-Based Revolution in Language 50,000 Years Ago," in *The Cradle of Language*, ed. Rudolf Botha and Chris Knight (New York: Oxford University Press, 2009), 136. Moreover, Neanderthals share with modern humans the key language-related changes or genetic mutations in FOXP2—results which indicate that such changes "predate the common ancestor (which existed about 300,000–400,000 years ago) of modern human and Neandertal populations." J. Krause et al., "The Derived *FOXP2* Variant of Modern Humans Was Shared with Neanderthals," *Current Biology* 17 (2007): 1908–12.

88. Dan Dediu and Stephen Levinson, "On the Antiquity of Language: The Reinterpretation of Neandertal Linguistic Capacities and Its Consequences," *Frontiers in Psychology* 5, no. 4 (2013): 397.

89. For evidence for an unknown African hominin from genetic admixture between them and humans, see Michael F. Hammer et al., "Genetic Evidence for Archaic Admixture in Africa," *Proceedings of the National Academy of Sciences* 108, no. 37 (September 13, 2011). For evidence for an unknown Asian hominin from genetic admixture between them and humans, see Callaway, "Mystery Humans." Callaway comments, "The results suggest that interbreeding went on between the members of several ancient human-like groups in Europe and Asia more than 30,000 years ago, including an as-yet-unknown human ancestor from Asia."

For instance, studies on the development of specialized bone tools (called *lissoirs* or burnishers) used to work and polish leather among Neanderthals indicate that a number of such advanced tool types predate the arrival of *Homo sapiens*.

This indicates that Neanderthals developed such tools independently of humans, and some researchers, such as evolutionary anthropologist Marie Soressi, have argued that it is likely that humans learned about certain tools from Neanderthals.[90]

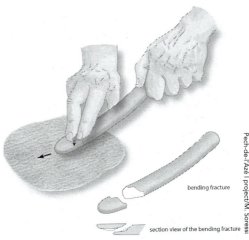

Pech-de-l'Azé I project/M. Soressi

bending fracture

section view of the bending fracture

Neanderthals were capable of inventing new tool types, such as the lissoirs shown here. In view of the numerous characteristics that Neanderthals and other non-human hominins shared with *Homo sapiens*, many anthropologists have increasingly come to question whether the popular notion of human uniqueness can be given any scientific meaning.

In addition to possessing capacities for language and technology to a degree that is equivalent to that of *Homo sapiens*, nonhuman hominins also enjoyed the capacity for art,[91] an awareness of mortality,[92] ritualized or ceremonial behavior,[93] and the capacity for symbolic thought.[94] Some hominin species even possessed certain key characteristics to a greater degree than humans. For instance, all of the nonhuman hominins were physically stronger than humans,[95] and Neanderthals had larger brains than humans. As paleoanthropologist Ian Tattersall comments, "Neanderthals who inhabited Europe toward the end of the Ice Age

---

90. See Marie Soressi et al., "Neandertals Made the First Specialized Bone Tools in Europe," *Proceedings of the National Academy of Sciences* 110, no. 35 (August 27, 2013).

91. See Joao Zilhao, "The Emergence of Ornaments and Art: An Archaeological Perspective on the Origins of 'Behavioral Modernity,'" *Journal of Archaeological Research* 15 (2007): 1–54; and Marco Peresani et al., "An Ochered Fossil Marine Shell from the Mousterian of Fumane Cave, Italy," *PLoS ONE* 8, no. 7 (July 2013): e68572.

92. Paul B. Pettitt, "The Neanderthal Dead: Exploring Mortuary Variability in Middle Palaeolithic Eurasia," *Before Farming* 1, no. 4 (2002): 20.

93. William Rendua, Cédric Beauvalc, and Isabelle Crevecoeurd, "Evidence Supporting an Intentional Neandertal Burial at La Chapelle-aux-Saints," *Proceedings of the National Acadamy of Sciences* 111 (2014): 81–86.

94. F. D'Errico et al., "Archaeological Evidence for the Emergence of Language, Symbolism, and Music—An Alternative Multidisciplinary Perspective," *Journal of World Prehistory* 17 (2003): 1–70.

95. Christopher Stringer and Robin McKie, *African Exodus: The Origins of Modern Humanity* (New York: Henry Holt: 1997), 97.

had brains that were, on average, even larger than ours are today. Classic Neanderthal brains averaged about 1500 ml in volume, while the current worldwide *average* is less than 1400 ml."[96] In light of findings in contemporary paleoanthropology, historian of anthropology Felipe Fernandez-Armesto concludes, "There no longer seems anything definingly special about specimens we class in the same genus as ourselves."[97]

Humans as the Unique "Image and Likeness of God"

While science does not appear to provide a clear basis on which to establish human uniqueness, in the Bible there is one designation the human species is given that nonhuman creatures are not. Genesis 1:26 says humans, unlike other beings, are created "as the image and likeness of God" (or *imago Dei*).[98] Throughout the history of biblical interpretation, theologians and Bible scholars have sought to understand the *imago Dei* in a number of different ways. While there has been little historical consensus with regard to the precise theological meaning of the phrase "image and likeness of God" as it applies to humans, one point of unequivocal consensus for more than two thousand years, observes Judaic scholar and historian Jeremy Cohen, is that "of all God's creatures, humans *alone* bear the image of God."[99] Theologian David Cunningham comments, "The biblical text very clearly attributes to human beings at least one description that it does not employ as an attribute of any other element of creation. This is the claim that human beings are created in the image and likeness of God."[100] The image and likeness of God in humans is thus somehow related to human uniqueness, but what exactly is the relationship?

---

96. Ian Tattersall, *The Last Neanderthal: The Rise, Success, and Mysterious Extinction of Our Closest Human Relatives* (Boulder, CO: Westview, 1999), 11.

97. Felipe Fernandez-Armesto, *So You Think You're Human: A Brief History of Humankind* (Oxford: Oxford University Press, 2004), 3–4.

98. Here I follow von Rad's translation speaking of humans "*as* the image of God" rather than "*in* the image of God." See Gerhard von Rad, *Genesis*, trans. J. H. Marks (London: SCM Press: 1961), 56.

99. Jeremy Cohen, "*Be Fertile and Increase: Fill the Earth and Master It*": *Ancient and Medieval Career of a Biblical Text* (Ithaca, NY: Cornell University Press, 1989), 1, emphasis in original.

100. David S. Cunningham, "The Way of All Flesh: Rethinking the *Imago Dei*," in *Creaturely Theology: On God, Humans and Other Animals*, ed. Celia Deane-Drummond and David Clough (London: SCM, 2009): 105. Theologian Oliver Putz likewise says, "Theologians have proposed numerous interpretations of what it means to be created in the image of God, virtually all of which agree on human uniqueness over and against nonhuman animals." Oliver Putz, "Moral Apes, Human Uniqueness, and the Image of God," *Zygon* 44, no. 3 (September 2009): 619; Ruth Page similarly says, "First the actual meaning of 'image of God' has varied so much during Christian history that no single clear reference emerges, and it seems to mean what people want it to mean. Second, the emphasis has made a clear distinction between humans and the rest of creation." Ruth Page, "The Human Genome and the Image of God," in *Brave New World? Theology, Ethics and the Human Genome*, ed. Celia Deane-Drummond (New York: T&T Clark, 2003): 71.

The Image of God in Humans as a Physical Resemblance or Shared Attributes

One ancient Jewish and Christian understanding of how the image of God relates to humans is to interpret the *imago Dei* as a physical resemblance. In other words, explains Bible scholar David Clines, "the phrase 'in our image, according to our likeness' in Genesis 1:26 means that man was created with the same physical form as the deity; of which he is a molded three-dimensional embodiment; delineated and exteriorized."[101] This is the understanding of the divine image within Rabbinic literature,[102] and one can also discern echoes of the physical resemblance interpretation in early church fathers such as Irenaeus of Lyons, who stressed that the whole human person is created as a physical copy of the man Jesus Christ, the true image of God.[103] Clines says that it might even be "suggested that the earliest interpretation of the image in physical terms was by the writer [of Gen 1] himself, when he spoke of Seth's being born according to the image . . . of Adam (5:3)."[104] Indeed, in Genesis 5:3, where Adam produced "a son in his own likeness, after his image," we find the exact same pairing of the terms "image and likeness" as in Genesis 1:26. According to Hebrew scholar James Barr, the point of the designation "image and likeness" in Genesis 5:3, is that Adam's son Seth "looked very much like his father." This offers "a powerful support to the physical interpretation and a serious difficulty for all others."[105] It is clear from this passage, explains Clines, that "it is the physical resemblance of father and son that is in view here, and if the difficult expression in Gen 1:26 is to be interpreted by the comparatively clear reference in 5:3 . . . a strong case for a physical meaning of the image develops."[106]

A second time-honored interpretation holds that it is not so much the entire physical body of humans that resembles God, but perhaps one particular attribute (or several attributes) that both humans and God share in common. This view—called the substantive or structural interpretation—sees the *imago Dei* as synonymous with one central characteristic or several key traits that make

---

101. David J. A. Clines, "The Image of God in Man," *Tyndale Bulletin* 19 (1968): 56.

102. See Alon Gottstein, "The Body as Image of God in Rabbinic Literature," *Harvard Theological Review* 87, no. 2 (April 1994): 171–95.

103. Irenaeus, *Against Heresies* 5.6.1. Irenaeus also says, "But man He fashioned with His own hands, taking of the purest and finest of earth, in measured wise mingling with the earth His own power; for He gave his frame the outline of His own form, that the visible appearance too should be godlike—for it was as an image of God that man was fashioned and set on earth—and that he might come to life, He breathed into his face the breath of life, so that the man became like God in inspiration as well as in frame." Irenaeus, *Proof of the Apostolic Preaching* 11.

104. Clines, "Image of God in Man," 57–58.

105. James Barr, *Biblical Faith and Natural Theology* (New York: Oxford University Press, 1993), 158.

106. Clines, "Image of God in Man," 58.

humans unique among or superior to other created beings. Many interpreters throughout the centuries have viewed the *imago Dei* predominantly in terms of characteristics and properties inherent to human nature and unique to humans. For instance, among early Jewish and Christian thinkers it was common to consider rationality as the one key capacity that humans share with God that sets them apart from the animals. The Jewish philosopher Philo (20 BCE–50 CE), for example, identifies the image of God with the mind or the rational aspect of the human, and the early Christian theologian Athanasius (296–373 CE) likewise proposes, "The divine image consists in the human person being a 'rational soul.'"[107] Augustine (354–430 CE) also advocates a substantive interpretation, writing "there is no doubt that man was made to the image of God that created him, not according to the body, nor according to any part of the soul, but according to the rational mind wherein the knowledge of God can exist."[108]

Other early church fathers considered additional unique features of human nature as the lens through which to interpret the image and likeness of God. For instance, Cyril of Alexandria (378–444 CE) observed that "it is on account of the fact that he is a rational animal, a lover of virtue, and Earth's sovereign that the human person is said to have been made in God's image."[109] Clement of Alexandria (150–215 CE), Ambrose (337–397 CE), Basil of Caesarea (329–379 CE), and Gregory of Nyssa (335–394 CE) all identified human beings' upright posture "as an aspect of the image of God in man."[110] Many early church fathers also suggested other fully embodied features that separate humans from the animals and thus, they reasoned, part of the image of God. These included the faculty of speech (Minucius Felix, 150–270 CE), the use of fire (Lactantius, 240–320 CE), and even the structure of the human hand, which Gregory of Nyssa argued was a necessary precursor for humans to develop the ability to speak and the mental faculty of reason.[111] More recent structural interpretations have focused on human sexuality,[112] metacognition,[113] the capacity for complex

107. Gottstein, "Body as Image of God," 176; Stanley Grenz, *The Social God and the Relational Self: A Trinitarian Theology of the Imago Dei* (Louisville: Westminster John Knox, 2001), 150.

108. Augustine, *On the Trinity* 12.7.12, quoted in Noreen Herzfeld, *In Our Image: Artificial Intelligence and the Human Spirit* (Minneapolis: Fortress, 2002), 16.

109. Quoted in F. Leron Shults, *Reforming Theological Anthropology: After the Philosophical Turn to Relationality* (Grand Rapids: Eerdmans, 2003), 224; original source uncited.

110. C. A. Patrides, "Renaissance Ideas on Man's Upright Form," *Journal of the History of Ideas* 19, no. 2 (April 1958): 257.

111. Matthew R. Goodrum, "Biblical Anthropology and the Idea of Human Prehistory in Late Antiquity," *History and Anthropology* 13, no. 2 (2002): 73.

112. Bible scholar Phyllis Trible explains that the author of Genesis 1, in attributing sexuality solely to humankind, consequently designates "male and female" as pertaining to the image of God. Phyllis Trible, *God and the Rhetoric of Sexuality* (Philadelphia: Fortress, 1978), 15. See also Grenz, *Social God*, 273.

113. Justin Barrett suggests higher order metacognition as the location of the image of God in humans. Barrett, "Evolution of Religious Brains."

language, and symbolic awareness as key characteristics that define the image and likeness of God in humans.[114]

The Image of God in Humans as What Humans Are Called to Do

Another interpretation of the image of God in humans holds that the *imago Dei* is not some capacity or quality that *Homo sapiens* intrinsically possess, but rather, it is a designation related to the vocation of humanity. Bible scholar Gerhard von Rad points out that the meaning of *imago Dei* focuses on the "purpose for which the image is given to humans."[115] The concept of the "image" as used in Genesis, explains Hebrew scholar Randall Garr, has a deep ancient Near Eastern background.[116] One illuminating ancient Near Eastern cognate of the Hebrew word for image (*selem*) is the Akkadian word *salmu*.[117] The Hebrew phrase "image of God" (*selem elohim*) used in Genesis 1:26–27 is the exact counterpart of the Akkadian expression *salam [God's name]* ("image of [Enlil, Marduk, etc.]"), an expression which often appears as an epithet of Mesopotamian kings. As the "image of god," the king in ancient Assyria and Babylonia "was understood to be

---

114. Recently the structural view has been exemplified by J. Wentzel van Huyssteen in his 2004 Gifford Lectures. Van Huyssteen engages in a research project where he explores "scientific notions of human distinctiveness" in order to ground "theological notions of human uniqueness" as they mutually inform the doctrine of the *imago Dei*. Recovering a biological basis underpinning what he holds to be the uniquely human capacities for consciousness, self-awareness and rationality, van Huyssteen "reenvisions" the *imago Dei* "as emerging from nature itself." J. Wentzel van Huyssteen, *Alone In the World?: Human Uniqueness in Science and Theology* (Grand Rapids: Eerdmans, 2006), 113. See also J. Wentzel van Huyssteen, "Human Origins and Religious Awareness," *Studia Theologica—Nordic Journal of Theology* 59, no. 2 (2005): 124. Gregory Peterson and Celia Deane-Drummond have recommended extending the *imago Dei* to nonhuman hominins and to certain cognitively sophisticated animals. Peterson recommends that theologians significantly rethink their understanding of the *imago Dei*. He concludes that they "change the locus of the image of God from human beings to nature" and consider the *imago Dei* within human beings as a smaller part of the much more broadly bestowed divine image. See Gregory Peterson, "The Evolution of Consciousness and the Theology of Nature," *Zygon* 34, no. 2 (June 1999): 299; Gregory Peterson, "Uniqueness, the Image of God and the Problem of Method: Engaging Van Huyssteen," *Zygon* 43, no. 2 (2008): 473. Deane-Drummond points to the recent discovery of *Homo floresiensis* who lived contemporaneously with humans and asks if these findings "undermine the meaning of humans as made in the image of God, *imago Dei*?" In a similar vein as Peterson, Deane-Drummond argues, "There is certainly support for the idea that all animals share in the likeness of the divine nature, even non-rational animals." Celia Deane-Drummond, "Are Animals Moral? Taking Soundings through Vice, Virtue, Conscience and *Imago Dei*," in *Creaturely Theology: On God, Humans and Other Animals*, ed. Celia Deane-Drummond and David Clough (London: SCM Press, 2009), 209. See also Celia Deane-Drummond, *The Wisdom of the Liminal: Evolution and Other Animals in Human Becoming* (Grand Rapids: Eeerdmans, 2014), 304–17.

115. Gerhard von Rad, *Old Testament Theology*, trans. D. M. G. Stalker (Louisville: Westminster John Knox, 2001), 144.

116. W. Randall Garr, *In His Own Image and Likeness: Humanity, Divinity, and Monotheism* (Leiden: Brill, 2003), 136.

117. Ibid., 137.

a special *representative* of the god or gods, possessing a divine mandate to rule, and hence divine authority; but he was not himself divine."[118] In the ancient Near Eastern context, adds Bible scholar Phyllis Bird, the appellation "image of the god" thus served to emphasize the "divinely sanctioned authority and god-like dignity" of the king.[119] Furthermore, says Bird, the Hebrew word *selem*, like the Akkadian *salmu*, is used in other contexts "to designate a statue or picture, a representation (of a god, animal, or other thing) that brings to mind, or stands in for, the thing it depicts or represents."[120] From the ancient linguistic context, Garr discerns that in the mind of the Hebrew author of Genesis 1, "humanity is envisioned to be, and created as, a token of divine presence and participation in the world."[121] In the same way that ancient "powerful earthly kings, to indicate their claims to dominion, erect an image of themselves in the provinces of their empire where they do not personally appear, so humanity is placed upon earth in God's image as God's sovereign emblem."[122] The *imago Dei* in humans is a type of kingly and priestly representative function or purpose that the human species fulfills. The human person and species, explains Old Testament scholar Gerhard von Rad, is "God's representative, summoned to maintain and enforce God's claim to dominion over the earth."[123] As Bible scholar Hans Walter Wolff says, "It is precisely in his *function* as ruler that man is God's image."[124] In this functional understanding of the image of God, the *imago Dei* is revealed not so much in what humans are, as in what humans are called to do.

The Image of God in Humans as Relationship

Other Old Testament scholars have asserted that the function of dominion is not in and of itself the substance of the *imago Dei*, but rather is the *result* of humans being created as the divine image.[125] Because the functional understanding describes what the image of God does rather than is, Westermann questions the comprehensiveness of the functional view and argues that the office of kingship or representation "is concerned with an individual in *relation* to a community."

118. Phyllis A. Bird, "Theological Anthropology in the Hebrew Bible," in *The Blackwell Companion to the Hebrew Bible*, ed. Leo G. Perdue (Malden, MA: Blackwell 2001), 260–61.

119. Ibid.

120. Ibid., 261.

121. W. Randall Garr, "The Nouns דמות and צלם," in *In His Own Image and Likeness: Humanity, Divinity, and Monotheism* (Leiden: Brill, 2003), 117.

122. Von Rad, *Genesis*, 59, 60.

123. Ibid.

124. Hans Walter Wolff, *Anthropology of the Old Testament* (Philadelphia: Fortress, 1974), 160–61; "Most Hebrew scholars came to the view, which is still the consensus, that the primary meaning of the 'image and likeness' language in Genesis refers to a task or function given to humanity." See also Shults, *Reforming Theological Anthropology*, 232.

125. Claus Westermann, *Genesis 1–11: A Continental Commentary*, trans. John J. Scullion (Philadelphia: Fortress, 1984), 153.

In this way, explains Westermann, the divine image and "the uniqueness of human beings, consists in their being God's counterparts. . . . Humans are created in such a way that their very existence is intended to be their relationship to God."[126] This third interpretation of the *imago Dei* (referred to as the *relational view*) points out that the functions of the image appear to be entailed through a certain kind of unique relationship that humans have with God and each other. The functions of stewardship and dominion, then, are the consequences, not the content, of the divine image.[127] In the relational view, the image of God consists first and foremost not within the human *capacity* for relationship but in the *relationship* of the Divine-human encounter. The functional understanding of the human as representative is deficient, says Westermann, because "man" in Genesis 1 "is not an individual, but a species." Yet an unresolved question remains for Westermann as he asks, "What can be meant by saying that 'man' represents, or takes the place of, God on earth? This could only make sense if 'man' (i.e., humankind) were to represent God before the rest of creation."[128]

The Image of God in Humans as God's Election of the Human Race

Since the turn of the twenty-first century, a number of scholars have developed an understanding of the *imago Dei* within the ancient Hebrew theological framework of divine election. As Hebrew scholar Nathan MacDonald observes, "A more convincing and consistent exegesis [and interpretation of Genesis 1:26–27] establishes a link between election and the image."[129] According to this understanding, the *imago Dei* stands for God's historical *election* or choosing of human beings from among the animals and setting them apart as God's representatives for the sake and fulfillment of God's purposes. "There is nothing special about man physically, nor is he distinct in having the breath of life," says MacDonald. "His election is distinct. . . . This alone is the distinguishing feature of humanity."[130]

---

126. Ibid., 158.

127. For example, Karl Barth, reflecting upon the meaning of Gen. 1:27, explains, "Could anything be more obvious than to conclude from this clear indication that the image and likeness of the being created by God signifies existence in confrontation, i.e., in this confrontation, in the juxtaposition and conjunction of man and man which is that of male and female?" In the confrontational I-and-Thou relationship of man and woman described in Gen. 2:7, Barth discerns a mirror unto God's own Trinitarian nature. Karl Barth, *Church Dogmatics*, trans. H. Knight et al. (Edinburgh: T&T Clark, 1960) 3/1.195.

128. Westermann, *Genesis 1–11*, 153.

129. Nathan MacDonald, "The *Imago Dei* and Election: Reading Genesis 1:26–28 and Old Testament Scholarship with Karl Barth," *International Journal of Systematic Theology* 10, no. 3 (July 2008): 303–27.

130. Ibid., 318.

The physical resemblance, substantive, functional, and relational interpretations can all be seen as emerging from—and can be unified through—viewing the "image and likeness of God" as God's choosing or election of the human species as a whole. The relational view emerges because the relationship between God and humans is precisely one of God's sovereign choosing. Within the ancient Near Eastern context in which Genesis 1:26–27 was written, the election of a person or a group of people likewise entails a specific function or vocation that the elected one is to fulfill (that of stewardship, priesthood, and dominion). To properly fulfill that vocation, the elected one must possess certain substantive capacities or preconditions that permit the chosen one to carry out the elected office. One may, in this way, understand characteristics or traits—such as rationality, metacognition, and the capacity for language—as prerequisites necessary for exercising stewardship, priesthood, and dominion.[131] The *imago Dei* as election also includes the physical resemblance interpretation because in the Old Testament election is always in relation to the physical lineage or genealogy of the chosen person or group of people.

When perceived in light of the original linguistic, historical, and cultural context of the Hebrew theological framework of biblical (or historical) election, the image and likeness of God in humans is not essentially recognized by reference to any capacities, qualities, skills, behaviors, or even souls (*nephesh*) that *Homo sapiens* might possess in distinction from animals or other nonhuman creatures. Rather, the *imago Dei* emerges as a designation given through the free historical action of God in his own choosing of *Homo sapiens* and his calling them out from among the multiplicity of life-forms (that he also created "from the dust") to serve as his representatives to creation and to uphold God's justice and orient the creation towards fellowship with him.[132] Election in the biblical understanding relates to a people (and the succeeding lineage) whom God has chosen in the midst of history for a special purpose within the wider context of God's design. This purpose of historical election is furthermore defined not in terms of privilege (or even individual salvation), but rather for the sake of service. For example, says Hebrew scholar Aubrey Johnson, the elected Israelite king is called to be "the guardian of the humble and the needy, the weak and the helpless," and the mission of the divinely elected king is to establish righteousness and justice throughout the land.[133]

Within the Bible, the service of the chosen or elect ones is rendered through their obedience to God's commandments (Gen. 2:16). By obeying

---

131. For a discussion of the necessary prerequisites or preconditions of election as *imago Dei*, see Joshua M. Moritz and Ralph Stearley, "The Elusive Horizon of Behavioral Modernity, the Boundaries of Cultural Humanity, and the Elected Image of God," *Science and Christian Belief* (forthcoming).

132. See Joshua M. Moritz, "Evolution, the End of Human Uniqueness, and the Election of the *Imago Dei*," *Theology and Science* 9, no. 3 (August 2011): 307–39.

133. Johnson, *Sacral Kingship in Ancient Israel*, 10.

God's commandments, the elected live in community or fellowship with God. Likewise, the mission of the elected is to represent God to the non-elect in terms of God's sacredness, authority, and dominion. For instance, with regard to Abraham, the non-elect are "all the families of the earth" (Gen. 12:3) who will be blessed through Abraham and Sarah's election; for Israel, the non-elect are the Gentile nations to whom Israel—as God's elect—is to bear God's light and justice. In this way, explains Bible scholar Jon Levenson, "chosenness" serves a larger purpose in that "the chosen [or elected] people does not withdraw from" the non-elect, "but exercises a special office within it, an office defined by the particular character and will of their universal God."[134]

Each of the structural elements describing biblical election within the Hebrew textual tradition—including divine blessing, the multiplication of progeny, the giving of commandments, and the promise of the land—are also present in the early chapters of Genesis as they describe the first humans who are created as the image and likeness of God (Gen. 1:28 and Gen. 2:15–16). In the same way that Abraham and Sarah are elected by God to be a nation (ethnicity or race) of priests and a light to the other nations (ethnicities or races), Adam and Eve, as the primal human pair, are chosen and called to be a race or species of priests to the nonhuman creatures. Acting as royal vice-regents on God's behalf, humans are the brethren of the nonhuman creatures under their dominion. The election of humans is not a testimony to the superiority of *Homo sapiens* but, rather, a witness to God's sovereign grace and love. As the elected high priests of creation, *Homo sapiens* are called to intercede before God for the sake of the entire created realm with the ultimate aim that all creatures should live in God's presence. Elected by God as God's kingly and priestly representatives, humans are to bear God's image, authority, sacredness, healing, and atoning salvation to the whole nonhuman creation. Consequently, viewing the *imago Dei* in light of biblical election entails that it is not human uniqueness that makes *Homo sapiens* the image of God, but rather, it is the image of God that makes humans unique.

The Destiny of Humanity

Investigating the meaning of Genesis 2, Old Testament scholar John Sailhamer explains, "The first point that the author is intent on making is that the human being, though a special creature made in God's image, was nevertheless a creature like the other creatures which God had made." Akin to the other creatures, "man's origin was from the dust of the ground." Like humanity's origin, says Sailhamer, in Genesis 3:19 "one can also see an anticipation of human destiny . . . when

---

134. Jon D. Levenson, "The Universal Horizon of Biblical Particularism," in *Ethnicity and the Bible*, ed. Mark G. Brett (Leiden: Brill, 2002), 155.

human beings would again return to the 'dust of the ground.'"[135] As humans and animals share a common origin, comments Bible scholar Ludwig Wächter, "humans and animals suffer the same fate: they are made of dust and must return to dust" (Eccl. 3:18–21).[136] Yet, in the Jewish and Christian traditions, dust is not the end of the story. As was discussed in the previous pages, Jews and Christians have long held that redemption is the destiny for both humans *and* animals. But what does the Jewish and Christian theological vision of redemption look like?

Redeeming Disembodied Souls

A common view of life after death, known as *anthropological dualism*, is the idea that when the physical body dies, the immaterial disembodied soul goes to heaven. Philosopher J. P. Moreland points out, "Throughout history, most people have been dualists, at least in the sense that they have taken a human to be the sort of being who could enter life after death while his or her corpse was left behind."[137] Neurobiologist and philosopher Owen Flanagan likewise states, "The belief in a nonphysical soul that comprises an individual's essence, that is not physical, and that survives bodily death is a feature of virtually all of the world's great religions."[138] And cognitive scientists, such as Justin Barrett have shown that belief in souls as distinguishable from bodies is cognitively innate (i.e., foundational to the way humans think) and anthropologically universal (i.e., found in all cultures of the world).[139] Some, such as philosopher Stewart Goetz have contended that "the Christian intellectual tradition, like other religious traditions, has been on the side of ordinary belief with its affirmation of the soul-body distinction."[140] In an effort to bridge traditional religious understandings of the soul with the natural sciences, a number of philosophers, such as Moreland and Scott Rae, have argued that certain human capacities are best explained by the existence of an immaterial soul. These soul-supported features

---

135. John Sailhamer, *The Pentateuch as Narrative: A Biblical-Theological Commentary* (Grand Rapids: Zondervan, 1992), 98.

136. Ludwig Wächter, "רפע apar, dust," in *Theological Dictionary of the Old Testament*, ed. Johannes Botterweck, Helmer Ringgren, and Heinz-Josef Fabry (Grand Rapids: Eerdmans 2001), 11.264.

137. J. P. Moreland, "Restoring the Soul to Christianity," *Christian Research Journal* 23, no. 1 (2000): 1.

138. *The Problem of the Soul: Two Visions of Mind and How to Reconcile Them* (New York: Basic Books, 2002), 168.

139. Justin Barrett, "Toward a Cognitive Science of Christianity," in *The Blackwell Companion to Science and Christianity*, ed. J. B. Stump and Alan G. Padgett (Malden, MA: Blackwell, 2012), 322.

140. Stewart Goetz, "Substance Dualism," in *In Search of the Soul: Four Views Of the Mind-Body Problem*, ed. Joel Green and Stuart Palmer (Downers Grove, IL: InterVarsity, 2005), 34. See also John W. Cooper, *Body, Soul, and Life Everlasting: Biblical Anthropology and the Monism-Dualism Debate* (Grand Rapids: Eerdmans, 1989). For a discussion and critique of Cooper's position see Nancey Murphy, *Bodies and Souls, or Spirited Bodies?* (Cambridge: Cambridge University Press, 2006), 20.

of human behavior include agency and freedom, consciousness and mentality, and the nature of personal identity.[141]

While "ordinary people" may still embrace various forms of metaphysical dualism where the mind or soul is seen as separate from the body,[142] there are very few dualists among contemporary neuroscientists. This is because the evidence from neuroscience has overwhelmingly demonstrated that the "mind" is intrinsically connected to the operations and processes of the physical brain. Numerous studies of neurological disorders, brain damage, and neuronal degeneration have shown that physical conditions can radically and permanently alter a person's degree of concern for others, patterns of dress, use of reason and common sense, political ideology, feelings of empathy, emotional dispositions, and intensity of religious devotion.[143] As neuropsychologist Malcolm Jeeves explains, research has established that if an individual undergoes "changes in the neural substrate, we may observe changes in personality and in emotion."[144] Decades of research in the cognitive neurosciences have similarly established embodied neurological foundations for mental abilities, agency, and freedom,[145] which were traditionally associated with the disembodied soul.[146] Even the "spiritual abilities" of prayer, mediation, religious belief, and mystical experience are vitally dependent on fundamental neural substrates.[147] Because the properly functioning brain is so acutely coupled to the properly functioning human self, philosopher of mind E. J. Lowe comments that "at present, physicalism is the dominant view in the philosophy of mind, with dualists of all kinds being very much in the minority and interactionist substance dualists especially rare."[148] Both scientists

---

141. J. P. Moreland and Scott B. Rae, *Body and Soul: Human Nature and the Crisis in Ethics* (Downers Grove, IL: InterVarsity, 2000), 122. See also J. P. Moreland, *Consciousness and the Existence of God: A Theistic Argument* (New York: Routledge, 2008).

142. Goetz, "Substance Dualism," 34.

143. George Lakoff, "How to Live With an Embodied Mind: When Causation, Mathematics, Morality, the Soul, and God Are Essentially Metaphorical Ideas," in *The Nature and Limits of Human Understanding*, ed. Anthony J. Sandford (London: T&T Clark, 2003).

144. Malcolm Jeeves, "Human Nature without a Soul?" *European Review* 12, no. 1 (2003): 52.

145. Jeffrey D. Schall, "Neural Basis of Deciding, Choosing and Acting," *Nature Reviews Neuroscience* 2, no. 1 (January 2001): 33–42.

146. See Philip Clayton, "Neuroscience, the Person and God: An Emergentist Account," *Zygon* 35, no. 3 (September 2000): 615–18.

147. Dimitrios Kapogiannisa et al., "Cognitive and Neural Foundations of Religious Belief," *Proceedings of the National Academy of Sciences* 106, no. 12 (March 24, 2009): 4876–81; Justin L. Barrett, "Exploring the Natural Foundations of Religion," *Trends in Cognitive Sciences* 4, no. 1 (2000): 29–34; Mario Beauregarda and V. Paquette, "Neural Correlates of a Mystical Experience in Carmelite Nuns," *Neuroscience Letters* 405, no. 3 (September 25, 2006): 186–90; Uffe Schjoedt et al., "Highly Religious Participants Recruit Areas of Social Cognition in Personal Prayer," *Social Cognitive and Affective Neuroscience* 4, no. 2 (June 1, 2009): 199–207; and Andrew Newberg and Eugene d'Aquili, *The Mystical Mind: Probing the Biology of Religious Experience* (Minneapolis: Fortress, 1999).

148. E. J. Lowe, "Dualism (Property Dualism, Substance Dualism)," in *Encyclopedia of Neuroscience*, ed. Marc D. Binder, Nobutaka Hirokawa, and Uwe Windhorst (Berlin: Springer, 2009), 1020.

and professional philosophers, says psychologist Susan Blackmore, "have consistently argued that dualism cannot be made to work, and indeed there are almost no dualist philosophers today."[149]

The Physical Resurrection of the Body

The majority of biblical scholars today agree with the consensus of scientists and philosophers that the human person is essentially an integrated unity of mind and body (known as a *psychosomatic unity*) rather than a dualist dichotomy of physical body and immaterial soul. They point out that the understanding of the human person as a unity or a whole is characteristic of the entire biblical witness. According to Levenson, the ancient Hebrew anthropology holds that "the human being is not an amalgam of perishable body and immortal soul, but a psychophysical unity who depends on God for life itself."[150] For instance, explains Westermann, in Genesis 2:7 the phrase "'And man became a living being' . . . is very important for the biblical understanding of humanity." Here, he says, "a person is created as a נפש חיה [*nephesh* or living soul]; *a 'living soul' is not put into one's body*. The person as a living being is to be understood as a *whole* and any idea that one is made up of body *and* soul is ruled out."[151] Both Early Jews and Early Christians, explains New Testament scholar N. T. Wright, retained this ancient Hebrew concept of the human person as psychosomatic unity and rejected metaphysical dualism in favor of a "more integrated anthropology."[152] Both the Apostle Paul, as "a Hebrew of Hebrews," and the other authors of the New Testament continued to uphold this monistic or wholistic view of anthropology.[153]

The New Testament understanding of the essential psychosomatic unity of the human person can be discerned in a key passage related to the destiny of the human person. Here the Apostle Paul is addressing the question "How are the dead raised? With what kind of body [*sōma*] will they come?" After a

---

149. Susan Blackmore, "Imitation Makes Us Human," in *What Makes Us Human?*, ed. Charles Pasternak (Oxford: Oneworld, 2007), 14.

150. Jon D. Levenson, "Genesis: Introduction and Annotations," in *The Jewish Study Bible: Jewish Publication Society Tanakh Translation*, ed. Adele Berlin, Marc Zvi Brettler, and Michael A. Fishbane (New York: Oxford University Press, 2004), 15.

151. Westermann, *Genesis 1-11*, 207, emphasis added. Similarly W. E. Vine, Merrill Unger, and William White conclude, "The Hebrew system of thought does not include the combination or opposition of the terms 'body' and 'soul.'" Vine, Unger, and White, "Soul," in *Vine's Complete Expository Dictionary* (Nashville: Thomas Nelson, 1984), 238. See Anthony A. Hoekema, *Created in God's Image* (Grand Rapids: Eerdmans, 1986), 212. See also Wolfhart Pannenberg, *Anthropology in Theological Perspective*, trans. Matthew J. O'Connell (Edinburgh: T&T Clark, 1999), 523.

152. N. T. Wright, *The New Testament and the People of God: Christian Origins and the Question of God* (Minneapolis: Fortress, 1992), 255.

153. John A. T. Robinson quoted in Joel B. Green, *Body, Soul and Human Life: The Nature of Humanity in the Bible* (Grand Rapids: Baker Academic, 2008), 6.

brief discussion of the different types of bodies and their constituent materials, he explains:

> So it is with the resurrection of the dead. What is sown perishable is raised imperishable. It is sown in dishonor; it is raised in glory. It is sown in weakness; it is raised in power. It is sown a soulish body [*sōma psychikon*]; it is raised a spiritual body [*sōma pneumatikon*]. If there is a soulish body [*sōma psychikon*], there is also a spiritual body [*sōma pneumatikon*]. So it is written: "The first man Adam became a living soul"; the last Adam, a life-giving spirit. (1 Cor. 15:42–45)

Instead of the contrast here being between the physical-material and spiritual-immaterial, Paul is juxtaposing the ensouled and yet material body (*sōma*) of this present life with the resurrected and yet material body (*sōma*) of the future that is enlivened by the Spirit of God. This is evident from the fact that Paul refers to the body of the resurrected Jesus—the last Adam—as a "life-giving spirit." The Gospels clearly claim that Jesus was *physically* raised from the dead, and from the historical context it is known that any notion of a *nonphysical* resurrection would have been unthinkable to the first century Jewish contemporaries of Paul.[154] Paul sets up a series of antitheses that compare the bodies humans have in this life to the bodies they will have in the resurrection life. As theologian Alan Padgett explains, "Our mortal bodies are corruptible, dishonorable (especially as a dead corpse), weak, and 'soulish' or physical. Our resurrection bodies will be glorious, powerful, 'spiritual,' and incorruptible (ἀφθαρσία), the same word Aristotle used for the [physical substance of the eternal] heavens."[155] As Adam was made from earthly material (dust), so the body of the resurrected Christ—"the final Adam"—is composed of celestial material. Because Christ is the first fruits of the resurrection from the dead, those who follow him will be raised in the same manner.

The biblical view of the human person is inextricably intertwined with the biblical view of human destiny. In both the Bible and the Christian theological tradition that immediately followed, the true Christian hope for human destiny lies not in the immortality of the soul or in a merely spiritually resurrected body without flesh and blood, but rather, as Augustine says, in the confidence human beings will, "in the resurrection, inhabit those very bodies in which they here toiled." The "same material components of which the present body is made," says Augustine, will be "reshaped into its most perfect possible form."[156] Every organ of the physical body will be transformed, glorified, and renewed as

---

154. For the physical nature of the resurrected Jesus in the Gospels, see Matt. 28:9; Luke 24:39, 42–43; and John 20:25, 27. For a discussion of first-century Jewish understandings of the resurrection of the dead, see N. T. Wright, *The Resurrection of the Son of God* (Minneapolis: Fortress, 2003).

155. Alan G. Padgett, "The Body in Resurrection: Science and Scripture on the 'Spiritual Body' (1 Cor 15:35–58," *Word & World* 22:2 (Spring 2002): 160.

156. Augustine, *Enchiridion on Faith, Hope, and Love* 23.87–90; Augustine, *Retractions* 1.16.2.

incorruptible.[157] For both Augustine and other early Christians, "the goal of life is not to escape from the body, but that the body as well as the soul should be saved from corruption and pass from sickness to health."[158] The key concept in the Christian idea of human redemption and destiny as physical resurrection, says Wright, is transformation. God "will transform our present humble bodies to be like [the] glorious body" of the resurrected Jesus.[159]

Conclusion

One of the central biblical teachings about human beings, says Gerhard von Rad, "is that man is dust and ashes before God."[160] Science agrees insofar as it understands that the species *Homo sapiens* in its essential physical nature is nothing materially mysterious or biologically baffling. Both science and Scripture also concur that humans are akin to the animals not only on the level of their physical existence but also in terms of possessing a spiritual dimension and a need for redemption. Yet, unlike the animals, humans are designated as the image and likeness of God. This chapter has explored several ways to understand the content and function of the *imago Dei* offered throughout the centuries. Related to the issues of human origins and vocation is the question of human destiny. This chapter examined both anthropological dualism and the view that the human person is a psychosomatic unity. While dualism is a common view among religious practitioners, it seems that the concept of an immaterial immortal human soul that absolutely distinguishes humans from animals lacks solid biblical support. Instead of perceiving a sharp divide between humans and animals in terms of origins, natures, or destinies, the Bible and the Christian theological tradition affirm that humans and animals have, in common, the source from whence they came and the hope of where they are going.

Discussion Questions

1. Reflect on your own experience with animals. Have you even been surprised by any humanlike qualities or actions of animals? Please explain your answer.
2. Do you think other humanoid species such as Neanderthals possessed the "image and likeness of God" according to the biblical meaning of that phrase? Why or why not?

---

157. "He, then, who created both sexes will restore both." Augustine, *City of God* 22.17.

158. W. Christian, "Augustine on the Creation of the World," *Harvard Theological Review* 46 (1953): 20.

159. N. T. Wright, *Surprised by Hope: Rethinking Heaven, the Resurrection, and the Mission of the Church* (New York: HarperOne, 2008), 100.

160. Gerhard von Rad, "Divine Likeness in the Old Testament," in *Theological Dictionary of the New Testament* (Grand Rapids: Eerdmans, 1991), 2:390.

3. Do you agree with the argument that since the activities of the mind depend on the brain there is no need to posit an *additional* immaterial soul to account for reason, personality, emotion, free will, or consciousness? What role did Ockham's Razor (the principle that the simplest explanation for a given phenomenon is most likely true) play in your thinking?

4. What do you think would be necessary in order for you to still be "you" after death—either by "surviving" death or by being bodily resurrected? Explain your answer.

5. Which hope for an afterlife—disembodied soul or resurrection of the body— do you think would offer you the most comfort in the face of death? Why?

Beyond the Classroom

With a group of friends, discuss the following question: Do you agree with the claim that eternal life would end up being boring and pointless? Why or why not? What kinds of activities might keep it forever interesting and meaningful?

Resources for Further Study

Books

Fernandez-Armesto, Felipe. *So You Think You're Human: A Brief History of Humankind.* Oxford: Oxford University Press, 2004.

Jeeves, Malcolm. *Human Nature: Reflections on the Integration of Psychology and Christianity.* Philadelphia: Templeton Foundation Press, 2006.

Jeeves, Malcolm, ed. *Rethinking Human Nature: A Multidisciplinary Approach.* Grand Rapids: Eerdmans, 2011.

Middleton, J. Richard. *The Liberating Image: The* Imago Dei *in Genesis 1.* Grand Rapids: Brazos, 2005.

Articles

Barrett, Justin. "Toward a Cognitive Science of Christianity." In *The Blackwell Companion to Science and Christianity*, edited by J. B. Stump and Alan G. Padgett, 319–34. Malden, MA: Blackwell, 2012.

Berry, R. J., and Malcolm Jeeves. "The Nature of Human Nature." *Science and Christian Belief* 20, no. 1 (2008): 3–47.

Hasker, William. "The Emergence of Persons." In *The Blackwell Companion to Science and Christianity*, edited by J. B. Stump and Alan G. Padgett, 480–90. Malden, MA: Blackwell, 2012.

Haught, John. "Christianity and Human Evolution." In *The Blackwell Companion to Science and Christianity*, edited by J. B. Stump and Alan G. Padgett, 295–305. Malden, MA: Blackwell, 2012.

Jeeves, Malcolm. "Neuroscience, Evolutionary Psychology, and the Image of God." *Perspectives on Science and Christian Faith* 57, no. 3 (2005): 170–86.

Moritz, Joshua M. "Evolution, the End of Human Uniqueness, and the Election of the *Imago Dei*." *Theology and Science* 9, no. 3 (August 2011): 307–39.

Internet Resources

"How Could Humans Have Evolved and Still Be Created in the 'Image of God'?" Accessible at *http://biologos.org/questions/image-of-god*.

Moritz, Joshua. "Chosen by God: What the Image and Likeness of God (*Imago Dei*) IS NOT." BioLogos Forum website, June 2012. Accessible at *http://biologos .org/blog/chosen-by-god-part-1*.

Moritz, Joshua. "'Let Us Make Man in Our Own Image': What Does It Mean to Be Human?" Voice of Light Productions. Accessible at *http://vimeo .com/41244016* (time: 01:01:40).

Wall-Scheffler, Cara. "How Did Humans Evolve?" The Faraday Institute for Science and Religion. Accessible at *https://www.faraday.st-edmunds.cam.ac.uk /Multimedia.php?Mode=Add&ItemID=478* (time: 01:28:15).

Wright, N. T. "On What It Means to Be an Image Bearer." BioLogos Forum website, June 16, 2012. Accessible at *https://www.youtube.com/watch?v=yp-Ku-_ ekAY* (time: 00:03:10).

CHAPTER 8

Miracles and the Laws of Nature

Miracles are so called not because they are the works of God but because they happen seldom and for that reason create wonder. If they should happen constantly according to certain laws impressed upon the nature of things, they would be no longer wonders or miracles but would be considered in philosophy as part of the phenomena of nature, notwithstanding that the cause of their causes might be unknown to us.

—*Isaac Newton*[1]

A "miracle" is an exception from lawfulness; hence, there where lawfulness does not exist, also its exception, i.e., a miracle, cannot exist.

—*Albert Einstein*[2]

In This Chapter

* What Is a Miracle?
* Does Science Prove That Miracles Are Physically Impossible?
* The Scientific Possibility of Miracles
* Discussion Questions
* Beyond the Classroom
* Resources for Further Study

The question of miracles is frequently posed as an issue that fundamentally divides science and religion. A common understanding of miracles, held by both religious believers and unbelievers alike, is that a miracle is an event that cannot

1. Quoted in Peter Harrison, "Newtonian Science, Miracles, and the Laws of Nature," *Journal of the History of Ideas* 56, no. 4 (October 1995): 531–53, at 539; original source uncited.

2. "*Dort, wo eine Gesetzmässigkeit nicht vorhanden ist, kann auch ihre Ausnahme, d.h. ein Wunder, nicht existieren.*" Quoted in D. Reichinstein, *Die Religion der Gebildeten* (Zurich: Verlag Aristoteles, 1941), 21. Cited in Max Jammer, *Einstein and Religion: Physics and Theology* (Princeton: Princeton University Press, 1999), 89.

be explained by science. If science can explain the causes behind a purported miraculous occurrence, then, many would say, it is not a true miracle. As leading young Earth creationist Henry Morris holds, "Miracles are *scientifically* impossible."[3] Or as John Maddox, editor of the journal *Nature*, writes, "Miracles, which are inexplicable and irreproducible phenomena, do not occur," because the definition of the concept excludes their possibility.[4] If a miracle is a scientifically impossible event, as Morris and Maddox state, it is not surprising that many scientists doubt that such events ever happened in the past or occur in the present. This was not how miracles were always regarded, however, nor is it how miracles are viewed in many contemporary religious traditions.

Within the major world religious traditions, there are many different ways miracles are understood. Western theistic conceptions of miracles are not easily adapted to beliefs about wondrous events found in the religious traditions of Hinduism and Buddhism. Part of the reason for this is because each of the various world religions has had a distinct history of interaction with the natural sciences. Certain key concepts in science, which became central in determining the meaning of miracles in Western theism, such as the idea that there are laws of nature, played no role in how the Eastern religions of Buddhism and Hinduism understood extraordinary "supernatural" occurrences. As Eastern religious scholar Gavin Flood observes, "The concept of miracle [in the West] entails the concept of a law of nature. Transplanting this definition into India, it is not clear that Indian religions [such as Buddhism and Hinduism] developed any concept directly akin to this."[5] In a similar way, says Buddhist scholar Rupert Gethin, "the Buddhist notion of 'miracle' (*pratiharya*) does not conform to this understanding."[6]

A number of specific questions about miracles emerge from a theistic religious context. How can believers in one creator God conceive of this God as being active in answering prayer? Are there any limits to the extent to which God can respond by acting in the physical world? What challenges does scientific knowledge raise for how one thinks of God performing miracles in the world, and how can God's action be understood in light of the laws of nature? This chapter explores these questions concerning miracles, with a particular focus on the Western theological and scientific traditions.

Perceptions of miracles and conceptions of the laws of nature have changed throughout the ages. While the Jewish and Christian Bible and the Christian theological tradition through the Middle Ages discerned no sharp divide

---

3. Henry Morris, *Miracles: Do They Still Happen? Why We Believe in Them* (Green Forest, AR: Master Books, 2003), 55, emphasis added. Morris nevertheless firmly believes that miracles have happened.

4. John Maddox, "Miracles Do Not Happen," *Nature* 310 (July 19, 1984): 171.

5. Gavin Flood, "Miracles in Hinduism," in *The Cambridge Companion to Miracles*, ed. Graham H. Twelftree (Cambridge: Cambridge University Press, 2011), 184.

6. Rupert Gethin, "Miracles in Buddhism," in *The Cambridge Companion to Miracles*, ed. Graham H. Twelftree (Cambridge: Cambridge University Press, 2011), 217.

between the natural and the supernatural, during the European Enlightenment many thinkers began to view miracles as violations of the laws of nature and thus came to question both the possibility of miracles and the credibility of any accounts claiming miraculous events had occurred. More recently, however, it has been shown that the Enlightenment concept of physical law is no longer scientifically valid. Consequently, arguments based on Enlightenment assumptions about natural law that reject the possibility of miracles are no longer sound. Beyond this, recent discoveries in quantum physics have raised new possibilities for how God's interaction with the world of nature can be understood.

What Is a Miracle?

In the theistic traditions of the West, the term *miracle*, often referred to as God's special providence, has taken on a number of meanings throughout the ages. A central dimension of all Western understanding of miracles has been how the various definitions relate to the concept of laws of nature. Since the idea that laws govern nature was originally a theological concept developed within the Jewish Scriptures, it is not surprising that the Hebrew Bible perceives no fundamental dichotomy between miracles and natural laws. Since God was the sovereign author of both, there could be no contradiction between the two. The biblical understanding of how miracles interact with the laws of nature continued to predominate in the West through the Middle Ages and into the early Modern period.

The Biblical Understanding of Miracles

While today it is commonly believed that miracles are supernatural events ruled out by the laws of nature, according to theologian Wolfhart Pannenberg, "this was not the meaning of the concept of miracle in Christian theology" or the Bible.[7] As theologian Alan Padgett explains, "The concept of 'miracle' in the Hebrew Bible and New Testament does not imply something beyond the capacity of nature to bring about."[8] Instead of viewing miracles as instances that are contrary to nature, says Pannenberg, "in the biblical writings, the word miracle refers to extraordinary events that function as 'signs' of God's sovereign power."[9] In the Old Testament, terms that are sometimes translated as "miracle" would be more accurately conveyed by the words "sign" (*oth*) or "wonder" (*mopheth*)—often paired together as "signs and wonders" (see Dan. 6:27). In the same way, the New Testament uses the Greek words "sign" (*sēmeion*) and "wonder" (*teras*) to speak of events that point to God's purposes and power (*dynamis*).

---

7. Wolfhart Pannenberg, "The Concept of Miracle," *Zygon* 37 (2002): 759–62, at 760.

8. Alan Padgett, "God and Miracle in an Age of Science," in *The Blackwell Companion to Science and Christianity*, ed. J. B. Stump and Alan G. Padgett (Malden, MA: Blackwell, 2012), 533.

9. Pannenberg, "Concept of Miracle," 760.

Within Scripture, there are a number of events labeled as a sign or a wonder, which do not entail extraordinary causes beyond the ordinary course of nature. For instance, the rainbow was given as a sign (*oth*) of God's covenant with Noah, and every living creature (Gen. 9:12–13) and circumcision was given as a sign (*oth*) of God's covenant with Abraham (Gen. 17:11). The prophet Isaiah walked three years naked through Jerusalem as a "sign and wonder," symbolically anticipating the troubles God would bring upon Egypt and Ethiopia (Isa. 20:3). The baby Jesus lying in a manger is a sign (*sēmeion*) for the shepherds (Luke 2:12). Other signs and wonders in Scripture, however, do appear to have causes that dramatically depart from the normal order of things. For example, the "signs and wonders" (Exod. 7:3) surrounding the Exodus of the Hebrew slaves from Egypt—such as the parting of the Red Sea—and the "sign" of Jesus turning water into wine (John 2:11) are events that seem to go beyond what nature can accomplish on its own powers.

How do special instances of God's objective actions within the physical world interact with the laws of nature? Here, it is important to remember (as discussed in chapter 2) that, in the biblical worldview, "nature" is always regarded as a creature of God and not as an independent entity standing over and against God's purposes. As Bible scholar Howard Clark Kee explains, in the Bible "there is no such thing as 'nature,' in the sense of a force, immanent in the world, by which its function is empowered and guided. Rather, the universe was created by God, is sustained by God, and its destiny is determined by God's will. His will is not perceived as a blueprint, which, once it has been drawn up, cannot be deviated from."[10] To see God as constrained by the regularity of the laws of nature is to ignore God's role as the creator of these laws in the first place. In the biblical view, it is the laws of nature that are constrained by the will of God through nature's obedience to God's word. The order and regularity of nature is a manifestation of nature's obedience to God's command, since, says Kee, "the will of God is not capricious, but orderly." Because the regular course of nature is an exemplification of the laws of the one creator God, "the writer of Genesis (8:22) is confident that the world will continue its pattern of daily, seasonal and vegetal cycles."[11] Thus, explains theologian Christopher Kaiser, "rather than viewing the acts of God and natural processes as mutually exclusive, a consistently biblical theology would view the laws of nature as an expression of God's activity in the world."[12] Nature is God's creature, and, says Kaiser, "the operations of God's

---

10. Howard Clark Kee, "The Biblical Understanding of Miracle," *Christian Scholar* 39, no. 1 (March 1956): 50.

11. Ibid. See Job 38:33; Ps. 148:1–12; Prov. 8:29; Jer. 31:35–36, 33:20–21. See also Christopher Kaiser, *Creation and the History of Science* (Grand Rapids: Eerdmans, 1991), 15–16.

12. Christopher Kaiser, "The Laws of Nature and the Nature of God," in *Facets of Faith and Science*, vol. 4, *Interpreting God's Action in the World* (Lanham, MD: University Press of America, 1996), 190.

creatures, even the most regular and predictable ones, are portrayed as the direct expression of God's word and ordinance."[13]

If the laws of nature are a deep expression of the will of God for the cosmos, then where do miracles fit into the picture? It would seem that an understanding of a miracle as a supernatural intervention is not an option here. As Kee says, "The biblical view of the relation of God to the world has no place . . . for miracle as a violation of natural law." In the Bible's understanding, says Kaiser, "whatever takes place in creation as the result of God-given laws *is* the work of God." Therefore it would make no theological sense for certain acts of God (miracles) to contravene other acts of God (the laws of nature).[14] In the biblical view, both miracles and the laws of nature have the same ultimate source and goal—to accomplish the will of God for creation. While the laws of nature realize God's purposes in *cosmic* history, miracles (sometimes referred to as special divine action) bring about God's purposes in *redemptive* history. Yet, observes Kee, "the events that constitute redemptive history are not in another sphere from the events of world history." Miracles, says Kee, are "simply one facet of God's action in history, of a purpose which began with the creation and will end with the completion of the work of redemption, through which the whole of God's creation will be subjected to His will."[15] In the biblical understanding, observes Padgett, "the greatness of a miracle . . . has to do with its importance for salvation . . . *not* how far it exceeds the capacity of natural things to bring it about."[16]

Miracles in the Early Church

Early Christians continued to affirm the biblical understanding of miracles as actions of God given as signs pointing to God's redemptive purposes. For early Christians, the God of nature and the God of miracles was the same. Agreeing with Athanasius (296–273 CE), early Christians held that "natural law itself could be interpreted as a manifestation of direct divine action" and that "the facts of nature are the acts of God."[17] Augustine (354–430 CE) was the first Christian thinker to attempt a formal definition of the term *miracle*. Writing that a miracle is "anything which appears unusual, beyond the expectation or ability of the one who marvels at it," Augustine explicitly emphasized that such events "do

---

13. Ibid., 191.

14. Ibid.

15. Kee, "Biblical Understanding of Miracle," 55.

16. Padgett, "God and Miracle in an Age of Science," 534.

17. Richard England, "Natural Selection, Teleology, and the Logos: From Darwin to the Oxford Neo-Darwinists, 1859–1909," in *Science in Theistic Contexts: Cognitive Dimensions*, ed. John Hedley Brooke, Margaret J. Osler, and Jitse van der Meer (Chicago: University of Chicago Press, 2001), 280, original source uncited.

not occur contrary to the nature of things."[18] While miraculous occurrences do not contravene the natural order of things, they may, says Augustine, still *appear* contrary to nature due to "our limited *knowledge* of the 'course of nature.'"[19] In Augustine's view, says historian of science and religion Peter Harrison, "there was no intrinsic difference between the miraculous and the mundane—miracles were distinguished only by their *effect* on observers."[20] Augustine maintains that if one were to know everything about the causes in nature, then the concept of miracles would itself disappear.[21] From God's point of view, says Augustine, there is no difference between miracles and the laws of nature since "God is the Creator of the nature of things as well as of the events that appear unusual to us."[22]

Like Augustine, Basil of Caesarea (329–379 CE) did not perceive miracles as contrary to the laws of nature since both are expressions of the will of the same God. For him, explains Kaiser, "the idea of laws of nature in no way detracted from the sense of the providence of God . . . in the world."[23] According to Basil, writes theologian Doru Costache, "the mode of God's activity in the world is not episodic but continuous; it does not suspend the laws of nature but is an essential part of them."[24] For Basil, God acts in, with, and through nature as one who has perfect knowledge of nature's laws. The Creator "is permanently at work within and through the natural possibilities of a universe that ultimately remains open to, and dependent on, him." While nature has been given a certain degree of autonomy and exists as a created reality outside of God, it is "by no means *separated* from its creator."[25] While Basil views the laws of nature as permanent, explains Kaiser, he does not view them as compulsory. "The laws of creation are at all times contingent on the will of God."[26]

Miracles in Medieval Christian Theology

After the turn of the first millennium, observes medieval historian Edward Grant, philosophers and theologians such as Adelard of Bath (1080–1152) and

---

18. Augustine, *City of God* 21.8; *Contra Faustum* 26.3.

19. Augustine, *City of God* 21.8.3; quoted in Pannenberg, "Concept of Miracle," 760.

20. Harrison, "Newtonian Science, Miracles," 533.

21. G. C. Berkouwer, *The Providence of God* (Grand Rapids: Eerdmans, 1952), 198.

22. Augustine, *De Genesi ad Litteram* 6.13.24. See also Pannenberg, "Concept of Miracle," 760.

23. Christopher B. Kaiser, *Toward a Theology of Scientific Endeavor: The Descent of Science* (Burlington, VT: Ashgate, 2007), 49.

24. Doru Costache, "Christian Worldview: Understandings from St. Basil the Great," *Phronema* 25 (2010): 41.

25. Ibid., 42.

26. Kaiser, *Toward a Theology of Scientific Endeavor*, 51. See also Robert M. Grant, *Miracle and Natural Law in Graeco-Roman and Early Christian Thought* (Amsterdam: North Holland Publishing, 1952), 26–28.

William of Conches (1090–1154) agreed with the early church fathers in that they "firmly believed that God had created a rational universe that operated in a lawful manner."[27] Both miraculous events and the regular laws of nature were seen as reflections of the direct activity of God. As twelfth-century theologian Gilbert de La Porree (1070–1154) explains, "All things have been made by God as their author, but certain things are called God's work just as they are, namely those that he makes by himself. . . . Others are called works of nature and they are created by God after some natural resemblance, as a seed from other seeds, a horse from other horses and similar things from similar things."[28] According to these medieval thinkers, one does not "by investigating natural causes . . . threaten God's omnipotence in any way." God is always free to perform a miracle that has unknown or even unknowable immediate causes. However, one cannot know that the causes of an event are unknowable until one comes to understand everything that there is to understand about causes that can be known. A miracle—as an event that appears contrary to the normal course of nature—cannot be recognized as such until one understands the causes that emerge from God's activity in the regular laws of nature.

For instance, when Adelard's nephew remarks, "the spontaneous appearance of life in a dish of soil was miraculous," Adelard responds by drawing a firm distinction between the actions of the Creator which have unknowable causes and the work of the Creator through nature of which the causes can be known. "It is the will of the Creator," says Adelard, "that herbs should sprout from the earth. But the same is not without a reason either . . . for whatever exists, is from Him and because of Him. But the natural order does not exist confusedly and without rational arrangement, nor is it lacking in disposition which, so far as human knowledge can go, should be consulted."[29] In other words, Adelard maintains, one should persist in seeking an explanation in terms of "natural causes," before attributing what one does not understand to the miraculous action of God. In seeking out the natural causes, explains Adelard, one "takes nothing away from God." When, however, an explanation according to God's action in knowable natural causes cannot be found and "*where human knowledge completely fails*, then the matter should be referred to God."[30]

---

27. Edward Grant, *Science and Religion, 400 B.C. to A.D. 1550: From Aristotle to Copernicus* (Baltimore: John Hopkins University Press, 2006), 163.

28. Gilbert De La Porree, quoted in James Hannam, *The Genesis of Science: How the Christian Middle Ages Launched the Scientific Revolution* (Washington, DC : Regnery, 2011), 57; original source uncited.

29. Quoted in Peter Hodgson, "The Church and Science: A Changing Relationship," *Heythrop Journal* 49, no. 4 (July 2008): 632–47; original source uncited.

30. Adelard, *Natural Questions* 4, emphasis in original; quoted in Christopher B. Kaiser, "Early Christian Belief in Creation and the Beliefs Sustaining the Modern Scientific Endeavor," in *The Blackwell Companion to Science and Christianity*, ed. J. B. Stump and Alan G. Padgett (Malden, MA: Blackwell, 2012), 10.

William agreed that one should not too quickly resort to miraculous explanations before endeavoring to understand God's regular actions through natural causes. He suggested that when one considers the reasons behind an event, he or she must look at both the primary and secondary causes. According to William, writes medieval historian James Hannam, "the primary cause, the ultimate reason why anything happens, is God. His omnipotence is such that he is the ultimate reality that underlies everything else. Nothing happens that is contrary to his will."[31] However, says William, the natural philosopher "can also ask in *what way* God has attained his aims. This is the secondary cause of an event. Nature obeys the laws that God ordained when he created the world. These 'natural laws' are the secondary causes that God usually uses." Consequently, the natural philosopher—later known as a scientist—can, for all intents and purposes, "ignore the possibility of miracles in his research even while admitting that they occasionally happen."[32]

Theologian and philosopher Thomas Aquinas (1225–1274) seeks to locate the essence of a miracle in the event itself rather than in the experience of the observer. Though he agrees with Augustine and others that miracles are not contrary to nature in any absolute sense, Aquinas nonetheless maintains that a miracle is "apart from the order implanted in things."[33] A miracle, for Aquinas, is an event where "we observe the effect but do not know its cause."[34] Miracles produce wonder precisely because their causes cannot be explained through the natural properties of objects. For something to be a genuine miracle, though, it is not enough for the causes to be hidden from just some individuals. A true miracle, explains Aquinas, must be an occurrence that has "a completely hidden cause in an unqualified way . . . not simply in relation to one person or another; it must have a cause hidden from *every man*." Moreover, predictable or repeatable events that have natural causes, even though the causes remain unknown, are not miraculous. Thus, says Aquinas, "when something is called a miracle, it means an occurrence beyond the order of all created nature. No one but God can do this; because whatever an angel or any other creature does by its own power is still within the order of created nature and therefore not a miracle."[35]

31. Hannam, *Genesis of Science*, 56.

32. Ibid., 57; original source uncited.

33. Aquinas, quoted in Harrison, "Newtonian Science, Miracles," 533; original source uncited.

34. Ibid.

35. Thomas Aquinas, *Summa Theoligica* I.110.4; quoted in J. A. Hardon, "The Concept of Miracle from St. Augustine to Modern Apologetics," *Theological Studies* 15, no. 2 (May 1954): 229–57, at 233.

Does Science Prove That Miracles Are Physically Impossible?

The biblical and medieval understanding of miracles prevailed during the rise of the natural sciences in the early modern period. During the European Enlightenment in the 1700s, however, as the laws of nature came to be viewed as independent from the will of the Creator, God's action within nature was increasingly conceptualized in terms of miraculous intervention as a violation of nature's laws.

Miracles and the Rise of Modern Science

As medieval theology and natural philosophy transitioned into early modern science, the laws of nature continued to be viewed as an expression of God's general will for creation, while miracles were seen as revealing God's purposes as they related to particular persons at specific times. For instance, Francis Bacon (1561–1626) affirmed "the origin of the laws of nature in God," and "the continuing efficacy of those laws for all time as a reflection of the sovereignty of the Lawgiver." In his mind, however, such laws were not "thought to diminish the immediacy of divine providence."[36] In the same way, says historian of science Thomas Dixon, early scientists such as René Descartes (1596–1650), Robert Boyle (1627–1691), and Isaac Newton (1642–1727) envisioned "nature as an orderly system of mechanical interactions governed by mathematical laws. And they hoped that people would see in this new vision the strongest possible evidence of divine power and intelligence." At the same time, explains Harrison, "those figures who were at the forefront of an advancing mechanical science were also the most staunch defenders of miracles."[37] Descartes held that "God sets up mathematical laws in nature as a king sets up laws in his kingdom." And the same God "who was responsible for determining the regular way in which nature would normally operate, was also quite capable of suspending or altering that normal course of nature whenever he so chose."[38] According to historian of science Margaret Osler, Boyle likewise declared that God is "the author of the universe, and the free establisher of the laws of motion." Boyle affirmed that "God continues to have power over the laws he created freely and that he can override them at will, as the biblical miracles demonstrate."[39]

---

36. Christopher Kaiser, *Toward a Theology of Scientific Endeavour: The Descent of Science* (Burlington, VT: Ashgate, 2007), 50.

37. Harrison, "Newtonian Science, Miracles," 531.

38. Thomas Dixon, *Science and Religion: A Very Short Introduction* (New York: Oxford University Press, 2008), 47.

39. Margaret Osler, "Varieties of Providentialism," in *The History of Science and Religion in the Western Tradition: An Encyclopedia*, ed. Gary Ferngren, Edward Larson, and Darrel Amundsen (New York: Garland, 2000), 64.

God established the laws of nature, says Boyle, and "yet he has not bound up his own hands by them."[40]

Isaac Newton and his followers "rejected [any] definition of miracle, according to which a miracle must involve a violation of laws of nature."[41] For Newton, explains Osler, "the existence of matter and its observed properties are completely dependent upon divine will."[42] In the laws of nature that he discovered, Newton saw "proof, not of an absentee clockmaker, but of God's continued presence in the world."[43] The force of gravity, which was described mathematically as Newton's Law of Universal Gravitation, was viewed as a direct manifestation of God's action. "Gravity," says Newton, "is not itself mechanical, but the immediate fiat and finger of God, and the execution of divine law."[44] Scientific devotee and promoter of Newton, Samuel Clarke (1675–1729) likewise contended that "all those things which we commonly say are the Effects of the *Natural Powers of Matter*, and *Laws of Motion*; of *Gravitation, Attraction*, or the like; are indeed . . . the Effects of *God's* acting upon Matter continually and every moment." According to Clarke "'Natural' and 'supernatural,' are distinctions merely in our conceptions of things." Consequently, a miracle "does not consist in any difficulty in the nature of the thing to be done, but merely in the unusualness of God's doing it."[45]

Miracles as Violations of the Laws of Nature

In the generations following Newton, many scientists, philosophers, and theologians came to agree on a definition of miracles that was defended by the philosopher David Hume (1711–1776). "Nothing is esteemed a miracle," says Hume, "if it ever happen in the common course of nature." Indeed, a miracle is "a *violation* of the laws of nature" or "a *transgression* of a law of nature by a particular volition of the Deity, or by the interposition of some invisible agent."[46] However, if the laws of nature cannot be violated or transgressed, miracles cannot and do not occur. Since, says Hume, the entirety of human experience testifies that the laws of nature are never broken, and "firm and unalterable experience has established these laws," a miracle—by the very definition of the term—is not

40. Harrison, "Newtonian Science, Miracles," 535.

41. Ibid., 532.

42. Osler, "Varieties of Providentialism," 64.

43. John Hedley Brooke, *Science and Religion: Some Historical Perspectives* (Cambridge: Cambridge University Press, 1991), 160.

44. In Newton's correspondence with Richard Bentley, in *Works of Richard Bentley*, ed. Alexander Dyce (London, 1838), 3:21, quoted in Harrison, "Newtonian Science, Miracles," 537.

45. Samuel Clarke, *The Evidences of Natural and Revealed Religion*, in *The Works of Samuel Clarke*, 2 vols. (London, 1738), 2:697, see also 601; quoted in Harrison, "Newtonian Science, Miracles," 538.

46. David Hume, "An Enquiry Concerning Human Understanding," in *Classics of Philosophy*, ed. Louis P. Pojman (Oxford: Oxford University Press, 1998), 714.

physically possible. Thus, argues Hume, "the proof against a miracle, from the very nature of the fact, is as entire as any argument from experience can possibly be imagined." Hume's definition creates an inherent logical contradiction in the very notion of a miracle. If a miracle (by definition) is thought of as a violation of the laws of nature, and these laws—as unalterable regularities (by definition)—cannot be violated, then miracles are impossible. As philosopher Steven Horst explains, "The problem is not so much that miracles have empirical evidence against them, but rather that there is a contradiction inherent in the very notion of an event that is an exception to an exceptionless law."[47]

In Hume's view of natural law, which is assumed in his argument against miracles, "an exceptionless regularity of some sort obtains throughout the universe, without restriction of time or place."[48] Hume's understanding of the laws of nature as inviolable and immutable was strongly advocated by the religious skeptic and physicist Pierre Simon Laplace (1749–1827). According to philosopher of science Nancey Murphy, Laplace "envisioned every atom in the universe as a component in an unfailingly precise cosmic clockwork mechanism."[49] In this view, known as *causal determinism*, if one could know all of the laws of nature and the situation of the universe at any given instant, then one would be able to predict exactly the situation of this same universe at a subsequent instant.[50] In other words, explains Dixon, "if we had perfect knowledge of the current state of the material world and of the laws that governed it, then in effect we would also have perfect knowledge of the future of the world (and that future would be as fixed and unalterable as the past)."[51] Unlike Bacon, Descartes, Boyle, and Newton, Laplace believed that a law-governed world must also be causally deterministic and this left no room for miracles. Thus, when Napoleon asked Laplace where God fit into his vision of science, he famously responded, "I have no need of that hypothesis."

Theological Responses to the Physical Impossibility of Miracles

Laplace and Hume's approach to the question of divine action forces one to choose either miracles or the laws of nature. Taking to heart Hume's understanding of miracles, a number of theologians since then have judged that "true

47. Steven Horst, "Miracles and Two Accounts of Scientific Laws," *Zygon* 49, no. 2 (June 2014): 323–47, at 325.

48. E. J. Lowe, "Miracles and the Laws of Nature," *Religious Studies* 23, no. 2 (1987): 263–78, at 269.

49. Nancey Murphy, *Beyond Liberalism and Fundamentalism: How Modern and Postmodern Philosophy Set the Theological Agenda* (Valley Forge, PA: Trinity Press International, 1996), 63.

50. Pierre Simon Laplace, *A Philosophical Essay on Probabilities* (New York: Springer-Verlag, 1995), 128.

51. Dixon, *Science and Religion*, 48.

miracles," as violations of the inviolable laws of nature, have never occurred. For instance, theologian Friedrich Schleiermacher (1768–1834) redefines "miracle" as "merely the religious name for event," rather than as an occurrence which violates the laws of nature. For Schleiermacher, a miracle is not an *objective* event but a *subjective* discernment that rests solely in the eye of the beholder.[52] Theologian Rudolf Bultmann (1884–1976) similarly opts for the laws of nature over and against miracles. Bultmann writes, "It is impossible to use electric light and the wireless [radio] and to avail ourselves of modern medical and surgical discoveries, and at the same time to believe in the New Testament world of spirits and miracles."[53] Bultmann asserts that "modern men take it for granted that the course of nature and history . . . is nowhere interrupted by the intervention of supernatural powers," and consequently the "miracles" narrated in the Bible must be "demythologized" or understood symbolically and not literally.[54]

A different theological response to Hume affirms, through faith, that with God anything is possible. According to the view known as interventionism, God occasionally suspends or violates the laws of nature to accomplish certain miracles. Advocating an interventionist position, theologian Donald Bloesch criticizes Bultmann for denying "the possibility of divine intervention into nature and history" and for uncritically accepting Hume and Laplace's understanding of the laws of nature.[55] While Bloesch offers no specific understanding of exactly how God intervenes to suspend the laws of nature, another interventionist theologian, Millard Erickson envisions God performing miracles through introducing supernatural forces to counter the regular natural forces. In a miraculous event, says Erickson, the natural laws "continue to operate, but supernatural force is introduced, negating the effect of the natural law."[56]

A third group of theologians focuses on the immanence (or nearness) of God within the processes of nature. In this view, natural processes themselves can be seen as "slow miracles" worked by the hand of God. Through such means, explains theologian Henry Drummond (1851–1897), "God had produced not only the mountains and valleys, the sky and the sea, the flowers and the stars," but also "that which of all other things in the universe commends itself, with increasing sureness as time goes on, to the reason and to the heart of Humanity—Love."[57] Drummond criticized interventionists as creating "gaps which they will fill up with God." If God is only to be found in special and occasional miraculous acts, he contends, "then he must be supposed to be absent from the world

52. Ibid., 44.

53. Rudolf Bultmann, *Kerygma and Myth: A Theological Debate* (New York: Harper & Row, 1961), 5.

54. Rudolf Bultmann, *Jesus Christ and Mythology* (New York: Scribner, 1958), 16.

55. Murphy, *Beyond Liberalism and Fundamentalism*, 70.

56. Millard J. Erickson, *Christian Theology* (Grand Rapids: Baker Academic, 2013), 380.

57. Henry Drummond, quoted in Dixon, *Science and Religion*, 44; original source uncited.

the majority of the time." Drummond thus held that a "nobler conception was of a God present in everything" rather than one who was primarily present in occasional miracles.[58] Theologian Aubrey Moore (1848–1890) similarly argued that "either God is everywhere present in nature or He is nowhere." While some Christian apologists "felt that a defense of orthodoxy involved the indications of gaps in the natural order where divine intervention must be invoked," Moore felt "that this quest for a God of the gaps was deistic rather than Christian."[59]

The Scientific Possibility of Miracles

Rather than trying to find a loophole within Hume's view of special divine action, many contemporary philosophers and theologians have contended that his definition of miracles is far too restrictive. Hume's understanding would seem to discount many major miracles in the Bible that can be affirmed as miracles of timing. Moreover, Hume's view incorrectly assumes that scientific knowledge of the laws of nature is complete, so that one would know what sort of event would constitute a violation. Lastly, Hume's concept of the laws of nature as causally deterministic has been rendered problematic by indeterministic understandings of the laws of nature that have emerged from quantum physics. Quantum theory has also inspired new ways of thinking about how God might act within and through the realm of nature.

Miracles of Timing

Alan Padgett points out that many miracles described in the Bible would not violate any laws of nature. Thus, says Padgett, "to insist on keeping Hume's definition of miracle as a violation of natural law would mean that some of the key miracles in biblical salvation history (for example, the return of Israel from exile) would not be miracles at all on this definition—which is absurd."[60] The biblical use of the terms "signs" and "wonders" includes events that were caused by human agents and natural occurrences that did not exceed ordinary causes. In this way, many of the miracles witnessed in the Bible could be considered "miracles of timing." Philosopher George Schlesinger explains, "As long as an event is genuinely startling and its timing constitutes a mind-boggling coincidence, in that it occurs precisely when there is a distinct call for it to promote some obvious divine objective, then that event amounts to a miracle."[61]

---

58. Ibid., 45.

59. England, "Natural Selection, Teleology, and the Logos," 280.

60. Padgett, "God and Miracle in an Age of Science," 534.

61. George Schlesinger, "Miracles," in *A Companion to Philosophy of Religion*, ed. Charles Taliaferro, Paul Draper, and Philip L. Quinn, 2nd ed. (Malden, MA: Blackwell, 2010), 398.

Examining the miracles listed in the biblical book of Exodus, physicist Colin Humphreys writes, "A natural explanation of the events of the Exodus doesn't . . . make them any less miraculous. . . . The ancient Israelites believed that their God worked in, with, and through natural events. What made certain natural events miraculous was their timing."[62] Consider, for instance, the miraculous Israelite crossing of the River Jordan:

> Now the Jordan is in flood all during harvest. Yet as soon as the priests who carried the Ark reached the Jordan and their feet touched the water's edge, the water from upstream stopped flowing. It piled up in a heap a great distance away, at a town called Adam [modern Damiya] in the vicinity of Zarethan while the water flowing down to the Sea of the Arabah (the Dead Sea) was completely cut off. So the people crossed over opposite Jericho. (Josh. 3:15–16)

Is an event such as this physically impossible? Are there any known natural causes that could have stopped the water from flowing so that the Israelites could pass? The author of Joshua emphasizes that the water didn't stop at the place where the Israelites were, but at a great distance away upstream—near ancient Adam (modern day Damiya). What might have stopped the water flowing at Damiya? Humphrey believes an event that happened nearly a century ago may provide a clue. On July 11, 1927, an earthquake which measured 6.5 on the Richter scale shook Jericho. During

According to the Bible, as the ancient Israelites approached Jericho from the east, the waters of the Jordan River backed up near Damiya (ancient Adam), allowing them to cross on dry land. A similar phenomenon occurred in 1927.

---

62. Colin Humphreys, *The Miracles of Exodus: A Scientist's Discovery of the Extraordinary Natural Causes of the Biblical Stories* (New York: Continuum, 2003), 5.

this particular earthquake, says Humphreys, "mudslides occurred along the Jordan near Damiya, about 30 kilometres [eighteen miles] north of Jericho. These temporarily stopped the river's flow." Such cut-offs of the Jordan River typically last one or two days and have also been recorded in 1834, 1546, 1267, and 1160. This kind of event can provide an explanation in terms of natural causes for *how* the Jordan River stopped, while the Bible gives a theological explanation for *why*. A natural explanation describing how the river stopped in no way detracts from the extraordinary timing of the event.

When Is Scientific Knowledge of the Laws of Nature Complete?

A different type of response to Hume questions his view of the laws of nature and focuses on achieving a better understanding of this phrase. What exactly would it take for an event to transgress a law of nature? To answer this, one first needs to know precisely what a law of nature is. However, as philosophers Michael Murray and Michael Rea point out, the issue of how to adequately define the phrase "law of nature" is currently "a vexing and disputed one in the philosophy of science."[63] Philosopher Richard Swinburne thus asks "whether there could be evidence that a law of nature has been violated."[64] To have evidence that a law of nature had been violated, says Swinburne, "we would have to have good reason to believe that an event has occurred contrary to the predictions of a law that we had good reason to believe to be a law of nature; and furthermore we would have to have good reason to believe that events similar to the event would not occur in circumstances similar to those of the original occurrence."[65] If an event happens which is contrary to a prediction of a given formula that had been considered a law of nature up until that point, and there is good reason to believe that similar events would occur in similar circumstances, then it would seem that the formula in question is, in fact, not a law of nature.

Consider, for instance, "the central dogma of molecular biology," which was asserted as a "fundamental 'biological law'" in 1956 by co-discoverer of the DNA double helix Francis Crick.[66] The central dogma holds that "there is no information transfer from protein to nucleic acid." In other words, genetic information flows in only one direction—from DNA (and RNA) to proteins, and never the other way around. While believed for many years to be

---

63. Michael Murray and Michael Rea, *An Introduction to the Philosophy of Religion* (New York: Cambridge University Press, 2008), 201.

64. Richard Swinburne, "Miracles," *Philosophical Quarterly* 18, no. 73 (October 1968): 320–28, at 320.

65. Ibid., 321.

66. Eugene Koonin, "Does the Central Dogma Still Stand?" *Biology Direct* 7, no. 27 (2012): 1.

a biological "law of nature" that operated without exception, biologist Eugene Koonin explains how recent studies have shown that "information potentially can be transferred from a protein sequence back to the genome." Consequently, says Koonin, "the Central Dogma of molecular biology is invalid as an 'absolute' principle: transfer of information from proteins (and specifically from protein sequences) to the genome *does* exist."[67] If it is shown that there are exceptions to what was once viewed as an exceptionless law of nature—such as the central dogma—it does not prove that the violations to the central dogma are miracles, but rather that the central dogma was never exceptionless in the first place.

As an example of how a biblical miracle has been perceived as violating the laws of nature, consider the parting of the Red Sea during Israel's escape from Egypt:

> Then Moses stretched out his hand over the sea, and the Lord drove the sea back by a strong east wind all night . . . and the waters were divided. And the people of Israel went into the midst of the sea on dry ground, the waters being a wall to them on their right hand and on their left. The Egyptians pursued and went in after them into the midst of the sea, all Pharaoh's horses, his chariots, and his horsemen. (Exod. 14:21–23)

As the "supreme instance of 'sign' in the Old Testament," there is no doubt that this pivotal event in Israel's deliverance from bondage is depicted as a genuine miracle.[68] Furthermore, this event seems to fit Hume's understanding of miracle as a violation of the laws of nature. As Horst points out, "the parting of the Red Sea" is an event that does "involve bodies with mass behaving in a fashion contrary to what the gravitation law would predict."[69] The law of gravity, as it applies to water, clearly appears to preclude a large body of water dividing to create a land bridge for several hours until quickly collapsing together again.

However, is it certain that the understanding of the laws of nature in this case is sufficient for one to declare that such laws have been violated? While for many years it looked like the parting of the Red Sea was an unambiguous violation of the law of gravity, recent scientific studies by researchers at the National Center for Atmospheric Research and the University of Colorado at Boulder have shown that large bodies of water, under certain conditions, can behave precisely as the Red Sea does in the biblical account.[70] Using geological

67. Ibid., 4.

68. Kee, "Biblical Understanding of Miracle," 52.

69. Horst, "Miracles and Two Accounts of Scientific Laws," 329.

70. Carl Drews, "Using Wind Setdown and Storm Surge on Lake Erie to Calibrate the Air-Sea Drag Coefficient," *PLoS ONE* 8, no. 8 (August 2013): e72510.

maps, geological surveys, and sediment cores to reconstruct the configuration of lagoons and rivers that were present during the Exodus period, researchers led by atmospheric scientist Carl Drews, ran a number of computer simulations to see what would happen when a digital wind was applied.[71] According to Drews, the results demonstrated that "a strong east wind, blowing overnight, could have pushed water back at a bend where an ancient river delta is believed to have merged with a coastal lagoon. With the water pushed back into both waterways, a land bridge would have opened at the bend, enabling people to walk across exposed mud flats to safety. As soon as the wind died down, the waters would have rushed back in."[72] Drews explains that it is possible that "a phenomenon known as wind setdown caused winds of rare duration and force to peel back the waters long enough for the Israelites to make their way to freedom across an exposed land bridge." After being parted for a period of about eight hours, the waters would then rush back together suddenly. Drews observes, "When the wind stops, suddenly that water comes back again, and you would get these walls of churning water, thundering in and crushing anybody who is left in the passage there." Even though "the wind moves the water in a way that's in accordance with physical laws," Drews's findings closely match the account of the chief Exodus miracle.

Another example of a biblical miracle that seemed impossible in light of the laws of nature is found in 1 Kings 18:38. In this passage, the prophet Elijah is challenging the prophets of the god Baal, and both Elijah and the prophets of Baal are preparing sacrifices for the respective gods. As Elijah prayed, "the fire of the Lord fell and burned up the sacrifice, the wood, the stones and the soil, and also licked up the water in the trench." The idea of a finger of fire materializing in the sky to consume the contents of an altar on the earth below (or a group of fifty soldiers as described in 2 Kings 1:12) has been understood as the kind of event that clearly defies what both common experience and science says is physically possible. Yet, again, the scientific discovery of previously unknown natural phenomena and the revealing of new laws of nature can bring what was thought to be a violation of the laws of nature into the realm of physical possibility.

A phenomenon known as a fire tornado, which scientists documented for the first time in November 2012, appears similar to "the fire of the Lord" described in 1 Kings 18.[73] Lead researcher of the fire tornado investigation,

---

71. Carl Drews and Weiqing Han, "Dynamics of Wind Setdown at Suez and the Eastern Nile Delta," *PLoS ONE* 5, no. 8 (August 2010): e12481.

72. Carl Drews, "Could Wind Have Parted the Red Sea?," *Weatherwise Magazine*, January/February 2011, *http://www.weatherwise.org/Archives/Back%20Issues/2011/January-February%202011/red-sea-full.html*.

73. Richard McRae, Jason Sharples, Stephen Wilkes, and Alan Walker, "An Australian Pyro-Tornadogenesis Event," *Natural Hazards* 65, no. 3 (2013): 1801–11.

Richard McRae, explains that while the more common fire whirl is attached to the hot ground, a fire tornado is an extremely rare event which, like a true tornado, is attached to the underside of a thunderstorm and can lift off the ground to touch down again in different locations. Fire from the sky—like that described in the book of Kings—is thus physically possible, but it was not known to be possible before 2012. The example of fire tornadoes, like that of wind setdown, shows that there are phenomena and laws of nature that remain unknown, which could have played some role in events described as miracles. It seems then, that scientists could never reach a point where they could be certain that something is physically impossible according to the laws of nature since science could never reach a point where all laws of nature are known.

The Rise of Quantum Physics and the Demise of Enlightenment Science

Can the natural phenomena of wind setdown or fire tornadoes be seen as direct manifestations of the hand of God acting in and through nature? In a causally deterministic universe, any physical events said to be caused by God would still constitute departures from the ordinary course of nature. To avoid interventionism, such miraculous events would have to have been written into the initial conditions of the big bang. This means that the timing of such events would have to be essential if they were to function within the context of salvation history. In other words, if Moses had shown up a day later, he would have missed the miracle of the Red Sea parting. And if Elijah had failed to place his altar in just the right place at just the right time, the rare fire tornado would have missed its mark. If causal determinism is true, a complete scientific description of the causes of such events could only invoke the "hand of God" as operating at the very beginning of the causal chain (as one might arrange a chain of dominoes before setting them in motion).

However, is universal causal determinism scientifically true? There are compelling scientific grounds for thinking determinism is false. From the eighteenth to the beginning of the twentieth century, scientists believed natural laws were causally deterministic. Moreover, for nearly two centuries, the reigning scientific paradigm, known as classical physics, or Newtonian physics, held that natural laws are universal in form (i.e., they apply without exception in all places and at all times) and state what must happen. Swinburne explains, however, that with the development of quantum theory, or quantum mechanics, in the twentieth century, physicists "have come to hold that the fundamental natural laws are statistical."[74] Instead of stating what *must* happen, the laws of nature are now seen as stating what will *probably* happen. As quantum physicist Erwin Schrödinger

---

74. Richard Swinburne, *The Concept of Miracle* (London: Macmillan, 1970), 2–3.

observes, "Physical laws rest on atomic statistics and are therefore only approximate."[75] Beyond this, the standard interpretation of quantum physics, known as the Copenhagen interpretation, holds that there is *causal indeterminism* at the most fundamental physical level. In the standard quantum physical understanding of the universe, chains of causation are truly incomplete. In other words, quantum events happen without there being anything prior that physically causes or determines them to happen. In this way, says philosopher of science Nancey Murphy, quantum physics demonstrates empirically that "individual events violate the *principle of sufficient reason.*" In other words, there is no sufficient reason or prior cause that can be given for what determines one quantum event to happen rather than another.[76]

Consider, for instance, the phenomenon of radioactive decay. For radioactive elements such as plutonium (Pu), the half-life is the length of time during which one atom of the element has a 50 percent chance of undergoing radioactive decay or during which 50 percent of a given sample of the element will decay. The element Pu-240 has a half-life of 6,560 years, which means that, in that period of time, half of the atoms will have decayed in a given sample. According to quantum theory, the most complete scientific description possible of a plutonium atom (or a sample of plutonium) does not suffice to determine when a given atom will decay or which specific atoms in the sample will decay at a particular moment. The theory only gives the probability that a specific atom, or part of the sample, has for decaying; nothing determines or causes which half will decay within the half-life period. According to the standard Copenhagen interpretation of quantum physics, Murray and Rea observe, it would be impossible to predict when a particular radioactive atom will decay because decay events are indeterministic; "there are no conditions that are sufficient for their occurrence."[77]

The absence of prior causes in quantum events is not due to a lack of knowledge or information about physical systems but is rather an inherent aspect of material reality.[78] Gaps in causal explanation at the quantum level are not due to any incompleteness of the theory itself. Instead, these causal gaps reveal a genuine openness in the structure of the natural world. In other words, the concept of quantum causal gaps is not due to a failure of current theory but is a result

75. Erwin Schrödinger, *What Is Life? The Physical Aspect of the Living Cell* (Cambridge: Cambridge University Press, 1944), 10.

76. Nancey Murphy, "Divine Action in the Natural Order: Buridan's Ass and Schrödinger's Cat," in *Chaos and Complexity: Scientific Perspectives on Divine Action*, ed. Robert J. Russell, Nancey Murphy, and Arthur Peacocke (Vatican City State: Vatican Observatory Publications; Berkeley, CA: Center for Theology and the Natural Sciences, 1995), 338.

77. Murray and Rea, *Introduction to the Philosophy of Religion*, 141.

78. David Hodgson, *The Mind Matters: Consciousness and Choice in a Quantum World* (Oxford: Clarendon, 1991), 33.

of its success. As physicist and theologian Robert John Russell observes, both quantum theory and the experimental data that support it "indicate that there is no exhaustive set of underlying natural causes."[79] Quantum physics, says Russell, reveals a "radical incompleteness" of causal structures at the most basic level of reality.[80] Consequently, says philosopher Thomas Tracy, there "is a growing consensus that classical deterministic explanations for [quantum] systems are no longer a viable alternative."[81]

According to Dixon, "quantum mechanics suggests that at the most basic level material reality is not deterministic (nor does it even seem to be 'material'). We are in a world of clouds, of wave functions, of probabilities—not the reassuringly picturable clockwork universe of the Enlightenment."[82] As a result, Hume's argument against miracles is founded upon an understanding of immutable and deterministic physical law that is no longer scientifically valid. As philosopher and theologian Mark Worthing comments, "Science, at least to the extent it is influenced by quantum mechanics, is no longer so certain as to what can and what cannot happen."[83] If, as quantum physics indicates, "the laws of nature are statistical and not deterministic, it is not in all cases so clear," says Swinburne, "what counts as a counter instance to them. How improbable does an event have to be to constitute a counter instance to a statistical law?"[84]

Beyond providing a critique of the Enlightenment science that serves as the foundation of Hume's argument, quantum physics offers a way of thinking about how God might act in and through natural law without having to intervene with the regular order. As physicist Ian Barbour explains, since causal indeterminacy is a fundamental feature of nature, God can act as the "determiner of indeterminacies."[85] The integration of indeterminism into the order of nature, observes Tracy, "provides a structure within which God's particular providential actions need not involve any miraculous suspension of natural law."[86] In this view, God could act in quantum transitions or events to

79. Robert John Russell, "Does the God Who Acts Really Act? New Approaches to Divine Action in Light of Science," *Theology Today* 54 (April 1997): 54.

80. Robert John Russell, "Quantum Physics in Philosophical and Theological Perspective," in *Physics, Philosophy and Theology: A Common Quest for Understanding*, ed. Robert J. Russell, William Stoeger, and George Coyne (Vatican City State: Vatican Observatory Publications, 1997), 347–48.

81. Thomas F. Tracy, "Particular Providence and the God of the Gaps," in *Chaos and Complexity*, ed. Russell, Murphy, and Peacocke, 315.

82. Dixon, *Science and Religion*, 50.

83. Mark Worthing, "Divine Action and the Problem of Miracles," *Christian Perspectives on Science and Technology*, July 2009, 10.

84. Swinburne, "Miracles," 322.

85. Ian G. Barbour, *When Science Meets Religion* (San Francisco: HarperSanFrancisco, 2000), 170.

86. Thomas Tracy, "Divine Action," in *A Companion to Philosophy of Religion*, ed. Taliaferro, Draper, and Quinn, 313.

designate which of the probabilistically permitted possibilities are actualized. Special divine action (or miracles) of this type would not contravene natural causes. Rather, says Tracy, "God would act to *determine* what the system of nature leaves undetermined."[87]

With God's action taking place at the quantum level, extraordinary miracles may be redefined as highly improbable occurrences or statistical anomalies within the present order of nature and not violations of laws of nature or interventions in nature. God, in selectively determining quantum events, does not displace natural causes that would otherwise have determined those events, and from a scientific point of view such events would appear to occur by chance. God's quantum activity—which will always be invisible to science—would thus be entirely compatible with whatever physics might say about the distribution of such events in regular probabilistic patterns. "As long as God's determination of quantum events preserves the probability distributions spelled out by the theory," observes Tracy, "no natural law has been ignored or overridden; indeed, if God determines all quantum transitions, then the probabilistic laws of quantum

This graph, superimposed on a William Blake watercolor of the creation, expresses laws of nature as statistical regularities: "miracles" are statistical anomalies.

mechanics will just be a description of the pattern of God's action." In this way, Tracy explains, "the world God has made could display both a reliable causal structure and an inherent openness to novelty, allowing for a seamless integration of natural law and ongoing direct involvement by God in shaping the course of events."[88]

According to this noninterventionist concept of special divine action, God's activity remains essentially hidden—being cloaked behind the veil of quantum

87. Thomas Tracy, "Theologies of Divine Action," in *The Oxford Handbook of Religion and Science,* ed. Philip Clayton and Zachary Simpson (Oxford: Oxford University Press, 2006), 607.

88. Tracy, "Divine Action," 313.

indeterminacy.[89] The notion that God's action is concealed from direct human observation is an idea with deep biblical roots:

> You are the God who performs miracles; you display your power among the peoples. . . . Your thunder was heard in the whirlwind, your lightning lit up the world. . . . Your path led through the sea, your way through the mighty waters, *though your footprints were not seen.* You led your people like a flock by the hand of Moses and Aaron. (Ps. 77: 14–20, emphasis added)

One theological reason for God's "invisible footprints," says Murphy, is that for faith to be possible, "God's relation with us requires a fine line between complete obviousness and complete hiddenness."[90] God's ultimate purposes in performing miracles are complex, and they include not just that persons should believe in him, but some further aims with respect to how such belief should take root and grow. As philosopher Laura Garcia points out, "Jesus' miracles were not performed for everyone he met, nor did he explain the parables to every person present, nor did he run after those who left his company after finding some of his teachings too strange." As God reveals himself to his creation through miracles, there is always room for doubt. Even as the disciples encountered the risen Jesus, "when they saw him they worshiped him, but some doubted" (Matt. 28:17). In the biblical vision of God's action, says Garcia, "God respects the freedom of His creatures, and refuses to impose on those who do not respond to his invitations to them (whether direct or indirect). . . . This silence of God could be more for our sake than for His, of course, since it could be that the requisite attitude of heart is more necessary for our ultimate good than simply acquiring true beliefs."[91]

Conclusion

Most current discussions of how miracles can be understood in light of modern science begin with Hume's definition of "miracle" as "a violation of the laws of nature." This interventionist concept of miracles is dependent on the idea that there are laws of nature and that these laws are fundamentally deterministic. Within the Western theistic tradition before Hume, miracles were not perceived

---

89. Robert John Russell, "Divine Action and Quantum Mechanics: A Fresh Assessment," in *Philosophy, Science and Divine Action*, ed. F. LeRon Shults, Nancey Murphy, and Robert John Russell (Leiden: Brill, 2009), 355.

90. Murphy, "Divine Action in the Natural Order," 291.

91. Laura Garcia, "St. John of the Cross and the Necessity of Divine Hiddenness," in *Divine Hiddenness: New Essays* (Cambridge: Cambridge University Press, 2002), 86.

as contraventions to the laws of nature since God was believed to be the author of both. More recently, quantum physics has revealed that the laws of nature are not deterministic, as Hume believed, but that "an indeterminacy in nature itself seems to be present at the quantum level."[92] Because nothing physically causes events to happen at the subatomic or quantum level, God would be free to act within the most fundamental physical processes while forever being veiled from the eyes of science. Such quantum divine action involves no violation of the laws of nature.

Discussion Questions

1. If a miracle is a scientifically impossible event, is it ever plausible to believe that such events have happened in the past and still occur in the present?
2. If miracles are possible, why do you think they don't happen more often?
3. Do you think instances of extraordinary coincidences of a beneficial nature, or "miracles of timing," can be considered genuine miracles? Why, or why not?
4. Does defining miracles as "coincidences caused by God" avoid the problems arising from Hume's notion of miracles as violations of the laws of nature?
5. Do you think the understanding of miracles informed by quantum physics makes it more believable that miracles have actually occurred? In other words, in your opinion, does viewing miracles as scientifically *improbable* rather than physically *impossible* make them more plausible?

Beyond the Classroom

Conduct the following thought experiment with a group:

Imagine that you are God, and you desire to create a world that is both *regular* or *law-like* and yet *open* to your continued involvement *without* violating such regularity or laws. Can you (as God) think of a way to create a world that is both regular and open to your continual involvement?

Possible answers to be offered by group leader at the end of the discussion:

1. Create laws of nature that can be occasionally suspended (similar to a presidential pardon).
2. Set up the history of events in such a way that they follow a precise sequence, so that wondrous events will happen at particular times in certain

---

92. Ian G. Barbour, "Five Models of God and Evolution," in *Philosophy, Science and Divine Action*, ed. Shults, Murphy, and Russell, 27.

specified locations. (Human free will, if allowed, could mean that such miracles are not witnessed as planned).

3. Create a world based on statistical regularity (or statistical laws), such as described by quantum mechanics, which would allow you (as God) to act in surprising or miraculous ways on the "edges of regularity" (on the ends of the probability distribution or bell curve). The need to keep the regularity intact would mean that miracles (as statistical anomalies) would have to be rare.

Resources for Further Study

Books

Grant, Robert M. *Miracle and Natural Law in Graeco-Roman and Early Christian Thought.* Amsterdam: North Holland Publishing, 1952.

Humphreys, Colin. *The Miracles of Exodus: A Scientist's Discovery of the Extraordinary Natural Causes of the Biblical Stories.* New York: Continuum, 2003.

Shults, F. LeRon, Nancey Murphy, and Robert John Russell, eds. *Philosophy, Science and Divine Action.* Leiden: Brill, 2009.

Ward, Keith. *Divine Action: Examining God's Role in an Open and Emergent Universe.* Philadelphia: Templeton Foundation Press, 2007.

Articles

Padgett, Alan. "God and Miracle in an Age of Science." In *The Blackwell Companion to Science and Christianity*, edited by J. B. Stump and Alan G. Padgett, 533–42. Malden, MA: Blackwell, 2012.

Tracy, Thomas. "Theologies of Divine Action." In *The Oxford Handbook of Religion and Science*, edited by Philip Clayton and Zachary Simpson, 579–95. Oxford: Oxford University Press, 2006.

Internet Resources

Humphreys, Colin. "Can Scientists Believe in Miracles?" Accessible at *https://www.faraday.st-edmunds.cam.ac.uk/Multimedia.php?ItemID=Item_Multimedia_1&Mode=Add&Play=MP3&width=720&height=460* (time: 00:46:27).

Louis, Ard. "Miracles and Science: The Long Shadow of David Hume." BioLogos Foundation. Accessible at *http://biologos.org/uploads/projects/louis_scholarly_essay.pdf.*

Moritz, Joshua. "Does God Really Act?" Voice of Light Productions. Accessible at *http://vimeo.com/41753716* (time: 00:54:45).

Russell, Robert John. "The God Who Acts." BioLogos Forum website, May 2012. Accessible at *http://biologos.org/blog/series/the-god-who-acts-robert-russell-on-divine-intervention-and-divine-action.*

Wright, N. T. "Can a Scientist Believe in the Resurrection?" Accessible at *https://www.faraday.st-edmunds.cam.ac.uk/Multimedia.php?ItemID=Item_Multimedia_151&Mode=Add&Play=MP3&width=720&height=460* (time: 01:15:48).

CHAPTER 9

God, the Problem of Suffering, and the Natural Sciences

And God saw everything that he had made, and, behold, it was very good.

—Genesis 1:31

Nature does not abhor evil; she embraces it. . . . Death, destruction and fury do not disturb the Mother of our world; they are merely parts of her plan. . . . For we are casualties of Nature's callous indifference to life, pawns who suffer and die to live out her schemes.

—Harold Bloom, science writer[1]

In This Chapter

- Does Anything Justify the Suffering of God's Creatures?
- Could God Have Created a World without Any Suffering Due to the Laws of Nature?
- Why Would an All-Loving God Create through Evolution?
- Discussion Questions
- Beyond the Classroom
- Resources for Further Study

Existence is marked by suffering. All of the major world religions affirm this basic truth. Religions diverge, however, on what they believe about the ultimate causes of suffering, whether such suffering should be considered evil, and how the consequences of suffering can be redeemed. Religious persons also disagree about the roles God and nature play in the tragic drama of the world's travails. In

---

1. Harold Bloom, *The Lucifer Principle: A Scientific Expedition into the Forces of History* (New York: Atlantic Monthly, 1997), 3.

the Eastern religious traditions, the cosmic law of *karma*—a transcendent, moral law of punitive retribution—is the answer to why humans, animals, and even gods suffer. In Hinduism, explain religious scholars Antti Laato and Johannes de Moor, "all human beings as well as all gods are regarded as being under the law of *karma*. Gods are powerless in this respect to [ultimately] change the distress of human beings because they themselves are subjected to suffering."[2] Buddhism, too, focuses on karma as a chief cause of suffering. In the Buddhist conception of the cosmos, says Eastern religious scholar Donald Lopez, "the universe has no beginning. It is the product of karma, the law of the cause and effect of actions, according to which virtuous actions create pleasure in the future and nonvirtuous actions create pain. It is a natural law, accounting for all the happiness and suffering in the world."[3]

In stark contrast to Eastern religious conceptions, observes philosopher Chad Meister, "the three major theistic religions affirm a creation event in which God brought the universe into being, and they describe God as being actively involved in the created order."[4] The Creator God of the theistic traditions is affirmed as all-knowing, all-powerful, all-good, and all-loving. Moreover, in the Jewish and Christian Scriptures, God observes his work in creation and declares all things to be "very good." A dilemma thus arises within the theistic worldview—namely, if there is a God, then why is there suffering? This philosophical predicament, known as the theodicy problem, arises from the combination of three considerations—an affirmation of God's goodness, confidence in God's unrivaled power, and the belief in the real occurrence of suffering. Philosopher David Hume (1711–1776) summarizes the theodicy problem that theists face: "A perfectly good and omnipotent God would not wish to create suffering and he would be able to prevent any suffering. But there is suffering, and an immense amount of it, in this world. Therefore there is no good and omnipotent creator."[5] This chapter examines the problem of theodicy as it relates to the natural sciences. It investigates the goals that God has in creating the cosmos, asks whether suffering in creation is necessary to accomplish these goals, and explores whether God's values and purposes in creation are ultimately considered worth it from the perspective of the creatures that suffer.

---

2. Antti Laato and Johannes de Moor, *Theodicy in the World of the Bible*, ed. Antti Laato and Johannes de Moor (Leiden: Brill, 2003), xx. For a discussion of karma as a Hindu response to theodicy, see Purushottama Bilimoria, "Toward an Indian Theodicy," in *The Blackwell Companion to the Problem of Evil*, ed. Justin P. McBrayer and Daniel Howard-Snyder (Malden, MA : Blackwell, 2013), 482–506.

3. Donald Lopez, *The Story of Buddhism: A Concise Guide to Its History and Teachings* (San Francisco: HarperSanFrancisco, 2001), 19.

4. Chad Meister, *Introducing Philosophy of Religion* (New York: Routledge, 2009), 151.

5. David Hume, quoted in Keith Ward, *Divine Action: Examining God's Role in an Open and Emergent Universe* (Philadelphia: Templeton Foundation Press, 2007), 38; original source uncited.

Does Anything Justify the Suffering of God's Creatures?

In the Jewish and Christian traditions, the Creator is held to be absolutely and perfectly good. In the New Testament, God's goodness is so fundamental to his nature that God's essence is said to be defined by "love" (1 John 4:8). In the biblical tradition, God desires love over fear, and, as philosophers Michael Murray and Michael Rea explain, "God is to be worshipped not primarily out of motives of fear or divine command, but rather because God is good and God manifests goodness in a way that no other thing does or can."[6] Moreover, the Creator is said to be good not only to a few select individuals who follow his will, or even to just humans, but rather, "the Lord is good to *all*: and his tender mercies are over *all* his works" (Ps. 145:9, emphasis added). God's goodness and love extends to all God's creatures—human and nonhuman alike. Indeed, the central Christian proclamation begins with the news that God's Son was sent because he "loved the *cosmos*" (John 3:16).

The Value of Creaturely Love as the Ultimate Goal of Creation

The Jewish Scriptures place love for God and for one another at the heart of the commandments, and the Christian Scriptures confess that "God is love." Philosophers have pointed out that the presupposition and ultimate goal of love is relationship—"perfect love requires a beloved."[7] In the biblical understanding, a loving relationship is characterized by patience, kindness, humility, sincerity, altruism or self-sacrifice, a long-suffering attitude, forgiveness, truth, perseverance, trust, faith, and freedom (1 Cor. 13:4–7; Exod. 34:6). An overarching goal of God's creation of the cosmos is that God's creatures might enter into a loving relationship with their Creator and with each other. From this conception of God's final purposes in creation, several values emerge that become crucial in addressing the question of why God permits suffering that is experienced by his creatures as evil—where "evil" refers to anything that does not seem necessary for any greater goods (i.e., pointless suffering) or that detracts from or diminishes that which is experienced as good.

What is required so that loving relationship may ultimately come to fruition in the cosmos that God created? At a minimum, the prerequisites for the biblical sense of love (Greek: *agapē*) seem to include freedom, independence, rationality,

6. Michael Murray and Michael Rea, *An Introduction to the Philosophy of Religion* (New York: Cambridge University Press, 2008), 27.

7. Richard Swinburne, cited in Murray and Rea, *Introduction to the Philosophy of Religion*, 74; original source uncited.

knowledge, and the capacity to develop moral character. Relational love must be freely given and, as such, it may be courted but can never be coerced. In the same way that a legitimate marriage requires that each party say "I do" without a gun being held to the potential spouse's head, a relationship of love in the biblical sense must be one of willing consent rather than of forced abduction. Freedom of consent within any loving relationship requires *knowledge* about that which is being consented to and also the ability to make *independent decisions* for oneself. The capacity for independent decision-making in turn necessitates a certain degree of *rationality*. *Agapē*, or love, which is said to define both God's essence and the kind of relationship that God desires with and for his creatures, also entails the formation of a number of moral virtues, such as patience, self-sacrifice, perseverance, and faith.

The Value of Creaturely Freedom and the Free Will Defense

Freedom is the ability to act or choose without overriding external or internal constraints that force one's decisions. If one intrinsically values love as a worthy end in and of itself, then one will extrinsically value freedom, since it is a key component of love. However, one might also consider freedom an intrinsic value, apart from love. The latter is certainly the case within Western democratic countries where freedom is upheld as an inalienable right, and the oppression of freedom (e.g., slavery) is seen as a great evil. In the biblical tradition, God values freedom as well and continually bestows freedom upon creatures (Gen. 2:16; Deut. 30:15; 2 Cor. 3:17). Is the price of autonomy worth the cost of suffering that can potentially stem from free decisions? A line of argument known as the free will defense, which goes back to Augustine of Hippo (354–430 CE), asserts that autonomy is indeed worth the cost of suffering. Philosopher and contemporary advocate of the free will defense Alvin Plantinga observes, "A world containing creatures who are significantly *free* (and *freely perform more* good than evil actions) is more valuable, all else being equal, than a world containing no free creatures at all."[8]

Could God have created free creatures that always choose to do what is right, without exception? Like the majority of classical theists, Plantinga does not think it makes any sense to understand God's omnipotence as including the power to do what is logically impossible. Moreover, Plantinga argues that it is even incoherent to argue that God can do what is logically impossible. For example, God cannot create a square triangle. God cannot create a stick that is not as long as itself. God cannot make contradictory statements true. God

---

8. Alvin Plantinga, *God, Freedom, and Evil* (Grand Rapids: Eerdmans, 1977), 30, emphasis in original.

cannot make a rock so big he cannot lift it. God is not able to be ignorant, to be unwise, or to cease to exist. God cannot have true knowledge of God's own nonexistence. Each of these scenarios is impossible, and the fact that God cannot do the logically impossible is not, Plantinga maintains, a genuine limitation of God's power. The reason it is not a limitation on God's power, explains philosopher Richard Swinburne, is because "a logically impossible action is not *an action*. It is what is described by a form of words which purport to describe an action, but *do not describe anything which it is coherent* to suppose could be done."[9] In the same way, it is not logically possible to create free creatures who are in fact not free. God could not have created a world with free moral creatures that never choose to do evil. "To create creatures capable of *moral good*," says Plantinga, "God must create creatures capable of moral evil; and He can't give these creatures the freedom to perform evil and at the same time prevent them from doing so."[10] In other words, God cannot cause or determine the actions of free creatures so that they only do what is right. God thus takes a true risk in creating morally free creatures, and this risk is logically impossible to avoid. "As it turned out," reflects Plantinga, "sadly enough, some of the free creatures God created went wrong in the exercise of their freedom; this is the source of moral evil. The fact that free creatures sometimes go wrong, however, counts neither against God's omnipotence nor against His goodness; for He could have forestalled the occurrence of moral evil only by removing the possibility of moral good."[11] Swinburne concurs: "If humans are to have the free choice of bringing about good or evil, and the free choice thereby of gradually forming their characters, then it is logically necessary that there be the possibility of the occurrence of moral evil unprevented by God."[12] In Plantinga and Swinburne's assessments, the significant degree of freedom humans and other creatures enjoy is worth the price. Others, however, might feel they would be willing to give up their freedom if it meant that there would be less suffering in the world.

The Value of Creaturely Independence, Soul-Making, and the Hiddenness of God

Another precondition for a loving relationship is independence. Swinburne, Keith Ward, and Atle Søvik emphasize "God's goal of creating independent human beings for a certain kind of love."[13] In a romantic relationship, one

---

9. Richard Swinburne, *The Coherence of Theism* (Oxford: Clarendon, 1977), 153, emphasis in original.

10. Plantinga, *God, Freedom, and Evil*, 30.

11. Ibid., 30.

12. Richard Swinburne, *The Existence of God* (New York: Oxford University Press, 1979), 238.

13. Atle Søvik, *The Problem of Evil and the Power of God* (Boston: Brill, 2011), 39.

desires to be loved for oneself—for who or what he or she is as an independent being. Ward observes, "A fully interpersonal relationship of love between distinct beings is only possible where created beings can reject love and choose self."[14] God desires to be loved for God's own sake and to love each individual creature for his or her own sake. This requires that created beings have the capacity to choose and make decisions apart from God. Søvik explains, "The more self-created we are, the more it is right to say that God loves us for who we are, as opposed to loving us for what he has made us into."[15] God's goal of creating creatures that could grow into independent beings and come to love God on their own is related to how instances of suffering arise from the free decisions of such beings. According to Ward, "it *was* possible for God to create *free* human beings without inclinations to evil, but it *was not* possible for God to create *independent* human beings without inclinations to evil."[16]

In the same way that independence is essential for the possibility of a loving relationship, independence is also vital for the possibility of creaturely freedom or autonomy. If the minds and wills of all creatures were absolutely unified with the divine will without any significant distinction, then creatures could not be truly free. According to theologian Wolfhart Pannenberg, "God stands by his creation, and does so indeed in a way that respects his creatures' independence."[17] In other words, maintains philosopher Paul Moser, "God remains hidden to some creatures because failure to hide would prevent those creatures from coming to know God in the proper way."[18] Following a line of argument that was first developed by the early church father Irenaeus (130–202 CE), philosopher John Hick argues that the Creator must be veiled from the immediate consciousness of creatures to ensure the amount of independence and freedom necessary for them to have opportunities to respond in faith. The world, says Hick, must be, at least to some extent, "as if there were no God. God must be a hidden deity, veiled by His creation." God must be knowable, Hick explains, "but only by a mode of knowledge that involves a free personal response" on the part of God's creatures. The veil that obscures God's direct presence from his creatures (known as an *epistemic distance*) is part of God's design—so that the world can serve as an ideal place for "soul-making."[19]

According to this view, the development of virtue, character, and trust is a product of challenge and response in faith, which is possible only through

---

14. Ward, *Divine Action*, 217.

15. Søvik, *Problem of Evil*, 255.

16. Ibid., 45–46; Ward, *Divine Action*, 217, emphasis in original.

17. Wolfhart Pannenberg, *Systematic Theology* (New York: T&T Clark, 2004), 3:643.

18. Paul Moser, "Divine Hiddenness Does Not Justify Atheism," in *Contemporary Debates in Philosophy of Religion*, ed. M. Peterson and R. VanArragon (Malden, MA: Blackwell, 2004), 49.

19. John Hick, *Evil and the God of Love* (New York: Harper & Row, 1966), 281. "Soul-Making" is the term that Hick uses to describe the process by which creatures grow in virtue and faith.

creaturely independence that is guaranteed by the veil hiding direct knowledge of God. The separation between God and creatures that is necessary to ensure a certain degree of creaturely independence may be experienced as freedom from God, but it also can make God appear distant or remote. As Pannenberg observes, "By ordaining his creation for independence, God took a risk himself, the risk that the autonomy of his creatures would make him seem to be nonessential and even nonexistent."[20]

The Value of Creaturely Rationality and Knowledge

To become an independent and autonomous self and be responsible for one's own personal growth, one must be able to understand and have some control over the world in which one lives. In this way, knowledge and rationality act as extrinsic goods in the service of the intrinsic goods of independence and love. Reason and knowledge, though, can also be considered as intrinsic goods in their own right. As Swinburne maintains, "it is intrinsically good for us—not merely instrumentally good—to have both moral knowledge and general theoretical knowledge, and that is a further reason why it is good that we should have the choice of seeking such knowledge or not bothering to do so."[21] The project of the natural sciences to gain knowledge and understanding is viewed by many as an inherently worthy task. Scientific knowledge or "true belief about how the world works," says Swinburne, "is a good thing to have."[22] And the same can be said of the study of logic and mathematics, which have rationality as their core.

According to Swinburne, one of the greatest intrinsic goods is "knowledge by experience (which includes the experience of pain)." Such knowledge is achieved through the process of learning because this type of knowing is "the best justified knowledge."[23] Learning the true causes and consequences of one's actions requires that the causes operate consistently and that the effects be predictable. "If agents are knowingly to bring about states of affairs, or to allow states of affairs to come about through neglecting to prevent them," says Swinburne, "they must know what consequences will follow from their actions."[24] The intrinsic value of knowledge through learning and the excitement and celebration of scientific discovery would be lost if God constructed the world such that each creature born into it arrived with all of the logic and knowledge they would ever need to know.

20. Pannenberg, *Systematic Theology*, 3:643.

21. Richard Swinburne, *Providence and the Problem of Evil* (New York: Oxford University Press, 1998), 97.

22. Ibid., 91.

23. Søvik, *Problem of Evil*, 30.

24. Swinburne, *Existence of God*, 247.

Yet, as the ancient proverb teaches, "with much wisdom comes much sorrow; and to increase knowledge is to increase suffering" (Eccles. 1:18). Learning through a process of trial and error can be painful. Moreover, the possibility of knowledge seems to require the possibility that certain types of suffering will arise from the knowledge that is gained. While knowledge of causes and effects can enable one to help others for the sake of good, knowledge can also show one how to create new types of pain and increase the suffering of others. Thus, while some affirm that the price of the possibility of knowledge and rationality is worth the potential cost of suffering, others would rather forego the prospect of knowledge, mathematics, and science if it meant a safeguard from certain types of suffering.

The Value of Creaturely Morality

According to the Jewish and Christian faiths, a central aim of God's creation of the cosmos is that it be inhabited by moral beings. "Morality," says Ward, "is grounded in the being and purposes of God."[25] Moral beings are fundamentally relational beings. Swinburne explains, "Moral inquiry takes the form of talking to other people of different kinds, hearing about their experiences, becoming involved in their lives."[26] While morality is something intrinsically valuable, it is also a key component of relational love. Ward observes, "The birth of morality is coterminous with the birth of the relational self," and, "that is an occurrence of such value and significance that the whole previous existence of the cosmos, though it has indeed its own beauty and value, can also be seen as preparing for the emergence of rational and responsible consciousness."[27]

The value of freedom is fulfilled in the life of moral discernment even as "freedom is a necessary condition of moral responsibility."[28] Within the biblical tradition, the knowledge that is most valued is the knowledge of good and evil. As Swinburne affirms, it is "especially important to have true beliefs about moral matters."[29] God's goodness and love can only be fully known through the moral mind. "The genesis of moral sense," says Ward, "can also be seen as the emergence of a genuine knowledge of objective goodness. For the theist, this will ultimately be knowledge of one Supreme Good, and it will enable the transformation of human lives by that knowledge."[30] Beings who possess the capacity for morality are "capable of conscious relationship to a Supreme Good." In this relationship with the Supreme Good as creatures grow in character and are

---

25. Keith Ward, *Pascal's Fire: Scientific Faith and Religious Understanding* (Oxford: Oneworld, 2006), 194.

26. Swinburne, *Providence and the Problem of Evil*, 96.

27. Ward, *Pascal's Fire*, 182.

28. Ibid., 67.

29. Swinburne, *Providence and the Problem of Evil*, 63.

30. Ward, *Pascal's Fire*, 183.

transformed from self-centeredness to other-centeredness, the goal of morality is fulfilled, and the ultimate meaning of existence is discovered.[31]

Yet the existence of morality entails a certain degree of suffering. Philosopher and theologian Nancey Murphy explains, "Dangers, hardships, pain, and other kinds of suffering are necessary conditions for development of the moral character prized by God."[32] It is not possible, maintains Hick, for God to "instantaneously create morally mature persons, since moral maturity almost certainly requires struggling, grappling with temptation over time, and probably participating in evil."[33] Murphy agrees that such a notion of an instant morally good character is incoherent. This is because, says Murphy, "the concepts of character and virtue are 'past-entailing predicates'; that is, they cannot apply *now* if certain things have not been true in the *past*."[34] Virtue and good character are not qualities that one is born with, but rather these are acquired characteristics that involve a lifetime of moral formation. But even if it were possible, says Hick, to instantaneously create moral beings (e.g., moral robots or genetically programmed humans), this would be less valuable than the type of morality gained through freedom, experience, struggle, and resistance to temptation. "One who has attained to goodness by meeting and eventually mastering temptations, and thus by rightly making responsible choices in concrete situations," says Hick, "is good in a richer and more valuable sense than would be one created *ab initio* [from the beginning] in a state either of innocence or virtue."[35] Murphy agrees: "Goodness slowly built up through personal histories of moral effort [is] more valuable in God's eyes than [creatures] with a nature created good" from the beginning.[36] The moral perfection of creatures "does not take place at the species level by a natural and inevitable evolution," but "through a hazardous adventure in individual freedom."[37]

Could God Have Created a World without Any Suffering Due to the Laws of Nature?

Among God's fundamental goals in creating the cosmos is that there would be creatures who could enjoy freedom, rationality, knowledge, independence, and morality—all for the sake of ultimately entering into loving relationship

---

31. Ibid., 195.

32. Nancey Murphy, "Science and the Problem of Evil: Suffering as a By-Product of a Finely Tuned Cosmos," in *Physics and Cosmology: Scientific Perspectives on the Problem of Natural Evil*, ed. Nancey Murphy, Robert J. Russell, and William Stoeger (Vatican City State: Vatican Observatory Publications, 2007), 140.

33. Michael Peterson, *God and Evil: An Introduction to the Issues* (Boulder, CO: Westview, 1998), 94.

34. Murphy, "Science and the Problem of Evil," emphasis in original.

35. Hick, *Evil and the God of Love*, 255.

36. Murphy, "Science and the Problem of Evil," 140.

37. Ibid.; Hick, *Evil and the God of Love*, 256.

with both God and with their fellow creatures (Deut. 6:5; Matt. 22:37; Mark 12:30–31; Luke 10:27). With knowledge of the moral good comes an awareness of its opposite. The dark side of free will and independence is the possibility of suffering created by free decisions—unconstrained by the goodness of God's will and uninfluenced by the power of God's presence—that tend away from the good. Rational knowledge might then be employed to amplify the effects of such bad decisions in order to create occasions of terrible suffering. Such instances of suffering caused by free and independent moral agents are known as *moral evils*. Beyond moral evils are incidents of suffering caused by the regular course of nature, known as *natural evils*. Much of human and animal suffering is in various ways the effect of the ordinary operation of the laws of nature. Children fall; the force of gravity is largely responsible for the fall that causes injury. Plate tectonics cause earthquakes and earthquakes cause tsunamis. People drown due to the physical properties of water. Why do God's purposes require laws of nature at all? Couldn't God have achieved his goals in creating the cosmos without natural evils? Or couldn't God at least have made a better world, one with less suffering due to natural causes?

The Need for Regular and Indeterministic Laws of Nature

Logically speaking, the world God made includes greater goods that could not be realized without the creation of a lawful, natural order that has the potential to generate natural evils. To reach his goal of creating beings capable of free and independent love, God must create a world that is both law-like and intelligible. Only beings that can come to understand the world, and partly control it, can take responsibility for their own personal growth. This is the only way the cosmos can be constructed, says Søvik, for it to give rise to "a form of being that is truly independent and autonomous."[38] Murphy explains, "The universe must be orderly enough to allow for human responsibility. If the world were completely unpredictable then there would be no meaningful human action."[39] For meaningful creaturely action, and for knowledge, rationality, freedom, independence and morality, one must be able to experience the effects of one's actions. Independent, rational, free, moral agents must be able to make sense of the world in which they act, anticipate the consequences of action, and consider alternative possibilities.

Imagine a world where God prevented every event that would cause pain or suffering. The result would be a cosmos in which the laws of nature would not operate consistently: "Sometimes gravity would operate, sometimes not; sometimes an object would be hard and solid, sometimes not."[40] In such a world,

---

38. Søvik, *Problem of Evil*, 41.

39. Murphy, "Science and the Problem of Evil," 141.

40. Hick, *Evil and the God of Love*, 306.

says Murphy, "there would be no point in trying to do science, and prediction of the consequences of our actions would be impossible."[41] Furthermore, observes Murphy, "if God acted in all cases to prevent suffering (e.g., putting out abandoned campfires to prevent fawns from being burned in forest fires) then humans would have no sense of responsibility for their actions."[42] If the world was completely unresponsive to certain bad choices that creatures make (e.g., secretly disabling the blaring stereo in the neighboring dorm room or leaving a restaurant without paying the bill), then creatures would lose the ability—and hence the freedom—to choose to do such things. The laws or regularities of nature are thus a necessary basis for free and meaningful action.

The law-like regularity of the world is also a prerequisite for the possibility of creaturely knowledge and morality. The normal cause-and-effect structure of the cosmos, while permitting the possibility of natural evils, is necessary so creatures may obtain the most valuable types of knowledge. "Natural evil," says Swinburne, "is needed to give us the choice of whether to acquire knowledge of the good and bad effects of our actions, and indeed in order to allow us to have very well-justified knowledge at all."[43] In this way, explains Søvik, "God, by the means of natural evils, gives us very well justified beliefs about the effects of our actions."[44] True beliefs or knowledge that emerges from the experience of the regularity of causes and effects is also related to moral knowledge. "For humans to have a choice between doing good and doing bad," observes Swinburne, "we need to have true beliefs about the effects of our actions, for the goodness or badness of an action is so often a matter of it having good or bad effects."[45] If God is to give creatures the choice between good and bad, "he must give us, or allow us to acquire, true beliefs about the effects of our actions—beliefs in which we have enough confidence to make it matter how we choose."[46]

Beyond the need for laws of nature to be regular, a certain kind of lawfulness is necessary in order to ensure creaturely freedom, independence, and moral action—specifically, what is needed is a lawfulness in which the future course of events is not already established from the beginning. "Radical freedom," maintains Ward, "is a condition of real moral responsibility and human autonomy," and "autonomy only truly exists if there are alternative possibilities of action, undetermined by any prior internal or external necessity."[47] In other words, the laws of nature must not absolutely control all occasions in the cosmos so that the physical history of the universe is precisely and completely determined in every

41. Murphy, "Science and the Problem of Evil," 141.

42. Ibid.

43. Swinburne, *Providence and the Problem of Evil*, 185.

44. Søvik, *Problem of Evil*, 30.

45. Swinburne, *Providence and the Problem of Evil*, 182.

46. Ibid.

47. Ward, *Pascal's Fire*, 210.

aspect. In this way, says Ward, "indeterminism seems to be a necessary condition of radical freedom."[48] Creaturely freedom, Søvik agrees, "requires an element of indeterminism, so that the future is not already decided before [such creatures] are born."[49] Indeterminism within the structure of physical causation, such as that observed in quantum physics, is likewise necessary for genuine morality. "The ascription of praise and blame," says Ward, "depends upon agents being *undetermined* by anything other than themselves, their knowledge of possibilities open to them, their awareness of right and wrong, and their capacity to choose without compulsion in crucial moments of moral choice."[50]

In addition, for God to accomplish his purposes in forming rational, independent, moral, and free beings, the regular patterns of the laws of nature must be statistical rather than absolutely uniform and without exception in all places and at all times. "In such a universe," says Ward, "intelligent creatures will not be wholly determined by a supreme intelligence. But neither will they be wholly free to do anything they wish in a universe without any structure, direction or goal. They will be free only within limits."[51] In this way, explains Ward, "God could create a universe in which there is much room for creative freedom and for the exercise of moral responsibility, and yet have a goal for the universe."[52] As Søvik asserts, "God chose to create our world, and in order to create creatures with the independent freedom that we have, he had to allow indeterminism and the possibility of pain and suffering."[53]

The Need for Amoral and Impersonal Laws of Nature

Given that laws of nature are required for God to accomplish his purposes, one might ask, "Could God have created a world with laws of nature that were more personal, perhaps so as to discriminate between the good actions of creatures and the bad actions?" For instance, one could imagine a world where the laws of nature were constructed to allow free choices, but where those free choices could not cause any harm or injury to other creatures. In this harm-free world, explain Murray and Rea, "good choices could be made, and the good consequences that follow from them allowed. But bad choices, while not prevented altogether, would be prevented from causing additional damage."[54] Could genuinely moral beings develop in such a universe? Murray and Rea think not. First, they observe, "if the world were structured this way, we would never be able to learn

---

48. Ibid., 69.

49. Søvik, *Problem of Evil*, 40.

50. Ward, *Pascal's Fire*, 92, emphasis in original.

51. Ibid., 69.

52. Ibid., 70.

53. Søvik, *Problem of Evil*, 46.

54. Murray and Rea, *Introduction to the Philosophy of Religion*, 173.

to do evil in the first place . . . the idea of trying to do so would never enter our minds." While at first this might appear to be an advantage favoring the production of moral creatures, in reality, say Murray and Rea, these conditions would prevent creatures "from being able to make genuinely morally significant choices between good and evil alternatives."[55] Philosopher Louis Pojman agrees, explaining that in this consequence-free world, "concepts like courage, honestly, love, benevolence, and kindness would make no sense because no one could do any harm. . . . [I]t would be wholly inadequate for character development."[56]

For the sake of encouraging moral character development, which emerges from one's reflection upon consequences, what if creatures were permitted to merely believe there were bad effects generated by their immoral actions when, in fact, there were not? Murray and Rea point out that such a world would quickly degenerate into a grand illusion where everyone lived within their own subjective realities and nothing would actually be as it appeared. A person in this situation would think she has made choices with evil consequences, while those consequences were in fact prevented by God. In this type of world, "what will happen," ask Murray and Rea, "when a person tries to apologize for punching you in the nose, or to return money that she has stolen from you, or to visit the grave of a murder victim?" Since God will have blocked the consequences,

> the apology will make no sense, the returned money will seem like an unexpected boon, and there will be no grave. Moreover, any attempt to discuss the blocked consequences will quickly reveal that all is not as it appears. To prevent everyone from discovering that no negative consequences in fact arise out of attempts to do evil, God would have to cause us to go mute, or to be misheard, every time we intended, in conversation, to refer back to earlier sinful deeds. Different newspapers would have to be delivered to different people. . . . [O]ur experience would have to contain increasingly more elaborate illusions, until we would finally (and probably rather quickly) reach a point where we each live in worlds that are largely experientially isolated from each other.[57]

Such an existence would hardly lend itself to the development of moral beings that could lovingly relate to each other in terms of truth, long-suffering, self-sacrifice, and forgiveness.

If a harm-free world would not be conducive to the construction of moral agents, then perhaps a better-suited world would be one where the laws of nature were based on principles of retributive justice. In this world of "instant karma," God could establish a natural order organized so that only those who deserve

---

55. Ibid.

56. Louis Pojman, *Philosophy of Religion* (Long Grove, IL: Waveland, 2009), 74–75.

57. Murray and Rea, *Introduction to the Philosophy of Religion*, 173.

to suffer do so. One can imagine God setting up the cosmos in such a way that free agents are followed around at all times by something like moral highway patrol officers, ready to immediately punish any creature that makes a morally evil choice and ready to reward creatures when they do what is right. Or one could imagine some type of natural condition that is immediately induced upon one's moral or immoral actions. Child abusers might be instantly stricken with an unattractive skin disease, while generous and benevolent persons instantly become more physically attractive. "Events in such a world," explains philosopher Thomas Tracy, "might or might not display the sorts of patterns familiar to us as natural law, but they would all conform to some putative principle of moral law—the *lex talionis* [or 'eye for an eye'], for example."[58] In this *lex talionis* world of instant karma, the punishing and rewarding of immoral and moral deeds would, in itself, be a type of law of nature.

Would an *instant karma* world such as this be well suited to the formation of moral and rational agents? Tracy believes it would not be. In an instant karma cosmos, observes Tracy, moral behavior would be achieved only through a type of coercion: "It would be difficult in such a world ever to do what is right simply for its own sake, since truly virtuous actions would bring a prompt and proportionate reward." Murray and Rea agree, observing that "under such conditions, any incentives for doing evil would be eliminated or at least overwhelmed by the presence of the moral police, and we would be psychologically unable to choose evil."[59] Consequently, says Tracy, "any world in which rational moral agency is possible must have a lawful, impersonal, and amoral structure." The laws of the universe, explains Ward, "must be morally neutral, posing challenges as well as opportunities that are roughly the same for all, and in which good and bad are inextricably intertwined in one reality that strives towards realization of its own inner potentialities."[60] In other words, says Tracy, in any cosmos that allows for the development of genuine moral agency, "it will be possible to get hurt simply by virtue of the lawful operation of the natural order. Suffering will not always be deserved; if it rains at all, it will rain on both the just and the unjust."[61]

The Need for Limited Divine Intervention

If a lawful, impersonal, and amoral structure is required to make possible the existence of free, moral, and rational beings, then God could not prevent all cases of suffering by systematically altering the laws that run the universe. But could God intervene more within the natural world to stop particular instances

---

58. Thomas Tracy, "The Lawfulness of Nature and the Problem of Evil," in *Physics and Cosmology*, ed. Murphy, Russell, and Stoeger, 165.

59. Murray and Rea, *Introduction to the Philosophy of Religion*, 185.

60. Ward, *Pascal's Fire*, 206.

61. Tracy, "Lawfulness of Nature," 165.

of evil and suffering? Why couldn't God act through miracles so as to remedy more suffering then he currently does? Without a certain degree of regularity in nature, there would be no possibility of free, independent, rational, moral, and loving creatures who can have a relationship with their Creator.[62] God can act at the quantum level without suspending any natural laws, but in order to keep the statistical regularity of the cosmos intact, God's miraculous actions must be restricted to the level of improbable anomalies. "There are limits," says Tracy, "on how extensively God can intervene miraculously and still maintain the lawful character of the created order."[63] The necessity for a regular and predictable cosmos demands certain restrictions on what God can do outside of that regularity without undoing it. As Ward explains, "God can perform particular divine acts in our law-like but open world, but such a world also places restrictions on divine action. In general, God does not want to disturb the regularities that he has created, and if he interrupts all the time, he ruins the system."[64] God's actions in remedying suffering must generally be hidden so that they fall within the range of the probabilistic limits of physical law. In the eyes of the physical sciences, such divine actions will appear as simply chance, and as events that are improbable, but not technically impossible.

Why, then, does God not intervene more to prevent more instances of intense suffering? The answer, says Ward, "is that God treasures the unique goods of this kind of world so highly that he does not want to disturb this value-creating system too much." The reason "why God sometimes helps and heals people and other times does not" is "that God can intervene sometimes without disturbing the independent system too much, but not at other times. Since the world is so complex, we can never know when God can intervene."[65] One could imagine that there is a specific balance or tipping point at which, if God performs one more miracle, all of the goods of a lawful context for rational, free, independent, and moral life will be lost. For all that the average observer in this world knows, the current cosmos could be at this point. According to Tracy, "Even if our world is poised at this balance point, it will appear to us that it includes an excess of evils" since one will always feel that certain evils or experiences of suffering could have been prevented. However, he says, "we are not in an epistemic position to judge [or in a place to know] whether or not" this is indeed the case.[66]

---

62. In a similar way, if faith is greatly valued by God, and if the veil obscuring God is necessary for the development of faith, and if God values freedom and law-like regularity is needed for freedom, then God may do *more miracles* where there is *more faith*; and God will not use miracles to bring people to initial faith or convince people of little faith (see also Matt. 13:58).

63. Tracy, "Lawfulness of Nature," 173.

64. Ward, *Divine Action*, 62; Ward, *Pascal's Fire*, 96; and Ward, *God, Faith & the New Millennium: Christian Belief in an Age of Science* (Oxford: Oneworld, 1998), 104. See discussion of Ward in Søvik, *Problem of Evil*, 41.

65. Søvik, *Problem of Evil*, 263.

66. Tracy, "Lawfulness of Nature," 173.

The Constraints of Cosmic Fine Tuning

Is it possible that God could have created a world with different laws of nature that would have yielded fewer instances of natural evil? Perhaps God could have created a law of gravity that was gentler to creatures, or laws that produce a few less hurricanes and earthquakes. In response, Murphy explains that even if life were possible in a universe with vastly different basic laws, there would still be suffering.[67] The reason is due to the constraints of cosmic fine-tuning. "Recent work on the 'fine-tuning' of the constants and basic laws of physics," says Murphy, "suggests that the laws themselves had to be almost exactly as they are in order that life exist in the universe."[68] Cosmic fine-tuning points to the physical impossibility of a cosmos with life and with natural laws and constants significantly different from those in the present universe. Prior to research in cosmic fine-tuning, it was possible to imagine that the world could have been vastly different in ways that would lessen suffering, but now it seems that the same physical laws that permit life are also those that permit suffering.

Consider the law of gravity, for example, which founder of the Gravity Research Foundation, Roger W. Babson, has named "our enemy number one." Babson considers gravity evil because its effects resulted in the drowning of both his younger sister and his grandson.[69] Yet physicists now know that the slightest change in the gravitational constant—as small as a difference of one part in 10^{40}—would render life in the cosmos impossible. Physicist and philosopher Don Howard explains, "The same laws that give rise to disasters also produce good. Gravity pulls a meteoroid down upon us. But gravity also structures the solar system so as to make possible life on Earth."[70] Gravity, though sometimes the cause of suffering, needs to be as strong as it is relative to other forces so that planets stay together and so that the tissues of human and animal bodies hold together.

As scientists learn more about the deep structure of the cosmos, it appears that the conditions under which life can appear in the cosmos are extraordinarily limited:

> Vanishingly small changes in any of a large number of variables (e.g., the gravitational constant, the mass density and expansion rate of the early universe), would have consequences in the unfolding history of the cosmos that rule out forming the structures that make life possible. . . . In order for the world to engender intelligent life it must be

---

67. Nancey Murphy, "Introduction," in *Physics and Cosmology*, ed. Murphy, Russell, and Stoeger, xii.

68. Ibid.; and Murphy, "Science and the Problem of Evil," 142.

69. Don Howard, "Physics as Theodicy," in *Physics and Cosmology*, ed. Murphy, Russell, and Stoeger, 325.

70. Ibid., 332.

put together in very much the way we find it, and it will, therefore, contain nearly the current range and volume of natural evils.[71]

Consequently, observes Murphy, "the better we understand the interconnectedness among natural systems in the universe, and especially their bearing on complex life, the clearer it becomes that it would be impossible to have a world that allowed for a free and loving human response to God, yet one without natural evil."[72]

Where Is God When Natural Disasters Strike?

The most notorious cases of suffering owing to the effects of nature are natural disasters. Consider, for example, the December 2004 tsunami in Southeast Asia that took the lives of more than 200,000 people and left millions more without homes, water, power, or sustenance. Among the lives taken during the most destructive tsunami in recorded history were those of the family of seven-year-old Karl Nilsson. The family was on vacation in the resort town of Phuket when the wave hit. In the moments before the tsunami struck, writes journalist Tom Martin, Karl had been playing in a hotel room with his two younger brothers, and his parents were only yards away. When the waters rushed in, the entire family was swept away. Karl somehow survived, but "stranded and alone in a foreign land, his life had been torn apart." Frightened, abandoned, with a broken collarbone, and shivering in his underwear, Karl had still hoped to find his family. He never did. "There was to be no happy ending," comments Martin, and, to this day, Karl lives in the wake of that tragedy.[73] In the fallout of such disasters, many have asked, "If God is a God of love, why is this happening? Why is God doing this?"[74]

If tsunamis come from earthquakes, and earthquakes come from plate tectonics, then is it possible that God could have accomplished his purposes in creating the cosmos, without plate tectonics? In light of the contemporary scientific understanding, it is difficult to imagine how any form of complex life could have arisen without plate tectonics. Scientists have found that plate tectonics is crucial to the origin of life, and, as biologist Peter Ward and astronomer Donald Brownlee observe, plate tectonics is a key factor explaining "why animal life exists here but not on other planets and their moons in our solar system."[75]

---

71. Tracy, "Lawfulness of Nature," 166.

72. Murphy, "Science and the Problem of Evil," 132.

73. Tom Martin, "Tragedy Goes on for Lost Child of Tsunami," *The Scotsman*, June 25, 2005, accessible at *http://www.scotsman.com/news/tragedy-goes-on-for-lost-child-of-tsunami-1-1391450.*

74. Denis Edwards, "Why Is God Doing This? Suffering, the Universe, and Christian Eschatology," in *Physics and Cosmology*, ed. Murphy, Russell, and Stoeger, 247.

75. Peter Ward and Donald Brownlee, *Rare Earth: Why Complex Life Is Uncommon in the Universe* (New York: Copernicus, 2000), 193–94.

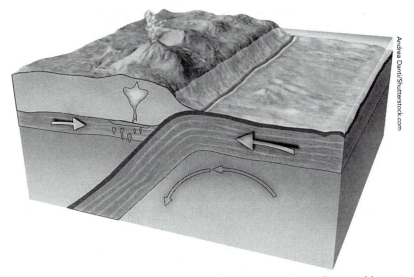

The processes of plate tectonics, such as the subduction zone illustrated here, cause natural disasters, including earthquake, tsunamis, and volcanoes. But without plate tectonics, scientists agree, there would be no life on Earth.

According to Brownlee and Ward, "the movement of the planetary crust across the surface of the planet is found in our solar system *only* on Earth, and it may be vanishingly rare in the Universe as a whole." And this is one key reason why life in the universe is rare as well.

Plate tectonics is necessary for the existence and sustenance of life for a number of reasons. "First," explain Brownlee and Ward, "plate tectonics promotes high levels of global biodiversity," and it is "the factor on Earth that is most critical to maintaining diversity through time." In addition to this, "plate tectonics provides our planet's global thermostat by recycling chemicals crucial to keeping the volume of carbon dioxide in our atmosphere relatively uniform, and thus it has been the single most important mechanism enabling liquid water to remain on Earth's surface for more than 4 billion years." A third factor is that "plate tectonics is the dominant force that causes changes in sea level, which, it turns out, are vital to the formation of minerals that keep the level of global carbon dioxide (and hence global temperature) in check." Another reason is that there would be no continents at all on Earth without plate tectonics, and "Earth might look much as it did during the first billion and a half years of its existence: a watery world, with only isolated volcanic islands dotting its surface." Moreover, say Brownlee and Ward, "without continents, we might by now have lost the most important ingredient for life, water, and in so doing come to resemble Venus." Lastly, "plate tectonics makes possible one of Earth's most potent defense systems: its magnetic field." Without the magnetic field, Earth "would be bombarded by a potentially lethal influx of cosmic radiation, and solar wind 'sputtering' (in which particles from the sun hit the upper atmosphere with high energy) might slowly eat away at the atmosphere, as it has on Mars."[76]

Earthquakes, then, are a crucial part of the constant recycling of planetary crust, which has the effect of producing a lush, habitable planet. While the downside of earthquakes is obvious, a number of philosophers and theologians have asked if God is really the one to blame. In other words, was God's creation of plate tectonics the cause of unavoidable suffering and devastation in December of 2004? Murphy thinks not. Overpopulation and poverty were also key culprits. Murphy points out that tectonically active areas are often overpopulated because the recycling of the crust in these locations makes fishing and coastal farming lucrative. When natural disasters strike it is the poor who suffer most. Consider the difference between the earthquake with a magnitude of 7.0 that struck Haiti on January 12, 2010 (killing more than 160,000 and displacing close to 1.5 million) and a larger earthquake (7.3-magnitude) that struck Japan on December 7, 2012 and yet caused no major injuries or destruction. The great difference in the level of suffering caused by these two tectonically similar events in two highly populated countries has to do with their relative levels of wealth and poverty. Poverty, says Murphy, is the primary reason "why such large populations live in regions most likely to suffer natural calamities."[77] And the existence of poverty is a result of the selfish use of human free will—rather than being caused or required by any laws of nature that God created. Where, then, was God in all of this? "God," answers Murphy, "is creator of a universe intended to support life, particularly life with the capacity to respond to him in love. The tsunami was an unwanted by-product of the natural conditions that make life possible on Earth."[78] Without earthquakes and oceans, which create the potential for suffering caused by tsunamis, there would be no life at all.

Why Would an All-Loving God Create through Evolution?

While suffering emerges from the effects of the regular operation of the laws of nature, scientists, philosophers, and theologians have also pointed out that much suffering arises from the evolutionary process. As biologist Richard Dawkins points out,

> The total amount of suffering per year in the natural world is beyond all decent contemplation. During the minute it takes me to compose

76. Ibid., 193–94.

77. Murphy, "Science and the Problem of Evil," 132.

78. "Tectonic shifts cause earthquakes and tsunamis, but they also build up the land masses that we call home." See Howard, "Physics as Theodicy," 332.

this sentence, thousands of animals are being eaten alive; others are running for their lives, whimpering with fear; others are being slowly devoured from within by rasping parasites; thousands of all kinds are dying of starvation, thirst and disease.[79]

A century earlier, reflecting on such instances of animal suffering, Charles Darwin wrote, "What a book a devil's chaplain might write on the clumsy, wasteful, blundering, low and horribly cruel works of Nature!"[80] Moreover, death, extinction, and ruthless competition all seem to be key components of the mechanism of natural selection. "There is no getting away from this," says philosopher of biology Michael Ruse, because "pain and suffering are right there at the heart of" natural selection, and "are intimately involved in the adaptive process."[81] Still, many contemporary Jewish, Christian, and Islamic theists affirm that evolution is the way God creates life.[82] The question remains, then, why would an all-loving God create life through evolution?

Are Animals Conscious of Suffering?

One way to address the problem of animal suffering was offered by the French philosopher and theologian, Nicolas Malebranche (1638–1715), a prominent early disciple of philosopher and scientist René Descartes (1596–1650). Driven by theological concern for innocent animal suffering, Malebranche reasons that "if God renders justice to all his creatures, then animals must be incapable of suffering, for they have neither committed wrong, nor have they the opportunity for compensation in a future life."[83] However, if innocent animals do not feel pain, then God's goodness and justice can be upheld. Malebranche and other followers of Descartes (known as Cartesians), argued that nonhuman animals are essentially machines (or automatons) that do not possess souls, have mental awareness, or feel pain. For many generations, numerous scientists, philosophers, and theologians judged the Cartesian solution to the problem of animal suffering adequate. And even through the 1980s, says philosopher of science

79. Richard Dawkins, *River Out of Eden: A Darwinian View of Life* (New York: Basic Books, 1995), 131.

80. Charles Darwin, quoted in Jerry A. Coyne, "Gould and God: Review of *A Devil's Chaplain* by Richard Dawkins," *Nature* 422 (April 24, 2003): 813; original source not cited.

81. Michael Ruse, *Can a Darwinian Be a Christian? The Relationship between Science and Religion* (Cambridge: Cambridge University Press, 2001), 131.

82. Robert John Russell, "Special Providence and Genetic Mutation: A New Defense of Theistic Evolution," in *Evolutionary and Molecular Biology: Scientific Perspectives on Divine Action*, ed. Robert John Russell, William R. Stoeger, SJ, and Francisco J. Ayala (Vatican City State: Vatican Observatory Publications; Berkeley, CA: Center for Theology and the Natural Sciences, 1998), 194.

83. Malebranche, quoted in Peter Harrison, "Animal Souls, Metempsychosis, and Theodicy in Seventeenth-Century English Thought," *Journal of the History of Philosophy* 31, no. 4 (October 1993): 519–44, at 523; original source not cited.

Bernard Rollin, scientific researchers remained uncertain as to whether animals experience pain. Moreover, comments Rollin, veterinarians trained in the United States before 1989 were generally instructed to ignore animal pain.[84]

Today, however, researchers in animal consciousness have judged the Cartesian view scientifically untenable. In light of contemporary studies, explain animal consciousness researchers Marc Bekoff, Colin Allen, and Gordon Burghardt, animals have been shown to have "intentions, consciousness, choice, deliberation, planning, and other mental processes."[85] It has likewise been empirically demonstrated and "is now widely accepted that animals can feel pain and suffering."[86] While it was long thought that pain, suffering, fear, and anxiety had their evolutionary origin with mammals, "anatomical, pharmacological and behavioral data," says biologist K. P. Chandroo and colleagues, "suggest that affective states of pain, fear and stress are likely to be experienced by fish in similar ways as in tetrapods [i.e., land vertebrates]." In other words, explains Chandroo and colleagues, "fish have the capacity to suffer."[87]

According to biologist C. M. Sherwin, researchers have found that even "invertebrates such as cockroaches, flies and slugs . . . exhibit behavioural and physiological responses indicative of pain; and, apparently, experience learned helplessness." Furthermore, explains Sherwin, "the similarity of these responses to those of vertebrates may indicate a level of consciousness or suffering that is not normally attributed to invertebrates."[88] Scientific investigations have revealed that the neurons required for the sensation of pain (called *nociceptors*) are present not only in mammals, birds, reptiles, amphibians, and fish, but also in some crustaceans and even a few insects.[89] The presence of opioid receptors (which work to alleviate pain) in numerous invertebrates from sea slugs to honeybees additionally indicates that such animals may experience pain as a deterrent and pleasure as a motivator.[90]

---

84. Bernard Rollin, *The Unheeded Cry: Animal Consciousness, Animal Pain, and Science* (New York: Oxford University Press, 1989).

85. Marc Bekoff, Colin Allen, and Gordon Burghardt, eds., *The Cognitive Animal: Empirical and Theoretical Perspectives on Animal Cognition* (Cambridge, MA: MIT Press 2002), xi.

86. Alain Boissy et al., "Assessment of Positive Emotions in Animals to Improve Their Welfare," *Physiology and Behavior* 92 (2007): 376.

87. K. P. Chandroo et al., "Can Fish Suffer? Perspectives on Sentience, Pain, Fear and Stress," *Applied Animal Behaviour Science* 86 (2004): 225.

88. C. M. Sherwin, "Can Invertebrates Suffer? Or, How Robust Is Argument-by-Analogy?" *Animal Welfare* 10, no. 1 (February 2001): 103–18. See also Jane A. Smith, "A Question of Pain in Invertebrates," *Institute for Laboratory Animals Journal* 33, nos. 1–2 (1991): 25–31.

89. S. Barr, P. Laming, J. T. Dick, and R. W. Elwood, "Nociception or Pain in a Decapod Crustacean?," *Animal Behaviour* 75 (2008): 745–51.

90. Lauritz Somme, "Sentience and Pain in Invertebrates," Report to the Norwegian Scientific Committee for Food Safety (2005), accessible at *https://web.archive.org/web/20100814211300/http://jillium.nfshost.com/library/pain.htm*. See also A. S. Levine and C. J. Billington, "Opioids as Agents of Reward-Related Feeding: A Consideration of the Evidence," *Physiology and Behavior* 82, no. 1 (2004): 57–61.

Does the Evolutionary Process Necessitate Animal Suffering?

Many standard accounts of Darwinian evolution emphasize the central role of death, pain, contingency, and selfishness, as being entailed in the very process by which organisms are created, and the "insights of Darwinian science suggest" that "competition, predation, and extinctions prove indeed to be necessary elements in the evolution of the sort of biosphere we know now."[91] Insofar as this dark side of natural history is essential to the mechanism of natural selection, and insofar as God uses evolution through natural selection to create life, then God is ultimately accountable for the pain and suffering that results from this process.[92]

One way around this dilemma is to argue, as Ruse has, that Darwinian natural selection is the "only way in which complex adaptation could be produced by [natural] law," and that God essentially had his hands tied when creating biological life.[93] Biologist Francisco J. Ayala has likewise contended that if we view cases of cruelty and evil in nature as a "consequence of the clumsy ways of the evolutionary process" then a major "burden is removed from the shoulders of believers."[94] Consequently, there is a ready-made theological answer to why evolutionary suffering exists—namely, the necessity of natural selection as the *only* means that God could use to produce adaptively complex life. "Physical evil exists," observes Ruse, "and Darwinism explains why God had no choice but to allow it to occur."[95]

Another potential response to the problem of animal suffering in evolution is to point to how, throughout the Old Testament, new life and new horizons emerge from death and suffering and, in the New Testament, the renewal of all creation is anchored upon the suffering and death of Jesus on the cross.[96] While the ultimate theological reasons for why it is necessary for suffering to precede new life remain obscured in the divine mystery, they are reasons nonetheless, and as such remain firmly rooted in the very heart of the Judeo-Christian scriptural tradition. That God might choose to create new life through evolutionary suffering, then, is in no way theologically inconsistent with the traditional Jewish

---

91. Christopher Southgate, "Re-Reading Genesis, John, and Job: A Christian Response to Darwinism," *Zygon* 46, no. 2 (June 2011): 370–95, at 384.

92. Ruse, *Can a Darwinian Be a Christian?*, 131.

93. Michael Ruse, "Darwinism and Christianity: Does Evil Spoil a Beautiful Friendship?" in *The Evolution of Evil*, ed. G. Bennett, M. J. Hewlett, T. Peters, and R. J. Russell (Göttingen: Vandenhoeck and Ruprecht, 2008), 86–98, at 97.

94. Francisco J. Ayala, *Darwin's Gift To Science and Religion* (Washington DC: National Academies Press, 2007), xi, 159.

95. Ruse, *Can a Darwinian Be a Christian?*, 136–37.

96. Niels Henrik Gregersen, "The Cross of Christ in an Evolutionary World," *Dialog: A Journal of Theology* 40, no. 3 (Fall 2001): 192–207.

and Christian understandings of how God acts within history.[97] Appealing to the theological and scriptural traditions in light of what is known of the evolutionary emergence of life through natural selection, one might discern "evolutionary disvalues as part of the 'shadow side' of creation."[98] In this way, says philosopher Holmes Rolston III, one response to evolutionary suffering is to accept that "struggle is the dark side of creativity."[99]

A third approach to the theodicy dilemma posed by evolution is to take a closer look at the science itself to understand how instances of animal suffering directly relate to the processes or mechanisms that drive biological change through time. Evolutionary biologist Jeffrey Schloss points out that "competition is neither a necessary nor a sufficient condition for natural selection. *Natural selection* is formally defined as the differential reproduction of genotypes (or information)." Moreover, says Schloss, "the claim that 'death drives evolutionary development' turns out to be problematic. . . . Scientifically death *does not* 'drive' evolution." The same can be said of suffering and extinction. In scientific principle, then, death, ruthless competition, parasitism, suffering, and extinction are not the *driving forces* of natural selection, but rather, are a consequence of *limited resources* and the *contingencies* of the natural world.[100] It is neither logically nor empirically the case that evolution by natural selection is built on competition and premature death. Much of the observed change in the gene frequencies of different populations over time occurs without any vital contribution from either of these phenomena. In making this scientific point Schloss does not believe the theological problem of suffering in evolution is resolved. As Schloss says: "This is not in any way to blunt the theological problems associated with competition, suffering, and death" as genuine features of the natural world. Nevertheless, says Schloss, "I am arguing that these [problematic instances of suffering] are not exacerbated by evolution" and, thus, this perspective can still "act as a resource for natural theodicy."[101] Schloss's point about what Darwinian evolution *does* and *does not* require manages to remove the direct burden of guilt for animal suffering from natural selection—and also from any God who would choose to create through this evolutionary

---

97. Christopher Southgate, *The Groaning of Creation: God, Evolution, and the Problem of Evil* (Louisville: Westminster John Knox, 2008), 76–78.

98. Southgate, "Re-Reading Genesis, John, and Job," 384.

99. Holmes Rolston III, "Naturalizing and Systematizing Evil," in *Is Nature Ever Evil? Religion, Science, and Value*, ed. Willem B. Drees (London: Routledge, 2003), 67–86, at 79.

100. Jeffrey Schloss, "Evolution, Creation, and the Sting of Death: A Response to John Laing," BioLogos Forum website, August 10, 2012, accessible at *http://biologos.org/blog/evolution -creation-and-the-sting-of-death-part-1*.

101. Michael Murray and Jeff Schloss, "Animal Suffering: Theological and Philosophical Perspectives," lecture given at the Faraday Institute of Science and Religion, July 22, 2011, accessible at *https://www.faraday.st-edmunds.cam.ac.uk/Multimedia.php?Mode=Add&ItemID=Item_Multimedia _430&width=720&height=460*, quote begins at 00:30:12.

process. However, one may still wonder, why God would allow resources to be so limited in the first place.[102] Given that competition for resources *does* tend to increase the *efficiency* of creation through natural selection, one might also ask why God's system of creativity has to be structured in such a way that *so much* evolutionary creativity should flow from selfish competition for these limited resources. One might likewise wonder why predation, though perhaps not technically *essential* to the dynamics of natural selection, must still play such a significant role in the evolutionary history of life. In other words, why should the system underlying life's evolutionary creation be so structured that "arms races" between predators and prey generate so much adaptive novelty?[103] Finally, one might ask why parasites should reap the evolutionary benefits of such ruthlessly selfish behaviors—taking "a tremendous toll of life with scarcely any return that we can see."[104] Though such evolutionary evils or "disvalues" may not be ultimately *necessary* for the creation of life through natural selection, they are certainly behaviors that move selection *more effectively along* nevertheless.

A fourth possible approach to the dilemma posed by God's creation of life through evolution is to evaluate several recent developments in evolutionary biology that deemphasize the creative role of natural selection. A number of evolutionary theories that focus on mechanisms of cooperation, horizontal gene transfer, self-organization, developmental constraints, epigenetic inheritance, and generic morphogenetic principles (e.g., biological structuralism) view natural selection as secondary to other forces that drive evolution.[105] Some of these perspectives see novel mechanisms of evolutionary change as playing a role equally important to genetic mutation and natural selection. For instance, evolutionary biologist Martin Nowak has recently made a case for adding "'natural cooperation' as a third fundamental principle of evolution beside mutation and natural selection."[106] In a similar way, biologist David Penny suggests that "the selfish aspect of evolution has been over-emphasized," and he points out that

---

102. One response is that the issue of limited resources appears to be inextricably intertwined with a number of anthropic conditions related to the fine-tuned structure of the universe. See, for example, Thomas Tracy's discussion of the "nomic condition" for the existence of finite persons in Tracy, "Lawfulness of Nature," 164–66.

103. Geerat Vermeij, *Evolution and Escalation: An Ecological History of Life* (Princeton: Princeton University Press, 1987).

104. Holmes Rolston III, "Disvalues in Nature," *The Monist* 75 (1992): 250–78, at 255.

105. For a detailed discussion of this approach see Joshua M. Moritz, "Evolutionary Evil and Dawkins' Black Box: Changing the Parameters of the Problem," in *The Evolution of Evil*, ed. Gaymon Bennett, Martinez J. Hewlett, Ted Peters, and Robert John Russell (Gottingen: Vandenhoeck & Ruprecht, 2008), 143–88. See also Joshua Moritz, "Animal Suffering, Evolution, and the Origins of Evil: Toward a 'Free Creatures' Defense," *Zygon* 49, no. 2 (June 2014): 348–80.

106. Martin Nowak, "Five Rules for the Evolution of Cooperation," *Science* 314 (December 2006): 1560–63, at 1563. Nowak continues, "Evolution is constructive because of cooperation. New levels of organization evolve when the competing units on the lower level begin to cooperate" (1563).

"symbiosis is extremely common in nature" and cooperation ubiquitous through-out evolutionary history.[107]

Other biologists who have stressed the centrality of alternative evolution-ary processes see natural selection as playing even less of a central role in the evolutionary saga. According to philosopher of biology Bruce Weber these sci-entists argue that "natural selection is a trimming force at best, rather than having a creative and directional role."[108] For instance, microbiologists such as Carl Woese and Kalin Vetsigian hold that cooperation through mutualistic relationships was and is *more important* in shaping life's history than natural selection. Consequently, the evolutionary drama should not be described pri-marily in terms of a violent struggle but rather as a continual exploration of mutualistic networks. "If Darwin had been a microbiologist," write Woese and Vestigan, "he surely would not have pictured a 'struggle' for existence as 'red in tooth and claw.' Our view of competition in a communal world as a dynami-cal process is very different from the widely understood notion of Darwinian evolution."[109] Woese and Goldenfeld describe a realm of mutualistic evolution beyond the neo-Darwinian framework, explaining that "the Modern Synthesis is, at best, a partial representation of population genetics; but, this on its own is a limited subset of the evolutionary process itself, and arguably the least inter-esting one."[110] Echoing Woese, Vestigan, and Goldenfeld, biologists Scott Gil-bert, Jan Sapp and Alfred Tauber explain that in light of the discoveries of the last few decades "classical conceptions of individuality are called into question by evidence of all-pervading symbiosis."[111] There are no competing "individu-als" in the classical Darwinian sense and even the higher "animals are com-posites of many species living, developing, and evolving together."[112] Instead of ruthless competition between individuals as the axis around which evolution revolves, one finds "a world of complex and intermingled *relationships*—not only among microbes, but also between microscopic and macroscopic life."[113]

---

107. David Penny, "Cooperation and Selfishness Both Occur during Molecular Evolution," *Biol-ogy Direct* 9, no. 26 (2014): 1–9, at 4. Penny continues, "Indeed an interesting question might be to invert the question and find any organism where some symbiosis does not occur!" (4).

108. Bruce Weber, "Complex Systems Dynamics in Evolution and Emergent Processes," in *Beyond Mechanism: Putting Life Back into Biology*, ed. Brian Henning and Adam Scarfe (Lanham, MD: Lexington Books, 2013), 67–74, at 70.

109. Kalin Vetsigian, Carl Woese, and Nigel Goldenfeld, "Collective Evolution and the Genetic Code," *Proceedings of the National Academy of Sciences*, 103, no. 28 (July 11, 2006): 10696–701, at 10697.

110. Carl Woese and Nigel Goldenfeld, "Life Is Physics: Evolution as a Collective Phenomenon Far from Equilibrium," *Annual Review of Condensed Matter Physics* 2 (2011): 375–99, at 383.

111. Scott Gilbert, Jan Sapp, and Alfred Tauber, "A Symbiotic View of Life: We Have Never Been Individuals" *Quarterly Review of Biology*, 87, no. 4 (December 2012): 325–41, at 327.

112. Ibid., 326.

113. Ibid.

According to these scientists "evolution was essentially communal from the very beginning" and the mutualistic dimension of the evolutionary process continues to this day.[114]

In this view of life history the influence of selfishness, contingency, individualism, and competition in the process of evolutionary creation is much mediated. When considered philosophically and theologically, reflects philosopher Sarah Coakley, "the phenomenon of cooperation, seen now to be as deeply inculcated in the propulsion of evolution—from the bacterial level upwards—as Darwin's celebrated principles of mutation and selection, provides a significant modification of the 'nature red in tooth and claw' image that Darwinism early accrued to itself."[115] While cooperative models of evolution may result in "no less suffering or 'wastage'" in the *observable* history of life, they do show that "there *is* an ever-present tendency *against* individualism or isolationism" within evolution and that "hostile competitiveness or individualism" plays a much smaller role in the grand evolutionary narrative of life's creation.[116]

A similar de-emphasis on the role of struggle, competition, and selfishness in evolution is found among biologists conducting research in the area of evolutionary-developmental biology (called "evo-devo"). These scientists maintain that the forms that organisms take as a result of both embryological development and evolution are constrained not so much by struggle, competition, and historical contingency as by relational laws that govern the development of body plans and interacting ecologies.[117] Under the influence of the modern synthesis, twentieth century neo-Darwinian evolutionary theory assumed "that organismal structures like segmented bodies, eyes, limbs, and hearts, evolved essentially *de novo*, multiple times, independently in various lineages, in close conformity with the requirements of function."[118] However, explain biologists Michael Rose and Todd Oakley, beginning in the 1980s and 1990s the "discovery of conserved developmental genetic processes for patterning the bodies of taxonomically and morphologically disparate organisms forced biologists to consider common descent at deeper levels of biological organization."[119]

In addition to deemphasizing the central role of selfishness and competition in the process of evolution, findings in evolutionary symbiosis, evolutionary

---

114. Vetsigian, Woese, and Goldenfeld, "Collective Evolution," 10701.

115. Sarah Coakley, "Evolution, Cooperation, and Divine Providence," in *Evolution, Games and God: The Principle of Cooperation*, ed. Sarah Coakley and Martin Nowak (Cambridge, MA: Harvard University Press, 2013), 375–85, at 382.

116. Ibid., 382.

117. Scott Gilbert and David Epel, *Ecological Developmental Biology: Integrating Epigenetics, Medicine, and Evolution* (Sunderland, MA: Sinauer, 2009).

118. Michael Rose and Todd Oakley, "The New Biology: Beyond the Modern Synthesis," *Biology Direct* 2, no. 30 (November 24, 2007): 9.

119. Ibid.

convergence, and evolutionary-developmental constraints have been interpreted as reducing the overall role of randomness in the evolutionary history of life. For example, Vetsigian, Woese, and Goldenfeld point out that that "communal evolution results in a genetic code that is much further from the mean of random distributions than the results of Darwinian evolution."[120] Some of these scientists have even argued that the vast spectrum of evolutionary incarnations that have emerged throughout time appear to be the expression of "deeper structures," "principles," or even "prior organizational templates" written in mathematically quantifiable laws of nature.[121]

The Value of Creation through Evolution

In light of the fact that neither natural selection nor other evolutionary mechanisms necessarily entail the suffering of nonhuman creatures in order for evolution to proceed, it appears that God's employing evolution in creation is not an automatic indictment of divine malevolence. Because there is no necessary link between the mechanisms of the evolutionary process and the suffering that is witnessed within evolutionary history, God's creation through evolution need not be valued negatively on account of the suffering that it causes. Beyond this, God's creation of the various forms of life through evolution can be interpreted as having a positive value in that it functions to magnify God's overarching goals and purposes in creating the cosmos. In light of God's purposes in creating physical reality even certain types of randomness can be seen as contributing positive value to a theological understanding of creation that employs both contingency and evolution. If God's goals in creating the cosmos include making beings with the capacity for freedom, rationality, and morality, then accomplishing such goals appears to require a regular structure for natural law combined with a degree of physical indeterminism. In a similar way, the Divine goal that creatures develop a high degree of independence and relational love is best achieved through a means where creatures are created with the capacity to create themselves. An *evolutionary* understanding of creation allows for distinct beings who, having played a key part in their own particular histories of emergence, can then independently love God for who God is *as God*, and in turn be loved

---

120. Vetsigian, Woese, and Goldenfeld, "Collective Evolution," 10701. Carl Woese and Nigel Goldenfeld likewise say that there is "compelling evidence that not only may mutations be nonrandom, but horizontal gene transfer, too, need not be random." Woese and Goldenfeld, "Life Is Physics," 391.

121. Simon Conway Morris, "Evolution and the Inevitability of Intelligent Life," in *The Cambridge Companion to Science and Religion*, ed. Peter Harrison (Cambridge: Cambridge University Press, 2010), 148–72, at 153. See also George McGhee, *Convergent Evolution: Limited Forms Most Beautiful* (Cambridge: MIT Press 2011); and Brian Goodwin, "Beyond the Darwinian Paradigm: Understanding Biological Forms," in *Evolution: The First Four Billion Years*, ed. Michael Ruse and Joseph Travis (Cambridge, MA: Harvard University Press, 2009), 299–312; Simon Conway Morris, *The Runes of Evolution: How the Universe Became Self-Aware* (West Conshohocken, PA: Templeton Press, 2015).

for who they are *as themselves*. An evolutionary creation appears to be required for God to create independent, moral, and rational creatures who can—on their own terms—enter into relational love and community with their Creator.[122] The evils that arise from contingency within the creative process are directly related to the values and goals that God aims to achieve in creating beings who can know and love God.

Within the Abrahamic faith traditions, one of God's central goals in creating the cosmos is the formation of independent creatures with the capacity to love. God desires beings who can independently love God and whom God can love for whom they themselves are, as independent beings. Independence requires that one be responsible for one's *own* growth—at least to some degree. Evolution is a process by which creatures are self-made to a very high degree. Through designing evolution as the mechanism of creation, God made creation to make itself.[123] An evolutionary creation is one where creatures can achieve a significant level of independence and thus develop a key precondition for the giving of self and receiving of the other within the dynamics of mutually relational love.

Consider, for instance, an evolutionary process known as *niche construction*, where an organism alters its environment through its behaviors and decisions in such a way that such changes impact the way both its own evolution and that of its descendants moves forward. Through niche construction, explains biologist Kevin Laland, animals "not only shape the nature of their world, but also in part determine the selection pressures to which they and their descendants are exposed."[124] In this way, the behavioral decisions, environmental alterations— whether physical, social, or nutritional—and subjective choices of animals "play

---

122. This addresses, in part, the question of why God did not create heaven first. According to Christopher Southgate "an evolutionary scheme was the only way to give rise to [certain] creaturely values" and to "creaturely selves." Although "heaven can eternally preserve those selves, subsisting in suffering-free relationship, it could not give rise to them in the first place." Southgate, *Groaning of Creation*, 90. Atle Søvik also points to the value of *independent* created beings as one reason why God created *both* heaven *and* earth. "The way that God creates *independent* beings is by means of evolution," and "the goal of independence [in creatures of the physical cosmos] is that it is a unique good that God wanted to create in addition to less independent beings [i.e., the angelic creation of heaven], since two different goods are better than one." Søvik, *Problem of Evil*, 42 and 262. See also Keith Ward, *Religion and Creation* (Oxford: Clarendon, 1996), 220.

123. The idea of God making creation to make itself is a notion that goes back to Basil of Caesarea's interpretation of Genesis 1 and 2. See Basil, *Homily* 7, 1. For a discussion see Colin E. Gunton, *The Triune Creator: A Historical and Systematic Study* (Grand Rapids: Eerdmans, 1998), 61. For a contemporary discussion, see see Niels Henrik Gregersen, "The Idea of Creation and the Theory of Autopoietic Processes," *Zygon* 33 (1998): 333–67. John Polkinghorne likewise argues, "In his great act of creation I believe that God allows the physical world to be itself, not in Manichaean opposition to him, but in that independence which is Love's gift of freedom to the one beloved." John Polkinghorne, *Science and Providence: God's Interaction with the World* (London: Templeton Press, 2005), 77.

124. Rachel Day, Kevin Laland, and John Odling-Smee, "Rethinking Adaptation: The Niche-Construction Perspective," *Perspectives in Biology and Medicine* 46, no. 80 (2002): 81.

a major role in introducing evolutionary change."[125] Evolutionary biologist Patrick Bateson elaborates specifically on how such "self-made" evolutionary change takes place:

> If a population of animals should change their habits (no doubt often on account of changes in their surroundings such as food supply, breeding sites, etc., but also sometimes due to their exploratory curiosity discovering new ways of life, such as new sources of food or new methods of exploitation) then, sooner or later, variations in the gene complex will turn up in the population to produce small alterations in the animal's structure which will make them more efficient in relation to their new behavioral pattern.[126]

Another goal in creation that God highly values is creaturely *freedom*. God's creation of beings through the evolutionary process works to enhance this goal as well. Because in an evolutionary scenario creatures are more *independent*, they are also freer. The increase of creaturely freedom is a general trend witnessed throughout the evolution of life on earth, and evolution appears to be designed to favor free will. According to psychologist Roy Baumeister, "The evolution of free will began when living things began to make choices. The difference between plants and animals illustrates an important early step. Plants don't change their location and don't need brains to help them decide where to go. Animals do. Free will is an advanced form of the simple process of controlling oneself, called agency."[127]

The physics underlying biological systems as they interact with their environments seems tailor-made to encourage the growth of freedom through agency. For instance, a recent series of experiments designed to investigate the behavioral middle ground between determinism and randomness started with the working assumption that "if there is anything remotely close to free will, it must exist somewhere between chance and necessity." The researchers' aim was to study a "simple" and well-known organism—the fruit fly—to find evidence that would decide between two alternate hypotheses: (1) the *robot hypothesis* that the brains of animals are "deterministic input/output systems" that function in a background of "random noise" given off as a by-product of "imperfectly wired" brain systems, genetic and historical variations, and random fluctuations in molecule number; and (2) the *behavior is random hypothesis* that "individual behavior

---

125. Patrick Bateson, "The Active Role of Behavior in Evolution," *Biology and Philosophy* 19 (2004): 283–98.

126. Patrick Bateson, "The Active Role of Behavior in Evolution," in *Evolutionary Processes and Metaphors*, ed. M. W. Ho, and S. W. Fox (London: Wiley, 1988), 191–207, at 196.

127. Roy Baumeister, "Do You Really Have Free Will? Of Course. Here's How it Evolved," *Slate*, September 25, 2013, accessible at *http://www.slate.com/articles/health_and_science/science/2013/09 /free_will_debate_what_does_free_will_mean_and_how_did_it_evolve.html*.

is fundamentally indeterministic (not fundamentally deterministic but noisy)" and that "precise prediction [is] principally (not only technically) impossible."[128]

To judge between these two hypotheses, researchers investigated turning behavior in tethered fruit flies—a neurologically and genetically well-understood behavioral system in an animal with a relatively simple brain, which nevertheless displays variability.[129] The findings, explains biologist Björn Brembs, revealed "a fractal order (resembling Lévy flights) in the temporal structure of spontaneous flight maneuvers in tethered *Drosophila* fruit flies." In other words, he says, fruit flies exhibit "spontaneous behavior" that "is not simply random," indicating a "general neural mechanism underlying spontaneous behavior."[130] Furthermore, the existence of this "neural initiator" (or center of agency) "falsifies the notion of behavioral determinism." As a consequence it is now clear that the "flies are more than simple input/output machines," and by virtue of their brain's "sensitivity to initial conditions," genuine spontaneity or "voluntariness is a biological trait even in flies."[131] In a very basic but real way, then, says Brembs, "a fruit fly possesses free will."[132]

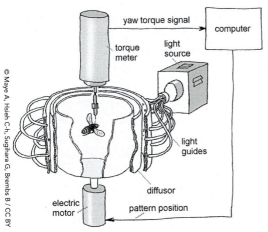

yaw torque signal

computer

torque meter

light source

light guides

light

diffusor

electric motor

pattern position

The apparatus shown here was used to measure the direction of fruit fly flight in a stimulus-free environment. In effect, the experiment demonstrated that fruit flies have free will.

The evolution of freedom works to enhance the evolution of knowledge, which, according to Jewish and Christian understandings, is another key goal that God desires for creatures. Freedom makes knowledge possible because, through freedom, one can experience the effects of one's various actions and learn how to cause things to happen. When creatures employ free will, says

---

128. Alexander Maye, Chih-hao Hsieh, George Sugihara, and Björn Brembs, "Order in Spontaneous Behavior," *PLoS ONE* 2, no. 5 (May 16, 2007): 1.

129. The researchers explain, "This system provides superb control over the perceived environment for a true assessment of the spontaneity of the behavior, while at the same time offering easily quantifiable behavioral dynamics." Ibid., 1–2.

130. Ibid.

131. Ibid., 6.

132. In a press release about his research team's findings, George Sugihara explains, "If there is anything remotely close to free will, it must exist somewhere between chance and necessity—which is exactly where fly behavior comes to lie." See "Do Fruit Flies Have Free Will? Scientists Measure Spontaneity in *Drosophila*," accessible at *http://brembs.net/spontaneous/release_short.pdf*.

Baumeister, they "must inhibit impulses and desires and find ways of satisfying them within the rules." Persons and animals must "also consciously imagine various future scenarios ('If I do this, then that will happen, whereupon I would do something else, leading to another result . . .') and guide their present actions based on disciplined imagination."[133] The evolutionary history of life on Earth has brought to fruition an increase in creaturely knowledge and rationality through freedom and independence. "Evolution," observes Baumeister, "has favored animals with psychological processes insofar as those processes help them pursue their goals. A more intelligent animal, for example, may be better able to find food and reproduce than a less intelligent one."[134]

Within an evolutionary framework, the combination of free will, rationality, and knowledge leads to the emergence of morality, which—according to the Jewish and Christian understandings—is another of God's central goals in creating the cosmos. The evolutionary process, explains Baumeister, leads to the development of increasingly moral beings by promoting "brainpower and social skills" over "physical strength, speed, and ferocity." Free will appears to exist for the sake of the moral life as it is lived out in community. "*Free will*," says Baumeister, "*is for following rules*. . . . It's what a creature might need in order to adjust its behavior to novel situations, to get what it wants while still following the complicated rules of the society." In order to thrive "and live harmoniously in a cultural group, an animal is best served by being able to inhibit its impulses and desires."[135] Free will, which consists of independent creaturely choices made through rationality and knowledge, is necessary for the self control that makes life in relational community possible. Relational or *agape* love, which Jews and Christians have long viewed as God's ultimate goal for creation, is the highest manifestation of morality and freedom.

In an evolutionary understanding of God's creation, independence, freedom, rationality, knowledge, morality, and the capacity to directly respond to God's will are not solely the possession of just one creaturely kind (i.e., *Homo sapiens*) but of many. As discussed in chapter 7, humans are not unique in their possession of freedom, rationality, culture, or moral action. And God values the moral actions of animals as he values those of humans. "Even if complicated by conflicting desires," says Swinburne, "animal actions of sympathy, affection, courage, and patience are great goods."[136] In this way, the hardships that animals face can lead to a similar type of character development and growth of virtue as that found in humans—with the difference being one of degree rather than kind. As

---

133. Baumeister, "Do You Really Have Free Will?"

134. Roy F. Baumeister, "Free Will in Scientific Psychology," in *Free Will and Consciousness: How Might They Work?*, ed. Roy F. Baumeister, Alfred R. Mele, and Kathleen D. Vohs (New York: Oxford University Press, 2010), 16.

135. Ibid., emphasis in original.

136. Swinburne, *Existence of God*, 244.

Swinburne observes, "God could have made a world in which animals got nothing but thrills out of life; but their life is richer for the complexity and difficulty of the tasks they face and the hardships to which they react appropriately."[137]

God's ultimate goals in creating an evolving universe appear to be present from the first moment of the cosmos. Ward reflects, "Conscious, self-aware, morally responsible persons are the mature development of what was embryonic in the earliest stages of the physical universe."[138] Written in the initial conditions of the big bang was the inevitable emergence of beings capable of loving relationship, who would accomplish their independence through a developmental process of making themselves. In this way, says Ward, "the fact of cosmic evolution can reasonably be seen to point to the possible goal of the cosmos as the emergence of a society of intelligent, morally free and potentially compassionate minds. That in turn points to the existence of one ultimate Mind, and one supreme Intelligence that is the origin and director of the process."[139]

In an evolutionary creation, the Creator is concerned not only with the spiritual development of human beings, but with that of *all* creatures that have at least some capacity to heed God's purposes. A world of many species of free creatures that can respond to God is truly a better or more valuable world than the "best of all possible worlds" that contains only one species of free creature who can regard or disregard the voice of its Creator. A world of many free creatures is a world in which God's plans and purposes are not wrapped up in the prerogatives and problems of one unique type of being (such as humans), but are instead akin to convergent endpoints of evolution that a spectrum of animal species can, and will, reach. A world of many free creatures with the potential to love each other and God is a world in which "the Glory of the Lord will be revealed and *all living things* will see it together" (Isa. 40:5, emphasis added).

Conclusion

This chapter has examined how suffering that is experienced as evil is related to the overarching values, goods, and goals that God—as understood within the Jewish and Christian faiths—has in creating the cosmos. These goals include the existence of life that would independently develop and, in time, come to possess the capacities for knowledge, rationality, morality, and interpersonal love. Due to the constraints imposed by logical possibility and cosmic fine-tuning, it seems that suffering is an unwanted but unavoidable by-product of conditions in the natural world that have to exist for there to be intelligent life at all. An independent world that is not absolutely controlled by the divine will "is the

---

137. Ibid., 245.
138. Ward, *Pascal's Fire*, 196.
139. Ibid., 197.

only world in which the unique beings that we are could become who we are."[140] The regularity of the laws of nature is necessary for the development of rationality, knowledge, freedom, and morality. Since the lawfulness of nature must be maintained for these values to be realized, God may not miraculously intervene beyond a certain threshold without the natural order falling apart. The price of moral freedom, rationality, and morality is the inevitability of suffering caused by both free agents and the impersonal, regularly operating laws of nature. Both humans and animals suffer the side effects of the impersonal and amoral laws of nature—allowing the potential for illness, starvation, and natural disasters—but these same laws permit generosity, forgiveness, and compassion. "The existence of a physical world with morally neutral general principles of causality (the laws of nature)," says Ward, "is necessary to the development of the sort of personal life that human beings have."[141] In other words, the only path leading to creatures that can freely and lovingly respond to God is through options that have evil as an unwanted but unavoidable by-product. "If God is to have living, intelligent, loving, free partners for relationship," explains Murphy, "then the universe God created had to be almost exactly as it is with respect to the ways in which nature produces human and animal suffering, and in which creatures are limited and subject to imperfections. *Natural and metaphysical evil are unavoidable by-products* of choices God had to make in order to achieve his purposes in having creatures who could know and love him."[142]

Discussion Questions

1. How have you tried to make sense of suffering in your own experience? Do you think suffering experienced as evil is a philosophical problem for one who holds an atheistic worldview? Why or why not?

2. Do you think persons would be sufficiently free to perform good actions and develop moral character (virtue) in a universe of instant karma (i.e., where moral law was immediately enforced)? Do you think persons would be sufficiently free to perform good actions and develop moral character (virtue) if the existence of God was an undeniable and obvious fact?

3. Do you think it was possible for God to create free and rational creatures without the possibility of any natural evils? Why or why not?

4. Do you believe nonhuman animals are conscious and can experience suffering? Would you consider this a form of evil? Is there a theodicy problem

140. Søvik, *Problem of Evil*, 263.

141. Ward, *Pascal's Fire*, 206.

142. Murphy, "Science and the Problem of Evil," 140, emphasis in original.

in cases where animals do not suffer or feel pain (i.e., in the case of many insects)?

5. In your opinion, are all the values discussed in this chapter (freedom, rationality, morality, independence, knowledge, and love) worth the potential for suffering?

Beyond the Classroom

With a group, watch these videos featuring lifelike, intelligent robots and discuss the questions that follow below:

Video 1: Realistic Robot. Accessible at *http://www.youtube.com/watch?v=Ih Vu2hxm07E* (time: 00:02:45).

Video 2 Realistic Female Android. Accessible at *http://www.youtube.com /watch?v=cy7xGwYdRk0* (time: 00:02:45).

Imagine a scientist who programmed an intelligent robot to "love" the scientist, to share the scientist's likes and dislikes (music tastes, humor, etc.), and to be the scientist's romantic lifelong companion.

1. What value can be placed on this love?
2. Is human love that is freely given (and not programmed) to another human more valuable than the love of an intelligent robot?
3. What role does freedom and independence play in determining the value of love?
4. Do you think freely given and independent love is a goal that may be worth suffering for?

Resources for Further Study

Books

Crenshaw, James. *Defending God: Biblical Responses to the Problem of Evil.* New York: Oxford University Press, 2005.

Murphy, Nancey, Robert John Russell, and William R. Stoeger, SJ, eds. *Physics and Cosmology: Scientific Perspectives on the Problem of Natural Evil.* Vatican City State: Vatican Observatory Publications, 2007.

Plantinga, Alvin. *God, Freedom, and Evil.* Grand Rapids: Eerdmans, 1977.

Swinburne, Richard. *Providence and the Problem of Evil.* New York: Oxford University Press, 1998.

Ward, Keith. *Pascal's Fire: Scientific Faith And Religious Understanding.* Oxford: Oneworld, 2006.

Articles

Moritz, Joshua. "Animal Suffering, Evolution, and the Origins of Evil: Toward a 'Free Creatures' Defense." *Zygon* 49, no. 2 (June 2014): 348–80.

Southgate, Christopher. "God and Evolutionary Evil: Theodicy in the Light of Darwinism." *Zygon* 37, no. 4 (2002): 803–24.

Internet Resources

Moritz, Joshua. "The Problem of Evil and the Natural Sciences." Voice of Light Productions. Accessible at *http://vimeo.com/44624343* (time: 01:08:08).

Schloss, Jeff, and Michael Murray. "Animal Suffering: Theological and Philosophical Perspectives." Faraday Institute for Science and Religion, July 22, 2011. Accessible at *https://www.faraday.st-edmunds.cam.ac.uk/Multimedia .php?Mode=Add&ItemID=Item_Multimedia_430&width=720&height=460* (time: 01:29:09).

CHAPTER 10

The End of All Things and the New Beginning

All the labors of the ages, all the devotion, all the inspiration, all the noon-day brightness of human genius, are destined to extinction in the vast death of the solar system, and . . . the whole temple of man's achievement must inevitably be buried beneath the debris of a universe in ruins.

—*Bertrand Russell, philosopher*[1]

And I saw a new heavens and a new Earth; for the first heavens and the first Earth had passed away.

—*Revelation 21:1*

In This Chapter

- The Cosmic Future: "A Foundation for Unyielding Despair"?
- Is the End of the Physical World the End of Religious Hope?
- Discussion Questions
- Beyond the Classroom
- Resources for Further Study

While all religions are concerned with the final fate of individual human beings, they differ in how they understand the ultimate future of the cosmos (an area of study called *eschatology*). Within the Eastern religious traditions, the universe is believed to be without any absolute beginning and without an ultimate end. Time is thought to be eternal and cyclical as the cosmos passes ceaselessly through an endless series of destructions and regenerations. Hindu scholar David Knipe explains, "Noticeably absent from . . . Hindu beliefs is the notion

---

1. Bertrand Russell, *Russell on Religion: Selections from the Writings of Bertrand Russell*, ed. Louis Greenspan and Stefan Andersson (New York: Routledge, 1999), 32.

of an end of time, a last day."[2] In the same way, observes Buddhist scholar Donald Lopez, "the Buddhist scriptures contain no classic account of an end time, an apocalypse," or "an eschaton [i.e., an end] in which the final purpose of human existence and of creation is fulfilled."[3] In contrast to the Eastern religious traditions, the theologies of the theistic religions are intensely rooted in a linear and historical view of time and space. From the perspective of theism, cosmic history is moving toward an ultimate fulfillment that will take place at the end of days (referred to as the *eschaton*). In the same way that Judaism, Christianity, and Islam affirm an absolute beginning to space and time, they also believe that space and time will come to final completion at the end of time.

What does science believe about the distant cosmic future? While it is popular to imagine an age of unending technological progress where science will eventually eradicate the worst of human suffering and social ills, physicists agree that even the most advanced technology imaginable cannot save life from the bleak fate of ultimate extinction. As philosopher Bertrand Russell eloquently expresses, "All the labors of the ages, all the devotion, all the inspiration, all the noonday brightness of human genius, are destined to extinction in the vast death of the solar system, and . . . the whole temple of man's achievement must inevitably be buried beneath the debris of a universe in ruins."[4] Russell's cosmic pessimism stems from his faith in the truth of science. If current understandings of physics are correct, in a few billion years the sun will expand to engulf the Earth. In a few billion more, the light of the sun itself will forever perish. Eventually, all the stars in the universe will slowly exhaust their fuel and die, shrouding the cosmos in eternal darkness. Finally, the universe will expand and cool to approach absolute zero temperature where any stable particles left will be isolated and alone in the vastness and blackness of space. "Only within the scaffolding of these truths," says Russell, "only on the firm foundation of unyielding despair can the soul's habitation be safely built."[5] With regard to the future of both humanity and the universe, the whole of the natural sciences appear to testify—against the confessions of religions—that the sure reality is the extinction of life. And yet the majority of religions place their hope in a future beyond the finality of the cosmos. This last chapter explores scientific and religious perspectives on the end of time, particularly focusing on Christian understandings of the ultimate transformation and resurrection of the present creation into the new creation.

---

2. David Knipe, "Hindu Eschatology," in *The Oxford Handbook of Eschatology*, ed. Jerry Wallis (New York: Oxford University Press, 2008), 171.

3. Donald Lopez, *The Story of Buddhism: A Concise Guide to its History and Teachings* (San Francisco: HarperSanFrancisco, 2001), 33.

4. Russell, *Russell on Religion*, 32.

5. Ibid.

The Cosmic Future: "A Foundation for Unyielding Despair"?

According to science, what does the cosmic future have in store? It is easy to take the current state of life's existence on Earth for granted. The present day inhabitants of the Earth live in a place in the universe and at a time in cosmic history that is ideal for the existence of complex life. However, from what physicists know of the evolution of stars like the sun, all life on Earth will one day come to an end. Astrophysicist William Stoeger observes, "If civilization and life on earth survive periodic impacts of large asteroids, or other possible global catastrophes, they will certainly not survive the eventual catastrophic changes in the sun."[6] As the sun ages over the next few billion years, it will heat up, slowly evaporating the seas, and eventually eradicating all life on Earth. According to astrophysicists Robert Smith and Klaus-Peter Schroeder, a 10 percent increase in the luminosity of the sun over the next billion years "will cause runaway evaporation until the oceans have boiled dry."[7] By 1.3 billion years from now, any remaining pockets of water will have boiled off into space, leaving Earth a dry and barren world. By this point, all eukaryotic life (i.e., life that is made up of cells that have nuclei) will have died out due to increased heat and radiation. Then, explains geophysicist Siegfried Franck, at around 1.6 billion years from the present, when the atmospheric carbon dioxide content reaches levels too low for photosynthesis, the lifespan of Earth's biosphere comes to its ultimate end with the extinction of prokaryotes (i.e., cells without nuclei).[8]

The Ultimate Physical Fate of the Earth and the Sun

Within the next 5 billion years, the sun will exhaust the hydrogen supply at its core and begin to expand into a red giant. As the sun expands, it will envelop the inner planets, destroying Mercury and Venus and, says Stoeger, "eventually will either envelop or nearly envelop Earth."[9] Six billion years from now (if the Earth has not been entirely consumed by the expanding sun), the atmosphere will have evaporated into space as meteorites rain down on the arid world. The entire realm of biological existence on Earth will have long since perished. Then after a billion years more, even the light of the sun itself will perish as its outer

---

6. William R. Stoeger, "Scientific Accounts of Ultimate Catastrophes in Our Life-Bearing Universe," in *The End of the World and the Ends of God*, ed. John Polkinghorne and Michael Welker (London: SCM, 2000), 24.

7. Robert Smith and Klaus-Peter Schroeder, "Distant Future of Sun and Earth Revisited," *Monthly Notices of the Royal Astronomical Society* 386, no. 1 (May 2008): 155–163, at 160.

8. Siegfried Franck, Christine Bounama, and Werner von Bloh, "Causes and Timing of Future Biosphere Extinction," *Biogeosciences Discussions* 2, no. 6 (2001): 1665–79, at 1673.

9. Stoeger, "Scientific Accounts of Ultimate Catastrophes," 25.

layers are ejected, its core cools to form a white dwarf, and it becomes a rigidly crystalline planetary nebula. At the end of its life, the luminosity of the sun will fall below three-trillionths of its current level, and it will fade gently away into the blackness of space.[10]

The Ultimate Physical Fate of the Universe

Perhaps through increased technological advances and long-range space flight, humans will find a new home elsewhere in the cosmos and will manage to escape the final destruction of the biosphere and of the planet Earth. Could the human race continue to exist throughout all eternity by travelling from planet to planet, ever in search of new suns and new earths? "Though the earth and the sun are destined for eventual destruction," says Stoeger, "we might be inclined to suppose—or at least hope—that the universe as a life-generating ensemble is eternal. However, from all that we know about the evolution and dynamics of the observable universe, and about the laws of nature that govern it, this is not true."[11] The calculations of physics point to the inescapable truth that—one way or another—the universe itself will, in time, no longer be a home fit for life. It is clear, comments astrophysicist Paul Davies, that "the universe is irreversibly running down."[12] According to Davies, "All the evidence points . . . to a universe that has a limited life span. It came into existence at some finite time in the past, it is currently vibrant with activity, but it is inevitably degenerating toward a heat death at some stage in the future."[13]

The ultimate physical fate of the cosmos depends on a number of factors, including the overall shape of the universe and how the competing effects of expansion and gravity interact. In the early 1990s, many scientists thought the universe might have enough matter and energy density that gravity would slow and eventually stop its expansion (a scenario known as a *closed universe*). In this situation, the universe would reach its maximum size, and then the force of gravity would pull matter together causing the cosmos to re-collapse upon itself until, about 100 billion years from now, all matter in the universe would contract into an infinitely dense point (called a singularity or black hole). In this "big crunch" scenario, explains Davies, "the universe would slowly transform itself into an all-encompassing cosmic furnace," and thus there would be no possible chance for the survival of any biological life or even artificial intelligence.[14]

---

10. Smith and Schroeder, "Distant Future of Sun and Earth Revisited," 160.

11. Stoeger, "Scientific Accounts of Ultimate Catastrophes," 27.

12. Paul Davies, *The Last Three Minutes: Conjectures about the Ultimate Fate of the Universe* (New York: Basic Books, 1994), 13.

13. Ibid., 18.

14. Ibid., 122.

The "big crunch," says Davies, "is not just the end of matter. It is the end of everything. Because time itself ceases at the big crunch, it is meaningless to ask what happens next, just as it is meaningless to ask what happened before the big bang." In the same way that the universe "came from nothing in the big bang," observes Davies, "it will disappear into nothing at the big crunch."[15]

A second cosmic scenario called the "big freeze" (or "heat death") will take place if the mass of the universe is less than the critical amount needed to slow and reverse the expansion of the cosmos (a scenario known as an *open universe*). In the case of the big freeze, says Stoeger, "the universe will expand forever, and eventually run down and disperse to the point that no further star formation, galaxy formation or anything else will occur."[16] After about 1 trillion years from now, with no more free hydrogen available, star formation will come to an end. Eventually, about 100 trillion years from now, the last star will burn out and, says Davies, "the era of light will be over forever."[17] In 10^{34} years from now, protons will begin to decay and the universe will be dominated by galactic-scale black holes. In about 10^{100} years, explains Davies, all black holes—even the supermassive ones—will evaporate, "their death pangs momentary flashes of light in the inky blackness of eternal cosmic night, a fleeting epitaph to the erstwhile existence of a billion blazing suns."[18] As the universe continues to expand in frozen, silent darkness and protons continue to decay, any remaining matter will become unstable and eventually evaporate.[19] Any "solid objects, like planets, that had avoided falling into a black hole would not last forever" explains Davies. "Instead, they would very gradually evaporate."[20] In this way, Davies observes, "the 10^{48} tons of ordinary matter that we presently observe spread throughout the universe is all destined to disappear either into black holes or through slow nuclear decay."[21] Given this scenario for the far future of the universe, says Davies, "it seems that any form of life must ultimately be doomed."[22]

A third cosmic scenario called the big rip was proposed in 2003. The big rip was developed in light of the role of "dark energy" or "phantom energy" in the increased acceleration of the expansion of the universe, which has been observed through space telescope data over the past decades. The big rip scenario suggests

---

15. Ibid., 123.

16. Stoeger, "Scientific Accounts of Ultimate Catastrophes," 27.

17. Davies, *Last Three Minutes*, 50.

18. Ibid., 90.

19. Fred C. Adams and Gregory Laughlin, "A Dying Universe: The Long-Term Fate and Evolution of Astrophysical Objects," *Reviews of Modern Physics* 69 (1997): 337–72.

20. Davies, *Last Three Minutes*, 96.

21. Ibid.

22. Ibid., 99. Davies discusses a number of approaches to how some form of artificial life might continue within this context.

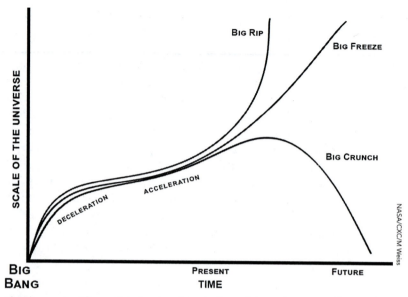

The three scientific models for the ultimate fate of the universe are illustrated in the above graph: the "big crunch," the "big freeze," and the "big rip." Whichever model proves true, life as we know it will not survive.

that around 20 billion years from now the acceleration caused by dark energy eventually becomes so strong that it completely overwhelms the effects of gravity and other physical forces. First, galaxies lose their constituent stars. Then solar systems fly apart. And finally, even atoms are torn apart.[23] In this scenario, explains philosopher of physics Rüdiger Vaas, phantom energy "tears space literally apart and leads irrevocably to a complete disruption of everything, even atomic nuclei."[24] While this third scenario for the future of the universe is still much debated,[25] it is clear that if the data are shown to support this theory and the big rip does happen to be in store for the cosmos, then there is ultimately no future for life. Vaas observes, "There is no mechanism by which life could stop such a process, so it seems to be doomed in this case."[26]

23. Robert Caldwell et al., "Phantom Energy: Dark Energy with $w < -1$ Causes a Cosmic Doomsday," *Physical Review Letters* 91, no. 7 (August 13, 2003): 071301.

24. Rüdiger Vaas, "Dark Energy and Life's Ultimate Future," in *The Future of Life and the Future of our Civilization*, ed. Vladimir Burdyuzha (Dordrecht: Springer, 2006), 231–47, at 239.

25. See George Ellis, R. Maartens, and M. MacCallum, *Relativistic Cosmology* (New York: Cambridge University Press, 2012), 389; Artyom Astashenok et al. "Phantom Cosmology without Big Rip Singularity," *Physical Letters B* 709 (2012): 396–403.

26. Rüdiger Vaas, "Dark Energy and Life's Ultimate Future," in *The Future of Life and the Future of Our Civilization*, ed. Vladimir Burdyuzha (Dordrecht: Springer 2006), 239–40.

Is the End of the Physical World the End of Religious Hope?

What stakes do the various world religions have in the future of the cosmos? For traditional Buddhists who seek *nirvana* (meaning "to extinguish") and Hindus who seek *moksha* (meaning "liberation"), the goal of individual salvation is to be released from and to put an end to the endless cosmic cycle of re-birth and re-death (called *samsara*). In this sense, the ultimate winding down of the cosmos for all eternity can be welcomed since a future with no more human births entails a future that finally brings a universal stop to the beginningless cycle of samsara. Beyond this, in Hinduism the hope that good karma would lead to a re-birth in heaven among the gods is a distinctly *other-worldly* hope that does not depend on the fate of this particular cosmos. Pure Land Buddhism likewise envisions the possibility of re-birth in other universes known as "pure lands" or "buddha fields."[27] Since, explains Lopez, "in Buddhist cosmology there are billions of universes like our own," the ultimate physical fate of this specific universe is of little consequence when considering the grand scheme of things.[28]

Other-worldly notions of the afterlife are present in theistic traditions as well—such as the Judeo-Christian conception of heaven and the Islamic notion of paradise. The traditional eschatological focus of the Abrahamic religions, however, has long been the physical resurrection of the body and the transformation of this cosmos at the end of days. The theistic affirmation of *physical* resurrection is one of the key dividing lines between Eastern and Western religions. Bible scholar N. T. Wright explains, "There is a world of difference between the Orthodox Jew who believes that all the righteous will be raised to new individual bodily life in the resurrection and the Buddhist who hopes after death to disappear like a drop in the ocean, losing one's own identity in the great nameless and formless Beyond."[29] As the central prayer of the Jewish liturgy confesses, "God keeps faith with those who sleep in the dust."[30] Christians, who have inherited from Judaism the belief in physical resurrection, likewise place their ultimate hope in the final transformation of this present creation into a new creation. Because Judaism and Christianity anticipate a transformation of this particular cosmos at the end of days, observes physicist and theologian John Polkinghorne, the predictions from science concerning the ultimate fate of the universe pose "a sharp question to theology concerning how the latter [Christianity] conceives of the ultimate fulfillment

---

27. Lopez, *Story of Buddhism*, 64.

28. Ibid., 86.

29. N. T. Wright, *Surprised by Hope: Rethinking Heaven, the Resurrection, and the Mission of the Church* (New York: HarperOne, 2008), 7.

30. Jon D. Levenson, *Resurrection and the Restoration of Israel: The Ultimate Victory of the God of Life* (New Haven: Yale University Press, 2006), 3.

of God's creation."[31] As theologian Ted Peters explains, in the Christian vision, "what happens to us depends on what happens to the cosmos. The resurrection to a spiritual body can only occur at the advent of the eschaton. If there is no cosmic transformation, then there is no resurrection, and if there is no resurrection then our faith is in vain and we of all people are most to be pitied (1 Cor. 15:14, 19)."[32] The Jewish and Christian hope in the resurrection and the life of the world to come entails that the fate of the cosmos predicted by science will not be the ultimate destiny of the universe.

The Physical Resurrection of Jesus as a Glimpse of Humanity's Future Resurrection

The Resurrection of Jesus Christ plays a central role in Christian eschatological thinking.[33] According to Christian understanding, the destiny of each individual human being is anticipated by the final fate of Jesus. In this way, one witnesses a glimpse of the final bodily resurrection—which both Christians and Jews expect to occur at the end of time—in the body of the risen Jesus. When asked what the future resurrection would look like, the author of Colossians points to the risen Christ as the paradigm case, referring to him as "the firstborn from among the dead" (Col. 1:18). In the same way that Jesus—called "the last [or eschatological] Adam"—was raised from the dead, the children of the first Adam follow. The Apostle Paul illustrates the change that will take place in the future resurrection by making an analogy to the transformation of a seed. In the same way that an acorn is buried (as one type of body) and transformed into an oak tree (as a different type of body), the resurrection at the end of time will witness a similar kind of bodily transformation:

> What you sow does not come to life unless it dies; and as for what you sow, you do not sow the body that is to be, but a bare seed, perhaps of wheat or of something else. . . . So it also is with the resurrection of the dead. It is sown a perishable body, it is raised an imperishable body; it is sown in dishonor, it is raised in glory; it is sown in weakness, it is raised in power. It is sown a soulish physical body [*sōma psychikon*], it is raised a spiritual physical body [*sōma pneumatikon*]. If there is a soulish physical body, there is also a spiritual physical body. So also it is written, "The first man, Adam, became a living soul." The last Adam became

---

31. John Polkinghorne, *The God of Hope and the End of the World* (New Haven: Yale University Press, 2002), xviii.

32. Ted Peters, "The Physical Body of Immortality," in *Science, Theology, and Ethics* (Burlington, VT: Ashgate, 2003), 315.

33. Polkinghorne, *God of Hope*, xx.

a life-giving spirit. However, the spiritual is not first, but the soulish; then the spiritual follows. (1 Cor 15:36–46)

In the Christian understanding, the resurrected body is not a complete *replacement* of the present physical body, but rather, the future bodily existence is somehow *continuous with* and directly related to the present—analogous to how an acorn is related to an oak tree while at the same time being very different. While the person raised from the dead is the same individual that lived before, the resurrection involves a transformation that is as radical as that which occurs when a seed grows into a tree.

The continuity between the present body and the future body is made explicit in the New Testament accounts of the Resurrection of Jesus. In the New Testament accounts, the conclusion that the risen Jesus had some sort of physical continuity with his previous bodily existence follows from the fact that his tomb was empty. In other words, the empty tomb of Jesus implies that the transformed and glorified Jesus is the same person that he was before, and not an entirely new creation of God. The implication from this is that the transformation of the resurrection involves a renewal of creation out of what has already existed (*creatio ex vetere*) rather than an entirely brand new creation out of nothing (*creatio ex nihilo*). Polkinghorne explains, "The Lord's risen body is the eschatological transformation of his dead body. This implies that the new creation does not arise from a radically novel creative act *ex nihilo*, but as a redemptive act *ex vetere*, out of the old."[34] The Christian understanding of eschatology as physical transformation, says Robert Russell, "is derived in large measure from a view of the Resurrection which emphasizes elements of continuity and discontinuity between the historical Jesus of Nazareth and the Risen Jesus. In this view, the empty tomb plays a key role in pointing to an irreducible element of physical/material continuity within an overarching discontinuity between the historical Jesus and the Risen Lord."[35]

New Testament accounts of the resurrected Jesus underscore this emphasis on both continuity and discontinuity in the resurrected life. In many ways, the risen Jesus is the same as the pre-risen Jesus. The resurrected Christ is described in a very physical manner—as eating broiled fish and even inviting the disciples to touch his hands and side. The risen Jesus interacts within space and time, walks on the ground as opposed to flying or floating, speaks words that propagate through the air in the normal fashion, and remembers the names of his friends and many other details from his previous life. Yet the risen Christ is also radically different from the pre-risen Jesus. According to three of the Gospel narratives and the account of Paul's dramatic vision of Christ, the risen Jesus is

---

34. Ibid., 116.

35. Robert John Russell, "Eschatology," in *The Blackwell Companion to Science and Christianity*, ed. J. B. Stump and Alan Padgett (Malden, MA: Blackwell, 2012), 544.

an "alien reality" and is not readily recognizable even by those who are close to him.[36] On the road to Emmaus, in his breaking of bread with the disciples, in his encounter with Mary Magdalene in the garden, and on the shore of the Sea of Galilee, one reads that there is something about Jesus' physical appearance that has changed. Beyond this, the risen Jesus is depicted as having supra-physical properties, such as the ability to enter locked rooms or appear and disappear at will. These appearances of "the resurrected Lord," says theologian Wolfhart Pannenberg, "were experienced as appearances coming from heaven," and they entailed Jesus' glorification.[37] From the way in which several of his followers worshiped him as soon as they saw him, it is clear that something had radically transformed the resurrected Jesus. Polkinghorne observes, "The character of the appearance narratives definitely excludes a mere notion of resuscitation. The risen Christ is transformed. . . . His presence is the manifestation of a glorified life that transcends the everyday existence of this present world. Yet his body still bears the marks of the passion."[38]

The Physical Resurrection of Jesus as a Glimpse of the New Creation

In the same way that the future bodily resurrection of humanity is anticipated by the Resurrection of Jesus, the Christian understanding of eschatology distinctly emphasizes that the final transformation of the whole universe has already been previewed in the physical Resurrection of Christ. Christians understand the event of Christ's Resurrection as a prefiguration of the time when—at the end of days—God will glorify and transfigure the entire realm of nature as the new creation. In the same way that there is both continuity and discontinuity between the pre-risen Jesus and the resurrected Christ, says Russell, "the new creation is neither a 'replacement' of the present creation—that is, not as a second *ex nihilo*— nor the mere working out of the natural evolutionary processes of the world. Instead, eschatology involves the complete transformation of the world by a radically new act of God beginning at the resurrection of Jesus and continuing into the future."[39] As the same body of Jesus that lay in the tomb was transformed into an imperishable and glorified resurrection body, so this same world humans presently inhabit will be transformed into the new creation of the eschaton.

In Scripture, death is mysteriously required for new life (see John 12:24). In the biblical conception, the death of the present body appears to be necessary for

---

36. Wolfhart Pannenberg, *Jesus—God and Man*, trans. Lewis L. Wilkins and Duane A. Priebe (Philadelphia: Westminster, 1968), 93.

37. Ibid., 92.

38. Polkinghorne, *God of Hope*, 73.

39. Russell, "Eschatology," 564.

the new life of the resurrection. The same understanding applies to the cosmos as a whole. The present world must fade away for the renewed world to come into existence. Consequently, in the New Testament the eventual destruction of the Earth and the passing away of the heavens are expected as a necessary fulfillment of God's future purposes: "The heavens will disappear with a roar; the elements will be destroyed by fire, and the earth and everything done in it will be laid bare. . . . That day will bring about the destruction of the heavens by fire, and the elements will melt in the heat. But in keeping with his promise we are looking forward to a renewed heavens and a renewed earth, where righteousness dwells" (2 Pet. 3:10–13). The author of Revelation likewise receives a vision of the future and beholds that the first heavens and the first earth pass away before the new heavens and new earth are unveiled (Rev. 21:1). The Apostle Paul writes that God has intentionally subjected the physical creation to "futility" in order that the "whole creation may be set free from its bondage to decay" to inherit the "glorious freedom" of resurrected existence (Rom. 8:20–21). The cosmos must die, the Christian faith affirms, but God will raise the cosmos to life again. In the face of "the sober estimates of the scientists that the universe as we know it today is running out of steam and cannot last forever," says Wright, "the gospel of Jesus Christ announces that what God did for Jesus at Easter he will do not only for all those who are 'in Christ' but also for the entire cosmos. It will be an act of new creation, parallel to and derived from the act of new creation when God raised Jesus from the dead."[40]

How the "Word Become Flesh" Changed the "Way of All Flesh"

Is the final resurrection and transformation of the cosmos just for the sake of human beings? The Christian Scriptures and many key thinkers in the theological tradition have understood redemption and resurrection to occur at the level of existence within which God became incarnate in Jesus Christ. Both the Bible and the early church testify that the crucial category of existence or being that God participated in (or "assumed") in Christ's Incarnation is the *flesh*—a term that was understood to mean biological life at its most basic and inclusive level. According to the traditional Christian understanding of the Incarnation, then, God in Jesus did not only come to save *human* creatures of flesh, but *all* creatures of flesh wherever they might exist throughout the entire cosmos.

John 1:14 is the most radical Christian expression of the early Jewish notion of the Messiah as God's agent for the renewal of the entirety of the living creation. As one reads the well-known words of the Gospel of John, "The Word became flesh," one must remember that in the original Greek, "the Word"

---

40. Wright, *Surprised by Hope*, 99.

did not merely become "man" (*anēr*) or even "human" (*anthropos*). Rather, the Word became "flesh" (*sarx*)—"the term which," according to Bible scholar Walter Houston, "defines the solidarity of humanity with the rest of creation in its bodiliness."[41] As Jesus the Messiah, "the Elect One of God" (John 1:34), took on *flesh*, he took on the most conceivably inclusive category of biological being and mode of existence known at the time when the Gospel of John was written. As God-in-Christ incarnated as "a living creature," the Creator God in the fleshly form of the last Adam entered into material solidarity with all "living creatures" of the cosmos.[42] Within its early Jewish, messianic context, the Incarnation is the event where the Word becomes flesh or biological life—as opposed to becoming exclusively human—and in so doing inclusively embraces a category of existence to which all living beings belong. As the Word becomes biological life, the boundary between humans and other living creatures thus becomes effectively blurred.

The early Christian church expanded on the theological implications of the redemptive significance of the atoning work of the Creator God in the flesh. Early Christians consistently viewed Jesus and the apostles as agents of reconciliation who anticipated the future new creation by spreading the gospel even to the nonhuman creation. A number of early Christian writings portray the mission of Jesus within the early Jewish messianic tradition of the "last Adam." Succeeding where the first Adam failed, Christ as the last Adam restores relationships with animals and inaugurates the "peaceable kingdom"—a reign which will be completed at the end of days when violence in nature will ultimately cease and all creatures will live together harmoniously in the presence of God (described in Hosea 2:16–23 and Isaiah 11). The New Testament proclaimed that "the gospel has already been announced to every creature under heaven" (Col. 1:23). Wright explains, "What has happened in the death and resurrection of Jesus Christ, in other words, is by no means limited to its effects on those human beings who believe the gospel and thereby find new life here and hereafter. It resonates out, in ways that we can't fully see or understand, into the vast recesses of the universe."[43]

Many early accounts of Jesus written around the time of the New Testament—narratives which were highly influential in the early church and remained so throughout the Middle Ages—reveal the character and identity of Jesus the Messiah as it was understood in many of the first Christian communities. For instance,

---

41. Walter Houston, "What Was the Meaning of Classifying Animals as Clean or Unclean?," in *Animals on the Agenda: Questions about Animals for Theology and Ethics*, ed. Andrew Linzey and Dorothy Yamamoto (Chicago: University of Illinois Press, 1998), 32.

42. This notion of "solidarity in flesh" is what theologian Niels Gregersen has called "deep incarnation"—connecting Christ with both an evolving creation and the whole cosmos. See Niels Gregersen, "The Cross of Christ in an Evolutionary World," *Dialog: A Journal of Theology* 40, no. 3 (2001).

43. Wright, *Surprised by Hope*, 97.

in the *Protoevangelium of James* the author recounts that at the birth of Jesus the animals in the surrounding countryside paused in reverent awe. In the highly influential *Infancy Gospel of Matthew*, dangerous wild beasts fulfill the Hebrew Scriptures as they worship the young Jesus and obey his commandments:[44]

> Lions and panthers adored him and accompanied them in the desert. Wherever Joseph and Mary went, they went before them showing them the way and bowing their heads; they showed their submission by wagging their tails, they worshipped him with great reverence. . . . And the lions kept walking with them, and with the oxen and the asses and the beasts of burden . . . and did not hurt a single one of them. . . . They were tame among the sheep and the rams which they had brought with them from Judea. . . . They walked among wolves and feared nothing; and not one of them was hurt by another.

Jesus meanwhile explains to his mother, "All the beasts of the forest must necessarily be docile before me."[45] As the animals travel with Jesus and his family, he feeds them and takes care of them until "all were satisfied . . . and they gave thanks to God."[46] Later in the gospel, the adult Jesus, speaking to an unbelieving crowd, declares, "how much better are these beasts than you, seeing that they recognize their Lord and glorify him; while you humans, who have been made in the image and likeness of God, do not know God! Beasts know me and are tame; humans see me and do not acknowledge me."[47]

Another early Christian account, which concerns Paul's interaction with a lion, comes from the *Acts of Paul*—an influential body of documents well-known in the early church, regarded as orthodox by many church fathers, and even included within the authoritative collection of New Testament Scriptures in certain parts of the ancient church.[48] This account describes how Paul acts as an agent of the messianic renewal of creation and even baptizes a nonhuman animal who seeks salvation. In this narrative, which clearly indicates that the resurrected life is not reserved for humans alone, "the author wanted to show by

---

44. *The Infancy Gospel of Matthew*, in *The Apocryphal New Testament: A Collection of Apocryphal Christian Literature in an English Translation*, ed. J. K. Elliott (Oxford: Clarendon, 1993), 84. *The Infancy Gospel of Matthew* is also known as *The Book about the Origin of the Blessed Mary and the Childhood of the Savior* and *The Gospel of Pseudo-Matthew*. This work was very influential in the Middle Ages and indeed, says Elliot, "much of medieval art is indecipherable without reference to books such as *Pseudo-Matthew.*"

45. *Infancy Gospel of Matthew*, 95.

46. Ibid., 96.

47. Ibid., 97.

48. For example, the *Acts of Paul* is listed in the canonical list of the Codex Claromontanus, and parts of the *Acts of Paul* are found in the Armenian Bible. See Elliott, *Apocryphal New Testament*, 350–53. The value of such stories for the present study, however, lies not primarily in their historicity, but in how they were regarded and received by the early church.

the baptism of the lion that, in the activity of Paul, the redemption of creation is realized, that is, God's *oikonomia* [or inbreaking eschatological community] attains its goal."[49]

While such early Christian accounts may sound foreign to many Christians in the present age, the church fathers were quite familiar with these stories and many accepted them as legitimate narratives of Jesus and the apostles that were judged to be in harmony with the documents of what would later become the authoritative New Testament. Following in this line of thought, Irenaeus of Lyons (130–202) sees the entire course of the created cosmos as a salvation history with Christ (the last Adam and renewed *imago Dei*) at the center. According to Irenaeus, within this cosmic salvation history, nonhuman creatures have firm footing as subjects of God's providence and redemptive concern. In the wake of Adam's fall, says Irenaeus, "God made a covenant with the whole world through Noah, pledging himself to all animals and humans."[50] The climax of this epic of redemption is Christ's symbolic reliving of the entire cosmic history—including the dynamics of creation and fall—within his own life. Through the Incarnation, as the Word becomes flesh, the entire world of flesh is brought into communion with God through Jesus' victory over sin and through Christ's final triumph over death in his Resurrection in the flesh.[51] For Irenaeus, as flesh is redeemed and resurrected through flesh, the words of Isaiah 40:5 and Luke 3:6 are fulfilled: "Then the glory of the Lord will be revealed, and all flesh [literally "all living things"] will see it together."

A few generations after Irenaeus, Athanasius (296–273) and Gregory of Nazianzus (330–390) likewise envisioned the final resurrection in terms of the categories of existence that God "took on" or "assumed" in the Incarnation. Athanasius argues that in Christ's Incarnation and Resurrection, "His *flesh* was saved, and made free the first of all, being made the body of the Word." Since God took on flesh, "we, being similarly corporeal therewith, are saved by the same."[52] It is not just humans who are saved through Christ's Incarnation and Resurrection, says Athanasius, but all flesh: "For the presence of the Savior in the flesh was the price of death and the saving of the whole creation."[53] The most influential theological understanding of the meaning of the Incarnation for salvation in the Eastern Christian tradition was defined by Gregory of Nazianzus's theological formula: "That which was not assumed (or taken on)

---

49. Tamas Adamik, "The Baptized Lion in the *Acts of Paul*," in *The Apocryphal Acts of Paul and Thecla*, ed. Jan N. Bremmer (Kampen: Kok Pharos, 1996), 65.

50. Irenaeus, *Demonstration of the Apostolic Preaching* 22.

51. Irenaeus, *Against Heresies* 4.34.1. "For the flesh of the Lord . . . confirmed the salvation of the flesh. Unless he had himself been flesh and blood . . . he could not have saved what had perished in Adam. By recapitulation his righteous flesh brought the flesh from slavery to sin into friendship with God" (5.14.1–2).

52. Athanasius, *Orations against the Arians* 61.

53. Athanasius, *Letter to Adelphius* 6.

is not healed (or saved); but that which is united to God is saved (or healed)."[54] In other words, redemption and resurrection occur at the same levels of existence in which God in Christ participated.

For the early church, the Greek term *cosmos* included not only the Earth but all of ordered creation. Christ's redemptive work was seen as having universal or cosmic significance in that, through Christ, God "reconciled all things to himself"—and not just those things on Earth (Col. 1:20). Christ's Incarnation and atonement brought all creation into the sphere of redemption. As early Christians affirmed that Jesus is "the living bread that came down out of heaven" and "the bread which [Jesus] gives for the life of the cosmos is [his] flesh" (John 6:51), it became clear to them that Jesus came to redeem all flesh within the cosmos. As one elect human from one elect species is chosen as the incarnate end point of the image of God in humanity, so all creatures of flesh throughout the entire cosmos are brought into God's salvific endeavor. Wright explains, "The point of 'election' was not to choose or call a people who would somehow mysteriously escape either the grim entail of Adam's sin or the results it brought in its train." The goal of God's elective choosing was to call a people through whom sin "and its results for the whole creation, might be brought to the point where they could at last be defeated, condemned, overcome." From the beginning, says Wright, it was God's plan that the process of election that started with Adam "would be narrowed down to a single point, to the Messiah himself," who would himself be "cast away" so that the whole of creation might be resurrected and redeemed.[55]

Conclusion

With regard to the future of both humanity and the universe, the whole of the natural sciences seem to testify that the sure reality is death. The far cosmic future is a tragic portrait of disintegration and physical failure. As Polkinghorne observes, "science presents us with a picture of a universe that, despite its present fruitfulness, will eventually end in the futility of cosmic collapse or decay."[56] When considering the meaning and purpose of human life in the grand scheme of things, physicist Steven Weinberg reflects, "It is very hard to realize that this all is just a tiny part of an overwhelmingly hostile universe. It is even harder to realize that this present universe . . . faces a future extinction of endless cold or intolerable heat. The more the universe seems comprehensible, the more it also seems pointless."[57] The theistic religions too affirm that the present world

---

54. Gregory of Nazianzus *Epistle, 101.*

55. N. T. Wright, *Paul and the Faithfulness of God* (Minneapolis: Fortress, 2013), 1208.

56. Polkinghorne, *God of Hope*, xviii.

57. Steven Weinberg, *The First Three Minutes: A Modern View of the Origin of the Universe* (New York: Basic Books, 1977), 154–55.

will end. Yet they also hope that a better world will take its place. Beyond this, Judaism and Christianity confess a hopeful future for this particular cosmos as the dying seed through which God will bring forth the resurrection of the dead and the life of the world to come. While both science and Scripture agree that the present physical universe was not built to last forever, as the vision of science reaches its limits, the eyes of faith lend sight to discern the prospect of a future cosmic hope. The faith of the Christian is centrally focused on Jesus of Nazareth and the foundational confession that the Incarnation, death, and Resurrection of Jesus has fundamental implications for the future of the whole material creation. According to the Christian vision, the Incarnation of God in Jesus is an expression of God's deep solidarity with all living creatures as God's own life inclusively embraces the category of existence to which all living beings belong.[58] In this view, as the Word becomes flesh (or biological life) God opens the way for all living things to inherit a future beyond death and disintegration. Just as Christ died, the cosmos itself will die. In the same way, though, the empty tomb and the bodily Resurrection of Jesus point to the future transformation and redemption of the entire material cosmos.

Discussion Questions

1. Considering the future of the physical universe as predicted by science, do you think there is any ground for ultimate hope? Explain your answer.
2. Do you believe that Bertrand Russell and Steven Weinberg's cosmic pessimism about the meaningless of life is warranted? Why or why not?
3. What do you personally think would need to either "survive" death or be brought back into being after death (in the case of bodily resurrection) for "you" to be really "you"? Your memories? Your personality? Your body or appearance? Your relationships—such as family and friends? Something else?

Beyond the Classroom

With a group of friends, consider the Christian vision of the future: a resurrected and transformed cosmos where risen human beings have glorified bodies that are imperishable and not limited by the typical restrictions of time or space. Do you think eternal life in such a state would be boring? Why or why not?

---

58. See Niels Henrik Gregersen, "*Cur Deus Caro*: Jesus and the Cosmos Story," *Theology and Science* 11, no. 4 (2013). And see Joshua M. Moritz, "Deep Incarnation and the Imago Dei: The Cosmic Scope of the Incarnation in Light of the Messiah as the Renewed Adam," *Theology and Science* 11, no. 4 (2013): 440.

Resources for Further Study

Books

Ellis, George, ed. *The Far-Future Universe: Eschatology from a Cosmic Perspective.* London: Templeton, 2002.

Leslie, John. *The End of the World: The Science and Ethics of Human Extinction.* London: Routledge, 1998.

Peters, Ted, Robert John Russell, and Michael Welker, eds. *Resurrection: Theological and Scientific Assessments.* Grand Rapids: Eerdmans, 2002.

Polkinghorne, John. *The God of Hope and the End of the World.* New Haven: Yale University Press, 2002.

Welker, Michael, and John Polkinghorne, eds. *The End of the World and the Ends of God: Science and Theology on Eschatology.* London: SCM, 2000.

Wright, N. T. *The Resurrection of the Son of God.* Minneapolis: Fortress, 2003.

Wright, N. T. *Surprised by Hope: Rethinking Heaven, the Resurrection, and the Mission of the Church.* New York: HarperOne, 2008.

Articles

Russell, Robert J. "Eschatology." In *The Blackwell Companion to Science and Christianity*, edited by J. B. Stump and Alan Padgett, 543–53. Malden, MA: Blackwell, 2012.

Saudek, Daniel. "Science and Eschatology in the Open Universe." *Science and Christian Belief* 23, no. 2 (2011): 133–57.

Internet Resources

Moritz, Joshua. "The End of the World: Theological and Scientific Perspectives on Cosmic Eschatology." Voice of Light Productions. Accessible at *http://vimeo.com/45346754* (time: 1:04:42).

Wright, N. T. "Can a Scientist Believe the Resurrection?" Faraday Institute for Science and Religion. Accessible at *http://www.faraday.st-edmunds.cam.ac.uk/CIS/Wright/* (time: 01:17:44).

Glossary

Abrahamic religions The religions of Judaism, Christianity, and Islam, all of which trace their history to Abraham in the Hebrew Bible.

abolitionism The movement in England and America in the eighteenth and nineteenth centuries to abolish the enslavement of Africans.

absolute zero The lowest possible temperature: –273.15 °C.

anthropic coincidences The observation that the constants of nature appear extraordinarily fine-tuned for the production of life; the life-friendly (or anthropic) character of the cosmos.

anthropological dualism The idea that when the physical body dies, the immaterial disembodied soul continues to live on in a nonphysical state.

a posteriori "From the later," meaning knowledge that follows from experience or observation.

a priori "From the earlier," meaning knowledge that is, in some sense, independent of experience or observation.

Aristotelian eternalism The view, following the Greek philosopher Aristotle (384–322 BCE), that both Earth and the cosmos are eternal and without beginning.

Aristotelian physics The view of the physical world, following Aristotle, which holds that motion in nature is caused by inherent principles in the elements earth, air, fire, water, and ether.

biblical election (or historical election) God's historical choosing of an individual or a group of people to accomplish certain purposes related to the divine plan of salvation.

big crunch Within physical cosmology, a possible far-future scenario in which the universe reaches its maximum size and then the force of gravity pulls matter together, causing the cosmos to collapse upon itself until all matter in the universe contracts into an infinitely dense point (or singularity).

big freeze Within physical cosmology, a possible far-future scenario in which the expansion of the cosmos continues forever and the energy within the universe dissipates until thermodynamic equilibrium (or maximum entropy) is reached.

big rip Within physical cosmology, a possible far-future scenario in which the acceleration of the expansion of the universe (related to dark energy) causes all matter to be torn apart, resulting in the violent destruction of the universe.

causal determinism   The idea that every event is necessitated by prior events and conditions; all events have a cause that is explainable in terms of previous events and the laws of nature.

causal indeterminism   The idea that events cannot be absolutely determined by prior causes and causal relations.

closed universe   In physical cosmology, a universe in which there is enough matter, and thus gravitational force, to halt the expansion initiated by the big bang.

cognitive ethology   The scientific study of the role of conscious awareness and intention in the behavior of nonhuman animals.

conflict thesis   The thesis that science and religion have experienced a long history of conflict or warfare.

convergence   (in evolution) When, in the course of evolutionary history, two or more lineages of different organisms arrive at the same biological outcome from very different starting points; when biological traits and forms develop independently in two or more unrelated or very distantly related evolutionary lineages.

Copenhagen interpretation of quantum physics   The standard view of quantum physics espoused by Neils Bohr and Werner Heisenberg, which holds that measurement outcomes at the quantum level are fundamentally indeterministic.

cosmogony   An account (traditionally given within a religious context) of why the world exists or how the present world came into being.

cosmology   The scientific study of the large-scale structure of the universe.

Council of Trent   (1545–1563) A Roman Catholic Church council aimed at countering a number of Protestant teachings.

creatio ex nihilo   The creation of something from absolutely nothing; an entirely brand-new creation; the Jewish and Christian idea that God created the universe from nothing.

creatio ex vetere   A renewal of creation out of what has already existed.

dark energy   (or phantom energy) In physical cosmology, a hypothetical form of energy that accelerates the rate of expansion of the universe; this energy has no electric charge and does not interact with electromagnetic radiation, such as light.

deism   The belief that God created the universe but does not intervene in the course of cosmic or earthly events.

demarcation problem   Within the philosophy of science, the problem of drawing a boundary between that which is to be counted as science and that which is not; what science is, how it works, and what makes science different from other ways of investigating the world.

development Within biology, the study of the process through which an embryo becomes an adult.

early modern period The period of history that follows the late Middle Ages, roughly from the Protestant Reformation around 1500 CE to the European Enlightenment around 1800 CE.

empirical A type of knowing that is acquired by means of observation.

entropy A measure of the disorder of a system; the tendency of systems to move toward thermodynamic equilibrium.

epistemology The branch of philosophy that studies the nature and limits of knowledge, and the justification of belief.

eugenics A movement popular in the first half of the twentieth century that aimed to influence human breeding patterns on a legal and social level so as to control the direction of human evolution.

evolutionary developmental biology (or evo-devo) The field of biology that studies the relationship between evolution and development.

exegesis The practice of interpreting a text.

extrinsic value (or instrumental value) The value or worth that is assigned to something in light of external factors; the value something has for the sake of something else.

fideism A view that denies that there is a legitimate place for science and reason within the content of religious faith and denies that religious faith has limits.

fine-tuning The name given to the observation that the physical constants of nature and the beginning state of the universe needed to have extremely precise values for the universe to be hospitable to life.

general relativity theory Albert Einstein's theory of gravitation, which pictured time as another dimension of space and described gravity as the bending of space-time.

genome The genetic material of an organism.

genotype An organism's hereditary information.

geocentrism A commonsense view of the solar system, which holds that the sun revolves around a stationary Earth.

God of the gaps When God is invoked to explain empirical gaps in scientific knowledge.

God's two books The understanding of the early and medieval Christian church that God has "written" two books through which God can be known:

the book of Scripture and the book of nature. In this view, both "books" are complementary ways in which God reveals himself to humans.

heliocentrism   A view of the solar system, espoused by Nicolaus Copernicus, which holds that the Earth revolves around a stationary sun.

historical geology   A view of Earth history that holds that the geological features of the planet have progressively changed through time in a linear and noncyclical manner.

image of God (or *imago Dei*)   Within Jewish and Christian theology, a term that applies uniquely to humans and denotes the relation between God and humanity.

Incarnation   Within Christian theology, the belief that the second person of the Trinity, also known as the Logos (or Word), "became flesh."

inductivism   The view of science described by Francis Bacon, which holds that the practice of science involves gathering experimental and observational facts about nature so one can infer general patterns or universal laws that describe the particular phenomena being observed.

intrinsic value   The value or worth that something has in itself or for its own sake.

karma   In Hinduism and Buddhism, a transcendent law that causes certain moral effects to follow from the actions of one's life, especially in relation to reincarnation or rebirth into the next life.

Lamarckian evolution   Change in species over time owing to the inheritance of acquired characteristics.

lex talionis   The law of retaliation; a principle of retributive justice where the punishment is equal to the offense (e.g., an eye for an eye).

logical empiricism (or logical positivism)   A movement in philosophy of science from the 1930s to the 1970s that aspired to develop an understanding of science that would allow one to speak of the verification or confirmation of certain items of empirical knowledge.

metacognition   Refers to the ability to think about thinking and to control and monitor one's own cognition.

metaphysics   A branch of philosophy referring to the study of phenomena and concepts that are beyond the physically observable universe.

modern evolutionary synthesis   An understanding of evolution developed in the first half of the twentieth century that combines insights from Darwinian natural selection, paleontology, and Mendelian genetics.

monogenism   A theory of human origins, which holds that all human races share a common descent or derive from a common ancestor.

moral evil   Instances of suffering or evil caused by free and independent agents.

multiverse   Within physical cosmology, a hypothetical set of infinite or finite possible universes.

natural evil   Incidents of suffering or evil caused by nature.

natural philosophy   The name for science in the ancient, medieval, and early modern periods; the branch of philosophy that sought to gain knowledge of physical reality and the material causes of things.

new creation   In Jewish and Christian theology, the transformed and resurrected cosmos that will follow the end of time.

normal science   The everyday practice of science within a framework provided by a given paradigm.

ontogeny   The developmental process through which two single cells first join to become one cell and then divide and develop to become a complex multicellular organism.

ontology   From the Greek *ontos*, meaning "being" or "existence," the branch of philosophy that addresses questions of being, existence, and the nature of reality.

open universe   In physical cosmology, a universe that continues to expand forever because there is insufficient matter, and thus insufficient gravitational force, to halt the expansion initiated by the big bang.

paleoanthropology   An interdisciplinary branch of anthropology concerned with early humans and their ancestors.

paradigm   A concept developed by the philosopher of science Thomas Kuhn, referring to the larger cultural context or worldview that influences the basic assumptions, metaphysical commitments, values, questions, and problems of science as well as the possible interpretations of data within science.

paradigm shift   A period of change where there is a dramatic and wide-ranging transformation in the scientific understanding of the world.

peaceable kingdom   A reign described in the Hebrew Bible (Hosea 2 and Isaiah 11) that will be completed at the end of days when violence in nature will ultimately cease and all creatures will harmoniously live together in the presence of God.

phenotype   An organism's observed properties or traits.

phylogeny   The evolutionary history of a particular group or species.

physicalism (or materialism)   The thesis that everything in the universe is physical.

polygenism   A theory of human origins that holds that the various human races have separate origins.

principle of sufficient reason   Stipulates that everything must have a reason or cause.

psychosomatic unity   The idea that the human person is essentially an integrated unity of mind/soul and body.

Scientific Revolution   The period from the 1500s through the 1700s, when medieval natural philosophy was transformed into early modern science.

scientism   A view that denies that there is a legitimate place for faith within the practice of science and denies that science has limits; the idea that any question that can be answered at all can best be answered by science.

singularity   An infinitely small point in which matter is infinitely compressed (e.g., in a black hole or during the big bang).

social Darwinism   A late-nineteenth-century movement aimed at applying the theory of natural selection to the development of society.

special providence (or special divine action)   Refers to God's extraordinary intervention into the course of events; particular acts of direct divine intervention.

steady-state theory   A theory of the cosmos that posited an unchanging universe with neither beginning nor end; developed by Fred Hoyle as a rival to big bang cosmology.

string theory   A mathematical theory of atomic physics that describes fundamental particles in terms of vibrating strings rather than as points.

symbiogenesis   The formation of new species through symbiotic relationships or cooperative synergism.

theodicy problem   The dilemma posed by the goodness of God and the omnipotence of God, in light of the reality of evil.

theory of mind   The capacity of an organism to attribute mental states to others; an understanding that others can see, feel, and know.

ultimate reality   Refers to the reality that is most absolute and fundamental (e.g., God, in theism).

underdetermination   In philosophy of science, a situation where the data alone does not determine which scientific interpretation is the correct one.

X-Club   A group of like-minded, agnostically oriented, and scientifically influential friends led by Thomas Henry Huxley whose goal was to place a secular science into the center of cultural life in Victorian England.

young Earth creationism   Within Judaism and Christianity, the view that the universe, Earth, and all the various forms of life were created instantaneously in six, twenty-four-hour days less than 10,000 year ago.

Index

Note: The abbreviations *n*, *i*, and *c* that follow page numbers indicate footnotes, illustrations, and charts, respectively.